Other Books by Carol Norén

The Woman in the Pulpit

What Happens Sunday Morning: A Layperson's Guide to Worship

IN TIMES OF CRISIS AND SORROW

A Minister's Manual Resource Guide

IN TIMES OF CRISIS AND SORROW

A Minister's Manual Resource Guide

Carol M. Norén

Foreword by James Cox

JOSSEY-BASS
A Wiley Company
San Francisco

Published by

JOSSEY-BASS
A Wiley Company
989 Market Street
San Francisco, CA 94103-1741

www.josseybass.com

Copyright © 2001 by John Wiley & Sons, Inc.
Jossey-Bass is a registered trademark of John Wiley & Sons, Inc.

Jossey-Bass books and products are available through most bookstores.
To contact Jossey-Bass directly, call (888) 378-2537, fax to (800) 605-2665,
or visit our website at www.josseybass.com.

Credits on page 325.

We have made all reasonable efforts to locate the copyright owners of sermons reprinted in this book from previous volumes of *The Minister's Manual*. We are prepared to fully credit the source in future reprints and pay appropriate fees for inclusion in this volume. Please contact the publisher.

Substantial discounts on bulk quantities of Jossey-Bass books are available to corporations, professional associations, and other organizations. For details and discount information, contact the special sales department at Jossey-Bass.

We at Jossey-Bass strive to use the most environmentally sensitive paper stocks available to us. Our publications are printed on acid-free recycled stock whenever possible, and our paper always meets or exceeds minimum GPO and EPA requirements.

Library of Congress Cataloging-in-Publication Data
Norén, Carol Marie.
In times of crisis and sorrow—A minister's manual resource guide / Carol M. Norén; foreword by James Cox.
p. cm.
Includes bibliographical references and index.
ISBN 0-7879-5420-9 (alk. paper)
1. Funeral service. 2. Funeral sermons. 3. Sermons, American—20th century. I. Title.
BV199.F8 N67 2001
259′.6—dc21   2001–01466
FIRST EDITION
HB Printing
10 9 8 7 6 5 4 3 2 1

CONTENTS

FOREWORD

At last, a comprehensive volume comes to the aid of pastors, priests, and rabbis who have the difficult but rewarding task of dealing with the issues of death and dying. When the solemn duties of consolation fall to the spiritual leader and congregation, the challenge may seem overwhelming. How does one know what is correct, what is meaningful, what is comforting, what is strengthening? Carol Norén has faced these questions, thoroughly researched traditional and contemporary approaches, looked with both a sympathetic and a critical eye at what is actually done, and now offers the best of her findings and her opinions on how to help people manage their inevitable bereavements.

No part of the ministry of consolation is left untouched. Tender service to the dying, to the immediate family and friends, and to the wider community receives careful attention. While the author deals with the total context of the funeral or memorial service, the focus is on the service itself. This includes scripture readings, prayers, eulogies, sermons, and testimonials. Actual examples of these items are included to provide specific and concrete materials that may spark and supplement the creativity of the person leading the funeral service. Students for the ministry, as well as practicing clergy, will find this volume informative, practically and helpfully detailed, and inspiring throughout. After serving as a pastor for many years in various settings and as a teacher of pastors, I give this volume my wholehearted recommendation.

James Cox, Senior Professor
The Southern Baptist Theological Seminary
Louisville, Kentucky

To Nils John "Big A" Anderson
and in memory of Signe Dahlgren Anderson

ACKNOWLEDGMENTS

This book would not have been possible without the assistance of clergy and laity around the globe who shared their stories of crisis and sorrow and bore witness to their hope in Christ. Many friends and colleagues at North Park Theological Seminary helped in the production of this work. Special thanks are owed to Jane K. Koonce and C. John Weborg, who read early versions of the manuscript and offered encouragement and advice; Dennis White and Carol Souliere, teaching assistants in homiletics; and Guylla Brown and Jeanine Brown, support staff, who gave invaluable help in manuscript production. Thanks also to Karen Westerfield-Tucker of Duke Divinity School and W. Richard Stegner of Garrett-Evangelical Theological Seminary, who offered theological and liturgical critiques in their respective fields. Tyler A. Strand of the Cathedral of the Holy Trinity in Manila; Raymond M. Krutz of Memorial Heights United Methodist Church in Rock Island, Illinois; Dennis K. Hagstrom of Advent Lutheran Church in Westminster, Colorado; and Bonnie Perry of All Saints Episcopal Church in Chicago, Illinois, all gave generously of their time and ideas. Olga Jonasson of the American College of Surgeons supplied me with resources on end-of-life care from the American Medical Association's Institute for Ethics. Other consultants included Andrew P. Norén, Chicago Police Department; Leak & Sons Funeral Home, Chicago, Illinois; and James Wilson and Mel and Marilyn Franklin of Barrington United Methodist Church, Barrington, Illinois. My thanks go to Sheryl Fullerton, Chandrika Madhavan, and others at Jossey-Bass for encouraging me to take on this project. Finally, I am grateful to James E. Loder,

Bess G. Hunnings, Eloise Leonard, and the late Frank Haronian, who have ministered to me in times of crisis and sorrow.

Chicago, Illinois   Carol M. Norén
May 2001

IN TIMES OF CRISIS AND SORROW

A Minister's Manual Resource Guide

Ministry in Difficult Times

On the first Monday morning of the year 2000, two faculty colleagues and I met in a conference room at North Park Theological Seminary. We were there to plan a memorial service for Jackson Blanchard, a staff member and friend who had died the previous day after a long battle with cancer. Jackson's brothers, who lived some distance away, had arranged for the cremation of their sister's body but had left the service entirely in our hands. The only directive Jackson herself had given was that her former pastor, along with Professor Klyne Snodgrass, one of the three people at this morning's meeting, was to "do" her funeral.

Klyne began our planning session by putting forth three questions for our consideration:

1. What do we want to accomplish?
2. Who should be involved?
3. What are we going to do?

The first question was the most crucial, for it would largely determine our answers to the second and third questions. Unfortunately, the first question was also the one most likely to be skipped by funeral home directors, by mourners still reeling from their loss, and by ministers as they schedule yet another obligation into the week. What *did* we want to accomplish? Each of us answered the question in turn. Klyne, a New Testament professor, said that the memorial service should offer comfort, hope, and challenge to those present. John Weborg, a professor of theology at North Park, answered that it should be a service of thanksgiving for our friend's life, and it should acknowledge that we grieve, but not as those without hope (1 Thess. 4:13). My own response was that the service should be primarily an act of worship, giving thanks for the ways in which Jackson's life revealed the nature and work of Jesus Christ. I wrote down our answers and we used them to guide us through the many questions that followed: What Scriptures would be read? Would the choir from our friend's church sing? Should we have a photo of her on display? Should there be another memorial service later on, when students returned for spring semester? Should we print bulletins? Who would host the reception afterward? In what ways could we show hospitality to Jackson's family, most of whom did not know the seminary community?

Our relationship to the person whose memorial service we were planning was in many ways like the relationships experienced by ministers and laity in a local church. Pastors, after all, become close to members of the congregations they serve and must deal with their own grief even as they minister to others. In our situation, we had the dimension of realizing that our seminary students would be watching us to see "how things ought to be done." But this expectation can also be claimed by parish ministers, whose church members look to them to model "good grief" and offer direction in times of loss.

Not all crises are directly related to bereavement, of course. Priests and ministers are called to speak words of comfort and hope in a variety of other situations. Sometimes we can anticipate people's pastoral needs; at other times, we are taken by surprise. In December 1995, the pastor of the church I was attending suggested that we have a special service on the 21st, the winter solstice. I smiled and asked, "Is this going to be *Christian* worship or an interfaith venture with the local pagans?" He said it was neither a non-Christian service nor an observance of the feast of St. Thomas, but rather an acknowledgment, on the darkest day of the year, that for many people it is hard to be merry as Christmas approaches. He named some of the burdens carried by families in the congregation: divorce, unemployment, difficulty adjusting to retirement, a first Christmas away from home, having to care for a parent with Alzheimer's disease, and so on. All of these situations represented different kinds of grief. The worship service he had in mind would speak particularly to those who were in dark times as it announced the Light of the World in whom we hope. The pastor, like the little committee now planning a coworker's memorial service, began with the question, What do we want to accomplish? The answer to that primary question led naturally to the questions of who should be involved and what exactly should be done.

In the pages that follow, I address the three questions put to us by our colleague that morning and attempt to answer them in a way that provides theologically sound and pastorally sensitive guidelines for clergy in times of crisis and sorrow. Although the book's primary focus is on worship as a means of extending pastoral care to those who mourn, it also addresses other losses besides death and suggests strategies for ministry.

The book is organized into two parts. Part One contains five chapters. The first chapter is the starting point for addressing the question, What are we trying to accomplish? As Christian clergy, our raison d'être is not necessarily the same as that of a funeral director, a newspaper reporter, or a relief organization. Each of these providers may be well-intentioned and give much-needed help, but the identity and mission of clergy are distinct from those of other providers. It is essential that we understand these distinctions and let them guide our decisions in offering pastoral care through worship.

Our theological foundations are the cornerstone for determining what we are called to do and say in the various crises faced by the congregations entrusted to our care. To proclaim our faith intelligibly, however, we must speak the language of the culture in which we minister. The second chapter discusses denominational, socioeconomic, generational, and other contexts that must be taken into account when striving for effective ministry. The culture and history of a congregation not only present the pastor with one or more dialects to learn, but also present implicit answers to the questions, Who should be involved? and What are we going to do? To assist the seminary graduate who is just beginning full-time parish work or the minister moving to a new church, the chapter discusses steps for learning the congregational culture, suggests local resources that may help the pastor address pastoral needs in crisis situations, and offers a pre-need funeral-planning sheet.

The third chapter explains four basic types of services that Christian clergy may conduct following the death of an individual. In addition to these basic types, paraliturgical acts and postfuneral services and gatherings may enter the picture, and the pastor must be equipped to deal with these.

The fourth chapter outlines four kinds of service for other times of crisis. Each service accomplishes something slightly different, so naturally the people who should be involved and the things that should be done will vary accordingly. Some crises and times of sorrow, such as natural calamities, scandals, volatile social or political issues, or crises that affect the community both inside and outside the church, require extra sensitivity and an unusual liturgy.

The fifth chapter gives an overview of pastoral issues, such as ministry to the dying and their caregivers, follow-up care of the bereaved and those in the aftermath of crisis, dealing with cultural and social pressures that may work against individual and congregational health, and issues of self-care. A pastor, after all, is not immune to the grief and sorrow experienced by parishioners. How we acknowledge our own neediness and receive ministry teaches those we serve as surely as our sermons and prayers do.

Part Two contains guidelines for writing sermons and designing worship services that are appropriate to the pastoral situations considered in the first five chapters. It also provides resources for funerals and other times of distress drawn from the best of more than seventy-five years of *The Minister's Manual,* a yearly publication that reflects and serves worship traditions across the English-speaking world. The resources presented in each edition are offered by pastors currently serving culturally and theologically diverse congregations. They include hymns, Scripture readings, prayers and litanies, quotations and illustrations, and sermons. Three types of homiletical resources are included in this section of the book: sermon briefs, or outlines, that may be adapted for local use; sermons that have actually been used in particular crises or funerals; and sermons about death, resurrection, and the ground of Christian hope. The latter may help the pastor teach a congregation the beliefs that can sustain them when crises come.

The chapters in Part One contain cross-references to the resources presented in Part Two so that readers will know where to look for material relevant to various services and pastoral care situations that can be adapted to the particular circumstances in their local church. The aim here is not to defend a single paradigm for ministry and worship in times of crisis and sorrow but to "equip the saints for the work of ministry, for building up the body of Christ" (Eph. 4:12) in whatever contexts God calls us to serve him.

PART ONE

UNDERSTANDING MINISTRY IN TIMES OF CRISIS AND SORROW

CHAPTER ONE

Theological Foundations
of Ministry to the Bereaved

My mother's cousin died recently, six months short of her ninety-seventh birthday. Baptized as an infant, Metha had grown up in an evangelical Protestant church and was an active member of the congregation until age and poor health kept her confined to her home. She was known for her piety and knowledge of the Bible as well as for her homemaking skills. Her children and grandchildren, whom she brought up in the Christian faith, helped plan the funeral. One of the two pastors who conducted the service had known her at least twenty years. The pews were filled with gray-haired people who were veteran disciples—Christians whom you'd expect to know what the faith does and does not teach. It seemed to me, therefore, both odd and perplexing that several different theologies of death and resurrection found expression in the fifty-minute service.

The funeral began with the familiar words of John 11:25: "I am the resurrection and the life. Those who believe in me, even though they die, will live." Jesus spoke these words to Martha, responding to her confidence that her brother would rise again in the resurrection at the last day. After speaking, Jesus raised Lazarus from the dead, though this was a transitory return to life and Lazarus undoubtedly had to die again.[1] What was the connection between this reading and my relative's funeral? It was the promise of new life, sooner or later, for those who believe in Jesus. No one expected the presiding minister to call Metha out of the casket in which she lay. As the service progressed, a granddaughter recounted Metha's readiness to "go home and be with the Lord," and her consternation that the Lord was taking his time in coming for her. The theological assumption here seemed to be that death comes only when God says it's time, and not before—an idea more palatable when the subject dies peacefully of old age than when a life is cut short in tragic circumstances.

Another young woman read the lyrics of a contemporary Christian song, written from the perspective of someone in heaven addressing mourners. The song exhorted the grieving family to end their weeping because the singer was now experiencing unbroken fellowship with Jesus and enjoying heaven's glories. The theology implicit in this song was that (1) the dead immediately experience eternal life in the presence of God, (2) they are conscious of both their new state and the world they have left behind, (3) they can and do communicate with us in this mortal life, and (4) mourning is therefore a sign of unbelief. Alert pastors will recognize the dangers of the second, third, and fourth theological premises: the second tempts the survivors to "play to the galleries," that is, to seek to please the departed rather than to please God; the third premise tempts the bereaved to dabble in seances, something condemned in Scripture; and the final premise is contrary to what Jesus himself did at the tomb of Lazarus.

The last hymn in the service was "Face to Face," a gospel song written in the 1920s. The second stanza is as follows:

> Only faintly now, I see Him,
> With the darkling veil between,
> But a blessed day is coming,
> When His glory shall be seen.
> Face to face I shall behold Him,
> Far beyond the starry sky;
> Face to face in all His glory,
> I shall see Him by and by![2]

The song seems to suggest that the "blessed day" that is coming is the second coming of Jesus Christ rather than the day an individual receives a heavenly reward, whether immediately after death or at the general resurrection described in 1 Thessalonians 4:16.

Absent from this theological smorgasbord was expression of the belief that death separates the body from the soul, with the disembodied soul enjoying some sort of immediate participation in heaven's joys while waiting to be clothed with a new, resurrection body at the end of the age. No one proclaimed that Metha's late husband had been waiting for her at heaven's gates and now welcomed her into paradise, where they would be together always. Nor did anyone borrow the biblical metaphor of sleep to say that the woman's soul was resting in peace until all the dead in Christ shall rise. I would not have been surprised, however, to have heard any or all of these beliefs proclaimed in the service. No one appeared to be troubled by the mixed messages being communicated, perhaps because there was not a pressing need to make sense of what had happened. This particular death was seen as a release from suffering and not as an enemy striking someone in the prime of life.

Without polling those who attended Metha's funeral, I cannot know exactly what they believe about death and resurrection, but the variety of interpretations expressed during the service suggest uncertainty, vagueness, and inconsistency. At this funeral there was no audible or visible demonstration of a desperate hunger to hear some word of solace from the pulpit. However, as one of my seminary professors used to remind us, we should keep in mind that in any congregation there may be someone whose heart is breaking, whether or not we are aware of it. There may be someone who will turn irrevocably toward or against Jesus Christ because of what happens in a worship service. Pastors and laity know that there are occasions when God's promises need to be proclaimed with all the clarity and conviction possible.

Such clarity was needed by the Rev. James Wilson, senior pastor of Barrington United Methodist Church, a large suburban congregation. The church was a beautiful, historic building on a hill; its steeple could be seen for miles. More than a landmark, the church was used throughout the week by choirs, a nursery program, and ministries for all ages. One morning, while some workers were restoring windows in the sanctuary, a heat gun used for stripping paint burned through a north wall. It smoldered quietly without attracting notice while the crew took its lunch break, but gradually spread within the walls and across the roof until suddenly the building burst into flames. The fire department and several neighboring towns' firefighters were called in, but to no avail. The film clip on the 6:00 news showed the moment the steeple crashed through the burning roof as reporters noted with relief that no one had been injured in the fire. That evening the congregation met in a nearby church of the same denomination, weeping, holding hands, and singing:

> The church is not a building,
> The church is not a steeple,
> The church is not a resting place,
> The church is a people.
> I am the church! You are the church!
> We are the church together![3]

The shock of losing a beloved building with lots of personal memories connected to it was bad enough. But James Wilson surely had other pastoral care needs to address: the anguish felt by the painters, the "if only" voiced and unvoiced; the disappointment of engaged couples whose weddings had to be relocated; and the tensions that arose in the months following as two congregations tried to share smaller premises. Then there were questions about insurance coverage, zoning ordinances, and the legal ramifications of it all. The pastor did not have *one* crisis to deal with; he had one after another. And in the midst of these crises he tried to offer pastoral care through worship and other means.

THE FAITH FROM WHICH WE SPEAK

As Christian clergy and worship leaders, we should know what we believe before we speak to people in crisis and sorrow. We need the confidence that the apostle Paul had when he wrote to Timothy, "I know whom I have believed." We must have the conviction of Paul reminding the church at Corinth, "We believe, therefore we speak." In order to give effective pastoral care, we must be able to account for the hope that is in us, presenting it with gentleness, reverence, and intelligibility. It is appropriate, then, to examine the theological assumptions that inform our decisions about how, when, and why we conduct funerals and other services in difficult times.

What *do* Christians believe about death, eternal life, and God's comfort in difficult times? Is any common theological ground shared by disciples of every stripe—beliefs that may be proclaimed and celebrated at the funeral of either a Southern Baptist or a Greek Orthodox Christian? On what basis do we announce God's providence in the midst of disaster? Although the Bible's plain sense is the foundation of Christian faith and practice, the ancient creeds of the Church—the Apostles' Creed and the Nicene Creed—offer shorthand summaries of the Christian hope announced and explicated in Scripture. In the Apostles' Creed, Christians confess:

> I believe in Jesus Christ, his only Son, our Lord, who was conceived by the Holy Spirit, born of the Virgin Mary, suffered under Pontius Pilate, was *crucified, died, and was buried;* [here some churches delete, "he descended to the dead/into hell;"] on the third day *he rose again*; he ascended into heaven and sitteth on the right hand of God the Father Almighty; *from thence he shall come to judge the quick and the dead* [italics added]. I believe in the Holy Spirit; the holy catholic church; *the communion of saints;* the forgiveness of sins; *the resurrection of the body; and the life everlasting.*

The Nicene Creed makes similar statements:

> He *suffered death and was burie*d. On the third day *he rose* again, according to the Scriptures, and ascended into heaven, and sitteth on the right hand of the Father. He will come again in glory *to judge the quick [living] and the dead,* and

his kingdom will have no end. . . . We look for *the resurrection of the dead, and the life of the world to come.*

As biblical theologian Christopher Seitz puts it, the relationship between Scripture and creed is mutually informing, mutually constraining, and mutually asserting.[4] The Apostles' Creed is recited by candidates for baptism. The Nicene Creed is repeated each Sunday by the majority of the world's Christians between the Liturgy of the Word and the Liturgy of the Table. Even denominations and independent congregations that do not recite these creeds as a regular part of worship will nevertheless concur with their content. What is more, these confessions of faith are simultaneously doxology and catechesis (that is, praise and instruction). As Geoffrey Wainwright has written, the creeds provide a hermeneutical grid through which the believer can interpret both the ample witness of Scripture and the Church and his or her own religious stance.[5] The creeds give general parameters for teaching about death, resurrection, and other doctrines, but they do not explore these subjects in depth.

IMPLICATIONS FOR MINISTRY IN TIMES OF CRISIS AND SORROW

There are several theological inferences that any thoughtful layperson can draw from the creeds.

The Centrality of Christ

First, and most important, in the creeds, belief in Jesus Christ and his Resurrection from the dead precede references to human destiny. This suggests that any statements about a Christian's life after death are made in reference to the nature and saving work of Christ. This is because the life, death, Resurrection, Ascension, and anticipated second coming of the Messiah are the primary subjects of the creeds as confessions of faith formulated by an undivided Church in its early history. It follows that the creeds thus have implications for the way ministers conduct funerals and minister in times of crisis. That is, the words of comfort and promise they speak should be founded on who Jesus Christ is. The Church finds its identity in proclaiming Christ as Lord, as the Sovereign over life and death. The person of Christ is the starting point for addressing all questions that arise in the face of grief. As a famous old hymn puts it:

The church's one foundation is Jesus Christ her Lord;
She is his new creation by water and the Word.
From heaven he came and sought her to be his holy bride;

With his own blood he bought her, and for her life he died.
Elect from every nation, yet one o'er all the earth;
Her charter of salvation, one Lord, one faith one birth;
One holy name she blesses, partakes one holy food,
And to one hope she presses, with every grace endued.[6]

A clergy friend of mine who died of pancreatic cancer in 1999 expressed the centrality of Jesus Christ in faith and hope another way. In her last letter to her congregation, the Rev. Joy Hoffman wrote, "I am going to die. My remaining mission is to die well to the honor of my God and King. To die well means not to love the circumstances of my death, but to accept that this manner of dying serves the purpose of God's salvation for me. I shall go down singing and so must you."[7] Joy Hoffman found meaning in her own life and death by looking first to her "God and King" rather than to her own reserves of courage. Her final sermon, "Ain't No Grave Gonna Hold This Body Down," is included in this book's section on Sunday messages in Part Two.

The Liminal Time After Death

A second tenet of the creeds that is often glossed over in contemporary ministry to the bereaved is the statement about the interval between the death of Jesus on the cross and his Resurrection: "He descended to the dead/into hell. The third day he rose from the dead." We are reminded of the ancient Jewish belief in Sheol, the abode of the dead. Hans Küng writes that "in the exegesis of the creed in the early Church and in the Middle Ages the *descendit* [descended] was sometimes taken to be synonymous with *mortuus et sepultus* [dead and buried] and not given a separate interpretation."[8] This transitional state, between the moment of dying and the Resurrection on Easter morning, is referred to in 1 Peter 3:18–4:6 and hinted at in John 5:25. Christ's sojourn among the dead is also alluded to in Acts 2:27 (quoting Ps. 16:8–11) and Revelation 5:13. Paul Sheppy, a British Baptist theologian who reflects a Reformed perspective, interprets the 1 Peter text to mean that the death of Jesus was total, as will be our death. "The sense of abandonment that Jesus feels [indicated by his cry of dereliction from the cross] is a recognition that death is a return to non-being."[9] One could also say that the time between Crucifixion and Resurrection was a liminal period during which God's saving purpose was challenged but not thwarted, because it concludes with Christ's victory over death and because even in this threshold state God's offer of mercy and salvation was extended to "the spirits in prison."[10] The period between Good Friday and Easter morning was a time of uncertainty, grief, and apprehension for the disciples. However, their confusion and pain could not negate the triumphant events of Easter.

In contemporary worship and pastoral care, this interval between death and resurrection may find expression in two aspects of ministry to the bereaved.

First, it serves to identify the believer (living or dead) with Jesus Christ. Just as our Lord underwent the pangs of death and separation, so do those who are baptized into Christ. And just as Jesus' very real death did not have the final word, neither does death have the final word for the believer.

In addition, the identification of the deceased with Christ may comfort those who mourn, for such identification directs us to Scripture that assures us that not even death can separate us from God's love and purpose (Rom. 8:38–39). Paul reminds us that if we have been united with Christ Jesus in a death like his, we shall certainly be united with him in a resurrection like his (Rom. 6:5). Identification with the crucified Christ may also be used to give voice to the tension between the present (already here) and future (not yet here) nature of the Kingdom of God. There is a temporal distance between the eternal life in which all believers presently share and the promise of glory in the new Jerusalem depicted in Revelation. We await the heavenly banquet even as we enjoy a foretaste of it in the Lord's Supper. Asserting that Christ was "crucified, died, and buried" and that "on the third day he rose again from the dead" legitimates the mourners' longing for the culmination yet to be realized: reunion with their loved ones before the throne of God.

The Coming Judgment

A third element of the creeds that pertains to death, resurrection, and justice is the coming judgment by God. Biblical texts referring to the Last Judgment are not popular fare in a postmodern culture and are rarely read in Protestant funeral services today. The parables of the sheep and the goats (Matt. 25:31–46) and the rich man and Lazarus (Luke 16:19–31) may be featured on Sunday morning as a means to spur the congregation into supporting one form or another of Christian social action. However, speaking of God's judgment in a time of grief is considered a clerical faux pas. Nevertheless, judgment is a vital part of the divine promise concerning the living and the dead. Without presuming to pass judgment on the eternal destiny of the deceased, proclaiming God's justice is a way of affirming God's sovereignty over life and death. In discussing burial liturgies, Wainwright underscores the belief in divine justice confessed in the creeds: "God [is] the universal creator and judge, the merciful redeemer and re-creator. . . . His authority as judge is grounded in his initial creative activity: it is because God is 'maker of all things' that he is 'judge of all men.' . . . To call God judge is to imply that he has a will and a purpose for his creation, and that human beings for their part have been given freedom and responsibility."[11] Eliminating judgment from consideration in a Christian theology of death and resurrection renders the cross meaningless, denies implicitly the goodness and righteousness of God, and devalues the faithful human response to the divine will. In the Christian funeral, belief in the ultimate reckoning before God may be comforting to the bereaved, particularly if passages such as 1 John 1:8–2:3 are read. The Sovereign who judges is also our Redeemer, and as 2 Peter 3:9 reminds us, the Lord is forbearing, not wishing that any should perish but that all should reach repentance.

The element of divine justice or judgment is both comfort and promise for crises other than bereavement. The creeds confess our understanding of salvation history and point forward to God's future. Anticipating that divine justice will ultimately prevail and that divine wisdom will sort things out can provide strong support when we are oppressed, bewildered, and searching for meaning. Proclaiming God's justice might enable those who are looking for someone to blame to let go of the desire for retribution. Confidence that God's purpose is being worked out even when we cannot see or understand it gives us strength to endure the pain of the present moment, for we believe that pain will not have the last word.

Parenthetically, people also need to hear when tragic events should *not* be considered manifestations of God's judgment, present or future. When overwhelmed by a disaster such as the Oklahoma City bombing or an earthquake in El Salvador, people may be tempted to follow two fruitless lines of thinking: asking why God caused or allowed it, or blaming themselves for circumstances beyond their control. Both approaches are attempts to cope with tragedy. Wise pastors will proclaim that the calamities are not God's judgment, but rather that divine judgment is in the righting of wrongs both now and in the future.

It is perhaps useful here to interject a brief discussion of heaven and hell, though the former is examined in greater detail later in this chapter. Heaven is the dwelling place of God and the angels, and ultimately of all those who have been redeemed through Christ. It is where they receive their eternal inheritance and reward.[12] Although Christian theology usually speaks of heaven as a place, it lays greater emphasis on heaven's essential quality, which is enjoyment of the presence of God. The Bible does not explicate heaven's relation to the physical universe; the depictions of the New Jerusalem in Revelation should be taken as evocative symbols pointing to a reality beyond human description.

Christian theology understands hell as the place or state into which unrepentant sinners pass after this life. Hell is the consequence of divine condemnation as opposed to being simply the abode of the dead. This concept of hell is implied but not stated within the Apostles' and Nicene Creeds. Jesus' teachings about hell employ metaphors: fire, darkness, gnashing of teeth, Gehenna, and so on. (Gehenna was a real place not far from Jerusalem, where human sacrifice had at one time been a part of idol worship; it was used as a garbage dump in Jesus' lifetime.) The "eternal punishment" of Matthew 25:31–46 stresses that hell is definitive, final, and decisive for all eternity. Furthermore, the damned are aware of their separation from God and their alienation causes them anguish. The Bible does not offer much specific information about hell—

or about heaven, for that matter—but what Scripture does say seems focused on communicating the irrevocable and dire consequences of not responding affirmatively to God's offer of salvation. Of those consequences, the one most clearly articulated in the New Testament is being cut off from God's delight.

In the context of offering pastoral care to the bereaved, a minister may give thanks that in Jesus Christ the separation from God caused by human sin is overcome. The great requiem masses of the past may be sung or quoted as reminders that everyone is accountable before God; but again, the funeral should not be an occasion to encourage worshipers to evaluate the particulars of the soul of the deceased. The pastor should acknowledge that "all have sinned and fall short of the glory of God" (Rom. 3:23) and pray for God's mercy to be extended to all. A corporate confession of sin may be appropriate in the funeral liturgy, but the day is past when a minister should attempt to emulate Jonathan Edwards's "Sinners in the Hands of an Angry God" during a funeral, when people are already bowed down with sorrow. There is a time for prophetic preaching and for communicating the serious consequences of sin, but to do so during a funeral only adds to grief.

The Communion of Saints

A fourth inference about death and resurrection to be drawn from the creeds concerns the communion of saints. The term is not found in the New Testament and, not surprisingly, there is considerable variation in what is meant by *the communion of saints* in different Christian traditions. Evangelical Protestants may use the word *saint* in its broadest sense, to denote any person in whom the Spirit of Christ dwells. Roman Catholics regard saints as "the signs of the presence and of the love of Christ. . . . It is thus that in the ancient Church prayer for the apostles, prophets, and martyrs became after their death a prayer *with* them in the communion of saints on behalf of the whole Church."[13] An Orthodox catechism employs similar reasoning to defend asking the saints to intercede for us: "Saints offer prayer to God for members of the Militant Church on earth. All that they can do for the living is pray. As long as the saints of the Triumphant Church pray to God without minimizing the redemptive, mediating work of Christ, it follows that the members of the Militant Church on earth can invoke the saints to pray and intercede to God for them."[14]

Veneration of departed saints is based on the assumption of their proximity to God, and some Christians pray *for* the dead, that they may grow in God's love and be made fit for heaven's joys. Despite the divergence of these viewpoints from traditional Protestant thought about the communion of saints, there is nevertheless common theological ground. All Christians will agree that the New Testament uses the term *saint* to refer to both Christians who are presently alive and those who have died in faith. For example, the catechism of the Episcopal

Church defines the communion of saints as "the whole family of God, the living and the dead, those whom we love and those whom we hurt, bound together by Christ in sacrament, prayer, and praise."[15] Through communion with the Father through the Son, the living and the dead share a common identity and inheritance (Col. 1:12). Hebrews 12:1 describes the saints as "a cloud of witnesses" encouraging believers to run the race that is before us, and in Revelation the saints are depicted surrounding the throne of the Lamb and singing praise to God. The martyrs' imprecatory prayer of Revelation 6:9–10 has been interpreted to presuppose that the saints nearer to God's presence have knowledge of what is happening on Earth, but it can also be construed to mean that they are aware, as we are, of the "already present" and "not yet" nature of salvation history.

What are the implications of the communion of saints for worship and ministry with the bereaved? Catholics, Orthodox, and Protestants alike believe that the saints in heaven worship God continually. We may be assured that when we worship God, we are engaged in activity with them and therefore enjoy a quality of "mystic, sweet communion" unavailable through any other means.[16] As we pray, "thy will be done on Earth as it is in heaven," we believe it is also the prayer of the faithful departed. Though separated from our sight, the saints are bound to us through the Lord to whom we claim allegiance and in whose name we were baptized. The reminder of this "tie that binds" can be of enormous comfort when the physical, visible connection has been broken. Furthermore, the godly example of the saints may serve as continued inspiration in the lives of those who remember them.

The Life Everlasting

A fifth tenet informing our ministry to the bereaved is belief in "the resurrection of the body and the life everlasting." The New Testament presents us with two main descriptions of life after death. First, it proclaims an immediate translation of the soul into the presence of God. This vision of unbroken communion with God is articulated in Jesus' promise to the thief on the cross that "today you shall be with me in Paradise" (Luke 23:43), in Paul's declaration that to be absent from the body is to be present to the Lord (1 Cor. 5:8), and in Stephen's plea, "Lord Jesus, receive my spirit" (Acts 7:59). This immortality of the soul is not to be confused with Platonism, for in Christian theology the disembodiment of the soul is a transitory stage. The physical, perishable body is committed to the Earth after death, where it returns to the dust (1 Cor. 15). The exact nature of the soul's existence is not defined but rather evoked in Scripture, but it is plain that it enjoys conscious and uninterrupted communion with God. Psalms 16:10–11, 23, and 73:23–26, and Romans 8:31–39, testify to the continuous fellowship and sustenance granted by the grace of God. John Calvin wrote of the limitations of human understanding of this phenomenon: "It is foolish and rash to inquire concerning unknown matters more deeply than God permits us to know. Scripture goes no farther than to say that Christ is present with [the souls of believers], and receives them into paradise (John 12:32) that they may obtain consolation, while the souls of the reprobate suffer such torments as they deserve."[17] Wainwright considers the disembodied existence of the soul from another perspective: "While I am not able to *imagine* human existence without bodily support, human self-consciousness points to a transcendence unsatisfied by all biochemical reductions and suggests at least a potential or incipient personality which grace may come to realize or perfect."[18]

Do the disembodied souls of Christians ascend to heaven, as the resurrected Christ did at the Ascension? A pastor may answer the question affirmatively by saying that we believe that to be in the presence of the Lord is to be in heaven. But we must be attentive to the unique theological significance of Jesus' ascension and not employ terms such as *ascend* and *clouds* so literally that they obscure rather than invoke the truth we claim, or foster trust in our limited human understanding rather than faith in Christ.

The second New Testament description of life after death is the bodily resurrection, when Christ will return to judge the living and the dead. Jesus alluded to this resurrection in John 5:28–29 and 6:40, 44, and 54. That the body and soul are distinct entities is asserted in the Gospels: "Do not fear those who kill the body but cannot kill the soul; rather fear him who can destroy both soul and body in hell" (Matt. 10:28; see also Luke 12:4–5). After Jesus' own bodily resurrection, his invitations to the disciples to touch his wounds and his breaking of bread with his followers demonstrate that he is no ghost or disembodied soul but rather a sign and pledge of what awaits all his followers at the end of the age. The Risen Christ is "the first fruits of those who have fallen asleep" (1 Cor. 15:20). The resurrection at the last day is a more prominent theme than the soul's intermediate fellowship, particularly in the Pauline Epistles and in Revelation.

In 1 Thessalonians 4:16, Paul describes the Rapture as a means of extending pastoral care to those who mourn. The congregation at Thessalonica was under persecution. They wondered when Christ would return and what would become of those who died before his coming. Paul's words reassured them that "those who are fallen asleep" are nevertheless heirs to God's promises in Christ. In 1 Corinthians 15:20–24, Paul speaks of the Rapture in the context of a longer discourse on the nature of the Resurrection. In Acts 24:15, the apostle tells Felix that there will be a resurrection of both the just and the unjust. In all of these examples, the resurrection of the body is anticipated as a future event, not as something that has already occurred to those who have died. It is for the eschatological event—the coming glory—that all creation groans together in travail (Rom. 8:22). The saints and martyrs depicted in Revelation already enjoy the felicity of the divine presence, but they too await the Kingdom's coming in its fullness when Christ will return to Earth and his followers will be clothed anew with resurrection bodies.

A third strain of belief concerning what happens after death may be found in the Old Testament. It should be acknowledged because Old Testament as well as New Testament texts are used by Christians to discuss death and resurrection. Belief in a physical or spiritual resurrection was not found in early Jewish thought. It was commonly held that the dead descended into Sheol, the abode of the dead. Sometimes this was conceived of as a hollow place under the earth. Other times it was acknowledged poetically, such as, "Abraham breathed his last and died in a good old age, an old man and full of years, and was gathered to his people" (Gen. 25:8). The dead did not praise the Lord (Ps. 115:17; see also Isa. 38:18) or experience conscious communion with God or the living. When David's infant son died, David commented, "Now he is dead; why should I fast? I shall go to him, but he will not return to me" (2 Sam. 12:23). Yet Sheol foreshadows the Christian belief in heaven and hell, for even in the abode of the dead there was not complete dissolution into nothingness. Saul was condemned for necromancy (1 Sam. 28), but Jewish tradition nevertheless accepted that he did consult the spirit of the dead Samuel. Theologian Walter Eichrodt describes Old Testament resurrection hope this way: "One receives the impression of a concept of faith which has not yet been elaborated or fixed in a dogmatic form, but is still elastic and bound up with the actual struggle for assurance of God. In the forefront stands the simple statement that death cannot forever cut off loyal Yahwists who have *fallen asleep* [italics added] from association with God, but must let them go free after Yahweh's final victory over his enemies. . . . The raising of the dead takes place in a way consonant with Israelite ideas of the human condition after death."[19] One can argue that belief in resurrection, which emerged gradually in Jewish thought, is a divine revelation that found its fullest expression in the Incarnation, death, and Resurrection of Jesus Christ.

FAITH REFLECTED IN MINISTRY TO PEOPLE IN LOSS AND CRISIS

What, then, are the theological implications for conducting Christian funerals and ministering in other times of crisis? In a funeral, the officiating clergy make clear that the soul of the deceased is being commended to God with thanksgiving. The body of the deceased is buried in hope of the resurrection that has been promised when Christ returns at the close of human history. Because the Lord will come to judge the living and the dead, the minister does not preempt divine prerogative by making evaluative comments about the deceased, except to pray for the divine mercy needed by all sinners. The promise of eternal life to all who believe in Jesus Christ can and should be announced, and the assurance of the deceased's unbroken communion with the Lord he or she loves should be reiterated as a comfort to those who mourn.

The Christian funeral is, first and foremost, a service to praise and glorify God, who in Christ reconciled the world to himself and offers new life to those who believe. This is the single biggest difference between Christian funerals and non-Christian memorial services. We are not present merely to pay our last respects but to worship God—Father, Son, and Holy Spirit. The occasion that draws us together is, at the same time, an opportunity to thank God for the person whose mortal life has ended, and to acknowledge before God what the deceased means to us. The Christian funeral is also a rite of passage for the bereaved. They receive instruction and affirmation for their altered status in the world, and are reminded to look with longing to the time when God's ultimate victory shall be accomplished.

The range of other crises in which a pastor may lead worship and extend comfort and hope is so broad that it is not easy to anticipate the demands of every possible occasion. Nevertheless, some of the same theological principles that guide ministry to the bereaved will apply in other crisis situations. As Christian leaders, our chief task is enabling people "to glorify God and enjoy him forever," to borrow a phrase from *The Westminster Catechism*. Our worship may include praise, lament, supplication, intercession, and even, occasionally, imprecation, but whatever the case, our words and actions are responses to the revelation of God's being, character, beneficence, and will.[20] Pastoral care in worship reminds those who are present of the Lord's faithfulness in the past, invokes the Spirit's sustenance in the present, and looks forward to God's unfolding purpose. In crisis as well as in sorrow, worship should include instruction and preparation of the saints for the challenges that lie ahead. Questions and anguish should not be suppressed but offered up to God reverently and honestly. Sometimes the most effective pastoral care is simply standing with one another at the foot of the cross, as novelist Susan Howatch has written, "[bringing] Christ to us and helping us see the crucified God."[21]

The person officiating at a funeral or in another time of crisis will do well to remember that while the creeds summarize the Christian faith, they make less use of metaphorical language than Scripture, hymnody, and prayers dealing with death and resurrection. Evocative phrases, such as *resting from their labors, fallen asleep, the new Jerusalem, pearly gates, streets of gold,* and so on, are based on the biblical witness but are prone to be misunderstood or misconstrued by worshipers taking them too literally. Metaphor is necessary to communicate a sense of what is ultimately beyond language and defies mortal comprehension, but every metaphor has its limits. The Bible does not teach that those who have died are literally asleep or in some twilight, Sheol-like state until the Last Judgment. Nor should the torments suffered by the rich man in Luke 16 necessarily be taken as a photographic depiction of hell as much as they should evoke a far worse possibility: eternal separation from God.

Some of our popular images for talking about heaven and hell are not found in the Bible at all; for example, heaven is never depicted simply as a reward for good behavior, something that is earned through human effort. On the contrary, when the writer of Revelation asks the identity of those in heaven, the answer given is, "These are they who have come out of the great tribulation; they have washed their robes and made them white in the blood of the Lamb" (Rev. 7:14). In other words, heaven is populated by those redeemed by Christ. Other folkloric notions about heaven abound. Harps and halos are not issued to everyone. St. Peter does not guard the gate or decide who is admitted. The dead do not become guardian angels for those they love who are still on Earth. A thoughtful pastor will be careful in the words he or she uses, recognizing that, given the limitations of language and the absence of firsthand experience, people are apt to take metaphors literally, to the detriment of their faith and witness. The theological significance of various symbols and actions in the funeral should be explained so that they proclaim and reinforce Christian belief rather than magical thinking.

Leaders of the Church should also be intentional in providing Bible studies, discussions, and Sunday morning worship that speaks to these issues in times other than those of crisis and sorrow. This will give people further opportunity to consider and understand "hard" texts about death and the afterlife. Parables about death and resurrection, direct pronouncements, metaphorical narrative, prophecy, and poetry require discernment and wisdom for right understanding.

Another strategy for helping worshipers discern the divine truth conveyed through imagery is to cultivate and create new, personal metaphors. For example, one Sunday I was preaching on John 14:1–7 and encouraging the congregation to identify with the anxiety voiced by Thomas: "Lord, we do not know where you are going; how can we know the way?" My listeners knew that the next day I was leaving for an extended stay in a country about which I knew little. I shared with them what I had tried to do to prepare for the trip, and the trepidation I felt about going. However, I said, there were two things that reassured me: first, someone had given me a map with directions to my destination; second, a trusted friend was already there and had promised to meet me when I arrived. The analogy was simple: the words of Jesus give us directions to the "many mansions" of heaven, and our Lord himself will meet us there. The act of creating and discovering indigenous imagery will help worshipers claim the gospel conveyed through language without being tripped up by misguided literalism, such as wondering what kind of trumpet will sound at the Last Judgment.

CONCLUSION

Ultimately, Christian ministry should model faith in the promises God has revealed and embrace the mystery that remains. "It could not be otherwise, else we should be God."[22] No less a believer than Paul uttered, "Now we see in a mirror dimly, but then face to face. Now I know in part; then I shall understand fully, even as I have been fully understood" (1 Cor. 13:12 RSV). We may also take comfort in and share with the bereaved the words of 1 John 3:2: "Beloved, we are God's children now; it does not yet appear what we shall be, but we know that when he appears we shall be like him, for we shall see him as he is." Ministering to people in times of crisis and sorrow does not require us to know all the answers; rather, it calls us to point to the Risen Christ who *is* the answer.

CHAPTER TWO

Communities of Faith

The Contexts of Crisis and Sorrow

Each year since I began teaching, I have taken students from my pastoral preaching or worship class to visit a local funeral home for a guided tour of the facility. It continues to amaze me that in nearly every class there is at least one person who has never seen the inside of a mortuary or even attended a church funeral. There is nervous laughter and whispering among the students as they are shown the casket selection room, and sticker shock when they view the itemized price list. The funeral director is patient and gracious in answering the usual questions. When course evaluations are turned in at the end of the semester, students rate the orientation at the funeral home as one of the most helpful experiences for their ministry.

My colleagues in the ministry field tell similar stories about introducing students to the world of the emergency room, the homeless shelter, and the county jail. A 1988 survey of five thousand seminarians in Catholic, Protestant, and Jewish schools revealed that the majority of students came from suburbs and small cities, not from rural communities with deep roots or from inner cities where they had lived in close proximity to people familiar with these institutions.[1] Average seminarians may not deliberately avoid buildings associated with high-stress occasions; they just may not have had occasion to enter them.

TELEVISION AS ERSATZ COMMUNITY

Not only are seminary students often unacquainted with the agencies people turn to in the most difficult moments of life, but like the population as a whole, they often have not been socialized in religious communities that teach them to negotiate the rites of passage initiated by death and disaster. Raised in a mobile society, often separated from the extended family, having minimal roots in a neighborhood, school, or church, their primary culture is television; and it is not television's raison d'être to equip clergy and laity to minister to the bereaved and those in crisis.

It is curious, then, that the funeral of Diana, Princess of Wales, in 1997, was one of the most-watched television broadcasts in world history. It had an enormous pedagogical impact on viewers, though that was not its intent. Commentators had to fill airtime when not much was happening or when an aspect of the service was self-evident. In addition to identifying celebrities entering Westminster Abbey, the anchors tried to provide a frame of reference for understanding words, acts, and symbols that might otherwise be unintelligible to viewers. The Princess of Wales's funeral was not taken straight from *The Book of Common Prayer* but was, rather, a unique service for a unique person. It communicated the significance of a set of beliefs and traditions, such as draping the coffin with the Queen's Standard, having the male family members process behind the coffin, and positioning the flag atop Buckingham Palace at half-mast. The commentators explained all of these practices to help viewers make sense of what was happening. There was also extensive coverage of the crowds gathered in London parks and along the procession route—weeping, singing, flower-bearing throngs. They were teaching viewers how to mourn as well as creating the illusion of community. On that day, the networks gave lengthy instruction on royal protocol, church music and liturgy, popular belief systems, and what constitutes "good" grief.

Though some of these lessons may be useful for ministers in the local church, crucial elements are missing. First and foremost, there was no consensus that the televised funeral was Christian worship, nor that it should have been. Second, there was no community discernment of how to worship God and give thanks for the life of the deceased. Third, there was no interaction between viewers and commentators, which could have facilitated mutual pastoral care.

The televised funeral implicitly communicated a worldview and a set of values, just as a funeral at a local church or funeral home does. The commentators helped to create and explain those values—something done face to face by individual Christians, families, congregations, and other institutions in a given culture. It is not necessary to analyze the extravaganza at Westminster Abbey in minute detail; we can see in it, however, the importance of knowing the culture's language, symbols, and traditions in order to understand and communicate with it. For the Christian minister who conducts worship and offers pastoral care, that means studying the many factors that formed and re-form the congregation.

An example from another aspect of church life may illustrate this need. A few years ago a friend showed me a long, lace-trimmed baby dress that her first grandson would wear when he was baptized. Fortunately I didn't blurt out my initial reaction: "You're going to put that thing on a boy?!" As I looked at the dress more carefully, I saw that it was embroidered in white with a long column of names and dates. My friend explained that the dress had been in her family for several generations and the embroidered names were of every baby who had been christened in the dress. Her local church understood this and rejoiced each time a new name was added to the dress, and to the community of faith. To an outsider who didn't know the history, seeing a baby boy in such a dress looked strange. To someone who knew the history, or was told the story, it had theological and personal meaning, and reinforced the community's self-understanding.

In times of crisis and sorrow, we don't want to run roughshod over people's feelings because we do not understand their history and symbols. Nor do we want to forget ritual acts that offer comfort and provide familiar signposts for those negotiating a difficult rite of passage. Knowing how Christians in previous centuries worshiped in the midst of bereavement helps us make informed and responsible choices in our ministry of worship today.

A BRIEF HISTORY OF CHRISTIAN FUNERARY PRACTICES

An abbreviated survey of the development of Christian burial customs and of the entire range of funerary practices will help the pastor identify and work with the cultural particularities of the congregation he or she presently serves. Some of the funeral and interment practices of the contemporary Church go back to the ancient Church. Five acts constituted most of the earliest Christian funerals:

1. There was prayer in the house, during which the corpse was washed and anointed and wrapped in white linen.

2. There was a funeral procession to the grave during daylight hours. The daylight march was in deliberate contrast to the Roman practice of holding funerals at night. Everyone in the Christian procession wore white garments (as they did for baptism). Carrying palm leaves, lights, and incense, they sang psalms of hope and alleluias of victory:

ritual actions communicating the belief that Jesus Christ had conquered death.

3. There was a short service of praise and thanksgiving around the body.

4. The Eucharist was celebrated and a kiss of peace was given to the corpse.

5. The body was placed in the ground with the feet toward the east, as a sign of hope in the coming of the Son of Righteousness. Often an agape, or love feast, followed the interment, and there were also later commemorations.[2]

Many of these practices are maintained to some extent in Western churches that have a formal liturgy. As in the early Church, most funerals and all interments are held during daylight hours. There is a procession with the body, usually by automobile or on foot. Clergy vestments are likely to be white, as they are for Easter. In more traditional communities and at state funerals, colors are worn that set mourners apart from the rest of the population. Black is the color for mourning in the dominant European American culture, but either black or white is customary in Filipino American, Hispanic, and African American communities. Some Asian Americans put on ethnic clothing for funerals, and other minorities, such as immigrants from Ghana, tie strips of black and white or blue and white cloth on their sleeves. Incense and candles are used around the body. Victory over death through Jesus Christ is proclaimed. Holy Communion is celebrated. Refreshments are shared by the mourners after the service and interment are complete.

The Middle Ages

The tone of the early Church funeral was one of hope and triumph, looking forward to the resurrection of the body and entrance into God's Kingdom. Christian funeral rites during the Middle Ages maintained the ritual elements of procession, prayer, Eucharist, and interment, but the mood of the service was quite different than the mood of funerals today. Primary emphases included the need for forgiveness, the fear of judgment, and contemplation of the destiny of the soul rather than of the body. From the third century on, the Church began to see penitential discipline performed in this life as a substitute for punishment in purgatory. The presence of a priest was essential at a burial in order to pray for absolution for the deceased, which was understood to be an extension of the priestly power to absolve the living.[3] At the Council of Lyons in 1274 and the Council of Florence in 1439, purgatory was defined and the words of the funeral liturgy were standardized, making prayers for the dead a central focus in the Mass. The illustration from Humbert of Romans included in Part Two of this book reflects the great concern about purgatory during this period.

The mood of medieval burial rites is not much in evidence at Christian funerals in North America today. There may be several reasons for this. First, the tendency is toward celebrating the life of a person rather than remembering the divine judgment to which everyone is subject. Lack of cultural and ecclesial consensus on what constitutes sin makes it unlikely that penitence and absolution will figure large in the service. However, the texts of ancient and medieval prayers may find expression in the music sung or played at a contemporary Christian funeral. The Dies Irae (Day of Wrath) and other parts of the requiem Mass which are sometimes sung by a choir or soloist at a Catholic funeral are inherited from the medieval Church. Even if there is not explicit reference to purgatory in the requiem Mass, it is understood that the form of this Mass was established "to draw the grace of heaven down upon the souls in purgatory."[4]

The Continental Reformation

In the sixteenth century, Martin Luther and other reformers wrote against Masses for the dead and the Roman rite of burial, yet Luther produced no manual for alternative services. For a long time, in Protestant Europe burial was left to the family, guilds, or local governments, because Protestant leaders wanted no part of "popish abominations" and the pomp of requiem Masses.[5] Luther did compose a few German and Latin chorales for funeral services, and proposed some general principles for Christian funerals. The theme of the service was to be faith in the resurrection rather than preoccupation with the dead body. The congregation was to participate in burials out of love for the deceased and the family. For clergy and laity alike, participation in a funeral was an act of pastoral care. John Calvin, like Luther, produced no order of service for funerals, but he did suggest that an appropriate sermon should be given in the churchyard and that attendance should be left to each person's discretion. An offering for the relief of the poor was often taken up.

It is not difficult to recognize the reformers' legacy in contemporary Christian burial practices. The roots of the involvement of people outside the community of faith, such as fraternal organizations and independent burial societies, can be traced to this culture. Attending a wake or funeral as an act of kindness to the bereaved rather than out of religious obligation or concern for one's own soul also comes, in part, from this period.

The English Reformation and the Rise of Nonconformity

In England, the Protestant Reformation brought other changes in burial practices. Thomas Cranmer's 1549 prayer book prescribed a churchyard procession, the liturgy of the Word, Holy Communion, and "cautious petitions for the departed." The emphases were on giving hope to the living rather than seeking absolution for the deceased, and commending the deceased to God.[6] These prescriptions were displaced in 1645 by the Presbyterian *Westminster Directory of*

Public Worship, which did away with all burial rites. The dead were now buried without ceremony, in part because of the Puritan distrust of liturgy, but also in reaction to fulsome praise of the deceased. The Savoy Conference of 1661 preceded revision of the 1552 burial rite with some modifications: it forbade use of the rite over the unbaptized, suicides, and the excommunicated. Baptists and other Nonconformists in England discontinued Holy Communion as part of their burial services. They introduced more extemporaneous prayer and added their own hymnody. Until 1880, Nonconformists could not be buried in Anglican parish cemeteries, so "Free Church" burials were often conducted by lay preachers in municipal cemeteries. This practice reinforced extemporaneous, highly contextual liturgy.

The plurality of funeral customs even within a single denomination today is in part a reflection of the extemporaneous and laissez faire practices of the Free Churches, along with an openness to receiving and integrating local customs. Hymns, gospel songs, and winsome preaching, rather than prescribed prayers, carry the funeral service in many traditions. The rarity of Holy Communion as part of the funeral in Baptist, Methodist, and other denominations can be traced, in part, to this period in English history, and also to the difficulty of "fencing the table" at a funeral.

North American Adaptations

It is worth noting a few developments in North American history that have influenced the way people mourn and the manner in which churches and communities minister to the bereaved. High infant mortality rates in seventeenth- and eighteenth-century New England meant that parents expected that two or three of their children would die before the age of ten. There was neither time, resources, nor the inclination to have elaborate mourning rites. The Puritans soberly counseled one another on the brevity of life and on the need to plead for divine mercy in the face of coming judgment.

An important turning point in the relationship between the bereaved and the community of faith was the emergence of the cemetery as a cultural institution in the nineteenth century. Prior to that time, the dead were interred in graveyards next to the church, in the church itself, or in the town common or a vacant lot. In the latter two locations, graves were often unmarked or built over as the need arose. In the rural South, it was common to have simple family burial grounds on private land. These were rarely maintained if the property changed hands. With rapidly increasing populations in northeastern cities, the interment of so many dead in city graveyards became a health hazard, so rural or garden cemeteries were created in the 1820s and 1830s. These were located away from population centers, sometimes in cooperation with horticultural societies. Cemeteries such as Mount Auburn in Cambridge and Spring Grove in Cincinnati gained renown for their natural beauty and impressive monuments, and an excursion to the cemetery was regarded as pleasant, uplifting, and instructive. Visitors might have the sense of visiting loved ones in a final resting place that was secure against developers. A coffin could not be carried on the shoulders all the way to such cemeteries, nor could the mourners walk such a distance, so livery companies hired out hacks and carriages for funeral processions. It was a mark of status to have vehicles specially designed and outfitted for this purpose. American funeral rites thus evolved from brief, simple interments adjacent to the church to more prolonged rites that offered the opportunity to display one's wealth along the way. The funeral was no longer the sole province of a religious leader (who was assisted by those who washed and dressed the dead, dug the grave, and built the coffin), and the finality of "earth to earth, ashes to ashes, dust to dust" was muted by the impression that the deceased had moved to an attractive, gated community.

These changes, along with the disestablishment that occurred between the Great Awakening and the Civil War, had enormous influence on ministry to people in times of crisis and sorrow.[7] No longer could a church declare who could or could not be buried in the churchyard, because most burials took place elsewhere. Ministers relied more on moral persuasion and less on dogma to nudge their listeners onto the road to heaven. The emphasis in evangelical Protestant hymnody and literature shifted from the person and work of Jesus Christ to an individual's experience of Jesus Christ. For example, the following eighteenth-century hymn became a favorite selection for funerals:

> O God, our help in ages past,
> Our hope for years to come,
> Our shelter from the stormy blast,
> And our eternal home! . . .
> Time, like an ever rolling stream,
> Bears all its sons away;
> They fly forgotten as a dream
> Dies at the opening day.[8]

By the end of the nineteenth century, many Protestants were singing about heaven this way:

> Sing the wondrous love of Jesus;
> Sing his mercy and his grace.
> In the mansions bright and blessed
> He'll prepare for us a place. . . .
> While we walk the pilgrim pathway,
> Clouds will overspread the sky;
> But when traveling days are over,

> Not a shadow, not a sigh. . . .
> When we all get to heaven,
> what a day of rejoicing that will be!
> When we all see Jesus,
> we'll sing and shout the victory![9]

It would not be an overstatement to say that death and dying were romanticized in both literature and life from the mid-nineteenth century until World War I. Popular fiction of the period, such as *Ten Nights in a Bar Room* and *Uncle Tom's Cabin,* entertained readers with the lingering and sentimental deaths of Mary Morgan and Little Eva. Christians in the community of faith functioned as distributors of "memorial literature," as seekers after testimony and last words, as ministers to the physical needs of the dying and their caregivers, and as reinforcers of rituals old and new.

In some respects, community participation in the rituals of death in America centered as much on the deathbed as on the grave.[10] It was customary for family and friends to keep vigil around the dying person, in order both to provide nursing care and to hear what testimony or edifying last words the person might say. Diaries and letters recorded in graphic detail the particulars of the illness or calamity that caused someone's death. This information was intended to valorize the dead and edify the survivors. For example, a Methodist preacher of the period wrote this to his brother:

> Our dear mother died yesterday about 1:45 o'clock in the afternoon. She did not regain the power of speech so that we could get a dying testimony from her. But on Saturday she had more rest and seemed to be very happy, occasionally folding her hands on her breast as in prayer, and speaking to herself. . . . We could not catch the words, but I thought I heard her say once, "and they crucified him," so she had no doubt communion with her Savior. She seemed to be happy occasionally and smiled, which visions as she saw we don't know. But the Lord she trusted has taken her to himself and she has entered on her eternal rest.[11]

What legacy of faith and practice have we inherited from our forebears? Almost nothing from our Puritan ancestors finds expression in our funerals today, except perhaps disdain for prescribed rituals and prayers among some evangelical groups. Fundamentalists and some ethnic minority preachers may, like the Puritans, emphasize the brevity of this life and the impending divine judgment, but this is not characteristic of funeral preaching per se. To some extent, we value the dying testimony of those Christians we would identify as heroic. The last words of Cotton Mather and Dwight L. Moody, included with other sermon illustrations in Part Two of this book, still inspire us. The testimony of Cassie Bernall, a teenager killed in the Columbine High School tragedy, has often been quoted from American pulpits, and the Columbine sermon by

Dennis Hagstrom in Part Two alludes to it. What our generation seems not to have inherited from our forebears is the hope that every Christian will give a dying witness, whatever the circumstances of his or her death.

CONTEMPORARY FUNERARY PRACTICES

It is easy to see how some developments of the nineteenth century have left their mark on the present-day community's ministry in times of sorrow. New churches are not built with adjacent cemeteries; the cultural expectation is that the dead will be interred elsewhere. The exception, of course, are columbaria, which have been integrated into church design as cremation has become more common. The funeral director has replaced the minister as keeper of records, liaison with government, and sometimes person officiating at the funeral or memorial service. Although it is no longer common to demonstrate our mourning by wearing black for months after a death, or by hanging a wreath or crepe on the door, we nevertheless try to demonstrate the depth of our love for the deceased by spending lavishly on the casket, grave marker, flowers, limousines to the cemetery, and so on. We also participate vicariously in the grief of others by leaving flowers, candles, or other memorabilia at disaster sites, and by signing condolence books for celebrities and royalty we've never met. Hagiographies and exposés of the deceased abound in popular culture, but the community of faith is no longer given to repeating the testimony of its saints. This was demonstrated during and after the funeral of Mother Teresa in 1997; people celebrated her good works and largely ignored her prophetic teaching.

Whereas previous generations lessened death's sting by sentimentalizing it and singing of "the sweet by-and-by," our culture has denied death through manifold strategies. We have done this by removing death from the family home to the hospital or nursing home, by employing euphemisms such as "passed on" and "expired," and by using computer technology to create the illusion that dead actors are speaking new lines, to name just a few means of denial. The distancing and denial of death, impersonal transactions with unknown record keepers, and the substitution of celebrity for relationship are detrimental to individuals and communities. People long for genuine community, and one way pastors minister to this need is through our words and acts in worship. Reminding people of their common roots, reinforcing the symbols that point to their hope in Christ, and enculturating newcomers are vitally important tasks, particularly in times of crisis and sorrow. To accomplish these tasks, however, we must be able to "read" the community we pastor.

In any congregation, past customs shape current practices—even if the community no longer remembers why things are done a certain way or ascribes new meaning to old symbols. Because the ethnic, political, social, and economic location of the congregation influences the Christian burial service, ministers may serve various congregations in a single denomination and find remarkably different funeral expectations and customs. For example, one of my colleagues tells of funerals in the farm community where he was a pastor. He noticed that sometimes—but not always—the men would kneel down and peer into the open grave. He wondered if their doing so depended on the kind of Christian the deceased had been, or whether it depended on the relationship the deceased had had with the men present. He finally asked one of the men the significance of this behavior. The answer surprised him with its simplicity. They were farmers. At graveside services in winter they were checking to see how far down the soil was frozen; they would use this information to plan for the coming growing season. There was no explicit theological or historical significance to their action. The pastor was able to draw on symbols and acts from their culture— earth, death, winter, spring, life—to communicate the promises of the gospel powerfully in that community.

It makes sense for pastors to have a plan for familiarizing themselves with the cultural context when going to serve a new congregation. Twenty or thirty years' experience in pastoral ministry may not equip you to deal with every contingency in your next church. The following steps will help you acquaint yourself with the particularities and needs of the culture in which you will offer pastoral care to the bereaved.

Talking with Your Predecessor: A Valuable Resource

First, lengthy conversation with the previous pastor is in order. Ask about deaths in the congregation in the preceding year or two. Was the burial service conducted in the church by the pastor or was it conducted elsewhere by another clergyperson? Have any other clergy been invited to assist in funeral services at the church, and if so, what has been the extent of their involvement? Are services most often held in the church, in a funeral home, or in a cemetery chapel, and has there been any change in custom in recent years? A cooperative predecessor, wanting the congregation to receive the best pastoral care possible, will gladly supply this information. The departing minister should also have a file of bulletins, memorial cards, obituaries, and other data pertaining to burial services of church members or other people. You should ask if there have been other losses or crises—an individual death or other event—that have had a major impact on the congregation as a whole, and you should inquire how the predecessor responded to these pastoral needs. The aim here is to have some case studies at hand, to familiarize yourself with ongoing situations, and to ensure that care is not interrupted. In one church in which I served, for instance, a little girl had died of cancer six months before my arrival. A paper trail documented what kind of funeral service had been performed and how often my predecessor had called on the bereaved family.

But the departing minister filled me in on other dynamics in the situation: that a particular group within the congregation had anointed the child, prayed for her, and claimed healing, and that some family members were suffering guilt as well as grief, fearful that their alleged lack of faith had contributed to the little girl's death. Still others in the congregation resented what they regarded as bullying tactics by the prayer group. The pastoral needs in this case went far beyond continuing to call on the parents.

Your predecessor may supply you with the congregation's guidelines for funerals conducted in the building, or with the church's guidelines for weddings, which may be used as a model for funerals. Many congregations have groups led by laypeople that prepare the after-funeral repast and minister to other needs of those who have just suffered a loss. The coordinators of such groups should be identified, as should the director of the altar guild, or whoever prepares the sanctuary for special services. A church directory, with notations of who is recently bereaved and who may have other special pastoral-care needs, is a useful resource. Having access to the minutes of the memorials committee, the church's rules about memorials, and a list of memorial items recently purchased will save you many headaches later on.

The departing pastor can supply information about outside agencies that are relevant to ministry to those who are in crisis and sorrow, such as the names of the hospitals, florists, and funeral homes most often patronized by the congregation. Even in a large city, chances are that only a few funeral homes are used by a majority of your members. If no information is available from your predecessor, you can nevertheless check the neighborhood telephone book for the names of funeral homes closest to your church building. The names themselves may give clues about the main constituencies the funeral homes serve. A congregation with a strong ethnic identity is apt to patronize funeral homes and other businesses with names of the same ethnicity. For example, a funeral home with an Irish name may be less likely to be used by Protestant congregations. Reading the obituary column of the local paper will yield still more information. For example, if one funeral home's death notices usually contain the phrase, "services have already been held," chances are it caters to orthodox Jews or Muslims, because people of these faiths bury their dead as quickly as possible. A funeral home that seems to be arranging mainly evening funerals is likely to serve the black community, in which evening services are commonplace. If someone outside the church phones and asks for your help in arranging a funeral service, you should direct them to a funeral home that understands and supports their ethnic and religious identity.

Some churches, particularly those in rural areas, own cemeteries adjacent to the church building or some distance from it. You should be provided with a copy of the cemetery bylaws and the names and addresses of cemetery trustees. Members of the congregation may be connected with family-owned cemeteries or private burial grounds. If so, the history, regulations, and phone numbers for the managers should be obtained. You should also be supplied with the names and telephone numbers of social service agencies so you can make referrals when appropriate. Agencies such as Compassionate Friends (for bereaved parents), Meals on Wheels, and Parents Without Partners may serve the various needs of those who have suffered a loss.

Ask your predecessor about crises other than death that the congregation has faced during his or her tenure. For example, what was said and done in worship the Sunday after the hurricane or the flood, or after a prominent member of the congregation was convicted, and so on? How did the concerns and needs of the congregation find expression in worship, and how have those crises been remembered since then? The departing pastor can identify current and developing crises, alerting you to pastoral care needs and giving you the names of support groups and relief agencies. It is also useful to know what crises are *not* talked about in the community of faith, and possible reasons for the silence. For example, if a previous pastor was involved in some sort of scandal, the congregation may be embarrassed to mention it to you. Even though the crisis has passed, silence may indicate a legacy of hurt and distrust, and these concerns should be addressed.

Networking with Other Area Clergy

What if you are a minister who is sent into an area to start a new church? There is no departing pastor on the scene to pass along this useful information, and what is more, a new church plant is more likely than a long-established congregation to be made up of people from diverse backgrounds and traditions. The strategy for the entrepreneurial pastor is therefore slightly different. Instead of talking with a predecessor, you should visit worship services at other area churches, regardless of whether they are of the same denomination as yours, and schedule appointments with their pastors. In these circumstances, neighboring clergy will probably not provide information about particular pastoral care needs in their own flocks, but they can nevertheless speak about local customs, cemetery policies, recent history, and agencies and businesses that may be involved in Christian burial and its attending needs.

Neighboring clergy can also supply you with vital information about cooperative ministries that function in times of crisis. During my teen years, local pastors banded together to work for reconciliation when race riots disrupted classes at the high school. Their influence came not so much from what they said as from their united appearance at the scene of trouble. Ministerial associations can serve as clearinghouses for giving aid to the homeless or meeting other needs, and they can organize a schedule for volunteer chaplaincies at hospitals that do not have regular chaplains on staff. Working together, area pastors can minister more effectively to people in crisis than they can working alone.

Meeting Funeral Directors and Other Key Leaders

You can be certain that you will meet funeral directors sooner or later, but it is wise to make their acquaintance before the first funeral at your new church. Nearly all funeral directors want a cordial and comfortable working relationship with area clergy; if nothing else, such a relationship is good for business. Funeral directors can take you around their facilities, let you know what services and features are available that are not obvious to the casual observer, identify trends and local customs, and supply you with a price list of their goods and services. Some funeral directors include the clergy honorarium in the total package billed to the bereaved; others assume that the family will give the honorarium directly to the pastor. You will want to find out what the local practice is, and perhaps negotiate a change. The funeral director can also warn you of potential local problems in ministering to the bereaved. For example, if cremation is chosen by a family but the local crematorium has not kept pace with the increasing demand for that service, the memorial service may have to be delayed or conducted without the remains available for committal. Or the funeral director may ask you to discourage friends and family members from serving as pallbearers because of the distance that must be walked between the hearse and the grave plot, or because the steps at your church are difficult for "amateurs" to negotiate while bearing a casket, particularly in winter.

A tour of the cemetery is also a good idea. Here you can ask how much mausoleum space and plots in various locations cost, whether burial vaults are required, what kinds of memorials and flowers are allowed, and how long flowers and other remembrances are left undisturbed on a grave. If the cemetery has its own chapel, you should tour it to determine its adequacy for the needs of your congregation, for the number who may attend a burial service, and for the standards of your worship tradition. The layout of the cemetery and its chapel can affect not only the type of service you can conduct but also the appropriateness of sermon illustrations and poetry you can use. For example, "Life's Record," a *Minister's Manual* sermon included in the section on sermon outlines in Part Two of this book, could easily be adapted for use in a garden cemetery with no markers, but it might sound countercultural if the mourners are surrounded by large, elaborate monuments.

You should also find out what hours the cemetery is open and whether the grave diggers are part of a union. This last bit of information is not irrelevant. Twice during my parish ministry cemetery workers went on strike. No burials took place until a settlement was reached. In the meantime, distressed families went through funeral services without the closure provided by a committal. One cemetery employee was a member of the congregation and he bore the brunt of people's anger toward his union—another situation requiring pastoral care.

To prepare yourself to minister effectively to people in other crisis situations, you should introduce yourself to workers in various other helping professions. One clergy friend of mine gained permission to ride in a police squad car for a few nights. He said it served several purposes: he learned about the local situations into which police were called, he forged relationships with the officers, and he observed effective—and ineffective—ways of interacting with people in times of great stress. Becoming acquainted with social workers and local government employees makes it easier to refer people appropriately and shows respect for the work these professionals do. It may also give you unexpected opportunities for ministry and evangelism. You can cultivate such relationships with members of your congregation who may already work in these fields, by asking for a tour of city hall or the county courthouse, and by inviting such professionals to speak to the local ministerial association.

Calling on Those Who Mourn

Once you are in place as the new pastor, visits to the recently bereaved should be among your top priorities in pastoral calling. This subject is dealt with in greater detail in Chapter Five. It is useful to remember that not only do such visits benefit the one who is grieving, but they also equip you to minister more effectively to the rest of the congregation. You may learn what theological questions should be addressed in your preaching ministry and adult classes. Local variations in denominational practice may be revealed. Areas of potential congregational conflict may come to light. Favorite hymns, Bible passages and translations, poetry, and prayers shared with you may become resources for your next funeral. It is likely that the grieving person will be grateful for your listening ear, regardless of how little or much is said, and the person's valuable role in the community will be affirmed as you acknowledge that vital information for ministry is being shared.

My predecessor conducted the funeral of an elderly widow the day before I moved into the parsonage. In the weeks that followed, I called on the widow's extended family. They knew I'd never known Addie, and I hadn't been at the funeral. But in visiting them, in addition to finding out about local funeral customs, I learned about divisions in the family that went back half a century or more. I was a safe listener for them because I brought no baggage with me. Listening to the mourners revealed priorities for pastoral care.

Listening to "War Stories"

Another priority in pastoral calling should be to visit the older, long-time members, who are a rich source of oral history about the congregation. Sometimes relegated to the sidelines or no longer able to attend worship regularly, they can serve as useful advisors to the new pastor, enabling you to learn from others' mistakes rather than your own. For instance, one church I pastored planned a special worship service at which the bishop would be present. It was to be followed by a reception in the fellowship hall. Someone volunteered to lend their silver tea service for the occasion. It sounded like a generous and innocent offer—until one of the senior saints of the congregation clued me in. The silver tea service was a symbol of a Hatfield-McCoy controversy in the church. Years earlier, the Hatfields had wanted to give the church a tea service as a memorial of a loved one, but they also wanted to dictate when and by whom it could be used. The church board wisely refused to accept the memorial on those terms. Now it was the McCoys who were offering to lend a tea service for this episcopal occasion. I was grateful to the elderly member who gave me the information, which made it possible for me to avoid resurrecting an old controversy. Long-time members can also help you exegete the church's music ministry, the altar guild, the pastor's discretionary fund and the budget as a whole, and policies for building use—all of which are relevant to your ministry to people in crisis and sorrow, as well as to Sunday morning worship.

Introducing Yourself to the Congregation

Early on in a new ministry, you may want to use the pastor's column in the church newsletter to discuss your availability to members and nonmembers in crisis situations and to acknowledge how you normally operate. Your usual office hours, day off, and phone and pager numbers should be included. Far from laying down the law to the congregation, such a column makes you more accessible and familiarizes the laity with the way you envision your work among them. It facilitates better communication with the congregation and helps people know what to do when there is a crisis or death in their family. If, for example, you are available to go with people to the funeral home to make arrangements, they should be informed of that option. You can also make known if you are available to accompany them to the police station, courthouse, or hospital, or into other stressful situations. Parishioners will be reassured to know who you have designated to handle funerals and to extend pastoral care when you are on vacation or otherwise away from the parish. Crises are less likely to escalate if people know which other staff members or lay ministers in the congregation may be telephoned in case of emergency. The pastor's column or an adult class may be forums for informing parishioners how decisions will be made about music, readings, and various kinds of participation in a service of Christian burial. The time to make such policies known is before a crisis; otherwise you may find yourself in a battle of wills, in which there are no good outcomes.

Helping People Plan

When a family goes to the funeral home to make arrangements for a burial, they will be asked a number of questions. Some of these are for preparing the obituary that will appear in the newspaper (if it will be composed by the funeral director rather than a member of the newspaper staff). Other questions are

. asked in order to expedite notification of those from whom death benefits may be due (such as the Department of Veterans Affairs or the Social Security Administration). Whether or not you accompany the family to this meeting, you will need some additional information in order to give effective pastoral care and ensure that the services you conduct go smoothly.

The Funeral Planning and Preference Sheet (Exhibit 2.1) may function as an official record kept in the church office. It can be filled out in the days preceding the funeral, thus serving as a reminder of what you will need for the service. It can also be filled out in advance by church members, thus serving as a will of sorts. The Funeral Planning and Preference Sheet can help you minister in at least two ways to a bereaved family that is already under great stress. First, in the initial shock of grief people are apt to feel helpless; their world has been disrupted. It can be quite therapeutic for them to answer questions about subjects on which they are authorities, such as "In what year did Aunt Reba marry Uncle Bert?" Answering such questions, or being asked to find a photograph to be displayed at the memorial service, restores a sense of control. Second, if the Planning and Preference Sheet was largely completed in advance by the now-deceased, you can use it to defuse potential arguments over, for example, which psalm Mother wanted at her service or whether she should be buried at Mount Hope or Holy Sepulchre. In addition, I have found that many elderly parishioners take satisfaction in having their say in their eventual funerals—what they want to be buried in, what hymns should be sung, and so on.

A final benefit to using the Funeral Planning and Preference Sheet is that it may alert you to cultural idioms you may not have encountered before. The planning sheet will have to be adapted, for instance, if you are ministering to Christians in the Hmong-American community, because in that culture there are three wake services each day for six days after the death, plus the funeral service itself on the seventh day.[12] The next chapter includes more extensive discussion of multicultural variations in worship, and Part Two contains suggested resources and brief, transliterated material for the pastor's use.

CONCLUSION

A good seminary offers courses in church history, tracing the development of Christian thought and practice. Other courses show seminarians how to conduct Christian worship, whether funerals, Sunday morning services, or other, occasional services. But no course or textbook has been written specifically for the congregation you serve, and every church, like every family, is unique. Learning the community's symbols, language, and history when you arrive will equip you to offer effective pastoral care and to proclaim the gospel of Jesus Christ in an idiom they recognize as their own.

Exhibit 2.1. The Funeral Planning and Preference Sheet

Full name _____ Occupation _____

Address _____ Telephone _____

Date of birth _____ Place of birth _____

Father's name _____ Mother's maiden name _____

Marital status _____ Name of spouse _____

Date of marriage _____ Place of marriage _____

Children's name _____

Other family members _____

Church membership _____

Approximately years _____

Church activities _____

Civic and other activities _____

Date of death _____ Place of death _____

Cause _____ Age: _____ Years _____ Months _____ Days

Organ/tissue donor? _____

Date and time of funeral/memorial _____ Place _____

Date and time of interment _____ Place _____

Funeral home _____ Clergy _____

Preferences regarding the service(s)

Scripture readings _____

Hymns _____

Other service music _____

Pallbearers _____

Clothing _____

Flowers _____

Memorial gifts _____

Disposition of body (burial, cremation, donation to science, and so on) _____

_____

If cremation, preferred disposition of remains (scattering, burial, and so on) _____

_____

Other preferences and notes _____

_____

A clear, portrait-style photo should be attached to the Funeral Planning and Preference Sheet, for possible use in the newspaper obituary or for display at the visitation or memorial service, and to guide the cosmetician at the funeral home.

CHAPTER THREE

Funerals and Other Memorial Services

One Sunday evening when I was a teenager, our church youth group was taken miniature golfing by the seminary intern. We listened impatiently as he explained at length the special rules by which we would play that night. As he concluded, "therefore . . . ," we spontaneously interrupted him by chanting, "with angels and archangels, and with all the company of heaven, we laud and magnify thy glorious name. . . ." It was the preface to the *Sanctus,* and we all knew it from memory because the choir chanted the same words to the same tune every time we had Holy Communion, the first Sunday of every month. No one had made us learn this part of the liturgy. We had never discussed the fact that we knew it by heart, or compared it with the rituals used by other denominations. We simply took it for granted that this was how Holy Communion was done.

For many years, when referring to funerals, or to the rest of the church's worship, clergy and laity could assume "this is how it is done." People did not used to change denominational affiliation as readily as they do today. Church boards did not revise their liturgies often—only every thirty to thirty-five years, in the tradition in which I was raised.

Times have changed. The far-reaching reforms of the Second Vatican Council have meant that Christians of every stripe are more likely than ever before to visit each other's churches and even to participate in the rites of passage— baptism, confirmation, weddings, and funerals—that occur in the context of worship. Denominations now borrow more freely from one another's liturgical traditions, and in the United States it is often assumed that whatever is new is best, whether one is buying a car or planning a worship service. The diversity of our congregations, along with the absence of meaningful community in a transient society, presents difficult challenges to clergy. The services we lead—particularly in times of crisis and sorrow—must create and nurture the congregation as a community united by faith in Jesus Christ. The primary focus in worship should be praise and thanksgiving to God, expressed in language and symbols that are intelligible and edifying to those gathered. This does not mean throwing out all the old prayer books and starting from scratch, but it does require us to know more than one prayer book, and to be able to make faithful and culturally sensitive choices in preparing liturgy for use in difficult times.

This chapter provides information on four kinds of funerary rites you may be asked to conduct: wake services, funerals, committal services, and memorial services. Throughout the chapter, pertinent denominational, regional, and ethnic variations that may be useful for effective ministry are noted. The choreography of a service is described when it cannot be assumed that such instructions would be included in a denominational service book to which you would have ready access—for example, directions for a military funeral are already available elsewhere, and in any case, a military chaplain would participate and give guidance. If you are asked to conduct one of these rites for the first time in a culture you don't know well, the directions provided here will be useful for your ministry.

THE WAKE SERVICE

It was customary for Christians in the early Church to wash and anoint the body, then wrap it in white cloths before the procession to the place of burial. This activity, which took place in private homes, was accompanied by prayer. It is the forerunner of all Christian devotional acts, public or private, that occur between death and the funeral itself. The term *wake* probably originates in the English parish festival and holiday formerly held in commemoration of a church's patron saint. It was a special time when ordinary routines were abandoned and the life and work of an exemplary Christian were remembered and celebrated. Wakes connected with funerals served several practical purposes. Prior to modern medical technology, the wake allowed time to make sure that the person was truly dead, not merely unconscious. It allowed an interval for building a coffin and sewing a shroud, and it permitted more distant family members and friends to travel to the funeral.

In contemporary North America, the term *visitation* is more in vogue than *wake* or *vigil*, though all three terms are used in this discussion. The general trend is toward a brief visitation period; instead of two evenings before the funeral, as would have been the case a generation ago, it is more often one evening, or simply an hour before the funeral itself begins. If the body is cremated and a memorial service rather than a funeral is held, the wake is sometimes eliminated altogether. The use and length of the wake varies from one region of the country to another, and from one ethnic group to another. Sensitivity to cultural expectations as well as to the theological foundations for this ministry is necessary. For example, in the Ghanian American community, it is considered insulting to bury a person less than a month after death, because quick burial is only for animals. Needless to say, the body is not on display for a month, and this practice is subject to state and local laws governing the disposition of human remains. Among Hmong immigrants, the wake is expected to be seven days long, with three wake services held per day.[1] In some parts of the country, funerals may be delayed until the family and friends can raise enough money to cover funeral expenses.[2]

A service during the visitation may be an unfamiliar practice to those not raised in the Orthodox, Roman Catholic, or traditional black (Protestant) churches, or to those not familiar with the various fraternal groups that may conduct services during the interval between the death of a person and the funeral. Such a service may even take some pastors by surprise. When Protestant clergy from the majority culture meet with the family to make decisions about the funeral service, chances are they do not organize a separate act of worship for the visitation period. With few exceptions, such as the Episcopal *Book of Common Prayer* and the United Methodist *Book of Worship*, denominational service books do not include prayers for a vigil.

It is appropriate, however, for Christian clergy to offer pastoral care through worship during the interval between the death and the funeral. Just as you would not stop visiting or praying for a person who is dying, you should not abandon those who mourn at any stage of this rite of passage. The most basic wake service, appropriate whatever the denominational affiliation of pastor and mourners, is to be present with the family when they first see their loved one's body in the coffin and to lead them in prayer. In some communities, this means escorting the next of kin to the funeral home (or church, if the wake takes place there). In other cases, you may arrange to meet the family at the entrance and escort them, with the funeral director, into the room where the visitation is to occur. The prayer said at that time may be extemporaneous; it should include thanksgiving for the life being commended to God, and petitions for divine comfort for those who mourn. It is rare in the United States for the wake to be held in the family's home, but when this is the case, being present when the hearse arrives is appropriate.

There are three other types of wake services in addition to praying with the family at the beginning of the visitation. The first type occurs in traditions where family and friends as well as the funeral director prepare the body for viewing. In the Korean American church, the pastor is expected to go to the hospital or home and conduct a brief prayer service with the family before the body is transported to the funeral home. In Korea, family and friends lay the body in the coffin; this ceremony is called *Ipkwonsik*. In the United States, this work is done primarily by the funeral director (though the family may place rings and other objects in the coffin), but the wake service itself is still called Ipkwonsik. It takes place at the beginning of the visitation period and includes prayers, hymns, reading of Scripture, a brief sermon, and time for testimonies.[3]

Even if there is not a wake service at the beginning of the visitation, family members and friends may have brought items they wish to place in the coffin. It is traditional for Roman Catholics to place a rosary in the hands of the deceased, but this is normally done by the funeral director as part of preparation for viewing. A deceased Orthodox priest will have a cross in his hand, the Gospel book resting on his chest, and the veil used to cover the eucharistic gifts during the divine liturgy covering his face.[4] The body of an Orthodox layperson is dressed in new clothes, symbolizing the new garment of incorruption (1 Cor. 15:53), and a *chapelet* is placed on the deceased person's brow. The chapelet is a strip of material on which Jesus Christ, the Virgin Mary, and John the Baptist are depicted, with the *Trisagion* ("O Holy God, Holy Mighty, Holy Immortal, have mercy upon us") inscribed on it. The strip of cloth is reminiscent of an athlete's or warrior's victory wreath. An icon is placed in the hand of the dead, symbolizing that "in life he beheld the Lord by anticipation, and now is gone to see him face to face in blessedness, with the saints."[5]

Among the traditional items other groups place in a coffin with the body before or during a wake service are a Bible, a prayer book, flowers, an eagle feather (used by some Native Americans), *paudau* cloth (Hmong), and *tapa* cloth (Fijians). Most of these items have some religious significance. Other items that may appear in or near the coffin include photographs (both of the deceased and of loved ones), balloons, and letters to the deceased. Occasionally, far less appropriate objects—such as bottles of liquor, teddy bears, money, cigarettes, and cookies—are added. There may be family arguments over which items should remain in the coffin for burial. To some extent, you can ward off these phenomena by good communication with the funeral director and by bringing up the issue with your congregation via newsletter, sermon, or adult class before attention is focused on a particular situation. For instance, a friend who accepted a pastoral call outside the United States discovered that in the host culture it was common for the bereaved to purchase counterfeit money, plane tickets, and a visa or passport out of hell and to place these items in the coffin. Rather than singling out a particular funeral, my friend planned an adult education series that would include what his denomination actually taught about death and resurrection.

How do you discern what is appropriate for the religious and social culture of your congregation? Two simple and logical questions may be asked. First, do the particular items placed in the coffin with the body express our faith in Christ, who is our hope in the midst of human grief? Items that suggest that the deceased is going to need money, whiskey, and so on in the future are contrary to Christian belief about the afterlife, so they do not belong in the coffin. Second, does allowing or even encouraging the placement of these objects extend pastoral care that ultimately nurtures Christian faith? For instance, the estranged son who wants to put a letter to his deceased father in the coffin may or may not believe that his father will read the letter, but this symbolic act may facilitate forgiveness and healing when you discuss it with the son during follow-up pastoral care.

It is common for the funeral director to remove eyeglasses, wedding rings, and other jewelry before the coffin is closed for the last time. These are later given to a designated family member for safekeeping. It is just as feasible for the funeral director to add artifacts of sentimental value at the last moment, after the visitation is over.

A second type of wake service is more formal than simple prayer with the family at the beginning of the visitation, and more public than the Ipkwonsik or other laying-out ritual. This service occurs at one or more set times during the interval between death and burial. It is most often held at the funeral home, but among some Christian groups it takes place at the church or in the family home, with or without the body of the deceased present. If the body is present, the coffin is nearly always open during the service, as it is during the rest of the visitation. Among many ethnic minority Protestants, this worship service is led by the pastor and consists of prayers, singing, Scripture reading, and a sermon. (Each edition of *The Minister's Manual* provides sermon briefs that may be suitable for a wake service; two examples, "The Evergreen Disciple" and "On Knowing God" are provided in Part Two of this book.) A wake service may be as brief as a half hour or it may last the entire night before the funeral. The latter is the norm in the Tongan American *Awakening Service* and the Fijian *Bikabika.* In addition to holding a formal wake service, Roman Catholics often pray the rosary together during the visitation. These prayers may be led by a priest or a layperson. Unlike the extemporaneous and private prayer with the family described earlier, the formal wake service is usually scheduled and announced in advance. The funeral home may be able to supply hymnbooks if the wake service takes place there, or it may be necessary for someone to be deputized to bring books from the church. At the agreed-upon hour, the funeral director will invite those present at the visitation to take their seats so that the service may begin. As pastor, you are not expected to stay for the entire visitation; however, it would be good for church members to take it upon themselves to make sure that the family is not left alone for extended periods during the wake. A person or group in the congregation may be willing to coordinate this effort.

A third type of wake service is the *transitional* service. The Orthodox and Roman Catholics have set prayers that are said when the body is moved from the funeral home (or family home) to the church. The Episcopal *Book of Common Prayer* and the Evangelical Lutheran Church in America's *Book of Worship* both contain a brief service for "reception of the body," which takes place when the coffin is being brought into the church for the funeral service. In other traditions, such as the United Methodist and Christian Reformed churches, optional transitional words are said only if and when a pall is being placed on the coffin. The pall—a large cloth sometimes adorned with a cross, butterfly, or other symbol of the resurrection—has both practical and theological significance. It communicates that all people are of equal rank before our Lord and need to be covered by his grace. *Pall* is also the name given to the small linen cloth covering the chalice at the Eucharist; by using it at a funeral, the church makes deliberate links between our own physical death and Christ's offering of himself so that we may have eternal life.

In many African and Asian immigrant groups, the transitional service takes place in the family home, when the pastor arrives to escort the family to the place of the funeral. It is the custom among some Roman Catholics and other groups for the cortège to make a detour between the funeral home and the church or cemetery chapel, past the home of the one who has just died. Consult with the family and the funeral director to determine whether there will be such a procession and whether you will ride with the funeral director or in your own car.

Resources for wake services are found in the next chapter. One relatively new publication that is particularly helpful is *The Silver Lining: Wake Services,* by J. Massyngbaerde Ford.[6] Some portions of Ford's services may be reprinted without requesting permission from the publisher each time, and many of the services are suitable for laity as well as clergy to lead.

THE FUNERAL

The Christian funeral is a worship service conducted with the body of the deceased present. Most often, the funeral is immediately followed by burial or cremation; the exception is when the body must be shipped somewhere else for burial. Whenever possible, the funeral of a Christian should take place in his or her church rather than in a funeral home. There are several compelling theological reasons for this. A funeral, like every other act of Christian worship, is for the congregation. It is a time to focus on God and on our life and death in light of God's love for us in Jesus Christ.[7] The church is where the congregation is used to gathering for worship and where it can more easily "own" the liturgy of death. It is where we mark out rites of passage in faith and life: baptism or dedication, confirmation, marriage, ordination. It is appropriate that the final rite of passage occur in the Christian's faith home. In the church, mourners are surrounded by symbols—altar and baptismal font or pool, paraments, the lighted paschal candle, stained glass windows, incense, holy water—that proclaim and reinforce Christ as ground of our hope. The Eucharist can be celebrated as a foretaste of the feast to come—the marriage supper of the Lamb in the Kingdom of God. Worship materials are immediately at hand to facilitate congregational participation in the service.[8] This makes the funeral an act of corporate worship rather than something done solely by the minister.

The Order of Service

The order of service will vary according to denomination, regional and ethnic custom, and discretion of the pastor. Most denominations publish their own service books with rubrics distinguishing "musts" from "mays." The pastor whose tradition does not have a service book or who needs to plan a service in which more than one denomination should be reflected may use the following sequence, which is characteristic of virtually all Protestant funeral services in North American culture:

- *Procession.* This may be led by the pastor, followed by the closed coffin and pallbearers, and possibly the family of the deceased and other participants in the service. Often the pastor will say the opening sentences while walking ahead of the coffin, or a choir will sing during the procession. In other cases, the coffin will already be in place at the bottom of the chancel stairs, outside the communion rail, facing the altar or with the head of the coffin to the congregation's left. The coffin may be covered with a pall or with flowers, but it should be closed during the service so as not to distract the congregation from worship or suggest that the body itself is being venerated. The pastor should process alone to the chancel while the funeral director or ushers lead the family to their seats.

- *Opening sentences.* These may be Scripture, prayer, or both. They serve to call the congregation to worship and to focus attention on God.

- *Invocation.* This is a brief prayer in which the Holy Spirit's presence in the service is invoked or acknowledged.

- *Readings from the Bible,* both Old and New Testaments.

- *Funeral message.* The word *message* is used here as a generic term that may include a sermon or homily on a given text, an obituary, a eulogy, or testimonies from family or friends.

- *Prayers.* These will include prayers of thanksgiving for the life of the deceased and prayers of comfort for the bereaved.

- *Dismissal with blessing.*

This sequence is not offered as a complete service, but it demonstrates the general flow of Protestant funerals. Hymns, solos, and instrumental music are usually added to the basic structure. Resources for each of these components, from both *The Minister's Manual* and other sources, are found in Part Two of this book. They will help you put together a service that is appropriate for your congregation. The structure of a funeral service is not so different from a Sunday morning preaching service. Some ethnic, regional, and other variations are noted shortly, but other than music, the major Sunday morning event missing from this sequence is Holy Communion. In a Roman Catholic funeral liturgy, the Eucharist is nearly always celebrated.[9] In Episcopal, Old Catholic, and Lutheran funerals, the Eucharist is frequently but not universally included. In the United Methodist and Evangelical Covenant Church worship books, there is provision for Holy Communion at funerals and memorial services, but it is rarely included. In most other Protestant traditions, the Eucharist is not part of the rites for the dead. These denominations often include Holy Communion infrequently in Sunday morning worship, and have a more informal mood in worship than the other traditions noted here.

The Time

Most funerals in North America take place during the day. The chief exception is among black Americans; about half choose to have evening services, with interment the next day.[10] In urban areas, if the funeral is followed by a cortège to the cemetery for immediate interment, it is scheduled to avoid rush-hour traffic.

The length of the service varies from a half hour, common among Pakistani Americans, to two to three hours in some traditional black and Holiness churches. In general, a service at a funeral home will be briefer than a service at a church; this is because congregational singing, recitation of a creed, and reading the psalter all take time, and these are more likely to happen when the service is in your own sanctuary.

Speakers

Who speaks during the service? As the person officiating, you will decide the nature and number of other speaking roles during the funeral. If you are relatively new to the congregation and the deceased had a close relationship with your predecessor, you may acknowledge that closeness by inviting that pastor to share leadership of the service.[11] If you are the predecessor, however, you should not accept an invitation to return and take charge of part or all of the funeral unless the invitation comes from your successor. If the family asks you to conduct the service, an appropriate reply is along the lines of, "I'm honored you want me to help you at this time. I think it would be best if you would discuss it with [the current pastor] and ask [him or her] to phone me if I can assist in the service in any way. In the meantime, know that I'm praying for all of you." Many denominations positively prohibit any clergy other than the current pastor from conducting services in the church, but even where written rules do not exist, professional courtesy and concern for the welfare of the congregation demand that you not encroach on your successor's ministry.

In addition to including other clergy who may have been close to the deceased, you may ask a lay reader or friend of the family to read one or more Scripture lessons, to give the obituary, or to offer a testimony. Among some ethnic groups, it is customary to invite other clergy of the same ethnicity to share in the service, even if they are not of the same denomination. One recent trend among some Protestants is to invite spontaneous testimony or sharing of a favorite memory of the deceased during the funeral itself. Unless the congregation is accustomed to offering religious testimony as part of the regular Sunday service, introducing it at the funeral is a poor idea. It puts pressure on the bereaved to perform, leads to later comparisons of one funeral with another, and can rapidly transform a service of worship into a lachrymose karaoke session.

The Congregation's Role

Christian funerals and memorial services are not private, because Christian worship is not private. The congregation should be encouraged to be present to proclaim its faith, stand in awe before the Lord of Life, and offer comfort to those who mourn. Having said that, it should be acknowledged that funeral services, unlike Sunday morning services, are apt to include a fair percentage of visitors with no religious affiliation. This makes the congregation's attendance and participation even more crucial, to help these visitors feel welcome and to lead in the hymns and other participatory acts of worship.

I learned this lesson the hard way. When I was serving two inner-city churches in Manchester, England, it happened that the first baby I baptized died six weeks later of sudden infant death syndrome. The parents were not active, long-time members of the church, though they were known to the congregation. On the day of the funeral, I looked across the tiny coffin to rows of empty pews. The only church members present were the organist, the caretaker, and the cradle roll secretary. The baby's immediate family was too distraught to sing the familiar hymns chosen for the occasion. Later, I rode in the hearse with the funeral director. As he led the procession from the church to the cemetery, I was surprised when we stopped in front of a local pub, and even more astonished when a crowd from the pub immediately surrounded the cortège, weeping, handing bouquets to the grieving parents, reaching in to touch the coffin. I asked the funeral director what was going on. "These are their pub friends," he replied. "They wanted to pay their last respects." When I asked why they hadn't come to the funeral, he said, "Well, miss, they didn't think they'd be welcome in your church."

Your congregation can make strangers welcome and engage in pastoral care at the funeral in a number of ways. Greeters may welcome people to the service and invite them to sign the guest book. Church members may serve as pallbearers, parking attendants, ushers, and nursery attendants during the service. The altar guild can make sure that packets of facial tissue are in the pews where mourners will sit. They can change the paraments for the service to white, and see that fresh candles are used for the altar and bier lights. Ushers may assist funeral home employees in arranging the floral tributes appropriately. The choir may present an anthem during worship. Other parishioners may take speaking parts in the service and assist in serving Holy Communion.

Additional Components

In some ethnic and racial groups, there are additional lay-led activities during funerals. In black churches, it is customary at the end of the service for ushers to carry all the floral arrangements to the back of the church and create a "corridor of flowers."[12] Ushers or deaconesses may also attend to the needs of mourners who become overwrought during the funeral. In the Chinese American funeral, a layperson is designated to take charge of the flower money or cloth money (sometimes called *white money*) received by the family in sympathy cards. The ushers may distribute red packets of dimes or quarters as people leave the service. This old custom signifies that the family's suffering or misfortune is now over.[13] In Japanese American funerals, the giving of money in sympathy cards is called *koden*. Again, someone is designated to receive the koden and keep track of the names of givers.

Other kinds of congregational participation fall more under the rubric of pastoral care; these are discussed in Chapter Five. In addition, some aspects of Christian rites for the dead pertain equally to funerals and memorials. These matters are discussed a little later in this chapter.

THE BURIAL OR COMMITTAL

The committal rite, whether it occurs at an open grave, a mausoleum, or a crematorium, is arguably more difficult for mourners than the wake or funeral. Until this moment, the separation from the deceased has been disguised or muted. The body has been embalmed, dressed, and arranged to present a semblance of sleep. Even if the coffin has been closed or absent until the funeral, the bereaved have been able to talk about the deceased as being there, that is, the final disposition has not yet taken place. In the committal service, Christians let go of the physical remains and commend the soul of the dead person to the mercy of God. It is true that in the future the mourners may visit the grave or columbarium, but for the present the prayers and readings at the committal mark closure and separation. This may be one reason for the recent trend toward private interments, and for the fact that many people who attend the funeral service forego the committal, even when invited. The sense of finality is strong.

Ground burial is still the most common choice in the United States, though cremation has become increasingly common. In 1961, 3.75 percent of American dead were cremated; by 1995, this had risen to 21 percent.[14] The cremation rate varies from one region of the country to another. In 1995, it was 16.3 percent in the Midwest, but as high as 60 percent on the West Coast.[15] Cremation is forbidden by Orthodox and Conservative Jews and some other religious groups, and is uncommon among the black population. Several factors account for the overall increase in cremations: cost considerations, an influx of immigrants for whom cremation is the preferred means of disposal, and the qualified lifting of the Roman Catholic Church's ban against cremation in the 1960s. (A separate appendix on cremation was appended to *Ordo Exsequiarum* by the Roman Catholic bishops in the United States in 1997.)

As with the funeral, there is a usual sequence to Protestant committal services in North America, regardless of denomination or ethnicity. The structure is as follows:

- *Procession to the place of committal.* This may include an automobile procession to the cemetery.
- *Scripture reading.* New Testament readings predominate. Suggested readings, along with other resources for committal services, are found in Part Two of this book.
- *Words of committal and commendation.* These are addressed to the mourners and speak for them, announcing that all who are gathered commend the dead person to Almighty God and commit his or her body to the ground, to the elements, or to its resting place.
- *Prayers.* These primarily ask God to receive the deceased into his eternal love and care, but they may also ask for strength for the mourners to live faithfully and for them to be comforted.
- *Benediction.* This is a prayer of blessing that closes the event.

Once people reach the place of committal, they wait a little distance from the grave for the funeral director and pallbearers to remove the coffin from the hearse. The minister then leads the procession to the grave or catafalque. The immediate family and close friends follow the pallbearers and may be seated on folding chairs or, if the committal is at a crematorium, in a front pew. The minister stands at the head of the coffin and faces it, waiting until the rest of the mourners have taken their places before beginning the service proper. At Korean American committals, the oldest son may walk alongside the pastor to the grave, carrying a picture of the deceased.

The committal service just outlined may be brief or long and may include hymn singing and another sermon, if that is the custom of the faith community. If there is a pall or American flag on the coffin, it is removed before the coffin is lowered into the ground. The pall is folded by the funeral director or pall-bearers and handed to the pastor once the service is ended. If a flag has been used, a representative of a veterans' organization or the funeral director folds it and ceremonially hands it to the next of kin, usually while someone plays "Taps" on a bugle.[16] At some cemeteries the pile of dirt near the grave is covered completely by an Astroturf blanket, but even when this is the case, there is often a board at the head of the grave with a small mound of earth deliberately placed on it for the committal. It is common for the pastor to cast this handful of earth onto the coffin while saying, "This body we commit to the ground, earth to earth, ashes to ashes, dust to dust." Sometimes this occurs simultaneously with the lowering of the coffin into the ground, but not always. In some communities, the pastor casts dirt three times, and in others the immediate family or everyone present casts it, symbolically filling in the grave. Cemetery Workers' Union regulations usually but not always preclude the mourning party from actually completing the job. Some Asian American and African American groups expect that everyone will remain until the cemetery workers finish their task.

A custom related to casting dirt is the placing of individual flowers on the coffin at the committal. This may be done by the pastor, by the immediate family, or by everyone present. At many Scandinavian funerals or committals, each mourner not only places a flower on the coffin but also speaks a few words of tribute and bows to the deceased. This is remarkably similar to the floral tribute and bowing that occurs at the close of a Japanese American funeral.[17]

Committal of a body at a crematorium—unusual in the United States but quite common in the United Kingdom and other parts of the world—follows nearly the same sequence as a ground burial, except the words of committal are likely to be, "We commit [his or her] body to be cremated, ashes to ashes, dust to dust," or "We commit [his or her] body to the elements." In England, there is usually a button inside the lectern that the pastor presses when saying the words of committal. The coffin, which is set on a small, elevated stage, is gradually hidden as curtains close in front of it. In some crematorium chapels there is a second button inside the lectern. Pressing it causes the coffin to move on a system of rollers into the retort (cremation chamber). Once the coffin has vanished completely, the curtains reopen—a rather macabre special effect, in my opinion. Elsewhere in the world, it has become increasingly common for mourners, whether gathered at a church or at a crematorium chapel, to take their leave of the coffin rather than to watch the coffin disappear.[18]

In the United States, committal services involving cremation are likely to involve the interment or scattering of ashes. If the ashes are being interred in

an urn in a columbarium or the ground, the words of committal may be modi-
fied slightly: "We commit the remains of [the person] to this prepared resting
place, that ashes may return to ashes, and dust to dust."[19] Cremains (the cremated remains) are packaged in one of three ways, depending on community
custom and eventual disposition. They may be in a sealed urn or canister, a
sealed metal or stone box, or an unsealed and temporary container. The last
option is chosen if the ashes are going to be scattered rather than interred. The
choreography of the committal is adapted for the situation. Six pallbearers are
obviously not needed to carry an urn or small box. Most often the funeral director carries the container to the place of interment, and the officiating clergy puts
the container in the niche or ground as the words of committal are said. Often
the funeral director or a cemetery worker covers the grave before the mourners
leave. In Japanese American funerals, the cremains are in a box covered with a
tied square of white cloth called a *furoshiki.* The cloth is left intact around the
box when it is sealed in the cemetery vault.[20]

If the cremains are to be scattered, the funeral director makes sure that the
ashes and fragments of bone are fine enough to be indistinguishable. Since cremation is considered to be the final disposition of human remains, there are few
laws limiting where the ashes may be scattered. You must obtain permission to
scatter them in a cemetery garden or on any property owned by someone else.
Scattering at sea must take place at least five hundred yards from shore; this
includes inland navigable waters, except for lakes.[21] Cremains should be suffi-
ciently dispersed or buried so that they are not recognizable by the public.
Mourners should not be downwind of the cremains as they are scattered, obviously. As you say the words of committal, the cremains are either poured out
or scattered by hand in a sowing motion, or a combination of the two. In cases
when the bereaved did not have a chance to view or touch the body of the
deceased before cremation, seeing the pastor touch the cremains in scattering
can be a powerful and healing experience.

MEMORIAL SERVICES

A Christian memorial service is very like a Christian funeral except that the body
of the deceased is not present. The structure of the service may be almost identical to the structure of the funeral; there may even be a procession consisting
of the pastor, other worship leaders, and the family of the deceased. Increasingly common in the United States, memorial services are chosen over funerals
for several reasons:

- The interment of the body was private or occurred a great distance from
  the church where the memorial service is being held.

- Family members or the community find it easier to focus on worship in a memorial service than at a funeral, where the body is present.

- The body has already been cremated, with or without a wake at the funeral home.

- The body was donated to a medical school or research facility.

- Family members or the community could not come together for a funeral immediately after the person's death.

- The design of the church would make it difficult to convey the coffin to the foot of the chancel steps.

- The church, pastor, or musicians were already booked when the funeral would have taken place.

- It is more economical to have a memorial service than a wake and funeral.[22]

Some communities of faith experience memorial services as more celebratory than funerals by focusing on the deceased's participation in the resurrection victory of Christ.[23] Because a memorial service usually occurs after the committal, the visible, tangible separation from the deceased has already occurred, whether hours, days, or weeks earlier. The bereaved may therefore be further along in the grieving process, though this is not necessarily the case. It is also common for the family to feel a letdown after the committal; the adrenaline or shock that operated immediately after the loved one's death has loosened its grip. For people in this condition, the memorial service can be an occasion when the rite of passage they are going through is acknowledged and God's comfort is extended through the pastor and the community. For others, a memorial service at a later date extends the absence of closure they feel. This is more likely to be the situation if memorial services are the exception rather than the rule in the mourners' church.

It should be noted that there may be both a funeral and a memorial service or ritual for the deceased. When this is the case, the memorial may take many forms, depending on custom, church mandate, and personal preference:

- The family of the deceased may sit as a group at the Sunday service following the funeral. The death may be announced, followed by silence, a brief prayer, and tolling of the church bell.

- Some other form of brief memorial may be incorporated into a Sunday service.

- A service may be held in the family home at a later date.

- The deceased may be remembered on the Sunday closest to the feasts of All Saints and All Souls (November 1 and 2), along with others who have died in the past twelve months.

The customs for secondary memorial services vary from one ethnic group or denomination to another. Japanese American, Korean American, and Pakistani American Christians have worship services to commemorate the first anniversary of a person's death. Tongan American Christians make a monetary gift to the church in memory of the departed on the first anniversary. Cambodian Americans and immigrants from the Philippines have even more memorial services, usually held at home; for Cambodian Americans, these occur on the 7th, 100th, and 365th days after someone's death, and for Philippine immigrants, they occur on the 9th, 40th, and 365th days. In Ghanian American congregations, the family comes forward and reads an account of the person's life one Sunday after the funeral.[24] In churches where fresh flowers are part of Sunday worship, people of any ethnic or denominational heritage may provide a floral arrangement in memory of their loved one on the Sunday closest to the anniversary of the person's death or birth.

RECURRING QUESTIONS AND SPECIAL CIRCUMSTANCES FOR FUNERALS

Some issues connected with Christian rites for the dead our grandparents never imagined—and a few perennial problems have been faced by pastors and congregations for generations. A sound biblical and theological foundation is needed to address such exigencies. As appropriate, liturgical resources and sermons for such situations are provided in Part Two of this book.

Services for Those Who Are Not Professed Christians

Being asked to conduct a funeral for someone who was not a professed Christian raises fundamental questions about the purpose of the Christian funeral and how we understand our ministry to the bereaved. Because a Christian funeral is a worship service in which we give thanks to God for the life of the one being remembered, an opportunity to proclaim the Gospel of Jesus Christ, and worship that extends pastoral care to the bereaved and guides them through a difficult rite of passage, I have no qualms about conducting services for non-Christians. The faith commitment (or lack thereof) of the deceased is not the stumbling block it would be at other Christian rites of passage, such as baptism or marriage, because the deceased is not making any vows to or before God in the name of Jesus Christ. Nor is the reputation or record of the dead person an issue; whatever kind of life this person led, he or she is a sinner in need of God's grace—and so am I. However, if I am asked to conduct services for a non-Christian, I do make clear that, as a minister of the Gospel, I conduct *Christian* worship, not generic, secular memorial services. We do not pay our respects to the deceased in a Christian funeral, as though he or she is being praised; instead, we praise and worship the Lord of Life.

A Service for Someone You Did Not Know

As with non-Christians, I see no impediment to conducting the funeral of someone I did not know. The exception would be if I were informed that the deceased had another religious commitment, such as Muslim or Buddhist; in that case, I would suggest that a leader from that faith community conduct the service instead. The funeral director or next of kin can normally supply you with biographical material to incorporate into an obituary or funeral meditation. It is unnecessary and counterproductive to announce, "Although I never knew [insert name of deceased]. . . ." Those closest to the deceased are already aware of the fact without you stating the obvious. In addition, who the dead person was is of less significance at a Christian service than who Jesus Christ is. The bereaved must ultimately draw comfort and meaning from the latter, not from the former.

Services for Stillborn or Miscarried Infants

Your congregation may or may not be familiar with such services, but they are an opportunity to offer pastoral care to devastated parents and family, and to commend the child into God's tender care. We need not raise questions about the state of the infant's soul or whether the baby was baptized. Conducting funerary rites for miscarried and stillborn children gives voice to our lament and our ultimate hope in Christ. Many of the resources for funerals of children, found in Part Two of this book, may be used for stillborn and miscarried infants as well. The United Methodist *Book of Worship* is one denominational service book that offers a special liturgy for this difficult occasion.

Services for Suicides

In the first few centuries of the Church, many Christians regarded suicide or making sure that some oppressor killed them as an acceptable way to follow Jesus.[25] In *The City of God,* Augustine wrote at length why suicide was not worthy of a Christian, and from 346 A.D. on, funeral rites—including burial in consecrated ground—were forbidden to those who had committed suicide. The Roman Catholic Church lifted the prohibition in 1983, but some Protestant traditions still follow the old practice.

There is no question that suicide is shocking and tragic. It leaves family and friends in critical need of pastoral care. It raises complex questions about biblical interpretation and precedents. But even if we regard suicide as the most grievous of sins, we cannot claim that it separates a person from the love of Christ (Rom. 8:31–39). Conducting the funeral for someone who has ended his or her life suddenly and dramatically does not mean that we condone suicide, any more than conducting an addict's funeral indicates that we endorse substance abuse. The cause of death should not determine whether or not we will conduct the funeral. If anything, the occurrence of a suicide should spur us on to lead our congregation in further study and discussion of theological, psychological, and legal issues connected with the subject.

Masonic and Other Rituals

The key issue here is not the relative merits of one fraternal group or another, nor is it the degree of involvement the deceased had (or mourners currently have) with such organizations. You are a minister of the Gospel, you conduct Christian worship, and all that happens in a funeral, or any other service, is to the glory of God and the edification of the worshipers. Therefore, although it may be appropriate for a Christian who is also a member of a lodge to have a role in the funeral service, such as reading one of the Scriptures, it is not appropriate for anything other than Christian worship to happen during the funeral. After all, if the deceased was a Ku Klux Klan member, you wouldn't incorporate cross burning into the service. If she was a Girl Scout, you wouldn't sell cookies at the committal.

Some churches unambiguously prohibit lodge rituals during their funerals and memorial services. *The Lutheran Book of Worship* (1978) states, "The ceremonies or tributes of social or fraternal societies have no place within the service of the Church."[26] The policy of the Church of the Brethren also frowns on them: "Services shared with fraternal groups or military units are not recommended. When the family insists on a service other than Christian worship, the services should be held separately."[27] Presbyterians have similar wording in their *Book of Common Worship:* "The ceremonies and rites of fraternal, civic or military organizations, if any, should occur at some other time and place."[28] This end may be accomplished by telling the family that the fraternal group may go through its rite during the visitation period, but not in conjunction with any wake service you are leading. Another option is for the group to have a memorial service later on, at their lodge. The Freemasons in some states have graveside services as well as funeral rites.[29] These should not be combined with the committal service for the same reason that they should not be part of the service in the church. You and your congregation would be wise to begin a discussion of fraternal orders and secret societies in relationship to Christianity before being faced with them in planning a funeral with a family. As with other matters, the discussion may be initiated through the church newsletter, a sermon, or an adult class.

Military, Fire Department, and Police Funerals

At first glance, these situations appear to be similar to Masonic rituals. Why should a person or group in special uniform fold a flag, play "Taps" on a bugle, march behind a piper, or do anything else that is not otherwise part of a Christian funeral? The difference is that churches appoint Christian clergy to minister to these groups; the services they conduct are, or should be, Christian worship using language and symbols of a particular culture. For example, a police chaplain may conduct a St. Jude service during the wake of an officer (St. Jude is the patron saint of police), and should be able to offer vocation-specific counseling and pastoral care to the late officer's family. When working with military, police, and fire department chaplains, care should be taken to preserve the christocentric focus of the funeral service rather than emphasizing the heroism or other merits of the deceased or advertising the organization's culture.

Accepting Honoraria for Funerals

Honoraria are not a simple matter. Although some pastors may quote, "The laborer deserves his wages" (1 Tim. 5:18), other ministers may claim that, like Paul, we should learn the secret of being content with either plenty or hunger, abundance or want (Phil. 4:11–12). Some denominations expressly forbid their clergy from accepting an honorarium for the funeral of a church member. In other traditions, the estimated honoraria for weddings and funerals are calculated as part of the pastor's total compensation. As noted in Chapter Two, some funeral homes include an honorarium for the pastor as part of the package price quoted to the family.

Obviously, the answer is not to snub a bereaved and grateful family that wants to do something for you, nor is it right to curry favor with a funeral director so that more funerals for the unchurched—and more fees—come your way. You also don't want a church member to feel that he or she cannot afford the additional expense of having you conduct a loved one's funeral. This is a matter for prayer and reflection on your own, with the church's staff, and possibly with the church's governing board. The church's wedding policy and fee schedule may suggest guidelines. If there are several people on the church staff, you may want to share any honoraria equally with them, because they are working behind the scenes and taking on extra duties to free your time for the funeral. Another possibility is putting a percentage of any honoraria received in a memorial fund or pastor's discretionary fund. Whatever decision is made by you and the leaders of your congregation, it should be made known to the general membership.

High-Tech Liturgy

People have been photographing the dead since the invention of the camera. When infant mortality rates were higher than they are today, it was not uncommon to take a photo of the dead baby, usually fully dressed and often held by the mother. This was one way of remembering the reality of the child's life, however brief. It is still common in some traditions to photograph the dead person in his or her coffin. There may be a number of reasons for this; for example, if a family member was unable to attend the rites for the dead, having a photograph may be a means of vicarious participation in the rite of passage that took place. A photograph may provide a catharsis for others, helping them come to terms with what has happened.[30] In some cases, a photograph may function somewhat like an icon for the bereaved, helping them to focus prayers of thanksgiving or intercession, or bringing to mind the faith manifested by the deceased. If a photograph is to be taken, it should be during the visitation, not the funeral. It should be done only with the permission of the family of the deceased, and if it is the custom for family members to be in the photograph with the deceased, no one should be coerced into getting into the picture.

What about videotaping the service? This should be discouraged. Photography is not an act of worship; more often it disrupts worship. It can be an intrusion into the privacy of mourners. Even so, the absence of a family member may be one argument for audio or video recording of the service. Many churches have a policy for videotaping of weddings, such as one stationery camera at the back or in a sound booth. The same policy could be in place for funerals and memorial services, with the added condition that the camera be aimed only at the chancel area from which worship is being led and not focused on the congregation. The most offensive funeral I ever attended had not one but two roving camcorders. Mourners were to file by the open coffin at the close of the service while the camera operators stood behind the coffin catching each individual on tape as he or she came forward. Only pity for the widow of the deceased prevented me from demonstrating my dismay to those doing the filming, who had destroyed any sense of worship.

In these days, when virtually anything is televised, the deceased may have made a video of himself or herself, with hopes that it would be played at the funeral. This is not Christian worship, even if the tape has the person saying religious things. If the deceased was a preacher or hymn writer, something from his or her work may be read or sung by others at the service, but in Christian worship, the living give thanks to God for the life and witness of the deceased rather than the deceased celebrating his or her life and witness. If the family is adamant about having a tape played, explain to them that they may arrange to do so during the wake (at a time other than when a wake service is taking place) or at an informal gathering after the service.

Other high-tech innovations being introduced into North American bereavement practices do not disrupt worship but attempt to present a substitute for it. One example of this is the memorial Web site, listed along with the location of the funeral home in the obituary column. Rather than traveling to a funeral home or church, having face to face contact with the bereaved, and worshiping God, people can simply log on and express their kind thoughts in the site's guest book; or they can go to one of many greeting card Web sites and send an electronic sympathy card to the mourners' e-mail addresses. This is not an adequate substitute for presence any more than chat rooms are a satisfactory substitute for family and friends.

Another example of synthetic sympathy made possible by technology is the drive-through visitation. At least one funeral home in Chicago has a facility where you can drive up to a closed-circuit television monitor and type in the name of the dead person you want to see, and a photograph of the body in the coffin will appear on screen. The drive-through visitation allows you to avoid any uncomfortable pauses in conversation with the bereaved, because you have no contact with them. Needless to say, no pastoral care is extended to them when friends simply order a video image in the same way they would order a burger and fries.

Security Concerns

U.S. citizens live in a violent society that places little value on human life per se. By contrast, Jesus taught that all people are precious in God's sight. One way we embody that teaching for mourners is by attending to their need for physical safety as well their need for spiritual comfort. Security may be an issue when conducting funerals if any of the following is a factor:

- The deceased was the victim or perpetrator of a crime.
- The deceased was a gang member or his or her family had a connection with a gang.
- The deceased was a public figure.
- The deceased had criminal associations.
- The deceased or the family of the deceased was or is wealthy by community reckoning.
- An enormous crowd is expected at the funeral home or church, so traffic control and neighborhood safety become issues.

The funeral director and local police are usually aware if any of these circumstances apply. The family should ask a friend (or you can recruit a church member) to house-sit for them during the hours they will be away from their home. This is advised because burglars are less apt to break into an occupied house, and a newspaper obituary announces to all the world when the family will not be home. It is also appropriate to ask police to drive by the house when the family will be at the funeral home, church, and cemetery. Additional security arrangements must be made if the body of the deceased is to be on display anywhere or transported from church or funeral home to a place of interment. If the deceased had any gang connections, for instance, members of a rival gang may attempt to steal or mutilate the body, vandalize the funeral home or church, or attack gang members or their families who are present. Policies for providing security for the family and deceased vary from one part of the country to another. In Chicago, for example, police may be posted for security outside the funeral home and church but do not serve as bouncers inside.[31] If there is difficulty obtaining police protection and crowd control, the funeral director can hire private security to maintain order. If possible, you should sit down with the family, funeral director, and law enforcement representatives before the wake to discuss what security procedures will be followed if trouble threatens.

Reporters

When a funeral requires special attention to security, the press may also be involved. If you already have a policy in place regarding photography and videotaping during the service, it may be brought to bear in dealing with mass media coverage. Before or after the funeral, reporters may approach you hoping for a statement that makes good copy. Your main concern in this situation will be fidelity to your calling and responsibility. This fidelity is manifested in several ways: bearing witness to our hope through Jesus Christ, representing the faith in terms intelligible to outsiders, maintaining confidences the bereaved have shared with you, refraining from placing individuals or the church in a legally compromising situation, and consulting with congregational leaders and other appropriate persons before an anticipated encounter with the press.

Pastoral Concerns in Conducting Funerals

The range of special circumstances that pastors encounter may be daunting to some readers. Fortunately, these are the exception, not the rule. However, whatever the denomination, ethnic or racial identity, or degree of formality in worship, all contemporary pastors will be challenged by two pastoral concerns in ministry to the bereaved: clarity and hospitality.

The need for clarity. The Christian funeral is an opportunity to proclaim the Gospel. That proclamation must be as straightforward and free from in-house code language as possible in order for visitors to understand it. Referring to texts by citation only is not advised; it effectively shuts out those who don't know the Bible well. Even if this is your usual method in Sunday morning preaching, it will not communicate effectively at a funeral, where your congregation is not taking notes. Simple language is also appreciated by the mourners, who may be too wracked by grief to take in a complicated exposition of a text. If congregational participation is expected, page numbers for hymns and prayers should be printed in a bulletin, as well as instructions for participation. The instructions may be as simple as an asterisk with the explanation "Please stand."

Hospitality as invitation. When you conduct a funeral or otherwise lead Christian worship, one thing you are doing is embodying and proclaiming God's gracious initiative toward us. It is a kind of hospitality to people in sorrow, reminiscent of the Risen Christ's invitation to his followers to "Come and have breakfast" by the Sea of Galilee. Jesus did not force-feed the disciples, and neither should we as we lead worship. We should invite participation, but we should not coerce people or shame them if, for whatever reason, they do not feel ready to take part.

Where does this become an issue in funerals? First, some mourners may question attending the service at all. Chinese American and Korean American parents may or may not attend a funeral of their own child because of the misfortune the death is perceived to bring upon the whole family.[32] In the rare situations where this is an issue, your task is to extend pastoral care in other ways to those who feel they cannot attend the service, not to bully them into going. Among the Orthodox and other ethnic and cultural groups, it is the custom for the family or the entire congregation to give the dead a final kiss of peace. If this is the custom where you are pastor, you may announce when it is to occur and invite anyone present who wishes to participate to do so; but physical and psychological space should be available to those who don't want to participate. Also, no pressure should be put on the bereaved or anyone else to speak at the wake, funeral, or repast.

CONCLUSION

The previous chapter suggested ways to listen to a culture and learn its language, symbols, and history. The purpose in this chapter has been to present the various settings in which the pastor speaks in times of bereavement. Fidelity to Christian teaching, sensitivity to pastoral care needs, and the desire for cultural intelligibility will inform your leadership. The same factors are brought to bear when conducting services in times of crisis, which is the main focus of the next chapter.

CHAPTER FOUR

Is There Any Word from the Lord?

Services for Difficult Times

In January 1986 I made a brief trip to Durham, North Carolina, to be interviewed for a faculty position at Duke University Divinity School. There was little downtime in the interview schedule; I was to meet with individuals and groups from breakfast time until mid-afternoon, when I would present a lecture to faculty and students. Then meetings would continue until 8:30 or 9:00 P.M. The following morning I was to preach in a seminary chapel service. At one point in that long first day, someone burst into the room and cried, "Have you heard the news? The shuttle crashed!" The *Challenger* had met with disaster moments after liftoff, and all on board had perished. The interview process continued, but a pall was cast over it. When I returned to my hotel room that night and turned on the television, it seemed that every station kept running videotape of the moment the *Challenger* broke apart.

Aside from my own feelings about the tragedy, I was in something of a dilemma. What was I going to say in chapel the next morning? I had prepared a sermon, of course, but my message had nothing to do with the *Challenger* disaster. Should I set it aside and try to compose something that spoke to the events of the day? Should I go ahead with the sermon I had ready and acknowledge the crash in the prayers of intercession? I did not know the people in the congregation—whether or how much they were grieving. They were not my pastoral responsibility, yet I assumed they would be evaluating my preaching content and style for pastoral sensitivity, among other things. I wasn't sure what was needed, what was expected, or what I should do.

It is easier in many respects to strategize for services pertaining to death than for those pertaining to crisis. There is little debate in local congregations about what constitutes death, but there may be differing opinions about what constitutes a crisis. Denominational service books have suggested liturgies for times of sorrow. Whatever our culture, customs surrounding death can provide a measure of security for those whose lives are torn by grief; but we have fewer resources at hand when we consider other chaotic or stressful experiences that may happen to individuals, the congregation, or the community. After reading Rosemary Radford Ruether's *Women-Church,* with its innovative rituals, a clergy friend and I used to joke that we, too, were going to create a set of new liturgies for rites of passage experienced by people in the congregation: acquiring one's first credit card, declaring bankruptcy, getting a tattoo, registering for the draft, winning the lottery, being indicted, and so on. Although we never got beyond composing extemporaneous collects for these occasions, the truth is that some of them represent genuine crises. For purposes of this discussion, I want to include under the heading *crisis* those occasions when events outside the normal liturgical calendar cause your congregation to inquire anxiously, "Is there any word from the Lord?" (Jer. 37:17).

"Is there any word from the Lord?" is indeed the right question to ask, because the Lord is the Christian's starting point for contemplating matters of faith and life. In discussing the Apostles' and Nicene Creeds earlier, we were reminded that in these creeds, belief in Jesus Christ and his Resurrection from the dead precedes references to human destiny. And just as Christians grapple with the mystery of death in light of who Jesus is, so do Christians look to the words and acts of the Redeemer to get their bearings in times of crisis. They look to you, their pastor, to remind them of the word from the Lord and to enable them to experience it anew in their current distress.

There will, of course, be events that cause individuals rather than the entire church to ask if there is any word from the Lord, but it is primarily the community of faith and its worship that are under consideration here. As with services connected with death, the denominational and ethnic identity of the congregation and other factors of local context will shape the liturgy and your leadership.

CRISIS AND THE CHURCH CALENDAR

Before I go into detail about the structure and choreography of the four types of crisis service, a general observation about planning worship in times of crisis is in order. In *Preaching in and out of Season,* Thomas G. Long and Neely Dixon McCarter acknowledge that the church operates under at least three calendars: the Christian year, the secular calendar, and the program calendar of local and denominational emphases.[1] The Christian year is an annual cycle beginning with the first Sunday in Advent and ending with Christ the King or Judgment Sunday. The lectionary most commonly used in the United States includes a three-year cycle of readings for each Sunday of every season of the year. The secular calendar overlaps with the church's worship and program on such days as Labor Day and the start of the school year, Mother's Day and Father's Day, Memorial Day and Independence Day, and so on. These days are not intrinsically religious, yet they are often baptized into our worship together. Finally, the program calendar of local and denominational emphases also finds expression in worship, as in Stewardship Month, Race Relations Sunday, Home Missions Week, and others.

Different elements may be added to the structure of the Sunday morning service to mark special days in these three calendars without changing the basic format of the worship service. It should also be noted that these calendars may find expression in the service not just in the sermon but also through various acts of worship. For example, on Mother's Day the pastor may preach about Mary, the Mother of Jesus. The congregation may sing "Happy the Home When God Is There."[2] There may be a special offering to support a maternity hospital in another land. Ushers may give flowers to every mother present.

Ministry in times of crisis should take its cues from the ways we observe the three calendars that shape the worship and other programs of the church. A crisis is usually (but not always) an interruption of the other calendars, but it is not an interruption of worship itself. Instead, in the course of worship we acknowledge the event or issue that has precipitated the question, "Is there any word from the Lord?" and then announce the prophet's answer—"There is"— through preaching and other parts of the liturgy.

FOUR MODELS FOR RESPONSE

Because the exigencies of different crises vary, it stands to reason that there will be more than one way for worship to proclaim hope and comfort in times of distress. There are at least four types of liturgical event in which you may be involved: the Sunday-after-the-crisis service, the ecumenical service, the community interfaith service, and the anniversary or commemorative service. Each event has its advantages and limitations, as we shall see. After these models are presented, other types of sociopolitical liturgies and paraliturgies connected with crisis and sorrow are presented and discussed.

The Sunday After

The Sunday-after-the-crisis service is the one you will have to prepare and lead most often, simply because Sunday worship is the service you lead most often. Ronald Allen describes the pressures the pastor may experience as he or she comes to grips with whatever has happened: "In extreme moments, the preacher may be immediately swamped by a host of unanticipated pastoral responsibilities, such as calling on the bereaved or helping organize community action. But important as such roles are, the Sunday service is coming and one of the minister's most significant functions in extremity is to help the community begin to make Christian sense of the events. The sermon deserves the best attention that time allows."[3]

Whether or not you scuttle an already-prepared sermon to address the crisis homiletically depends on the answers to several questions:

• *Does the text with which you have been working have words to address the crisis?* Sometimes it is easy to make a connection between the text and the crisis at hand. For example, on the Sunday closest to the nationwide publication of *The Starr Report,* the Gospel reading suggested by the ecumenical Common Lectionary was Luke 15:1–10. The themes of lostness and restoration spoke clearly to the situation.

• *How close is the crisis to your congregation?* If church members are talking about the crisis, they are probably invested in it. If it isn't a subject they bring up, they may not be aware of the crisis or their hunger for a word from the Lord. In the latter case, you may want to raise their awareness through a topical sermon or adult class, but you are less likely to replace an already-prepared message, as though they already own the urgency of the situation. For example, in the early part of 2001, people in the United States were well aware of the foot-and-mouth disease crisis in Europe, but Americans did not experience it as a crisis in their own lives.

• *What other parts of worship may address the crisis?* In the chapel service the day after the *Challenger* disaster, I decided to preach the lectionary-based sermon I had prepared and address the grief and shock over the tragedy through the prayers of intercession. On the Sundays following the sinking of the submarine *Kursk* in 2000, "Eternal Father, Strong to Save" was sung in many churches.

• *What will be the duration of the crisis, that is, is it an unfolding situation that may be addressed at other times in worship or elsewhere?* When I lived in the north of England, the troubles in Northern Ireland were never far from public consciousness. No one expected a quick or durable resolution. The pain of that situation was noted occasionally in sermons, often mentioned in community prayer, and addressed through the other aspects of the church's ministry, such as conferences and youth trips. Samuel D. Proctor's book *Preaching About Crises in the Community*[4] offers useful suggestions for preaching in contexts where people must carry on indefinitely in an unresolved crisis.

Let me give some examples of crisis situations and how clergy responded in the Sunday-after framework. In the first chapter I mentioned a large suburban congregation whose church building burned down. The crisis was so acute that the pastor did not wait until the Sunday after to begin addressing it; a special service was held just hours after the flames were extinguished. The sermon, hymns, and prayers were not based on lectionary texts, but they all proclaimed God's sovereignty and providence in the midst of the disaster.[5] The Sunday morning after the fire was All Saints Day. The pastor used the appointed readings to preach about lessons we learn from the saints—Christians who were faithful "in spite of dungeon, fire and sword"—and about the evidence of God's grace at work through present-day saints who ministered in the midst of the current situation. (Two of his related sermons, "They Said So!" and "Holding It Together," are included in the section on crisis sermons in Part Two of this book.) In the weeks and months following the fire, the crisis was not forgotten—how could it be? However, the congregation resumed following its calendars and the crisis was addressed in other ways: through meetings of the trustees and other decision-making committees, through pastoral care of individuals and groups, and through changes in the rest of the church's programs.

A second Sunday-after situation in recent years was the massacre at Columbine High School in April 1999. For the Rev. Dennis Hagstrom's Lutheran congregation, just north of Denver, the crisis was close to home. They needed to hear the situation addressed directly in the Sunday sermon. Pastor Hagstrom found that the Gospel text for that Sunday, John 10:1–10, spoke comfort and hope in the midst of the tragedy. Therefore, he preached from the lectionary, and the rest of the liturgy, coordinated with the sermon text, reinforced the theme of the service. (His sermon, "Columbine," is included in the section on crisis sermons in Part Two.) As for the rest of the church calendar, the night after the shooting the confirmation class met as usual, but the regular lesson was scrapped and Pastor Hagstrom led the group in discussion of the tragedy and in prayer for those involved.[6]

On January 17, 1995, an earthquake wrought devastation around Kobe, Japan. At that time I was part of a U.S. congregation that was 50 percent *nisei* and *sansei* (second- and third-generation Japanese Americans). On the Sunday following the earthquake, the associate pastor, who was a native of Kobe, gave a report based on information he had received from the pastor of the Methodist church in Kobe. He led the congregation in prayer, and an offering for earthquake victims was collected. The remainder of the worship service continued as planned. In this situation, the pastors were sensitive to several dynamics in the congregational culture: that half of the congregation had roots in that part of the world, but the other half did not; that esteem and concern for the associate pastor was held by everyone in the congregation; and that there was opportunity to address the crisis through concrete action and simultaneously strengthen ties with a sister church on the other side of the world. Other than a subsequent update in the church newsletter, the crisis was not mentioned again, in worship or elsewhere in the church's program.

Planning a service for the Sunday after a crisis event requires discernment and a good understanding by the pastor of the congregational culture and its worldview. The pastors of the half-nisei and -sansei congregation, for example, already knew that in general the laity were shy about praying extemporaneously before others, but they were glad to be led in prayer by a minister. The pastors also knew that the congregation was full of doers; they were more willing to take action for a cause than to meditate on an issue. So the service for that Sunday was designed to be an authentic expression of worship by that congregational culture as they acknowledged a calamity.

Another element of discernment is knowing what will and will not be considered a crisis. Karl Barth's adage about the preacher having the Bible in one hand and the newspaper in the other has sometimes been misunderstood and misused by clergy. For instance, the pastor may perceive an unexpected or developing event as a crisis worthy of preempting other things in the worship calendar, while the congregation may be aware of the event but face it with equanimity or apathy. The reverse can also be true, of course. As stated earlier, the more church members talk about a situation, the more likely it is that they perceive it as important. It is also true that the mass media increase or diminish the perceived significance of a crisis by the amount of coverage they give the event. Monitoring mass media and listening to the congregation talk, therefore, will help you gauge whether a Sunday-after service is advisable.

The Ecumenical Service

Ecumenical services led by area clergy of different Christian traditions are most commonly associated with Thanksgiving and Good Friday services, but they may also occur in response to crises. Two situations may prompt such a service:

1. The crisis is local but affects people across denominational lines. The clergy and congregations believe that a Christian response through worship is appropriate.

2. The crisis is not sudden and unexpected so much as it is progressive. The ecumenical service is not only an act of worship, but it also expresses the hope that God's power will be manifested before things get worse. The service may also equip the worshipers for specific action.

Countless ecumenical crisis services were held when Martin Luther King Jr. was assassinated in 1968. Racism was not a new crisis, of course, but the death of King and the riots that followed brought communities—particularly white communities—to a new awareness of how deeply their communities and the nation were divided.

A more recent example of an ecumenical crisis service was prompted by a severe drought in the southern and western United States. Television news showed Christians of every stripe in one Texas community gathering on the town square once a week to pray for rain.[7] In this instance, ecumenical worship was also a rallying point for action; these same Christians worked together to build a pipeline from a nearby town that had more water.

Your pastoral task at an ecumenical service is somewhat different from your role in the Sunday-after service with your own congregation. It is impossible to monitor the pastoral care needs of participants for follow-up as you would at home. You cannot appeal to in-house history to give coherence to the crisis, and you may assume that the congregation will be self-selective, that is, it will be made up of people who feel some ownership of the crisis, rather than people attending out of custom. The local church calendar is not being displaced or incorporated, because most ecumenical crisis services do not occur on Sunday morning. The decisions about the worship service do not rest solely in your hands. However, in ecumenical worship your presence makes a powerful witness to common identity and neediness before God, and to Christian belief that the Holy Spirit will lead us forward together in the work that lies ahead.

Theologically, the ecumenical crisis service should be unambiguously christocentric and unambiguously worship. As such, when you take part in planning such a service, you would do well to employ theological guidelines suggested by Geoffrey Wainwright in a lecture on preaching as worship. He lists four characteristics of Christian preaching and worship: they are *doxological, anamnetic, epicletic,* and *eschatological.*[8] By doxological, Wainwright (quoting John Chrysostom) means that everything is done with one goal in view: the glory of God. In an ecumenical crisis service, this may mean that while the circumstances giving occasion for the service are not brushed aside, the congregation is led to more than contemplation of the circumstances; they are moved to praise God's providence in the midst of crisis (Ps. 73:25, 26). Wainwright uses the term *anamnetic* in the sense of reminding the worshiping community of the gospel on which it is founded, embodied in the teaching, person, and work of Jesus Christ.[9] This means that the speakers in Christian worship must not attempt to comfort those in crisis solely by evoking memories of easier times but must point to the Lord who is the hope of the world. For worship to be epicletic, those present assume that no human situation has the permanence of the Word of God (Isa. 40:8). The preacher invokes the help of the Holy Spirit to discern which word from Scripture needs to be proclaimed at a particular time—in this case, in response to the present crisis.[10] Eschatological worship looks forward to God's future as promised in the Bible. It proclaims with confidence that because God is faithful, the present crisis will not have the last word. There is reason for hope rather than panic or despair. The prayer services related to the Texas drought, for example, were anamnetic in their use of texts such as James 5:7, 16–18, and eschatological in evoking the imagery of Isaiah 35.

We might add to Wainwright's list two theological elements that have a legitimate place in the ecumenical crisis service. The first is *lament:* honesty before

God about the experiences, emotions, and questions we bring to this time of worship. Lament in no way cancels out the necessary doxological character of the service; we need look no further than the Psalms for examples of lament and praise coexisting in a single discourse. Pastoral prayer, a psalm read responsively, or a prepared recitation of the particulars of the crisis are ways of articulating the crisis in the context of worship. This allows lament to occur without letting it take over the service and compromise the transition that should occur (as it does in Ps. 22, for example) from lament to praise. "The Difference Christ Makes," a sermon by Lance Webb, is included in the section on sermon briefs in Part Two. It demonstrates this movement from lament to praise.

A second element that may be incorporated into the ecumenical crisis service is an *invitation to respond* to the word in one way or another. This differs from the liturgical response that might occur in the Sunday morning service, such as saying a creed or coming forward for baptism. At the crisis service, worshipers may be invited to contribute to a relief offering, to work on a project to get the community through a crisis, to forge new relationships, and so on. For example, people involved in the ecumenical prayer services during the drought in Texas took on a new project together—laying a pipeline—and forged new relationships with volunteer laborers from a nearby prison. They celebrated the signs of God's purpose being worked out in the midst of a difficult time.

The Community Interfaith Service

This type of service occurs less frequently than the Sunday-after or ecumenical crisis service. Religious pluralism is manifested in its leadership, and it draws nonreligious attendees as well as people who are members of faith communities. Other characteristics common to this type of crisis service are as follows:

- The crisis is perceived as more global than in the ecumenical service.
- The crisis may be a single event, such as a plane crash, or an ongoing, developing situation, such as world hunger.
- The service may be planned and led in part by major players in the crisis whose religious commitments, if any, are unknown.
- Ongoing pastoral care of those attending the service is not a factor, or it is perceived as a job for specialists such as social workers, lobbyists, and the legal system.
- There is more likely to be an anniversary service or other public follow-up to the community interfaith service than to a Sunday-after or ecumenical service.

The community interfaith crisis service often presents the Christian pastor with a paradox. On the one hand, if you are invited to have a role in planning and leading such a service, it is almost certainly by virtue of your vocation. On the other hand, you may be expected to soft-pedal your christocentric orientation, or not express it at all. Leaders of other religious groups are faced with the same dilemma regarding their faith commitments. The result, sometimes, is a service that has less to do with worship than with crisis. Lament becomes the prominent note, and preaching becomes opaque, that is, no transcendent reality is invoked, nor is any "God larger than and sovereign over history, no God whose powerful yet gentle presence can give us courage" when speaking of the situation that was the impetus for the service.[11]

A report suggesting such a community service was published by the Associated Press after a Concorde jet crashed near Paris in July 2000. Many of the passengers were from the German city of Moenchengladbach. The German chancellor spoke at a hastily arranged service on the grounds of the World's Fair in Hanover. "Today, Germany is shaken," were the only words from his address quoted in the press release. There were three other lament quotes in the article.[12] In fairness to those involved in this crisis service, they had no control over what was included in the Associated Press article. Another memorial service at the Madeleine Church in Paris, reported on television news, more clearly invoked God's presence and comfort in crisis. Airline employees, relatives, and French and German government officials attended, and the primary leader was the Roman Catholic auxiliary bishop of Paris. Nevertheless, the tendency in interfaith services is to make lament and supplication the two liturgical priorities. Any anamnesis is focused on remembering how the crisis came about and reciting the details. Epiclesis is a factor in asking God's help in getting through the crisis, though sometimes divine intervention in the crisis is also invoked. The eschatological dimension in interfaith services is likely to be rather humanistic, resolving that the future will be different because of human effort, rather than proclaiming God's sovereignty over history. When death figures as part of the crisis, references to the afterlife are often nebulous and not based on Scripture.

It should be acknowledged that not every community interfaith service in time of crisis has all the characteristics outlined here. For example, in 1999 an Episcopal church in Chicago hosted "an interfaith service for the beetle-infested trees of Ravenswood"[13] after the discovery of Asian long-horn beetles in the area resulted in the destruction of many of the neighborhood's oldest, largest trees. The service was anchored in the community, though the situation precipitating the service had a global dimension. Native American, African, and Judeo-Christian worship materials were used in worship, which took place in the church and was led primarily by the pastor. There were readings from both the Old and New Testaments, though there were no explicit references to Jesus Christ. Lament was balanced with thanksgiving for the goodness of creation. There was, however, theological dissonance between the final hymn, "O God, Our Help in Ages Past," and the closing prayer:

Those who are dead are never gone,
They are there in the thickening shadow.
The dead are not under the earth:
They are in the tree that rustles. . . .
They are in the hut, they are in the crowd,
The dead are not dead.[14]

When you are asked to participate in a community interfaith worship service in response to a crisis, you will probably have less influence shaping the service than you would in an ecumenical service. Given that your participation will be limited, it is crucial that in the portion of the service for which you have responsibility you point to the Lord who has borne our griefs and carried our sorrows, the God who has a word for us in the present situation, and the Sovereign to whom the future belongs.

There may also be times that a Christian pastor decides not to participate in an interfaith service, such as when it is evident in advance that his or her witness to faith will be compromised. A few times in my ministry when I did not know what would be said or done in a service other than my own role, during the service there were ritual words and acts in which I could not participate. In these cases, I sat or stood quietly until the service ended, and voiced my concerns to the planners afterward.

The Anniversary Service

Of the four main types of crisis service, the anniversary service is the one that a North American pastor is least likely to have occasion to lead. An anniversary service is apt to resemble the community interfaith service in that it may involve leadership and attendance from people outside the faith community, and it usually occurs in response to an event of global dimensions. A memorial may be dedicated at this service. Such was the case at the service in Oklahoma City on the anniversary of the 1995 bombing. Anniversary services may be reported by the mass media and have a didactic as well as a liturgical function, as in special services marking the anniversary of D-Day and other patriotic holidays. Through the service, the history of the crisis is repeated and passed on to the next generation. "Remembrance of the Dead," by Grace Donovan, found in the section on sermon briefs in Part Two, is an example of a sermon suitable for an anniversary service.

The order of worship at a crisis anniversary service may be simple and fairly spontaneous, or it may resemble a dedication of church furnishings and ornaments. I participated in an instance of the former when I was living in Stockholm in 1995. A year earlier the ferry *Estonia* had sunk in the Baltic, with tremendous loss of life. The crisis was one of responsibility as well as grief: Who was to blame and how should they be held accountable? On the anniversary of the disaster, a brief period of silence was observed across the country. In the school where I worked, the chief administrator called us to attention, and after the period of silence, clergy and laity of various traditions offered extemporaneous prayers.

Denominational service books often include liturgies for longer and more structured observances. These may contain the following elements:

- Praise (usually hymns)
- Invocation
- Scripture lessons
- A sermon
- Presentation of item to be dedicated
- Prayer of dedication (including thanksgiving, dedication, supplication, and ascription of glory)
- Final hymn

At the crisis anniversary service, a memorial or political address may replace the sermon or be given in addition to the sermon. Representatives from government or from the community immediately affected by the crisis may speak briefly. There is often a moment of silence as everyone present remembers the crisis. If no lasting memorial is being dedicated, other liturgical acts may be incorporated into the service: the lighting of candles, the laying of a wreath, the releasing of balloons, the playing of "Taps" on the bugle, and so on.

Some of the liturgical concerns of the community interfaith service also apply to the anniversary service. Is the crisis being remembered before God or simply being remembered? Do those attending the service have an opportunity to participate in worship through the singing of hymns or other acts? Is the Word of God speaking to the situation, or does the occasion use Scripture as a footnote for another canon being proclaimed? Do the prayers invoke God's presence and direction in finding our way forward, or are they thinly veiled political speeches? As a pastor invited to participate in an anniversary service, you may have limited influence on the rest of the liturgy, but you can nevertheless determine that the part you play will be Christian worship offered to the glory of God.

OTHER LITURGIES AND PARALITURGIES

Some services related to crisis and sorrow do not fall neatly into any of the categories already discussed. Some may occur on Sunday morning, if you are addressing ongoing crises or problems shared by everyone in your congregation.

Others are likely to occur outside your church building and be attended by people invested in the crisis who are not necessarily part of your congregation. Another type of liturgy is a more pastoral office conducted in the home of someone in time of great stress. All of these liturgies may be opportunities to praise God and offer hope through Jesus Christ.

Community Concerns as Crisis

The crisis liturgy that occurs on Sunday morning is suggested by Proctor in *Preaching About Crises in the Community.* He talks about three "crises and priorities" that should be addressed in preaching: the priority of eliminating poverty amid plenty, the priority of education, and the priority of family stability.[15] At first glance, these appear to be ongoing social issues in which the Church has a stake, but not crises that would call for setting aside the church's calendars. We can easily imagine, however, local manifestations of these priorities that would evoke the question, "Is there any word from the Lord?" from church members. For example, a situation that would bring poverty amid plenty into focus might be conflict over whether the church should have a homeless shelter or food pantry on its premises. The dropout rate at the local high school, the need for a tutoring program at the church, or school board elections would make education a high-stress issue. A scandal that destroys the family of a church leader or evidence of domestic violence would raise the stakes in the priority of family stability from ongoing issue to immediate crisis.

In structure, the liturgy for such crises is not different from that of the Sunday-after worship service, which in most Protestant denominations contains the following elements, though the order may vary slightly:

- Prelude
- Call to worship or greeting
- Hymn of praise
- Invocation or other opening prayer
- Act of praise, such as a choir anthem
- Readings from the Bible
- Sermon
- Pastoral prayer
- Offertory
- The Lord's Prayer
- Hymn
- Benediction
- Postlude

This order may be augmented with more hymns, as well as with baptism or Holy Communion, testimonies, the saying of a creed, a prayer of confession, and so on. Suggestions for hymns and Scripture readings for this kind of service are found in Part Two.

One difference between the reasons for Sunday-after services and the priorities and crises Proctor has in mind is that the former involve crises that strike unexpectedly whereas the preaching and worship Proctor describes are for situations the congregation has experienced before and expects to encounter again. A second difference is that your primary sphere of ministry after a Sunday-after service is likely to be follow-up care with your own congregation. In the crisis and priority service Proctor has in mind, your sphere of ministry extends beyond the parish and engages political and economic powers in the larger community. For example, in January 2001 the public learned of the child born from the Rev. Jesse Jackson's adulterous liaison with a former aide. Operation PUSH (People United to Save Humanity) in Chicago held a sociopolitical crisis liturgy. It may be identified as such, rather than as a Sunday-after crisis service, for two reasons: first, the precipitating event was characteristic of the larger, ongoing problem of family stability mentioned by Proctor; and second, Jackson's ongoing influence in the larger political community will be affected by the news of his adultery and by the reaction of Operation PUSH.

Sociopolitical Paraliturgies

Another type of sociopolitical liturgy may be prompted by a crisis event either within your congregation or outside it. It names as a theological issue something that may or may not be perceived by other people as mainly a religious issue. It may take place somewhere other than in the church. Possible reasons for this are that the act of worship may simultaneously be a political demonstration, there may not be unanimity in the congregation about the subject of the crisis, or those attending the service may have other faith commitments that make holding the service on neutral ground appropriate. Some contemporary issues that may prompt crisis liturgies are abortion, homosexuality, capital punishment, war, famine, a world economic summit, or the AIDS epidemic.

Because the AIDS crisis is often linked to homosexuality (regardless of one's view on those issues), I offer an example of a liturgy that deals with both. The service is taken from *Equal Rites: Lesbian and Gay Worship, Ceremonies, and Celebrations*. The liturgy in question, "Telling Love's Story: Remembering and Responding to AIDS,"[16] has many elements common to the structure of a Sunday service:

- *Preparation.* This includes gathering candles, red ribbons, and straight pins to give to each participant, and placing large candles, a loaf of bread, and a glass of water on a cloth that is significant for the occasion.

- *Naming the circle.* Participants give their own names and the name of someone afflicted with HIV/AIDS and then pin a red ribbon on themselves to honor that person.

- *Calling to gather.* One person lights the large candle from the small one and then talks about the AIDS epidemic.

- *Song.* "They Are Falling All Around Me," by Bernice Johnson Reagon, is suggested.

- *A reading.* "Face of AIDS," from *A Shallow Pool of Time,* by Fran Peavey, is recommended.

- *A responsive reading* (nonbiblical).

- *Listening to a song.* "The Letter," by Ruben Blades, is recommended.

- *A poem.* "The Concert," by Ken Cierpial, is suggested.

- *A time of extemporaneous reflection.*

- *Prayers of the faithful.* A litany is provided.

- *Sharing of bread and water.* These are identified as symbols of nourishment.

- *Lighting of candles.* Each person lights a small candle and then speaks.

- *Prayer of hope.*

- *Song.* "We Shall Not Give Up the Fight" is suggested.

- *Greeting of peace.* Participants hug one another.

- *Sending forth.*

At first glance, this order does not look so different from the shape of a Sunday morning service. Ritual acts begin and conclude this assembly. The candles, water, and bread employed in the rite are all used in orthodox Christian worship, though they are used differently. There is singing, an address by one person, music, and prayer. These acts add up to something that seems familiar.

Having acknowledged the similarity, this service cannot be called Christian worship. Nothing from the Bible is read. The name of Jesus is never uttered. The songs are neither praise nor supplication, and there is nothing to suggest that they are intrinsically religious. Other than a few phrases in the prayers, there is little sense of transcendence, of "a God larger than and sovereign over history," to repeat the phrase from Sider and King quoted earlier in this chapter.[17] I would not participate in this crisis service—not because of my views on the crisis but because of my convictions about Christian worship. It might more accurately be called a paraliturgy—that is, it bears a resemblance to Christian worship but does not contain the same substance. If I were asked to conduct such a service, I would try to minimize any sting of refusal by suggesting an alternative Christian liturgy.

By contrast, we may consider two other sociopolitical crisis services related to the same issue. In March 1999 the Rev. Gregory Dell, a United Methodist minister in Chicago, was brought to ecclesiastical trial for conducting same-sex union services, which are forbidden by the denomination's *Book of Discipline.* The trial was a turning point in the United Methodist Church's debate about human sexuality. On the day the trial began, supporters of the church's official position and supporters of Pastor Dell held separate worship events outside the building and elsewhere. Both informal services contained Scripture readings, music, prayer, testimony, benediction, and charge. While the two groups' different convictions were clearly manifested in their liturgies, no one who was present would accuse either of not being Christian worship. Why? Because in both groups' services, the crisis in question was lifted up before God. Prayers for the Holy Spirit's discernment were prayed for in Jesus' name. The Word of God was read for guidance and encouragement. The songs sung were, for the most part, from the denominational hymnal.

What can we learn from all the sociopolitical liturgies mentioned here? They impel me to reflect theologically on the extent to which the life, values, and experiences of the congregation should find expression in any of the services I conduct. The question is not whether I am sympathetic to one political viewpoint or another, to one person's experience over another's; the question is whether the issue displaces worship or is offered up to God in the course of worship. As Marva Dawn has written, "It is absolutely essential that the Church keep God as the subject of worship since to be Christian means to believe that the God revealed in Jesus Christ is everything to us—Creator, Provider, and Sustainer; Deliverer, Redeemer, and Lord; Sanctifier, Inspirer, and Empowerer."[18]

The sociopolitical liturgies in *Equal Rites* are useful in that they employ accessible, simple language to give voice to the fear and grief shared by those both inside and outside the household of faith. Portions of the liturgies may be incorporated into your own crisis worship services or inspire your own creativity in developing liturgy that is contextual and christocentric. Guidelines for selecting hymns and other resources for this type of liturgy are found in Part Two.

Pastoral Office as Crisis Liturgy

A final crisis liturgy to be considered is the pastoral office, conducted privately with only those immediately involved in the crisis. (The word *office* is used here in the sense of a religious or ceremonial observance.) This office may be as informal as extemporaneous prayer at the end of a counseling session or during a follow-up visit with a family after a funeral or other crisis service. Other more structured service resources are also available. The "Service of Hope After Loss of Pregnancy" in *The United Methodist Book of Worship* is one example of such a service. Neither a funeral nor a memorial service, it contains readings from the Old and New Testaments, prayers, a time for witnessing, a hymn, and a blessing.[19] This service is an example of worship that facilitates a rite of passage, just as weddings and baptisms do. The event is acknowledged and mourned before God, and God's healing love is invoked for the blessing of those in crisis. Pastors may also find useful some of the healing rites in Chapter Eight of Ruether's *Women-Church,* such as the "Rite of Healing from Rape" or the "Rededication of a House After a Burglary or Other Violence." These services can be beneficial as part of your ongoing pastoral care for someone who has suffered such trauma. Ruether herself indicates that some rituals of healing should be done with a small group of friends as a means of opening the person in crisis to the healing life forces of creation and redemption.[20]

You may find that a pastoral office develops of its own accord out of a crisis situation. For instance, if you are sitting with the family of someone on trial, your counsel, Scripture readings, and prayers are likely to change as events in the courtroom progress. One value in recording the sequence that occurs is that it may serve you in other pastoral situations where the liturgical task is less explicitly to respond to events as they happen and more to help people work through events that have already occurred. A general sequence for this pastoral office is as follows:

- *Scripture sentence.* Psalm 34:18, Psalm 46:1, or 2 Corinthians 1:3a and 4 may be appropriate, as well as some of the opening sentences noted in Part Two of this book.

- *Prayer of confession or lament.* If everyone present knows from memory a confession from a denominational service book, it may be recited in unison, or the pastor or others present may pray extemporaneously, acknowledging their brokenness and need before God.

- *Scripture reading.* Isaiah 40:28–31, Psalm 116, Mark 4:35–41, or Colossians 1:11–20 are among the texts that may be appropriate.

- *Witness.* Those present may witness to God's sustaining power. In some cases, a ritual act, such as lighting a candle or exchanging a hug, makes visible the gracious work of the Holy Spirit in those involved.

- *Prayer of thanksgiving, intercession, or both.* Again, this prayer may be said by the pastor or others present.

- The Lord's Prayer

- A blessing

CONCLUSION

The people you serve need not recognize or care about the taxonomy of these crisis services as they care about the services pertaining to death. They will, however, be anxious to hear if there is "any word from the Lord" in difficult times. As pastor, your familiarity with the different types of services will help you discern how to speak God's Word and give voice to people's hope in a worship framework appropriate to the situation.

CHAPTER FIVE

Pastoral Care Issues

An elderly church member once told me a story of something that happened to him during World War II. John was part of a Welsh regiment that was gathering its dead and wounded during a lull in the fighting. He discovered that a friend of his had been mortally wounded. As he cradled the dying man in his arms, the soldier looked at him and gasped, "Sing *Cwm Rhondda* for me." Tentatively, John began to sing:

> Guide me, O Thou Great Jehovah,
> Pilgrim through this barren land;
> I am weak, but thou art mighty—
> Hold me with thy pow'rful hand:
> Bread of heaven, Bread of heaven,
> Feed me till I want no more,
> Feed me till I want no more.

Other soldiers joined in—both Welsh and German—their voices growing stronger as they sang the young man home:

> When I tread the verge of Jordan,
> Bid my anxious fears subside;
> Death of death, and hell's destruction,
> Land me safe on Canaan's side.

Songs of praises, songs of praises,
I will ever give to thee;
I will ever give to thee.[1]

The battlefield was as hellish a place as can be imagined, but the Church was manifested as the men lifted their voices in praise to God and in ministry to the dying. We could claim that this was pastoral care to the bereaved; John and the other soldiers present were given hope and purpose as they recalled God's promises together. More than thirty years after the war's end, John pointed to that episode as a turning point in his faith.

The issue under consideration in this chapter is pastoral care in times of crisis and sorrow. The story just told by an elderly church member underscores the purpose of the care offered by Christian pastors and laity: to glorify God and equip the saints for faithful living in this earthly pilgrimage. This purpose may seem self-evident to some, but it bears repeating in a culture where lesser goals may distract us from our true calling.

Except for military chaplains, few clergy have occasion to offer pastoral care on a battlefield such as the one John experienced. Ministry to the dying, the bereaved, and people in times of stress has many of the same dynamics, however. Death "concentrates the mind wonderfully," to paraphrase Dr. Johnson.[2] People in crisis want to hear the truth—truth that will sustain them through their ordeal. They want to be connected with others when circumstances make them feel most alone. They want the comfort of knowing that God loves them and the assurance that he has a good purpose for them (Rom. 8:28, 31–39). Communion with God through prayer, praise, and hearing God's word may help meet all these pastoral care needs and thus equip the saints.

Five aspects of pastoral care in times of crisis and sorrow are considered in this chapter: ministry to the dying and their caregivers, follow-up care in bereavement, the congregation as pastoral caregivers, pastoral self-care, and pastoral care in crisis situations. These are kinds of care that anyone serving a local church will be called upon to give, as opposed to the pastoral care of death row inmates and guards that would pertain to prison chaplains, for instance. A separate book could be written about each of these aspects of care, but my intention here is to provide a starting place for reflecting on ways to minister effectively in your own context.

MINISTRY TO THE DYING AND THEIR CAREGIVERS

The writings of two women in the 1960s dramatically changed our culture's perceptions of death and the process of dying. Elisabeth Kübler-Ross's landmark work, *On Death and Dying,* categorized the stages a person goes through upon hearing a diagnosis of terminal illness.[3] It spawned countless other books on how to make the last stage of life one of growth and meaning. The other writer, Jessica Mitford, produced *The American Way of Death,* an exposé of alleged exploitation by the funeral industry, and the public's willingness to buy—literally and metaphorically—into the industry's worldview. Kübler-Ross's work has provided ministers and caregivers with a framework for dealing with the emotional and physical needs of the dying person. Mitford's lampoon may make us better able to liberate the bereaved from the idolatry of consumerism. The Kübler-Ross school and its growth and healing center, Shanti Nilaya (Final Home of Peace), aim to help terminally ill people live meaningful and pain-free lives until they die.[4] Their mission, while philanthropic, is not Christian.[5] And Jessica Mitford, as Thomas Long pointed out, was a "secular rationalist, Jessica the anti-ritualist, Jessica who remained at heart the stiff-lipped Edwardian aristocrat with little tolerance for 'folk' ceremonies of mystery and wonder."[6] In other words, Mitford was not concerned with ministry to the dying or with providing transcendent meaning for the community. The Christian pastor should read these two significant authors, but also read beyond them for guidance in giving pastoral care based on our faith.

Thomas Oden suggests that "the same pastoral competencies that are needed amid death and bereavement are also found in effective ministry generally: empathetic listening; gentle, unconditional acceptance; internal congruence; ownership of feelings; witnessing to God's comfort; candor and honesty; confrontation when appropriate."[7] The way in which these competencies are to be manifested is suggested by individual circumstances, such as the length and nature of your prior relationship with the dying person, the person's ability to communicate, and the apparent imminence of the person's death. For example, during my ministry in Manchester, England, I served part-time as the Nonconformist chaplain at a local hospital. It was a trauma center and, for some odd reason, anyone brought in unconscious or otherwise unable or unwilling to state a religious preference was put in my "book." This meant I would find myself at the bedsides of critically ill or injured Sikhs, atheists, and Muslims as well as dying Baptists and Methodists. It would have been inappropriate and insensitive to extend pastoral care to these people in the same way I would to a long-time member of my own congregation, just as we do not speak to strangers in other circumstances as we do to close friends and family. Simple courtesy meant that interaction began with my introducing myself. The response of the ill or dying person suggested the next step. Praying silently for the Holy Spirit to work and speak through me at each bedside was one way to embody God's gracious initiative toward the person, whatever his or her religious convictions and reaction to my presence.

It is common today for seminaries to require clinical pastoral education for their master of divinity students. Such programs offer specialized training in ministering to people who are hospitalized or in other institutions. This training is a vital part of ministerial education; after all, a Gallup survey commissioned by the National Hospice Organization in 1996 revealed that 90 percent of respondents said they wanted to die at home, but since 1980, 75 percent of deaths in America have occurred in institutions.[8] We want that 75 percent to have access to the best pastoral care possible. A full-time hospital chaplain's work is not identical to that of a pastor visiting a parishioner, because the chaplain is not likely to have a prior relationship with the patient or an ongoing relationship with the family after the patient recovers or dies. Given that for most readers the majority of your ministry to the dying will be with people you already know to some degree, how can you best equip the saints for holy living and dying? Which of Oden's pastoral competencies should come to the forefront, and when?

Manifesting God's Love to the Dying

In *Spiritual Care,* Dietrich Bonhoeffer gives a succinct answer: "What the sick need to know . . . is that they are special and uniquely lodged in God's hand, and that God is the giver of life whether in this world or the next."[9] It can be difficult for the sick person to acknowledge the need for this reassurance, both because of the tendency in our culture to avoid dealing with one's own death, and because the dying person may mistake the need for reassurance for a failure in his or her faith. As one hospice psychologist has observed, "The approach of death sometimes rekindles old fears and insecurities. It's understandable that as one loses one's defenses and protective mechanisms, one becomes extremely vulnerable."[10] As a pastor, you must discern ways to articulate God's sovereignty and love—Bonhoeffer's being "lodged in God's hand"—without exposing or exploiting the vulnerability of the dying person. Though there are other possibilities, four means of showing the compassion of Jesus Christ during the final moments of someone's life are through touch, speech, worship, and private counsel.

Touch. The compassion of Jesus Christ may be expressed in a number of ways. First, like Mother Theresa of Calcutta, you can present the love of Christ palpably, by being unafraid to touch or be physically near the dying person. Whereas medical personnel may have to wear gloves and a mask to carry out their duties, in most instances the clergy should be unmasked to do their best work. In describing his life-threatening illness, Norman Cousins wrote, "There was the utter void created by the longing—ineradicable, unremitting, pervasive—for warmth of human contact. A warm smile and an outstretched hand were valued even above the offerings of modern science, but the latter were far more accessible than the former."[11] Jesus and his disciples laid hands on the sick, and so can you, when you minister in Jesus' name (Matt. 8:3; Mark 7:31–37; James

5:14; and others). In those infrequent situations where a dying person shrinks from any human touch, however, it is kindest not to override the person's wishes.

Speech. Address the dying person directly, even if he or she is unable to speak or appears to be unresponsive. Speaking across the bed to family members while ignoring the person between you excludes him or her at a time when being recognized as an individual precious to God and the community is vital. If the person can speak, maintaining eye contact and being attentive to what he or she says, even if garbled or unintelligible, further communicates divine compassion.

Conversation does not need to be lengthy. Sitting next to the bed (as opposed to standing over the patient), you can clasp the person's hand or touch the person's arm and greet him or her by name. If the patient does not appear to recognize you, or cannot respond verbally, simply identify yourself and say something like, "I've come to pray with you." Refrain from putting the dying person to the test by saying things such as, "Do you know who I am?" or "Squeeze my hand if you understand what I'm saying." This only adds embarrassment and distress to the suffering person who comprehends you quite well but is physically unable to do what you ask.

Worship. Another part of ministry to the dying and their families is leading them in worship. Many denominational service books include a liturgy for the sick and dying. If you are a minister in a less formal tradition, you can nevertheless be prepared to conduct a brief devotional: readings from Scripture, a pastoral prayer that includes thanksgiving and supplication, and an invitation to everyone present to join in saying the Lord's Prayer or the Apostles' Creed. This simple liturgy proclaims the gospel to the dying person one last time in this life. It reminds him or her of Christ's promises. It gathers up the anxieties and concerns of everyone present and offers them to the Lord. It gives glory to God. In some traditions, the Viaticum (Holy Communion) is given to those who are in likelihood of immediate death, to strengthen them with grace for their journey into eternity.[12] You may also anoint the dying person with oil, symbolically conveying Christ, who is at once the source of the Spirit and the exemplar of the life of the Christian.[13]

Private Counsel. If family and friends are present, you can request a few moments alone with the dying person. Bonhoeffer suggests that the pastor should ask if the person is distressed and would like to make a confession, and follow up by asking if the person is wholly certain of salvation through Christ and takes comfort in it. The inquiry should end with absolution for all sins and assurance of the hope of life eternal.[14] Oden does not frame the situation in language as priestly as Bonhoeffer's, but he does suggest that you extend the opportunity for the dying person to express whatever regrets and fears may remain, and then reassure him or her of the pardon available through Christ.

At the time of death, it is appropriate for you to pray and lead others in further prayers. Again, many denominational service books have prayers for this occasion. They include a prayer for mercy for the one who has died, the Lord's Prayer, and a commendation of the soul to God, such as the following:

> Depart, O Christian soul, out of this world;
> In the Name of God the Father Almighty who created you;
> In the Name of Jesus Christ who redeemed you;
> In the Name of the Holy Spirit who sanctifies you.
> May your rest be this day in peace,
> And your dwelling place in the Paradise of God.
> Into your hands, O merciful Savior, we commend your servant *N.*
>   Acknowledge, we humbly beseech you, a sheep of your own fold,
>   a lamb of your own flock, a sinner of your own redeeming. Receive
>   him into the arms of your mercy, into the blessed rest of everlasting
>   peace, and into the glorious company of the saints in light. *Amen.*
> May his soul and the souls of all the departed, through the mercy of God,
>   rest in peace. *Amen.*[15]

These prayers are fitting in that they acknowledge that whether we live or die, we are the Lord's and he is worthy of our worship. Prayers at the time of death also minister to the bereaved who are gathered around, for in acknowledging the death and commending the person's soul to God, the bereaved begin to be equipped for their new status and role in the world.

Ministering to the Needs of Caregivers

You may also have opportunity to offer pastoral care to those closest to the dying person. They are likely to feel overwhelmed with conflicting feelings: dread at the prospect of their loved one's death, guilt or anger over unresolved issues with the dying person, tension with other family members about division of responsibilities and decision making, anxiety about the future, and exhausted relief when the ordeal ends, to name just a few. Perhaps the most significant ministry you can have with them is your *presence*: just showing up at the hospital or nursing home or wherever they are keeping vigil. Oden identifies the pastor's special, representative roles in visiting the sick: teaching, praying, healing, and consoling in Christ's name on behalf of the whole community. But the same can be said about your role in visiting those who care for the sick.[16] They, too, need a listening ear, plus the reassurance that God is with them in their suffering and will strengthen them for whatever lies ahead. As pastor, you can pray with them for discernment when difficult decisions must be made. The liturgical resources for pastoral care included in Part Two may be used to help them bring their needs and concerns before God. You can also facilitate, organize, and equip your congregation to offer respite care; and of course you have the freedom to plan Sunday morning worship and sermons that will instruct them in the faith that will sustain them in times of crisis and sorrow.

In addition, there may be opportunities to extend pastoral care to other professionals who are caregivers—doctors, nurses, social workers, and so on—and to those who have some relationship with the person who has died. One poignant but rewarding experience in my own ministry was being summoned to a nursing home because Orville, a member of the church I served, was "sinking fast." When I arrived, the nurse at the desk said she'd been trying to reach Orville's closest relative, but no one was answering the phone. I told her I had another number where this relative might be reached and went back to my car to get the church directory. When I returned, the nurse's eyes were brimming as she said, "I'm so sorry; Orville just died." I felt terrible, having unnecessarily missed seeing him by only a few minutes, but I nevertheless asked her to take me to Orville's room. Aides were disconnecting the medical apparatus that had surrounded him. I walked to the bed, laid my hand on the man's grizzled head, and said, "I'm going to say a prayer for Orville. You are welcome to join me, if you wish." The nurse stayed. I thanked God for Orville's life, for the blessing his faith had been to those around him, and for the care he had received at the nursing home. I commended his soul to God and prayed for comfort for his relatives and for all who mourned. After concluding the prayer, I asked if I could sit by his bed for a few minutes. The nurse left.

It was then I heard a man's voice from behind a curtain that divided the room: "Are you still there?" I'd been unaware that there was another patient in the room. He asked me to draw back the drape, which had been closed when Orville went into cardiac arrest. Merrill was middle-aged and dying slowly of a degenerative disorder. He said he rarely had visitors but had become friends with Orville in the few weeks the old man had been there. He was grieving. I realized that my opportunity that afternoon was to share the gospel and offer God's comfort not to a member of my church but to a stranger who had cared for him and was suffering very real sorrow at his death.

Follow-Up Care in Bereavement

During the period between a church member's death and the funeral or memorial service, you will spend a fair amount of time with the immediate family of the deceased. There are a number of areas that don't pertain directly to worship planning in which you may offer pastoral care and guidance. Some of these concerns are immediate needs while others are more long-term. Among the immediate issues are questions about organ donation, autopsy, viewing the body, and family dynamics.

Organ Donation. Ideally, the question of organ donation should be discussed with a terminally ill person and the family long before the brief window of opportunity at the time of death. If the person has filled out a Funeral Planning and Preference Sheet (Exhibit 2.1), signed a living will, given someone medical power of attorney, or indicated a preference regarding organ donation on the back of his or her driver's license, the matter may be settled fairly simply. In circumstances of sudden or violent death, the traumatized family may not consider the possibility of organ donation unless you or medical personnel bring it to their awareness. Hospital staff are not supposed to put people under pressure to agree to donation, and neither should you; however, there are at least two legitimate pastoral concerns that make your involvement in this decision appropriate. The first concern is the comfort the dying person or the bereaved may have in knowing the magnitude of this final gift to the world. Sometimes even the most ravaged individual can donate corneas, middle ears, or other tissues that remain viable.[17] In a terminal illness, it is not uncommon for a person to feel that the body has betrayed him or her; the possibility of organ or tissue donation can then have redemptive power. Second, you are likely to encounter people with some degree of confusion about the resurrection of the body who are therefore concerned that their loved one's body remain intact. This misapprehension is an opportunity for instruction in Christian beliefs as well as assuagement of fears. Some people, for example, misread 1 Corinthians 15 and 1 Thessalonians 4 and suppose that an intact earthly body is needed at the general resurrection. Leading them through a careful study of these texts, emphasizing that the resurrection body will be a new, imperishable body, can relieve their anxiety without pushing them toward gruesome or argumentative questions, such as whether John the Baptist, who was decapitated, will be lacking a head at the resurrection. All major Christian traditions affirm the value of organ and tissue donation—which may further reassure those people who are uncertain.

Autopsy. Autopsy is another matter that often distresses the bereaved, particularly Mexican Americans and other groups with an aversion to disturbing the body after death.[18] The laws governing autopsies vary from one state to another, but in general an autopsy under a coroner's direction may be required when the circumstances of a death are violent, suspicious, or unexplained, or when a death is medically unattended and a doctor is unable to certify the cause of death. Homicides, accidents, and suicides come under the same jurisdiction.[19] As a pastor, one of your tasks may be to explain to the bereaved the legal requirement of an autopsy and to reiterate Christian beliefs about the resurrection of the body.

There are also circumstances in which an autopsy may be optional. It may be requested by a teaching and research hospital in the interest of learning more about the cause of death or to explore alternatives for treatment of the disease from which the person died. The family may also inquire about an autopsy if they want to learn whether genetic or infectious conditions led to death, to obtain DNA analysis for determining paternity or maternity, or to resolve questions about possible malpractice—although hospitals generally do not perform autopsies simply at a family's request, nor will they generally perform an autopsy on someone whose death had no connection with the hospital and for whom an autopsy is not required by law. It is possible for the funeral director to arrange for a private autopsy to be done by an independent pathologist. This may cost between $1,700 and $3,000 and is rarely covered by insurance. The cost is greater if an exhumation is involved.[20] Your role in cases of elective autopsy is to help the family weigh the options and, if an autopsy is ordered, to give the family prayerful support as they receive what could be additional distressing news.

Viewing the Body. A third immediate pastoral care issue that may present itself is the decision about whether to view the body, and when to view it—either before or after it has been moved to the funeral home. The trend toward memorial services rather than a wake followed by a funeral was noted in earlier chapters. In some cases, a person has died in a hospital or nursing home without family members present and arrangements have been made to have the body transferred immediately to a funeral home or crematorium. In such cases, the body may be cremated without any of those who are closest to the person seeing him or her dead. There is nothing intrinsically right or wrong about not viewing the body, although it is tragic when a person dies alone. In my own experience both as a pastor and as a bereaved person, I have found that it is harder for people to come to terms with the reality of a loved one's death when they have not viewed the body, or at least talked with someone who viewed the body. Far from being macabre, seeing the empty shell of a loved one shortly after he or she has died can be a therapeutic and faith-affirming moment. People have told me what a blessing it was to see that the person who had suffered was now at rest, and about the strong sense of God's presence they had in those moments. In *A Severe Mercy,* Sheldon Vanauken wrote about the experience of being at his wife's bedside when she died:

> As the light had grown stronger, she had grown weaker. Perhaps she was taken up into the light, for now the faint moan in her breathing ceased. Then her breathing slowed. My face was close to hers. Then each of three breaths was

lighter than the one before. There were no more. I knew on the instant of her dying that she was dead. . . . As I stood there in that suddenly empty room, I was suddenly swept with a tide of absolute *knowing* that Davy still was. I do not mean that I thought her body might still live; I knew it didn't. But past faith and belief, I *knew* quite overwhelmingly that she herself—her soul—still was.[21]

Hospitals, nursing homes, and hospices telephone the next of kin when a patient in their care has died without another family member present. They are usually willing to leave the patient's body in the room for a few hours until loved ones arrive for a final visit. If the family is present at the time of death, the nurses may ask them to leave the room briefly while they disconnect any medical apparatus, close the person's eyes, and otherwise arrange things to give the body a natural, peaceful appearance. Even if it is impossible for the family to get to the hospital or nursing home before the body is moved, and if there is to be no open-casket visitation, funeral directors may allow the next of kin to see the body of their loved one before it is cremated or placed in the casket. It is a good idea for you to discuss this option with the funeral director before the situation arises.

There may be instances, such as after a crime or accident, when a mangled body must be identified by someone, and police or medical personnel believe it would be too traumatic for the family to view their loved one this way. As their pastor, you may be asked to make the identification for the family. If this happens, you can count on the family pressing you for details afterward, particularly if there will be no cosmetic reconstruction and viewing at the funeral home. This is not a morbid obsession on the part of the bereaved but rather an attempt to come to terms with what has happened and to confront their loss. Without belaboring aspects of the person's appearance that were particularly distressing, you can truthfully give information similar to Sherwin B. Nuland's description of a dead body: that the appearance of a newly lifeless face cannot be mistaken for unconsciousness, that the vibrant spirit is gone, and that the corpse looks as though his or her essence has left, and it has.[22]

Handling Family Tensions. Family dynamics may present the need for immediate pastoral care. This is especially true if someone is being blamed for the death or if one family member shouldered an undue share of responsibility for caring for the one who has just died. If you anticipate this sort of situation, it is a good idea to bring your spouse or a respected member of the congregation with you to the wake or family home. This enhances the possibility of separating warring factions and protecting them from words that can leave lifelong scars. For instance, I recall a tragic situation with a large family in which the youngest child died in an accident while the mother thought the older children were watching him. Their grief was compounded by accusations and guilt. If you have had an ongoing relationship with the bereaved family, you will probably know in advance some of the potential conflicts just following a death. Make yourself available as a nonjudgmental, safe listener. This can defuse volatile situations and pave the way for referrals to mental health professionals for more intensive counseling when appropriate. You may want to maintain a list of referral possibilities for this purpose.

People grieve in different ways, even when they are part of the same culture or family. If a family has called you to minister to them in a time of sorrow and crisis, they are looking to you for leadership as well as comfort and hope. An appropriate exercise of your pastoral authority is to grant them permission to express their grief in whatever ways they need to, without pressure to maintain a stiff upper lip or show how much they cared about the deceased. There are only two behavioral boundaries for those who mourn: first, they must not deliberately exacerbate the grief of others (by demanding that another family member stop crying, for example); and second, they must not compromise Christian worship by disruptive activity (such as throwing themselves on the coffin or demanding that it not be lowered into the ground). It is possible to set and maintain these boundaries with the prearranged help of a few carefully chosen people. The ushers or pallbearers, for example, can be warned of the possibility of disruptive behavior and can gently comfort, restrain, or (if necessary) remove the distraught mourner.

Long-Term Pastoral Care to the Bereaved

After the funeral or memorial service, you can assist those who mourn in a variety of ways. First, pastoral care may be given indirectly during Sunday morning worship. In some churches, the names of deceased members are mentioned during the intercessions on the anniversary of their death. All Saints Day and All Souls Day are other times when the church may remember and give thanks for those who have entered the Church Triumphant during the previous year. Even if you are ministering in a denomination that does not observe the two practices just mentioned, it is possible to arrange for a favorite hymn of the deceased to be sung on the anniversary of the death. However, I would advise you not to announce that this was so-and-so's favorite hymn or favorite passage of scripture or whatever, because the congregation is apt to keep score regarding who gets mentioned and who doesn't. Such competitiveness is not conducive to worship or pastoral care.

Another, more direct kind of ongoing pastoral care is also in order. In the weeks and months after the funeral, calling on the bereaved is appropriate and usually appreciated. You may share with the family a hymn, text, prayer, or sermon that communicated God's promises to you when you yourself experienced a loss. In the course of your visits, mention the person who has died and perhaps share a favorite memory of him or her. This invites the bereaved family members to talk through their grief. A composition by Terry Kettering expresses this need vividly:

The Elephant in the Room
There's an elephant in the room.
It is large and squatting, so it is hard to get around it.
Yet, we squeeze by with, "How are you?" and "I'm fine" . . .
And a thousand other forms of trivial chatter.
We talk about the weather.
We talk about work.
We talk about everything else—except the elephant in the room.
We all know it is there.
We are thinking about the elephant as we talk.
It is constantly on our minds,
For you see, it is a very big elephant.
But we do not talk about the elephant in the room.
Oh, please, say her name.
Oh, please, say "Barbara" again.
Oh, please, let's talk about the elephant in the room.
For if we talk about her death,
Perhaps we can talk about her life.
Can I say "Barbara," and not have you look away?
For if I cannot, you are leaving me
Alone . . . in a room . . .
With an elephant.[23]

I also make a practice, in my personal devotions, of praying for a bereaved person or family every day for the first year after their loss. I do this because I know that the first year without their loved one can be a trial, and because I believe the Holy Spirit can provide them with sustenance far beyond my limited ability and resources. Sending a brief note on the anniversary of the death can help the family get through what can be a very difficult day. It can reassure them that others have not forgotten.

THE CONGREGATION AS PASTORAL CAREGIVERS

Finally, it is essential that we recognize that ministry to the bereaved does not belong solely to us as pastors; it also belongs to the congregation and larger community. We have a responsibility to equip the members of our congregation to minister to one another in times of crisis and sorrow. We should have information available about grief support groups, social service agencies, and attorneys to help them through these rites of passage. Some of these resources may already be sitting in the pews.

When Matthew recorded Jesus' parable of the Great Judgment (Matt. 25:31–46) he was not writing only for clergy. Church members with any biblical knowledge assume this. They want to help others in need and do what Jesus commands, but many of them are leery of taking on additional responsibilities with no term limit. One of the ways you can equip them for ministry without overextending them is suggesting ways they can give pastoral care to mourners and others in crisis. Bereavement ministries are discussed here, and crisis ministry is discussed later in the chapter.

Caregiving During the Time of the Wake and Funeral

The third chapter noted ways the congregation can be involved during the wake and funeral service, by being present, assisting in leading worship, ushering, and so on. There are also countless nonliturgical ways they can give care during this period: by running errands for the bereaved family, cutting the grass and doing other maintenance around the family's house, meeting out-of-town relatives at the airport, offering a spare bedroom or picking up the tab for a hotel room for those relatives, lending a car or offering chauffeur service, baby-sitting, providing a hairdresser who will go to the house, providing meals or organizing a roster of people who will do so, taking photos of all the floral tributes and noting who gave them, and addressing envelopes for the acknowledgment cards sent after the funeral. These are but a few of the acts of kindness your church members can extend, and none of them requires a lengthy contract. Steve Sjogren's *Conspiracy of Kindness*[24] may give your congregation additional ideas for serving people in their time of need.

The most common lay ministry to the bereaved family is providing the repast, or "funeral meats," after the committal service. As Bonhoeffer points out, after the body of the deceased has been laid to rest, a sense of desolation can overcome the mourners.[25] The services are over, but the bereaved need to be reincorporated into the community in order to continue the rite of passage that occurs when a loved one dies. The after-funeral meal, which is preferably served at the church, receives the bereaved person with his or her changed status as part of table fellowship with other believers. The shared meal is in the tradition of the agape meal eaten by the early Church following the burial of its saints. There are other reasons for providing hospitality for mourners. First, left to their own devices, they may forget to eat, or they may feel too overwhelmed to prepare a meal. Second, it may be very painful to go straight from the cemetery to the family home, where one chair at the table is conspicuously empty.

The repast after the committal may also be an occasion for informal sharing of memories. One practice that has gained popularity in recent years is having an "open microphone," so that anyone who wishes to speak about the deceased or give testimony may do so. The sharing of funny or poignant stories celebrates the life of the person who has died, and reassures the family that they are not alone in missing him or her. Someone from the congregation may serve as host of this time of reminiscing. If an open microphone is not feasible or wanted by the family, someone can circulate with a cassette recorder, and offer people the opportunity to recall on tape a favorite memory of the deceased, or speak words of comfort to the family. Such recordings will be prized by the bereaved, particularly if the tape can be copied and circulated to friends and family members who were not able to be present. Other laity can set up a display of photographs and other items about the person who has died, making sure that everything on display is returned to the family after the repast.

Phoning members of the congregation in order to recruit people to take on these various tasks every time there is a funeral is not good stewardship of your time. It is easier to coordinate congregational caregiving by having a system set up before the need arises. One church I know has a "Martha Society," the function of which is to recruit and deploy laity to help in times of crisis and sorrow. Another church has divided its membership list into twelve teams—one for each month of the year. Each team has a coordinator who organizes the team for whatever relief ministries are needed during that month. Regardless of how your congregation chooses to mobilize itself to give pastoral care to the bereaved, it is wise to have one person whose ongoing job is to oversee the kitchen, or all audiovisual equipment, or the church vehicles, or other spaces and equipment for which maintenance must be monitored or special skills may be necessary to meet insurance requirements.

Long-Term Congregational Care

When an elderly woman in the congregation is widowed, the congregation can readily guess what some of her day-to-day needs might be: snow shoveling or grass mowing, home security, assistance with financial management, and other household chores. In *Worship as Pastoral Care,* William Willimon notes that other women who have suffered the same loss seem to gravitate toward the new widow, giving her moral support and education for her new role in the community, even if they are not educating her deliberately.[26]

It can be a greater challenge for the congregation to discern ways to help people in other situations get on with life. When a crisis or bereavement shatters a family, it isn't difficult to imagine what kind of help the children may require: baby-sitting, transportation, someone to participate in father-son or mother-daughter activities at school or with scouting groups, counseling, and so on. The coordinator of congregational care may be alert to what church members can do for others after a time of crisis or sorrow. But as the pastor, you may have to take the lead in considering how mourners may be reincorporated into congregational life and participate in ministry themselves.

For example, Laurie and Bill's daughter Emily was born with Down's syndrome, a serious heart defect, and other health problems. The congregation supported them with prayer and loving acts for nearly a year, through Emily's hospitalizations and eventual death. Not long after Emily died, it was time for vacation Bible school (VBS). Laurie had always worked with the toddlers' class. The Christian education committee debated among themselves: Should they send Laurie notice of the VBS planning meeting, or should they assume it would be too painful for her to be around children the same age as her daughter? The pastor decided to phone Laurie and ask her preference. It was a good thing he did this, because Laurie wanted to "get back to normal." Spending time with other peoples' children was indeed painful for her, but it was also healing. It would have been far more painful to have been removed from her former role in the church, to feel isolated in her grief.

Through your preaching, administration, and example, you can show the congregation gracious ways to help the bereaved person or family find their place in the community. Inviting without assuming is generally a safe strategy. The newly single person may decide for himself or herself that the couples class is no longer the best fit, for example; but people from that group can nevertheless continue the relationship in another venue.

Support Groups for the Survivors

Another pastoral care resource for bereaved people is the grief support group. Sometimes these groups generate spontaneously, when a death has a deep impact on people outside the immediate family. It is more common, however, for the pastor to announce that a group will be started for any who are grieving and those who are interested should come to an initial meeting. A church-related support group often contracts to meet for a certain number of weeks or sessions. Those who wish to continue beyond that time may meet informally or join a newly forming group. The group may study denominational material on grief, do Bible study and intercessory prayer, or simply talk through what they have experienced. You may feel responsible for leading them, but their time together may be more useful if a competent layperson who has suffered a similar loss in the past guides the group.

There are other grief support groups that are not under the auspices of any particular church. The chaplain of the local hospital can help you connect with existing groups in your area. Some groups minister to the needs of people who have suffered particular losses. Compassionate Friends, for example, is directed to the needs of parents who have experienced the death of a child. Candlelighters is made up of parents whose children are victims of cancer. The Guild for Infant Survival is for people who have lost children to crib death, or sudden infant death syndrome.[27] Web sites for some of these groups are listed in the Bibliography.

PASTORAL SELF-CARE

Thus far, the discussion of pastoral care has been about what you, the pastor, can do for others, and about what you can equip the congregation to do for others. But you must also pay attention to the pastoral care you yourself need, especially in bereavement. It is unfortunate that too few Protestant clergy have spiritual directors or other clergy with whom they are willing to unburden themselves. Perhaps some are worried about repercussions in career advancement if it becomes known they have sought care when reeling from a loss. Others may fear that their congregations (or they themselves) will take it as a sign of unbelief if they acknowledge their own anguish when a loved one dies. They may think they must not manifest sorrow at the death of a church member with whom they were especially close. But grief denied is only grief delayed, and grief made worse by pride and guilt. Susan Howatch, a British novelist, depicts the dangers of repressed grief in *Absolute Truths.* The main character is Charles Ashworth, an Anglican bishop whose wife died suddenly:

> I was the bishop. I had to behave in a certain way, the tradition had to be upheld and I had to set an example to my community. I knew that. . . . "I'm all right," I said later to my doctor—and indeed to everyone who flocked to my rescue. "It's a terrible shock, but I've got everything under control." I was floundering around in reality now, that violent world where death tore gaping holes in the fabric of life, but fortunately my position as bishop meant that I knew how to reduce it to order. There were rituals to be observed, traditions to be embraced, standards to be maintained. Clinging to the formalities like a limpet I began to plan a faultless funeral.
>
> There were so many people everywhere. I behaved perfectly, saying all the right things, but I wished the people could be somewhere else. . . . I went on behaving perfectly. I talked about how wonderful everyone was being. I even made theological remarks about the outpouring of grace which can result from a tragedy. No one would have guessed how alienated I felt, how dislocated, devastated and adrift.[28]

Ashworth was blessed to have an astute spiritual director and another clergyman who recognized his stifled grief and extended pastoral care. Gradually, he was able to own his loss and receive the help they offered. Like Charles Ashworth, you and I are not granted a clergy exemption from grief. The question then is, What will we do about it?

I believe we may look to the life and ministry of Jesus and the early Church for guidance. The examples recorded in Scripture do not all pertain to grief or to pastoral self-care, but they do inform both.

First, we may recall what Jesus did when his friend Lazarus died: he wept. The leader of the disciples was not ashamed of his tears, nor were those around him put off by them. If the Son of God—the Resurrection and the Life—was deeply moved, it is absurd for us in our human weakness to pretend that we're above such feeling. In Acts 9, the story of Tabitha shows the widows who loved her weeping over her death. All of these widows were Christian women who believed in everlasting life through Jesus Christ. Their sorrow was authentic, as was their joy when Tabitha was raised. In the same way, we should be honest with ourselves and those around us. Seeing a masked actor in the pulpit does not inspire congregational trust, no matter how good you think your act is or how necessary the part. What is more, your authenticity in grief, however you express it, gives your people permission to be equally genuine in their times of sorrow.

Second, we may consider the example of Jesus and the disciples in their stewardship of time. After his baptism, Jesus began his ministry with forty days of fasting and praying in the wilderness—preparation for the work that lay ahead. He often went away to pray by himself (Matt. 14:23, 26:36; Mark 6:46; and so on) and to rest. There would always be more people desiring healing, more crowds wanting to listen to him, more children to bless. But time spent alone with God provided the refreshment necessary for the next challenge. We may also consider the Lord's timing in the interval between the Resurrection and Pentecost. Surely the Holy Spirit could have been poured out immediately, but that was not God's plan. Instead, the apostles were given forty days to process what had happened, punctuated by appearances of the Risen Christ. After the Ascension, there was another interval for prayer together and waiting on God. They had been through a series of cataclysmic events. The liminal period between Easter and Pentecost prepared them for the gift of the Spirit and the ministry that followed. When Paul had his Damascus Road experience, God had him wait for three days in Damascus before sending Ananias to heal and baptize him.

All of these examples infer that the need for downtime and spiritual recharging are part of God's design for human beings. There will always be people and projects clamoring for our attention, but we will serve our Lord best when we keep Sabbath time to be renewed by his Spirit, particularly in times of great stress and change. Personal bereavement is one of those times. Grief cannot be rushed. Part of faithful ministry is equipping others to step in and take leadership when we cannot and should not try.

Third, we would do well to remember that Jesus did not baptize himself, nor did Paul. The New Testament has no stories of the sick laying hands on themselves and healing themselves. We don't even read of people washing their own feet. The model for ministry demonstrated by Jesus and the early church is mutual service and submission to the ministry of others. Our congregations will benefit from seeing their pastors model receptivity to the grace-filled words and deeds of others. They will be hurt if we spurn their attempts to minister to us.

If offers of human help are slow in coming, we can bear witness to the sustaining power of the Holy Spirit when people know we are going through a difficult time, and we can ask others to pray for us. Paul's Epistles provide us with examples of this acknowledgment of need (such as Phil. 4:10–20).

These examples suggest that authentic expression of grief, liminal time, and receptivity to the ministry of others are necessary parts of pastoral self-care. If there is one occasion when the three converge, it is in the funeral of a family member or a very close friend. Put simply, you should *never* serve as chaplain to your own family.[29] It is detrimental to your family's, your own, and the congregation's spiritual health.

When a family member dies, the remaining members need a pastor—someone to hear their confessions, to assure them of absolution, to confide in, and perhaps to mediate any tensions between them and you. They need ministry and direction from someone whose own vision is not occluded by grief and proximity to the loss. Traditionally, doctors do not operate on members of their own family, and for good reason. The introjection of their own needs precludes optimal performance of the task at hand. The same holds true for pastors when there is a death in the family. Furthermore, your relatives need you to be there in the familial relationship so they won't be deprived of a sister or brother in addition to losing the one who has died. You cannot wear two hats simultaneously.

Officiating at the funeral of a family member is bad for your own spiritual health. The funeral is, among other things, a rite of passage for the bereaved, when they are given guidance for their new status in the world. You cannot give yourself guidance, leadership, or comfort. The greater your suppressed grief is, if you try to conduct the service, the more likely it is that you will have to concentrate on performing well in spite of your grief. This distracts your attention from the worship of God and deprives you of the opportunity to hear words of divine comfort spoken by another.

Functioning as family chaplain is also almost always detrimental to the congregation's health, whether the occasion is a funeral, a wedding, or the baptism of a relative. Their next of kin have not conducted these rites for them, so when they see you insist on officiating for your relatives, it appears to make the occasions more special and even holy. Their focus is on your relationship to the people at the center of the events as much as or more than on the act of worship itself. At a funeral, the spotlight will be turned on you—How well are you holding up? Are you about to break down? and What should be done to help you if you do?—so that the praise of God and thanksgiving for the life being remembered become secondary at best. Your congregation deserves better pastoral leadership than this, so let someone else give it on these occasions.

In the last analysis, pastoral self-care is an oxymoron. When we are bowed down with grief, the best thing we can do is allow others to minister to us in Jesus' name.

PASTORAL CARE IN CRISIS SITUATIONS

Chapter Three noted different types of worship that are appropriate for addressing or remembering crisis, but as important as worship is, it is not the only means of providing pastoral and congregational care that will help people through difficult times. A crisis, such as bereavement, is a rite of passage for those at the center of it. It represents disruption of and separation from the security of established routines, whether the cause is natural disaster, war, or personal calamity. Willimon quotes Arnold Van Gennep's *Les Rites de Passage,* in which he describes three stages experienced by mourners:

1. *Separation* from the one who has died
2. *Transition:* a liminal period when normal routines and activities stop, when rituals acknowledge both the death of someone and the new status and roles of those left behind
3. *Reincorporation* into the mainstream of life[30]

For those directly affected by other crises, the same dynamics are at work. A significant difference, however, is that a much larger number of people are likely to be affected, and the crisis may be more protracted, begetting other crises.

For example, in August 2000, the governor of Montana declared the entire state a disaster area because of wildfires exacerbated by drought. Only a small percentage of the ecosystem was destroyed by flames; however, the fire and smoke drastically affected the tourist industry. The air quality was detrimental to people's health. Work routines and school calendars were disrupted. The crisis had an enormous and ongoing impact on people living a long way from the burning trees.

How would you extend pastoral care and facilitate the rite of passage for the people affected by wildfires in Montana, or in a community devastated by a hurricane, or in other critical situations? Obviously you wouldn't stand up and announce, "We're now entering stage 2," or superimpose a procedural checklist and follow it without sensitivity to the needs and dynamics peculiar to the event at hand. There are nevertheless pastoral care needs that are common to every crisis. If you and other caregivers in your congregation attend to these needs, you will indeed glorify God and equip the saints for faithful living.

Be There

The first need is for your presence. People under great stress may feel as though God has abandoned them. Even Jesus experienced this sense of being alone, as witnessed by his words as he hung on the cross: "My God, my God, why hast thou forsaken me?" (Matt. 27:46; Mark 15:34). If hell may be summarized as separation from God, a crisis evokes a sense of damnation in its power to make people feel cut off from their Lord. You can serve a priestly function in crisis by visibly representing the Christ whose steadfast love never ceases, whose mercies never come to an end, and whose faithfulness is great (Lam. 3:22–23).

The ministry of presence requires courage. A North Carolina pastor risked personal safety when he discerned that God was calling him to stay on Hatteras Island during Hurricane Emily in 1993. The Rev. Jim Huskins wrote:

> My mother, Stella (79 years old), was living with us. Her welfare was a great concern to us. At the same time, I felt that I should stay on the Island because the road could be washed out by the ocean tide and I might not be able to get back on the Island for several days after the storm. A lot of the local folks did not plan to leave the island and would most likely be cut off without help. I knew my wife and mother would not leave unless I did. I was really troubled by my choices.
>
> I went across the street from the parsonage to the church to pray. As I sought guidance in my decision making, I could only hear the words to the song that we sing so often: "When through the deep waters I cause thee to go, The rivers of woe shall not thee overflow."[31] After prayer I returned to the house and told Linda and my Mom that I felt I was supposed to stay.[32]

Pastor Huskins had no economic investments to protect by staying on the island, as his parishioners did. By remaining there through the hurricane and its aftermath, he showed the congregation that he—and God—were deeply invested in them. This gave them comfort and strength, which were just as significant as the relief efforts their pastor helped organize. It is no coincidence that government leaders and candidates for office routinely show up to view disaster areas and speak words of sympathy and encouragement. They know that presence matters.

Communicate

A second kind of pastoral care you can extend in crisis is communication: keeping those affected apprised of information as it becomes available. Parents of children who died in the Columbine High School massacre could tell you the agony of waiting hours for some word about their teenagers. Not knowing is, for most people, harder than knowing the worst. Even in crises that are not life-threatening but life-changing, such as a scandal that rocks the church, a succinct statement of the facts can minimize the rumor mill's potential for worsening the situation.

Encouraging open communication can ward off mob action in a crisis. A Federal Emergency Management Agency (FEMA) report published in 1984 documents the correlation between adequate, timely communication and warding off hypervigilance (a form of stress that in its most extreme form manifests panic):

Probably the most widespread myth about disasters is the belief that people will panic in the face of great danger. As a result of this belief, officials put out warning bulletins most cautiously. They frequently withhold warning to the last minute in the belief that the inevitable irrational panic is only slightly less damaging than the disaster itself. . . . Even in large-scale disasters, when emergency warnings are given to large numbers of people, hypervigilance and the accompanying symptoms of severe cognitive impairment have seldom been observed, despite the readiness of some influential journalists to raise the specter of mass panic.[33]

Your communication role as pastor is not to duplicate the work of FEMA or other emergency workers; however, your church can serve as a meeting place and information clearinghouse during a crisis. This function can be as simple as setting up a large bulletin board for posting official updates and personal messages, and arranging for someone to receive and post them. What is more, because of your prior relationship with the people in question, you can tend to the spiritual and emotional needs of people receiving bad news far better than a stranger making an announcement over the radio.

Other professions are gradually becoming more aware of interpersonal dynamics in giving and receiving information. The American Medical Association now has a curriculum with a six-step protocol for communicating bad news to patients: getting started, finding out what the patient knows, finding out how much the patient wants to know, sharing information, responding to feelings, and planning and follow-up.[34] As a pastor speaking to parishioners, you have the advantage of shared beliefs that will help put the information in perspective and discern the appropriate and faithful response. For example, in Pastor Huskins's situation, a parishioner would receive unwelcome news that the hurricane had destroyed the family home more easily from the pastor than from a stranger. Huskins would surround the person with other known and trusted church members, who would embody the love of the Lord, who promises, "I will never fail you nor forsake you" (Heb. 13:5). The difficult reality of the situation would not be avoided but would be viewed in light of faith in God's providence.

Connect

A third pastoral care strategy is networking with others to provide for immediate physical needs in a time of crisis. Your congregation will recognize that not only does such ministry rise to the Lord's challenge in Matthew 25:31–46, but it can also be an opportunity for low-key evangelism. The reality is that people remember the kindness shown to them in times of great stress. For small-scale crises, such as a family's home being destroyed by fire, the congregation may be able to draw on its own resources to supply food, temporary shelter, and other necessities. For larger emergencies, you and your parishioners will have to join forces with other churches and relief organizations.

For Pastor Huskins, for example, ministering after the hurricane was initiated by meeting with an interfaith council and the local coast guard chief, and then approaching FEMA and county officials about using one of his churches as an interfaith recovery center. One phone line and Huskins's personal computer were used until Red Cross supplies arrived with other volunteers and technical support.[35] Huskins said, "The calls never stopped for the next six months." His little congregation could not have sustained the massive relief effort on its own; they had to forge a network of care to embody the compassion of Christ to hurricane victims.

Maintain the Familiar

People in crisis are in a state where boundaries and routines have been disrupted. They are apt to experience life as chaotic, and this adds to their distress. Rogers and Nehnevajsa's FEMA report notes that the life of individuals, organizations, communities, and societies tends to keep unfolding in a basic and characteristic rhythm of repeated, or nearly repeated, actions.[36] We are all creatures of habit who tend to organize our universe in terms of predictable roles, institutions, and routines. Maintaining or reestablishing familiar patterns in the midst of crisis helps everyone involved move through the rite of passage with a greater feeling of security. We may remember that Jesus' disciples initially went back to their fishing boats after the Crucifixion and Resurrection. Doing the familiar lent a dimension of security in an insecure world. When the Risen Lord appeared to the disciples by the Sea of Galilee, he did not scold them for seeking refuge in old patterns, but used another familiar routine—breaking bread with them—to comfort and equip them for further ministry (John 21:21–19).

How can this approach be played out in the ministry of your church? For the Lutheran congregation in Colorado that was mentioned in Chapter Four, it meant going ahead with the scheduled confirmation class shortly after the Columbine High School massacre. The crisis was acknowledged and ministry took place, but the maintenance of established routines was an act of pastoral care. For the suburban congregation whose building burned, it meant transplanting their Sunday morning program to another location and continuing their programs as best they could in spite of the crisis. For Epworth United Methodist Church, which helps provide temporary shelter for homeless families in Durham, North Carolina, it has meant giving each family unit its own room in the church so that story-telling, prayers, and other bedtime routines with the children can occur in the family's private "home."

Creating some semblance of normalcy is not a denial of the magnitude of the crisis. It is rather an act of pastoral care that helps people negotiate their way through otherwise chaotic circumstances.

CARE FOR CAREGIVERS

It says in Mark 6 that after our Lord's disciples had preached and cast out demons and healed the sick, Jesus said to them, "Come away by yourselves to a lonely place, and rest a while." Not even those closest to Jesus worked twenty-four/seven. Theologian Stanley Hauerwas has ironically described clergy as being "one large, quivering mass of availability." Never taking time off does not mean we are being faithful, nor are we being responsible if we expect the same of the laity in ministry with us. Failure to provide respite for caregivers and ourselves leads to resentment, withdrawal, and burnout.

When someone in the congregation is the chief caregiver for an ill person, the need for volunteers to share the load and give the caregiver a break is easy for all to understand. The need may not be as obvious in a time of crisis, but it is just as real. Pastor Huskins described his growing awareness of the need for respite for those ministering to people after the hurricane. The sheer magnitude of the disaster, listening to story after story, and helping people process applications for aid made some volunteers begin to weep on the job. He located some trained counselors with whom the volunteers could unload and find relief. Counseling, recreational opportunities, and simple Sabbath time will help equip the saints in your church to extend pastoral care to others in crisis. This is, in some respects, analogous to the USO providing entertainment for military personnel, or the Salvation Army canteen truck offering refreshments to firefighters at the scene of a major blaze.

WORSHIPING TOGETHER

It may seem that we are coming full circle by mentioning worship and other ritual acts again. However, what I have in mind here are chiefly those ritual acts that are lay-initiated, even spontaneous. It is important to create a place in the midst of crisis for celebrating the symbolic acts of other Christians that mediate hope to the entire community. These gestures may or may not be intrinsically religious, but they bear witness to the divine promise of "strength for today and bright hope for tomorrow."[37]

James Wilson, pastor of the church that burned to the ground, described one such symbolic act in the sermon he preached the Sunday following the fire. As he stood in front of the gutted building the morning after the fire, a little girl stopped by with her mother and gave him five dollars she had saved "to rebuild the church."[38] It was a gesture that touched the heart of the minister and all who heard about it, and we could say it pointed them toward reincorporation, or new life on the other side of the crisis.

A more traditional ritual act was depicted in the *Chicago Tribune* at the time the Russian submarine *Kursk* sank in the Barents Sea. A photo showed a Murmansk citizen holding a religious icon and crossing himself as he prayed for the trapped seamen.[39] His pious gesture was not part of a demonstration organized by the Russian Orthodox Church but an individual's sign of faith. Orthodox Christians believe that icons serve as an existential link between the worshipper and God, and many icons are regarded as "wonder working."[40] We could interpret the man's ritual act as a silent witness that only the power of Christ and the saints could effect a miraculous rescue, or paradoxically, that though he held the icon in his hands, ultimately all who live or die are in God's hands. The Russian man's symbolic gesture sustained him, and perhaps others, during the crisis, and pointed to ultimate hope beyond it.

Of course, not all ritual acts, planned or spontaneous, promote healing, equip the saints, or glorify God. Collecting grim souvenirs after a plane crash or placing flowers and balloons at an accident scene may be ways of confronting the reality of what has happened, but neither points people toward God's future. Ultimately, both Christian worship and pastoral care, whether clergy-led or lay-generated, lead people to praise God for the eternal promise we have in Christ Jesus our Lord.

CONCLUSION

All of these possibilities for offering pastoral care in times of sorrow and crisis bear witness to our faith in Christ and follow the example our Savior provided during his earthly ministry. Jesus spoke directly to people and touched them, he manifested God's love for them, and he ministered to those who mourned. He was present with people in their hours of greatest distress: speaking the truth, showing them how to serve one another, keeping the Sabbath, reassuring them and drawing them to God in worship. As men and women called to minister in Jesus' name, let us strive to pattern ourselves after our Lord's example, praying that we "may grow into his likeness and evermore dwell in him, and he in us."[41]

PART TWO

RESOURCES FOR TIMES OF CRISIS AND SORROW FROM THE MINISTER'S MANUAL AND ELSEWHERE

When I graduated from seminary, I was fortunate to serve as associate pastor with someone who was a meticulous record keeper in addition to being gifted for ministry in other ways. During my first week on the job, he showed me his office copy of the Evangelical United Brethren (EUB) hymnal used by our formerly EUB congregation. (In 1968, the EUB Church and the Methodist Church joined together to become the United Methodist Church.) Each hymn was marked with the dates it had been used in worship and with suggestions for future use. By making these notations, my fellow pastor avoided selecting any hymn too often or too seldom. A quick glance at the page reminded him which music went over well with the congregation, which hymns were too difficult to sing, and which music had been scored for instrumentalists in the church. His work made that hymnal a more valuable resource than it had been the day it arrived from the publisher. I began marking my own hymnal in the same way. Doing so helped me make wiser choices when planning worship. My choices, however, were limited to what were in that book. Because there were only three hymns in the section on eternal life, I had to look further afield for music suitable for funerals and memorial services, and to guess what other selections in the hymnal might be appropriate. I wished for an easier way to put together a worship service.

I longed for some fresh ideas for preaching at funerals, too. The basic homiletics course I had taken in seminary hadn't covered preaching at funerals, and because I had attended services led by others, I knew that not all pastors approached the task the same way. At that time I was unaware of *The Minister's Manual,* a new set of homilies and outlines published every year to help stimulate the creativity of clergy in local churches. I didn't know my way around the service books of other denominations or how to develop the seemingly extemporaneous liturgy of pastors in churches that do not use a book of worship. The senior pastor's marked-up hymnal was a good starting point, but I needed more help and resources, especially in planning worship for times of crisis and sorrow.

Many pastors cope with the need for resources by collecting files of material suitable for funerals, baptisms, weddings, and so on. This is a good idea, but it doesn't guarantee you will have multiple options for each part of the service. For instance, your funeral file might end up with twelve good sermon illustrations, one committal, and no prayers. When called on to conduct a funeral, you want to be ready to witness to the hope and comfort available through Jesus Christ, and not be frustrated because the limited resources in your files are already overused.

This section of the book supplements the marked-up hymnal and filing system you may already use. The material is organized similar to *The Minister's Manual,* which identifies a Sunday and then offers a sermon based on a lectionary text for that day. The sermon is followed by several illustrations of the same sermon theme, a topical sermon and sermon "briefs," hymn suggestions, and worship aids. The resources provided here expand on the format of *The Minister's Manual.* They are presented in the following order:

- *Sermons and sermon briefs.* Guidelines are presented for composing different types of messages for funerals and crisis-related services. Examples of each type are offered, including several of the best from more than fifty years of *The Minister's Manual,* as well as messages for particularly difficult occasions, such as suicide or the death of a child. An index for this section is provided at the end of the book.

- *Illustrations and poetry.* Many of these illustrations and poems are suitable for a crisis or funeral, so they are not arranged according to type. An index of authors is provided at the end of the book.

Part Two also includes resources for other acts of worship you are likely to use in designing a funeral or crises-related service, or in extending pastoral care in more private settings. The liturgical resources provided here are found in the following areas:

- Opening sentences and calls to worship
- Scripture readings (arranged in canonical order and noting, where applicable, particular occasions when the passage would be appropriate)
- Invocations
- Benedictions
- Pastoral prayers
- Committal prayers
- Music, including a catalog of hymns from denominational and other major hymnals published in the United States, recordings, choral music, and instrumental music

Prayers for services of Holy Communion are not included because the traditions that most often include the Eucharist in a funeral have their own prescribed liturgies for this purpose.

Beyond the basic general worship structure, two other kinds of resources are offered: material for funerals of infants and children (including stillbirths and miscarriages), and liturgical resources for pastoral care. The latter may be used in ministering to people in the days after the funeral or crisis.

Pastors in North America minister in increasingly diverse settings, often among people whose first language is not English. Although we cannot conduct entire services in languages we do not know, it is nevertheless good to be able to say at least a few words in the tongue of the bereaved. Hearing "the songs of Zion in a strange land" extends pastoral care in a special way. For this reason, brief resources in Spanish and Korean are integrated into the rest of the worship materials provided, along with a pronunciation guide and English translation.

The resources in this collection may be used in several ways. First, you may compare them with your own predominant method for preparing services and discuss or reflect on the theological ramifications. Second, you can read through a category of sermons to become comfortable with trying a style or structure you have not used before. Third, any sermon can be used to spur your imagination as you begin working with the same text—a function *The Minister's Manual* has served for more than half a century.

Sermons and Sermon Briefs

What is the purpose of preaching when some people in the congregation may be too traumatized to take in much of what is being said? This is a legitimate question. Preachers and scholars have answered it in different ways throughout Christian history. Crisis sermons have on occasion been used as opportunities to frighten listeners into repenting and amending their lives. *Execution and Humiliation Sermons,* a book in my seminary's library, provided examples of "preaching the terrors" to witnesses of these occasions.[1] Most contemporary pastors want funerals and other crises to be opportunities to speak words of comfort and hope, but they may be uncertain of the best way to accomplish this. A helpful starting point for consideration of the question, "What is the purpose?" is found in the 1964 edition of *The Minister's Manual,* which quotes George E. Sweazey's ten reasons for a Christian funeral:

1. Give comfort, because sorrow and death are real.
2. Give thanks for one whom God gave to us.
3. Give tribute of appreciation and pride for who that person was.
4. Give a new hold on God, and on his love and care.
5. Give a closer tie with heaven through one more person who is there.
6. Give fresh assurance of what is ahead.
7. Give a turning point from which those who have been overwhelmed with sorrow can start back to normal life again.
8. Give a reminder of life's great purposes and destiny so that all who are present may take up life again with higher purposes.
9. Give comfort through the presence of sympathetic friends.
10. Give an emotional release that will bring calm and repose.

The editor of *The Minister's Manual* that year noted that these reasons are also helpful in preparing funeral meditations, and many of them apply to preaching in other times of crisis as well. They are all valid claims, but one sermon cannot hope to cover all ten of them. The service in its entirety may do that. If nothing else is accomplished, the purpose of a sermon at a Christian funeral or crisis-related service is to glorify God through proclamation of the gospel of Jesus Christ. It may also have a share in extending pastoral care to those who have gathered for worship in a time of special need. In addition, it may remember before God the person who has died or the crisis on everyone's mind. Within these three basic guidelines—proclaiming the gospel to the glory of God, extending pastoral care, and remembering before God—there is room for great cultural, denominational, and personal variety.

BIOGRAPHICAL MESSAGES

There is enormous variety in contemporary Christian preaching. One popular method, especially in free church traditions, is the predominantly biographical message. The sermon begins with the preacher sharing something personal about the one who has died. The person's uniqueness is acknowledged, sometimes at length, and the survivors may be mentioned or addressed directly. The preacher then refers to one of the texts read earlier in the service. The text is not explored in depth but is used thematically to illustrate the idea of Christian hope through the redeeming work of Jesus Christ. Quite often the message concludes with another personal reference, linking the deceased to the promise that has been proclaimed.

The appeal of the biographical message is that it is the most clearly personalized of the three types of funeral sermons outlined here. It invites the listener to remember and thank God for the person who has died. The dangers of the biographical message are several: it may focus so much on the deceased that almost nothing is said about God or the ground of our hope; it can give the impression that the merits and accomplishments of the deceased earned him or her a place in heaven, when that is not what the Christian faith teaches; and at its most extreme, it can give the mistaken impression that the dead person is being worshiped.

Funeral Sermon for Jimmy Marius

We have met here not to extol the virtues of some great man, but rather to remember a child who experienced neither the joys nor the griefs of becoming a man, although he lived among us for sixty-five years. I have known Jimmy for twenty-one of those years. He knew that I was the "preacher," his pastor, yet he always called me "Uncle Sherwood." Why? I have no idea, but I'm glad I never tried to correct him. I'm glad he felt that close to me.

Richard Marius is director of the expository writing program at Harvard University. He writes the following about his brother, Jimmy, the subject of this sermon:

> James Henri Marius was a Down's syndrome child. My mother and father moved to a farm at a place called Dixie Lee Junction in east Tennessee in 1950 so he could grow up in the tranquillity of what was then a remote neighborhood. In time my family began attending the Midway Baptist Church, which adjoined one of our fields, and Jimmy—as we called him—became a fixture there. He had only one desire, which was to be loved; and he was much loved by the family and by the community. He died on the night of December 23, 1991, and about three hundred people turned out for his funeral on the evening of December 26. As it happened, December 26 was my late father's birthday. My brother John and I commented to each other that it was in a way a good birthday present for Dad because our family and our community had fulfilled Dad's greatest wish, that Jimmy be loved and cared for as long as he lived.

Jimmy was different—*unique* would probably be a better word. I'm not sure he knew how unique he was. He seemed to accept himself as he was, apparently giving little heed to the opinions of others. There were times he seemed to think we were the "different ones" and considered us rather silly. Perhaps we may conclude that he belongs in the category of the "little ones" Christ spoke of. We may even consider him "one of the least of these." I'm not wise enough to know how much Jimmy understood about sin, repentance, faith, and salvation. But this is one thing I am sure of: Jimmy trusted the Lord Jesus Christ with all of his heart, mind, and spirit. Jesus had some harsh words for those who would reject one of these little ones: "Better for him that a millstone were hanged about his neck, and that he were drowned in the depth of the sea."

Jimmy's needs were simple; it didn't take much to please him. Three things he wanted with him at all times. He took his Bible with him everywhere, even to bed. He received a new Bible every Christmas, and even though he could not read, the old one was just about worn out. The second thing he carried was a pencil, unsharpened. He preferred striped ones. One Christmas, Virginia and I looked all over town trying to find him some striped pencils, but we couldn't. The third thing was a fan. Even on the coldest days you would see Jimmy sitting in church fanning himself. It may have seemed odd to others, but he seemed to get a lot of joy from it.

Jimmy loved the church and always knew when it was time to go to worship. He looked forward to "family night"; that was when everyone brought a covered dish and we ate supper together. One icy, snowy Sunday morning Henry was afraid to drive on the slick roads and told Jimmy that church services had been cancelled because of the dangerous road conditions. In a little while Jimmy heard the church bell ringing and was so distressed about missing church that Henry carried him piggyback up the hill, across the field, and through the snow to the church.

Jimmy loved to sing. It did not bother him that he could not harmonize with others, neither did it bother those who sat near him. His favorite song must have been "At Calvary," the song that Ella sang so beautifully a moment ago. He requested that it be sung every time he had an opportunity.

Some may think Jimmy's life was unproductive. On the contrary, he unconsciously taught us many things: to be more compassionate toward the hurting, more patient with the weak, more tolerant toward the slow, and more aware of the feelings and needs of those we look upon as being less fortunate than we are. Perhaps you could add many other lessons to these I have mentioned.

We are sad because of Jimmy's death, yet we are comforted because we know that Jimmy is not "different" anymore. John, the beloved apostle, reminds us, "It doth not yet appear what we shall be: but we know that, when he shall appear, we shall be like him: for we shall see him as he is" (1 John 3:2).

Little was required of Jimmy because he possessed little. He could not discuss the profound subjects of life, death, and eternity. But you can, and because you possess much, much is required of you. Out there in eternity you will stand before the same God Jimmy is with today.—E. M. Sherwood

Funeral Sermon for a Christian Mother

[She left three children between ten and fifteen years of age.]

There was once a small boy whose mother died when he was four years old. This boy grew through childhood and youth to manhood, and after the busy years of maturity he became an old man. There was never a time that he didn't miss his mother, but in a certain way he always possessed her more wonderfully than if she had lived.

How did he possess her? In four ways. First, she personified his ideals. You see, loveliness of character was no longer an abstract thing—loveliness of character was his mother. He learned to know what love is because love was his mother. He learned to know what faith is because faith was his mother. And so with all the Christian virtues and graces. Then, second, she carried his burdens. Though she could not be seen, his mother was always taking the load off his shoulders and from his heart. She bore the heartaches of his childhood, the perplexities of his youth, and the burdens of his later years.

Then, third, she gave him courage. Sometimes life goes to pieces, or the bottom drops out of things. One cannot always be sure of the seen person by one's side. But this boy learned early that he could depend on his mother. She gave him courage. And then, fourth, she always went before him. He would have to do his best because his mother was always out beyond him in his best. She was the courier that always went ahead into the promised land.

And so this mother became the heroine of the boy, the man, the old man. And she never failed him.—M.K.W. Heicher

Funeral Sermon for Edward McDowell

We are here to give thanks and remember before God the life of Edward McDowell. He was born at Halstead Place in Horton, the youngest of five children. Ed was educated at the Grange School. After school he worked for a short time in a manufacturing merchant's before going to Technical College, where he won first prize and a medal in Worsted. He then lectured for a spell at Sheffield College of Art in Textile Merchandise.

Ed was brought up at Slackside Wesleyan Reform Church, where his family were deeply involved, especially in the musical side of things. It was through music that he met Emma; he was in *The Yeoman of the Guard,* and his character played Emma's father! He married Emma just over sixty-four years ago, and together they brought up Anne.

Ed had already moved down to Devon before they were married. He was developing Dartington Mill and bringing it up-to-date. He became a director and manager of Dartington Hall Ltd. During the war he worked first for the Admiralty and then the RAF before returning to Dartington.

In 1954 Ed came back to Bradford to work at James Ives of Yeadon. He was production manager there as well as lecturing in Textile Calculations and Textile Technology. Apart from a short spell back in Devon in Buckfastleigh, Ed spent the rest of his working life at James Ives until he retired in 1975.

Ed and Emma lived around Horton Bank, and following an accident which greatly affected Emma, Ed cared for her faithfully.

Ed was always deeply involved in the life of the local church. He sang all over Devon with Anne and Emma, and he preached in the local chapels. Up here he was for many years an Elder and Church Secretary at Wesley Place down in Great Horton. He fulfilled these and numerous other duties readily and carried them out in his own quiet, efficient way.

After living at the top of Hollingwood Lane Ed moved into Snape House, then Woodleigh, finally living at the Beeches on Beacon Road. Really, the last few years have not been fair on Ed. Many of the things he liked doing were denied him after his stroke, and life had not been easy. Ed's health had deteriorated recently, and he was faithfully cared for at the Beeches and visited by Anne. Ed died there last Sunday night. He was ninety-one years old.

Anne, we offer you our sympathy and assure you of our prayers. We feel a whole range of emotions: relief that his suffering is over, perhaps. Sadness that someone we loved and who is important to us is no longer around. You all knew Ed, as a father, a grandfather, perhaps a great-grandfather, in more ways than one. Knowing him has influenced you and enriched you. You knew the breadth of his talents and skills. Ed was bright; he loved painting and music and walking. He loved his church and his family. Perhaps it was partly his faith, but he became a sort of surrogate grandfather to his wider family, giving a support which was greatly appreciated.

Ed was a very gentle man, not easily annoyed. On one occasion his grandsons were playing football and knocked Ed off his ladder, spilling paint everywhere. He picked himself up and said, with great feeling, "You stupid boys." That was about as angry as he got. I remember well how, when I first knew Ed, talking to him there was a laugh or a chuckle in virtually every sentence.

But Ed was no soft touch. He told me on more than one occasion of an incident when he was captain of Dartington Hall Cricket Club. There was a tradition that anyone from the opposing team who scored a century was given a bat. One young man ground his way slowly to a century, which he duly got, but he had taken so much time that it ruined the game. He got his bat, but the team was not invited back again!

Ed had a strong Christian faith. It was constant throughout his life. Such a faith does not provide easy answers, but it does provide a framework to live by. And it is the source of hope. For Jesus Christ came that we might have life in all its fullness. That means that Christians are involved in all sorts of ways in working for justice and equality. It also means we have the hope of fullness of life. As St. Paul says, where we shall fully know, even as we have been fully known. I take that to mean that we are free to become the people we were always meant to be. We will be at one with all those who have gone before and will come after. We will be able to do this because Christ has died and is risen, and has opened the way for us. He is for us the Way, the Truth, and the Life.

So let us give thanks to God for the life of Edward McDowell, for all that he was and all that he achieved. And let us live for those around us, for those who need us most, in the strength of Jesus Christ. Amen.—Richard Parkes

Funeral Sermon for Joyce K. Voth

Dear friends in Christ: Grace and peace be yours in abundance through the knowledge of God and Jesus our Lord.

Joyce Kuhn Borchardt Voth has brought us together on this spring Tuesday afternoon. We join in this service of worship to remember and to celebrate the life of one of God's precious daughters. Because Joyce was a Christian, we come to this house of worship in order to hear God's Word, offer up our prayers, and sing those wonderful hymns that are so important to those who cast their grief upon God. When death occurs we are drawn to the solace of the eternal promises given us in Jesus Christ our Lord and Savior.

Joyce died at the age of sixty-three years, six months, and one day. This is no longer considered elderly. We are saddened that chronic ill health ended her life at this time. There is always more living to do. But it can be said that Joyce did live through the seasons of life: the innocent years of childhood, growing to adulthood, her marriage and the birth of her four children, her move to Colorado with her family, the renewed life that came with grandchildren, her years of widowhood, and these last several years when her physical health and strength were not what they should have been. Joyce's life fit very well into the pattern described by the author of Ecclesiastes when he wrote so many centuries ago, "To everything there is a season. There is a time to be born and a time to die, a time to laugh and a time to cry." Joyce had time to live on this earth, a time to live and to enjoy. Beth, Elaine, Jay, and Barry, as well as her grandchildren and great-grandchildren shared that time, shared her life through its seasons. We wish, naturally, that there could be other times of life and joy. And when death occurs we often ask: "Why must there be a season of weeping and a time to die?" She was so much a part of our lives; we will miss her. But in the order of creation, for everything and everyone there is a season, a time to live and a time to die.

When it is time for one person to die, how do we sum up that particular life? The writer of Ecclesiastes continues: "I know that there is nothing better for [workers] than to be happy and enjoy themselves as long as they live; moreover, it is God's gift that all should eat and drink and take pleasure in their toil" (3:12–13). The life we live is a gift from God and it is intended to bring us joy and fulfillment, even though there are times when there may be pain and tears. Joyce packed a lot of living into almost sixty-four years. These words from Ecclesiastes paint a true picture of her life. She was a devoted and loving wife for thirty-five years, supporting her husband in the suffering of fatal illness. She was a warm and caring mother who fit the description in Proverbs: "Strength and dignity are her clothing, and she laughs at the time to come. She opens her mouth with wisdom, and the teaching of kindness is on her tongue. She looks well to the ways of her household, and does not eat the bread of idleness. Her children rise up and call her happy; her husband too, and he praises her: 'Many women have done excellently, but you surpass them all.' Charm is deceitful, and beauty is vain, but a woman who fears the Lord is to be praised" (Prov. 31:25–31).

Next to God, her children and their families were at the very center of Joyce's life. We who counted it a privilege to be her friends always knew what the kids, grandkids, and great-grandkids were doing, and when she was going to Phoenix to visit Elaine, or Las Vegas to visit Beth and Barry. There was pride in her eyes and in her voice when anyone in her family did well or demonstrated their God-given talents. Her family was her greatest pride and joy.

Joyce had her own interests and hobbies as well. She loved her friends, whether in the neighborhood, here at church, or at the library. She loved to play scrabble, do crossword puzzles, work on crafts, walk for charity, and read. Truly, Joyce was a voracious reader! There were books all around her house, calling her to new, wonderful places and exciting events. Thinking again of Ecclesiastes, there must have been veritable "pleasure in all her toil" for the last ten years at the Westminster Public Library, surrounded by shelves and shelves of books.

Today as we bid farewell to Joyce, yet another book comes to mind, the book St. Paul describes in Philippians: "Help these women, for they have struggled beside me in the work of the gospel, together with . . . the rest of my coworkers, whose names are in the book of life" (Phil. 4:3). The book of life is the biblical image of the permanent record of those who belong to God through the saving work of Jesus Christ. It numbers those who have died with Christ in baptism and been raised to new life, and who have lived as faithful children of God. Since her baptism in 1934, Joyce has had her name recorded there along with so many others who Christ claims as his own.

Two weeks ago today, at about this time, Joyce received Jesus Christ in Holy Communion for the last time. She was preparing to go to the hospital one more time to try and save her life. I asked her if she was afraid. She said no. God had been with her all her life and God would take care of her. Whatever happened would happen. Since she was in God's hands there was nothing to fear. On Easter Sunday evening, the night before surgery, she again said that God's Love for her would carry her through, whether she survived the surgery or not. This was the simple faith of a librarian who knew that her name was recorded forever in God's book of life.

It is Easter, the season of resurrection, and I think that this is a wonderful time to celebrate the life Joyce lived. Yes, there is "a time to be born and a time to die." Could there be any better time for a Christian to die and be born again into eternal life than Easter? Even though there are tears, the Crucified and Risen Christ lives in our hearts and, as he has promised, prepares a place for us in his heavenly dwellings, just as he prepared a place for Joyce. Amen.—Dennis K. Hagstrom

Funeral Sermon for a Child

Although the events that occurred in this incident happened thousands of years ago, the details are recorded in the Bible for a reason. That reason is to give you and me hope and comfort today. This story tells us much, but I want to focus on three facts that I believe will be of comfort to you.

First, Ashley is at peace; she is not suffering. The Bible says that in heaven there is no suffering, no pain, no tears. Your little one is in the presence of Jesus. Our Lord loved little children and is loving your child. And as much as I know you would rather be the ones to hold her now, there is no other place she would rather be right now than in heaven.

Second, I can say with confidence that your child is in heaven. Hell is for those who reject God. Ashley was too young to make a conscious choice to reject God. Your child was too young to commit a sin, and was therefore carried directly into the presence of God by her guardian angel. Your child wants to be with Jesus, and she wants you to be with him, too.

Finally, you can see your child again in heaven. I said a moment ago that your daughter was brought directly into heaven because she was not old enough to sin. What about us? We've been around for a while. Anybody with a brain can look around us and realize that none of what we see appeared simply by chance. The universe is too vast and the human body too complex for life to have evolved haphazardly. There is a Creator, and we know it.

We have a moral obligation to the Creator to acknowledge him. We are responsible to the one who made us. The Bible says if we reject him, he will reject us (2 Tim. 2:12). But on the other hand, Jesus said if we believe in him, he will bring us to the Father in heaven when we die (Matt. 10:32).

Your child was too young to either believe in or reject God. It is my belief that God, in his grace, brought Ashley to heaven simply because of her young age. King David had the same confidence when he said, "I shall go to him, but he shall not come to me." Your child is in heaven because she was too young to make that choice on her own. But what about you? What have you done about your obligation to God? Have you rejected God, or do you believe in him?

When I say believe, I am talking about more than just acknowledging that God exists. Even the devil is convinced that God exists. To believe in God means you acknowledge him on his terms. God's conditions are rather strict. Many people do not like them, but they are true and binding nonetheless.

Turn to Christ. And do not neglect turning to one another. I have seen the closeness in this family, and you need to remain close. Turn to one another for help, support, and encouragement. Don't allow yourselves not to grieve. Let it happen. Let God help you through one another.—Dan S. Lloyd[2]

Funeral Sermon for a Little Child

"God's loved ones are very precious to him, and he does not lightly let them die," the psalmist tells us (Ps. 116:15 LB).

We are gathered here today because we love Robin, who has become precious to us in the short time we have known her, and because we love Jeff and Lori and Seth, and we grieve with them the painful loss of their daughter and sister. Along with the grief come questions—Why did this happen? Where is God in all of this? Does he know, does he care, about the pain—all of the anticipation and hope for her coming, and the grief at her being born with less than full health—and then raised hope, that the surgery would repair her heart—and then hope dashed with the sudden finality that the surgery had not succeeded and she was no longer with us? Some of the *why* questions may go unanswered, but there are some things that we do know, truths about which our aching hearts can be assured, and in which I invite you, Jeff and Lori and Seth, as well as the rest of us, to take comfort.

Think with me, please, about what we know of the heart attitude of Jesus toward little children. Listen while I read to you from Mark, chapter 10. Jesus dearly loved and welcomed children to himself, and in fact he says that we need to be like them, like Robin, in order to enter his Kingdom. He welcomed them, took them up in his arms, and received them to himself, close to his heart. We can be confident, I believe, that God has lovingly received and welcomed little Robin back to himself. And at the same time as we miss her hugs and smiles—and ache with the pain of her absence—we are assured that she is safe and cared for, in the arms of Jesus. Jesus loves Robin, this we know.

What else do we know? In John's Gospel he records the words of Jesus telling about that place to which he takes his loved ones when they die—that place where one day there will be all kinds of family reunions, the place where we and Jeff and Lori and Seth can one day be reunited. On the occasion at which Jesus spoke the words I will read to you in a minute, he spoke to people whose hearts were deeply troubled, like ours are today. In John, chapter 14, the disciples were confused and upset—they were grieving, anticipating the loss of someone they loved. Listen to what Jesus said to them: "Do not let your hearts be troubled—I go to prepare a place for you"—for Robin, and for the rest of us who love Jesus. "I will come again and take you to myself, so that where I am, there you may be also." And the way to that place, the way to our final home, is through the person of Jesus. But while we wait, with the pain and loss, with the unanswered questions, Jesus offers a gift. Just a little later, on the same evening when Jesus spoke those words to his troubled friends, he said, "Let not your hearts be troubled."

But how can our hearts not be troubled? It still hurts, deeply. Does anyone understand? Can anyone understand the pain of watching a child suffer? Perhaps only those who have experienced a similar loss. But we know there is one who does understand, who watched his only son go through intense suffering, and death—who fully understands, and knows and cares for Jeff and Lori. God the Father experienced the suffering and death of his son Jesus, and we know that his parent heart understands their suffering.

What do we know from the life of Jesus that tells us of his understanding of our grief and pain? He is referred to by the prophet Isaiah as a "man of sorrows, acquainted with grief"—as well as the one who has "borne our grief and carried our sorrow." But the understanding of Jesus is not just sympathy. With it comes the power demonstrated in his defeating death on the cross and rising again, so that death doesn't have the last word. There is life beyond this life—eternal life—which God offers to anyone who will receive it through Jesus. This too we know.

Do we know why Robin was born with less than perfect health? No. Do we know why the heart surgery didn't work, and why she died, after we had come to love her? Why she had to suffer? No.

But do we know that Robin is safe, and welcomed and cared for in the home Jesus prepared for her? Yes, that we do know. But what about those who are left here? Does God, does Jesus understand our pain and loss—the hole left in the home and hearts of Jeff and Lori and Seth? Yes, he understands, and cares, deeply. And is there hope of ever seeing her again—of reunion with her one day? Yes, that too we know, because Jesus overcame death, and offers to take us to that same home one day.

Let me read to you the words of a familiar hymn that expresses well the heart of these things that we know:

> Children of the Heavenly Father safely in his bosom gather;
> Nestling bird nor star in heaven such a refuge e'er was given.
> God his own doth tend and nourish, in his holy courts they flourish;
> From all evil things he spares them, in his mighty arms he bears them.
> Neither life nor death shall ever from the Lord his children sever;
> Unto them his grace he showeth, and their sorrows all he knoweth.
> Though he giveth or he taketh, God his children ne'er forsaketh;
> His the loving purpose solely to preserve them pure and holy.

God's loved ones are very precious to him and he does not lightly let them die. Jeff, Lori, Seth, we grieve with you, but we also hold on to hope with you—hope in Jesus, who is Robin's life, and our life.—Martha Berg

Funeral Sermon for Christopher

I must confess my own inadequacy in the face of today's task. No amount of seminary training is adequate to lead a funeral for a child. But my job today is simple and easy compared to that of Chris's parents and brothers. No amount of living with him and loving him would have been enough for his family to feel like it was time to let go. There is no way to rehearse for today—no way for any of us to be prepared—for what we must do. We come with our feelings tender and our hearts aching, and with not a little fear and uncertainty. Nevertheless, we persevere because the only way out is through the pain. We pluck up our courage and go through the pain of saying good-bye because we know that on the other side of grief, life will be good again. It will never be the same as it was, but there will again be laughter and hope. I have a few thoughts to share with you. I offer no glib answers or pious platitudes. There are no words magical enough to take away the pain, or profound enough to explain Christopher's death in simple terms. But I believe there is a source of comfort and strength that can make this time bearable. I want to speak first to the family, but I invite you all to listen in.

It is never easy to say the last good-bye to a loved one. When an elderly parent or grandparent dies, we at least have the consolation that they lived long and died full of years. We expect to attend the funerals of our parents. We never anticipate burying our children. It is almost too difficult, and yet we must do it.

This is a heart-wrenching distortion of our expectations in life. It breaks the pattern we think is normal and ours by right. To see a life cut so short is difficult to understand. Why should a healthy boy die at Christmas, so soon after his tenth birthday? It doesn't seem fair. There is so much he never had a chance to do, to learn, to experience. Why should this sometimes loud and exuberant little person be silent and still at his age? Why should the world be deprived of his artistry, his fearlessness, his skill at sports?

Right now you are probably still numb. As the numbness wears off there will be strong feelings. You may feel cheated because you will never see him doing, learning, and experiencing the possibilities in life. You may be frustrated that this one whose daredevil exploits often put him in such danger should survive them only to die from a silent and stealthy disease—and angry that modern medicine couldn't prevent an illness from taking even a "tough little guy" like Chris.

There is a big why question that hides behind our lesser questions and our anger and disappointment. The biggest why of all is, Why would a good and loving and all-powerful God allow something like this to happen? We don't often say it out loud, for fear of being sacrilegious.

I'm not here to defend God against charges of injustice. I believe that God is big enough to hear your questions, your anger, even your accusations. The psalms are full of angry prayers. I believe also that God is the only one big enough to help you shoulder your burden. The presence of family and friends will be indispensable in the weeks ahead. But there will be times when no one is around to hold your hand, to talk with you and keep you busy in the silence; you will need someone larger than life to lean on.

We are just passing through the season of Christmas. I believe there is comfort and hope we can take from the Christmas story and the life of Jesus. The miracle of Christmas is that God chose to enter our world of uncertainty, disappointment, and pain in a personal way. The writer of Hebrews puts it this way: "Since the children have flesh and blood, he, too, shared in their humanity so that by his death he might destroy him who holds the power of death—that is, the devil—and free those who all their lives were held in slavery by their fear of death. For surely it is not angels he helps, but Abraham's descendants. For this reason he had to be made like his brothers in every way" (Heb. 2:14–17). I believe that because Jesus himself suffered and was tempted just as we are, he is able to help us.

There is comfort, too, in the way Jesus related to children. He showed a special interest in them and demonstrated the constant care of God. One day some people brought their little children to Jesus so he could touch them, but his followers told them to stop. When Jesus saw this, he was upset and said to them, "Let the little children come to me. Don't stop them, because the Kingdom of God belongs to people who are like these children." Jesus took the children in his hands, put his hands on them, and blessed them (Mark 10:13–16).

In the end, the child of the manger in Bethlehem who blessed other children died a cruel death on a Roman cross. His Heavenly Father could have saved him but did not, in order to show at the apex of humanity's wickedness that the forgiveness of God would prevail. Those who watched him die thought that his death was senseless and useless. His mother stood grieving at the foot of the cross, helpless to stop his death. His disciples couldn't understand why he had been taken from them at the height of his life. Three days later they began to understand. The Resurrection gave meaning to Jesus' death—and his Resurrection gives hope to all who have sat grieving since then. Death is no longer the end of life, but a new beginning. Death no longer has the sting it once held. Death has been swallowed up in victory. Victory for Christopher. Victory for all who dare to believe.

I know that you don't feel victorious now. It is too soon. For now your comfort comes from knowing that God walks with us in our pain. The angel that announced the birth of the Christ child said he would be called Emmanuel, which means "God with Us"—not far away in heaven and out of touch with humanity, but here and now, in our pain and sorrow. The Word became flesh and dwelt among us because God loved the world that much. God loves not only the world in general but you and me and Chris.

It is in times like this that faith is so important. Faith doesn't always answer why, but it allows us to continue in the face of unanswered questions. It allows us to go on believing despite the emptiness that surrounds such a death as this, until life begins to take on meaning again. I encourage you to draw on your spiritual resources of the present and to rediscover those from your past. Don't let helplessness lead to hopelessness. Rather, lean on the everlasting arms of God, who walks with us to strengthen us and lead us into the future.

I have just a word to say to Christopher's friends, and I invite the family to listen in.

We are reminded today just how precious and fragile is the fabric of our lives. Death reminds us that life cannot be taken for granted. We may not have tomorrow to enjoy. We may not have next week to get around those things we have been putting off in hope of a better time. The past trails behind us like a shadow, the future is but a light over the horizon. All we really have is today. All we really have is now. Although the chances of a death like Christopher's taking us by surprise is very small, we never know when we will draw our last breath. We do not know for sure how long our parents, our children, our friends and loved ones will be with us. We don't know for sure if there will be another chance to settle an argument, to give a hug or say "I love you." Christopher's life was unfinished by all the measures we usually make of life. Your relationship with him was unfinished, too. Perhaps there was something you meant to do, something that you intended to say: a word of praise, a word of friendship, a thank you, or "I'm sorry." I suggest to you that it's not entirely too late. Go ahead and say those words in the privacy of your heart. Or write him a note. Compose a poem to celebrate what he meant to you. Draw him a picture. In your own way, tell him what he meant to you and that you will miss him.

To everyone here I say, Chris is gone from sight but not from memory. His voice is silent, but you will hear him still. His life will echo in your thoughts the rest of your lives. At first the echoes will be painful. They will remind you of your loss and you will feel the emptiness acutely. In time they will be treasured memories. Until then, be gentle with one another. Time alone will not heal this wound, but time and love surely will.—Alan Hoskins

Funeral Sermon for a Suicide

It is not easy for us to conceive a more melancholy moment than the one we now share, sitting together at the edge of understanding, attempting to find some answer, some human meaning, in the silence of someone who was precious to us and is gone. We come to this sad moment bewildered by what has happened but also ill-prepared, because it was so totally unexpected and so ultimately final. The grim reality that grips us has left our senses numbed and our ability to think confused. Suddenly life is not what we expected or thought we had a right to hope it would be.

It seems so inappropriate for us to say we knew John, to speak of him in the past tense. But that is part of our new reality: We did know John. We know his Christian name was John David, the name used in his baptism, which links him to Jesus Christ. We know that he would have been seventeen years old if he had lived until March 21. We know that he was a junior at the local high school, that he was an average student, and that he was a member of the track team. We knew his love for animals, his taste for pizza, and his distaste for affluence. We knew him as a son, as a brother, and as a friend. Yes, we knew John. What we don't know is why he took his own life.

Why? This is the question we are all asking ourselves and one another. If we could only answer this question, somehow our grief might be more bearable, somehow our guilt might not rise up and accuse us so arrestingly, somehow the gloom that hangs over us like a starless night might be lifted. Why? It is so natural for us to ask this question, as if its answer could release us from the ache of John's death.

But, my friends, the answer to this nagging question that goes on repeating itself in our thoughts and our conversations would not satisfy our heart's desire. To know why would solve very little. An answer would only give rise to the same question. No reason would be enough to set our minds at ease. No reason why would return sparkle to our eyes and laughter to our voices.

But if we cannot know why, what questions can we ask and what answers can we expect? Some questions we hesitate to ask for fear of the answers we may get, and some answers we give are worse than no answers. Any one of us might give the answer that was given to a Frenchman who, at the turn of the century, went to a physician and said, "Doctor, you've got to help me. I can't go on with life. Please help me end it all." And the doctor said, "Now, now, my friend, you mustn't talk that way. You must laugh and smile and enjoy life. Make friends. Mix with people. Why not go to the circus tonight and see the great clown Debereau? He will make you laugh and forget your troubles." The man looked into the face of the physician with his sad eyes and said in a painful whisper, "But, doctor, I am Debereau."

The right questions that are often left unasked and the wrong answers that surround the lives of people like Debereau take their toll among us. Our own feelings of inadequacy and the fear of asking or saying the wrong thing often force us into silence. It is a painful thing to struggle with the issue of suicide. It is even more painful when we are as preoccupied with it as we are in this moment. The word itself, if spoken at all, may be spoken only in a sigh. The sense of shame, the burden of failure, the feelings of guilt, the look on our faces of hopelessness, the grief of loss—all, like waves, wash over us, tossing us back and forth between anger and despair.

What, then, can we say? We are not the first people ever to come face to face with the stark reality of our finitude. It was Paul who long ago cried out for release from life that seemed hemmed in on all sides. "Who will deliver me from this body of death?" he said. And before these words could fade into silence, he answered his own question with a doxology: "Thanks be to God through Jesus Christ our Lord" (Rom. 7:24–25).

What is it that allows Paul to give thanks on every occasion? Is it not the belief that God's claim for each one of us is ultimate, that nothing can separate us from the love of God—not death, not life, not angels, not principalities, not things present, not things to come, not powers, not heights, not depths, not anything—not even suicide.

It is true. The church has not always affirmed that God's grace can reach behind every event to the person, that God can rescue us from this body of death even when that death comes from our own hands. Our attitude about suicide often springs from presuming to know more about God than we actually are capable of knowing. What we have let our attitude and lack of charity do in the case of suicide is reach conclusions that our faith will not support. We must never forget that the Christian faith itself originated in an act of willing acceptance of death, a death which, we say, atoned for the sins of others. We must ever remember that Jesus taught his followers that their death, when done for the sake of a friend, was an expression of the highest form of love.

It was a long, long time ago, to be sure, but there was a time when, because of Jesus' own acceptance of his death, many of his followers willed their own death and even sought it. These people are known to us as martyrs, but what is more important, many of them now carry the title "Saint" in front of their name. We are tempted to make a distinction between the will and the deed, between the desire and the act, but in so doing we should be aware that Jesus refused such distinctions. None of this should be understood as counseling others to go and do likewise. Suicide is a very serious, irreversible act. But it is not the sin that many want to make it. If it were, we are all to be pitied, because deep within each one of us, as far away from our own consciousness as denial can keep it, is a profound yearning for death. Many things in life awaken a longing for death in each one of us, which is why suicide, according to Paul Tillich, "actualizes an impulse latent in all life. This is the reason for the presence of suicidal fantasies in most people."[3]

And so, my friends, I use this occasion with some sense of inappropriateness— at the death of one of God's children and a member of our Christian family, whom we love and will see no more—to affirm the value of John's life to us and to God, if not to John himself. We cannot know all the circumstances that surrounded John's decision to end his life, but we can know this: "None of us lives to himself, and none of us dies to himself. If we live, we live to the Lord, and if we die, we die to the Lord; so, then, whether we live or whether we die, we are the Lord's. For to this end Christ died and lived again, that he might be Lord both of the dead and of the living" (Rom. 14:7–9). "Thanks be to God, who gives us the victory through our Lord Jesus Christ" (1 Cor. 15:57).—W. Guy Delaney[4]

SCRIPTURE-CENTERED MESSAGES

A second sermon method for funerals is the Scripture-centered message. A congregation and pastor may favor this type of preaching for several reasons. It may be, for example, that their worship tradition includes providing a *eulogy* (also called *naming* or *witnessing*) in addition to the actual sermon, so the uniqueness of the deceased is not neglected in the Scripture-centered sermon because it has already been mentioned in the eulogy. Another reason for giving a Scripture-centered message could be the belief that preaching should bear witness solely to the gospel, not to the person who has died. Other reasons for choosing a Scripture-centered message are that little or nothing is known about the deceased, or the deceased was so notoriously wicked that to mention his or her life would be to name and judge the person's sins. Whatever the reason for its use, a Scripture-centered message is immediately preceded by the sermon text, read by the pastor. The sermon may be a line-by-line analysis or a more general announcement of the gospel as manifested in the reading. Any mention of the deceased is brief, and usually at the end of the sermon. Because the particular circumstances giving rise to the sermon are not in the foreground, Scripture-centered messages are versatile. Many can be adapted for funerals or other crises. "Not Made with Hands" and "The God of the Living" are examples of Scripture-centered funeral preaching. "Our Very Present Help" is an example of a message that is equally appropriate for funeral or crisis.

One appeal of the Scripture-centered message is that we "preach not ourselves but Christ as Lord" (2 Cor. 4:5). The Scripture-centered message is less *reminiscence* and more *invitation.* The listeners are placed on common footing before the Lord, who knows them all equally and intimately, rather than led to compare notes about who knew the deceased best, or to speculate how well the preacher knew the deceased. At the same time, a Scripture-centered message can impress some worshipers as impersonal or indifferent, and therefore even hurtful. I remember a family member returning from the funeral of a close friend and saying indignantly, "The minister never said one word about Bob. It was as though Bob didn't matter." Therefore, if we choose to preach Scripture-centered messages, we must ensure that there is opportunity elsewhere in the service, whether in an obituary or in the prayers, for naming the deceased with thanksgiving.

The God of the Living

TEXT: Luke 20:38

Perhaps all of us have heard someone say, at one time or another, that we know little or nothing about heaven. We might better be amazed at how much we know concerning the future life. It is largely a matter of going to the right source for our knowledge.

Science, groping now on the edge of the spiritual, may one day come up with some information, but not yet. Knowledge may have its source in authority. Jesus is such an authority, and it is to be noted that no statement that he ever made has been convincingly refuted, and none has been retracted.

On one occasion, Jesus was in argumentative conversation with a group of Sadducees concerning the resurrection from the dead. He ended the argument by referring to the God of Abraham and Isaac and Jacob, and then said, "He is not a God of the dead, but of the living."

Consider that statement as related to our hour of bereavement: He is a God of the living.

I. Jesus speaks of the God of Abraham and Isaac and Jacob, and then adds, "He is not a God of the dead, but of the living." Abraham is still Abraham, Isaac is still Isaac: this is an assertion of their continuing personality. The person who enters the eternal city is the person who was here. In the transition, he or she may discard a worn-out physical body. The grain of wheat, wrote Paul, is not quickened unless it dies, but God giveth it a body even as it pleaseth him. The transition is an ennoblement. The essential self remains. The person continues. There is great comfort in that assertion.

II. Jesus' statement means that our departed loved ones and friends are experiencing growth. A living thing is a growing thing. A living person is a growing person. She is growing in the direction of the Divine Person, which extends the process of growth into eternity and infinity. This is far beyond our comprehension, but we can grasp the idea as John grasped it when he said, "It doth not yet appear what we shall be, but we know that when he shall appear, we shall be like him."

III. Growth and continuing personality demand activity. The rest of heaven is surely not the rest of inactivity. The God of the inactive would be the God of the dead. Our God is the God of the living. Activity in the realm of love, in a realm where one is uninhibited by pain and distress and sorrow, activity unto the end which God appoints, is surely an attractive aspect of eternity. We get foregleams of this sometimes in this world when a bit of work that we do takes on a kind of divine radiance and a beauty that makes life marvelously worthwhile. This may not come often, but when the experience comes it is a harbinger of heaven.

This is the life that our loved one now enjoys—a life of continuing personality, growth, and activity. God is the Lord of her life. This is a great comfort to us.—M.K.W. Heicher

Things Missing in Heaven

TEXT: Rev. 21:1–7

What a number of "conspicuous absences" there are to be in "the homeland!"

No more sea! John was in Patmos, and the sea rolled between him and his kinsmen. The sea was a minister of estrangement. But in the home country every cause of separation is to be done away with, and the family life is to be one of inconceivable intimacy. No more sea!

And no more pain! Its work is done, and therefore the worker is put away. When the building is completed, the scaffolding can be removed. When the patient is in good health, the medicine bottles can be dispensed with. And so shall it be with pain and all its attendants. "The inhabitant never says: 'I am sick!'"

And no more death. "The last enemy that shall be destroyed is Death" (1 Cor. 15:26). Yes, he too shall drop his scythe, and his lax hand shall destroy no more forever. Death himself shall die! And all things that have shared his work shall die with him. "The former things have passed away" (Rev. 21:1). The wedding peal that welcomes the Lamb's bride will also ring the funeral knell of Death and all his company.—John Henry Jowett

The God of Comfort

TEXT: 2 Cor. 1:3–7

"Life is completely fair; it breaks everybody's heart." To the breaking of hearts Paul offers his God: "the God of all comfort who comforts us in all our afflictions, so that we may be able to comfort those who are in any affliction, with the comfort with which we ourselves are comforted by God" (1:3–4). Paul offers this God and Jesus Christ, the one whose broken heart has become the gateway to life.

Ministry begins in suffering. The grace of God is poured from broken heart to broken heart. Unbroken hearts are quite unusable for ministry; they are like shiny pottery vessels with no openings either to receive or to give the healing balms of God. For the desolation of hearts, only God's consolation will finally do—a consolation brought by Christ and his servants.

Ten times in five verses we see the word *comfort*. Do you get the idea of its importance? The New Testament word is *paraklesis*. You may remember that word from some other place: Jesus talking of God sending us another Paraclete, another like him (John 14:16ff). Paraclete literally means "one called [*klesis*] alongside [*para*]." Wayne Oates says that God's presence comes in two forms: as *overagainstness* (the Holy Other meeting you face-to-face) and as *alongsideness* (God coming to walk by your side as friend).

Jesus was the supreme: Paraclete of God, alongsideness made flesh, God's Son who came to Earth and walked beside us as friend.

But this friendship was a suffering friendship. Jesus was the Suffering Servant envisioned by the prophet, a man of sorrows and acquainted with grief, one who bore our sins and bore them away, the one whom we would despise and reject but by whose stripes we find our healing.

It is his broken heart that becomes our passage to the grace of God. He is the Christ of sorrow and comfort. I love the way H.C.G. Moule expanded on the following climactic moment from Bunyan's *The Pilgrim's Progress*. Christ is the Man at the Gate:

> "Here is a poor burthened sinner," said the Pilgrim; "I would know, Sir, if you are willing to let me in."
>
> [And we would say with the pilgrim] "Here are stricken and broken hearts; we have heard, Sir, that your heart was once broken, and has stood open ever since, and that its great rift is turned into a gate by which men go in and find peace. We would know if you are willing to let us in."
>
> "I am willing with all my heart," said the Man: and with that he opened the gate.

The broken heart of the Son of Man has become the open gate to eternal life. It has also been the occasion of our being called into the ministry of Jesus

Christ, the ministry that is not for professionals only but for the whole people of God.—H. Stephen Shoemaker

How Shall We Think of Our Christian Dead?

TEXT: Rev. 14:13

Truth is available by legitimate inference from what we know of God's dealings and from direct statements of Scripture, to comfort aching hearts and to satisfy the minds of those who live by faith in Jesus Christ. I want to offer you a great text and then lead you to some little windows that our New Testament opens to our faith.

Our text is a beatitude, one of the greatest of the many beatitudes of the Bible, a summary of the whole future of those who have fallen asleep in Christ, an assurance that we need not worry about their welfare or their happiness. If we had nothing else than this, we would have adequate grounds for confidence.

But we have more than this. There are a number of little windows that the New Testament opens to our faith—windows that illumine the assuring message of the text, windows through which insight is gained as we try to think about our Christian dead.

Here is a window that the New Testament opens to our faith: *Our Christian dead are alive—radiantly alive with the life that Christ shares* (John 11:25, 26, 14:1–3, 17:3).

Another window: *Our Christian dead are endowed with bodies adapted to that life* (1 Cor. 15:35–44, 49).

Another window: *Our Christian dead are intimately and indissolubly related to God.* (1) They live in his fellowship constantly (Rev. 21:3). (2) Their status and security are assured (Rev. 7:14, 15a). (3) They are in God's service (Rev. 7:15b). (4) All of their needs are satisfied (Rev. 7:16a). (5) God throws his protection over them (Rev. 7:16b). (6) God shall heal them of all sorrow (Rev. 21:4).

Here is a final window that the New Testament opens to our faith: *Our Christian dead live active, interesting, developing lives.*

I wonder whether we have ever fully understood just what John is trying to say to us about our Christian dead in the seventh chapter of Revelation, verse 17.

Our own faith in the future is strengthened as we hold to such convictions as these concerning our Christian dead. Paul's words closing the fifteenth chapter of 1 Corinthians take on new meaning when he speaks across the years to us: "Wherefore my beloved brethren, be ye steadfast. . . ." Holding such convictions, we are braced and undergirded for the days remaining to us, believing the effort to be worth all that is required, and looking with unwavering expectation toward whatever the future holds for us. For God is in it all! And God is at the end of it all!—Adapted from Wallace Alston

Encounter with Grief

TEXT: John 16:22

John's account of the Last Supper is an eloquent and moving one, ending with the address of Jesus to his troubled disciples. It is apparent that Jesus sought to fortify his friends with courage and faith for the tragedy to come. The shadows of the cross hung heavily over the upper room, yet Jesus sounded this note of hope: John 16:22.

There is grim honesty and realism in the Master's words—"So you have sorrow now"—and no offer to obscure tragedy or deny its reality. Jesus faced life and the future quite frankly, knowing there would be sorrow in the experience of his disciples. Indeed, no one can escape his own appointed encounter with grief. Death is one of life's inevitables and we have no choice but to face its implications both for ourselves and for our loved ones.

Jesus did not stop with the words, "So you have sorrow now." He went on to say, "I will see you again." It was a stirring affirmation of his faith that there is no death for beauty, truth, and goodness living in a human soul. Our grief is for ourselves, not for them. "I will see you again."

And so, "your hearts will rejoice." Oh, to be sure, we will grieve for a while. Grief is inescapable if we have loved. I think Jesus would say, "Go ahead and grieve." After all, he wept. One cannot be callous where love is involved.

The pain we feel at the moment is to be the tool and instrument of our later healing. Nevertheless, grief that is legitimate at its beginning may, if prolonged, impair recovery of spirit. While it is normal for anyone to be plunged into grief by the death of a beloved, it is by no means a sign of emotional health to be so permanently inconsolable that he retreats from the human enterprise.

Surely the disciples found enough to live by despite their grief. They found that Jesus had spoken truly when he said, "And no one will take your joy from you." Indeed, their grief was the source of their growth. Because of it, they became stronger, wiser, and better able to minister to the lives of others.
—Harold Blake Walker

A Better Country

TEXT: Heb. 11:13, 16

Our mother, sister, friend has passed over the boundary line into a better country. That better country is the dwelling place of her soul. That is a good phrase—the better country.

Some have taken it in hand to describe that country. A notable example is that of John in the book of Revelation. He describes the country partly in negatives: "God shall wipe away all tears from their eyes; and there shall be no more death, neither sorrow, nor crying, neither shall there be any more pain." That is good knowledge to have of the better country.

Then John writes as though it were "a great city, having the glory of God; and her light was like unto a stone most precious, even like a jasper stone, clear as crystal, and the street of the city was pure gold." This is all imagery, figure of speech; it has entered into the Christian tradition and it is good.

But today I should like to look into the better country from another point of view than that of negation of pain and sorrow, from another angle than that of materialistic imagery.

It is the soul of our loved one that enters the better country. The soul! Two things I point out about the soul—any soul, her soul, yours, mine. The soul responds. The soul forms attachments.

Concerning the responses: There are three things to which the soul of man responds. Let us begin with beauty. We can understand that. The response to beauty anywhere we find it is not the response of our bodies, or very seldom. The gateway may be the eye or ear, but the appreciation is an action of the soul. And always our response is limited, restricted. We look up to the mountains and we love their beauty, but it seems that something holds us back from full appreciation. There is beauty beyond to grasp, if only we could grasp it. Beauty is always offering something beyond us. If we somehow or other attain the beautiful, there is higher beauty to attain.

Now in the better country, the soul is unimpeded in its appreciative quest for beauty.

So it is with truth. Our souls desire truth. We are not satisfied without it. Of course we often get sidetracked after other things. We get carried away in superficial things; nevertheless, the soul's real desire is for truth.

Poet Alfred Lord Tennyson revealed something of our real nature when he said:

> Flower in the crannied wall,
> I pluck you out of the crannies,
> Hold you here, root and all, in my hand,
> Little flower—but *if* I could understand
> What you are, root and all, and all in all,
> I should know what God and man is.

That's it: we want to know, and every flower and every pebble might tell us the truth, if only we could grasp it.

Now in the better country, the soul of our dear one is uninhibited in the grasp of truth.

Then there is goodness. Sometime in her life, perhaps many times, she wanted intensely to be good. That was the soul's movement. We know that the best thing is goodness. We also know that the highest goodness is that of God.

In the better country we are unrestrained in our movement toward goodness.

Would you have a loved one return from that better country, where she is unimpeded in her quest for beauty, uninhibited in her grasp of truth, unrestrained in her growth toward goodness?

You would not desire her return. Rather do you glory in her passing into that better country.

The soul of a person not only responds to beauty, truth, goodness. The soul also forms attachments—attachments that are personal, with parents, brothers, sisters, sons, daughters, grandchildren, friends. The soul also has a relationship with God. Deep inside, these attachments are not physical. They are spiritual. Love is a spiritual thing. Love belongs to the heavenlies. Love is eternal. Love is Godlike. God is love.

These attachments of love are not broken when one goes into a better country. Rather, they are strengthened, enlarged, made more enduring.

"Now we see in a glass darkly, then face to face: now I know in part: but then shall I know fully even as also I am known."—M.K.W. Heicher

The Death of His Saints

TEXT: Ps. 116:15

The word *saints* does not mean those extraordinary characters who to many of us are not attractive because their lives seem distorted and unreal, but just ordinary people who, trusting in God, have lived well and who, on such a day as this, we delight to honor.

Death does not seem precious to us, yet perhaps it should. We may be looking from a different point of view than does the Lord. We are apt to think of death as a kind of blind alley, a dead-end street; but from the Lord's point of view it is not. Death is a thoroughfare. It is going through. It is stepping upward. It is going into another room. It is journeying into a better country.

The door of death seems very dark and drab to us, because from our angle only the light of Earth falls upon it and that light is mostly darkness. Remember that from the other side the light of heaven shines upon the door. It is bright and splendid. It might be a very precious and lovely thing to see one coming through that door from the other side.

Think of the things the saint leaves behind when passing through the door of death: pain and illness, sin and evil, sorrow and tears, limitations and frustrations. Think of the blessings acquired: wholeness, righteousness, joy, and achievement.

We know that there are good things left behind—chiefly friendships, kinships, human loves—but let us not be too sure that these are not still enjoyed. At least they shall be renewed. It seems that there is nothing worth keeping that shall not be kept.

Let us have faith that in the eternal city there is the presence of Christ. God himself is there in some fashion far beyond his presence with us here. There, too, truth is still to be discovered, and beauty is to be appreciated and perhaps created, and there is always higher goodness to be attained. Truth and beauty and goodness are ever beyond us and calling us to greater activity and a larger quest. I believe this is so. Think not of heaven as a do-nothing place. I foresee it as a place of great activity. From the Lord's point of view it must be a great blessing, a very precious thing, to enter the heavenly kingdom.

And from his point of view it may be well for us that our loved ones have gone through the door. This may kindle our own hope of glory. This may strengthen our own faith. We take our bereavement and we transmute it into activity and consecrate it unto good, and we ourselves live better lives.

We could go on with such meditation for a long time, for the happiness of the new country must be beyond our imagining and the blessings of eternity must be inexhaustible.

Precious in the sight of the Lord is the entrance of [the deceased] into the eternal kingdom.—M.K.W. Heicher

Dearer Than Life

TEXT: Acts 20:24

How dear is life! There is a physical enjoyment of life. Good health, a fine appetite, the joy of just living are experienced by many people. Our Father's world, the grandeur and beauty of nature, the privilege of friends, the joys of home life! How much good books add to life! Good conversation, creative thinking and expression.

There are three great uses of life. There is the nonuse of it. There are those who pamper it, coddle it, seek to save it that it might be used selfishly, indulgently, chiefly for their own ease or pleasure. There is the abuse of life. We wrong it, waste it, pour it out in riotous living. There is the noble use of life. To spend it for God's glory, bring it to its highest fulfillments, use it in the service of our fellow men, dedicate it to the great ends that God intended. When so used, the law of self-preservation is supplanted by the higher law of loving sacrifice.

The apostle Paul illustrates this noble use of life in an outstanding way. He counted his life dear, but not unto himself.

Duty is dearer than life. Duty is an august, a noble, a majestic word. It has a priority that should be in a man's soul. Obligation is at the heart of it. It is deeper than one's wishes or desires or feelings. Duty involves conscience, faithfulness, loyalty. When a man does his full duty, he is not far from being the noblest creation of God.

The welfare of others is dearer than life. Robert E. Speer, in his "Merrick Lectures," says, "Service is the man of truth and purity spending himself upon the highest use of life, namely, the uplifting of life and the making of men. We have the best ground for regarding this as the supreme service, the real purpose of life."

And when men settle, in the secrecies of their own souls, the great issue whether they will serve others before self, that they will ally themselves with the great moral forces of the universe and spend and be spent in the unselfish service of others; when men hear and obey the still small voice that speaks to them, then they are counting unselfish service dearer than life.

The cause of Christ is dearer than life. Jesus made this plain to those who wanted to come after him so that they might follow in his steps. "He that loveth father or mother more than me is not worthy of me; and he that loveth son or daughter more than me is not worthy of me; and he that taketh not his cross and followeth after me is not worthy of me." "He that findeth his life shall lose it and he that loseth his life for my sake shall find it." Only one person gave himself to redeem men from sin's guilt and power. No founder of any other religion dreamed of dying for his followers. The ethnic religions may contain some fine truths, but not one of them has a Redeemer. Jesus Christ alone laid down his life that men might have life abundant and eternal. And ever since Jesus lived and died, men have been counting their lives not dear unto themselves but rather dear for his sake and the gospel's.

Some worldly classmates said to one of their number about to sail for China, "Why do you throw your life away in that God-forsaken country?" The young man replied, "Christ poured out his life for me and for them; why should I not go?"

> For all through life I see a Cross,
> Where sons of God yield up their breath;
> There is no gain except by loss,
> There is no life except by death;
> There is no vision except by faith;
> Nor glory but by bearing shame,
> Nor justice but by taking blame;
> And that Eternal Passion saith,
> "Be emptied of glory and right and name."
> —Rev. Dr. F. S. Downs

Not Made with Hands

TEXT: 2 Cor. 5:1–5

I'm glad that we share a belief that one of the ways God speaks to us is through the Holy Scriptures, and furthermore, that part of what God says to us in the Bible is there for our comfort. Our passage from the apostle Paul is a practical and theological reflection in which many people do find comfort.

Paul was not always in the mood for comfort, but he managed here in spite of himself. He told the Corinthians, at some other place, that he was better at building up than he was at tearing down. This brief passage is part of that reality.

Paul had a keen eye for what mattered, and much about which we worry day by day really doesn't matter. He could look beyond the limitations of our earthly existence and set the value of life here and now in the context of eternity.

One fact about which he was certain is that there is more to human life than the body in which we live during our years on Earth. This body is important and essential in the way God has created us. We won't overlook that, and we don't want to. Paul was quick to remind us that when this body fails—and it will—it's not the end of us by any means. "For we know that if the earthly tent we live in is destroyed, we have a building from God, a house not made with hands, eternal in the heavens" (v. 1).

The "tent," when set up properly and well cared for, can last and give those who use it protection and enjoyment, but there are no delusions about its durability. A tent is something humanmade, not permanent; we cannot live there long. Paul contrasts a tent with a *house that God builds*—a heavenly, eternal home. This eternal home with God is promised to all who are children of God. We want it, and we need it. "Here indeed we groan, and long to put on our heavenly dwelling" (v. 2).

Life lived in relationship with God is so rich and full. When we begin to understand just how wonderful it is, we don't want to lose out on such life—ever, and we don't have to. God's children don't lose out on it. Instead, what happens is that, in God's vast plan, mortality is "swallowed up by life" (v. 4). The essence of who one is is transformed into fullness in the heavenly realms—no more weaknesses or limitations.

It's hard to believe, isn't it? "[The one] who has prepared us for this very thing is God, who has given us the Spirit as a guarantee" (v. 5). Through the Holy Spirit of God there are constant renewals in our lives and in the lives of many people we know, and these take place in an imperfect world. If this goes on here in this life and we can know a sense of renewal and resurrection in this life, how much greater will be the transformation God has waiting for his children in heaven! The best of life in the present is only a foretaste of all that God has prepared for God's own.

Dear friends, your loved one and our friend has moved out of his tent and into a most elegant heavenly home, a heavenly body in which he can celebrate his wholeness even as he joins the celestial choirs singing praise to God. He has begun to receive the gifts of eternity; he is in a new home, not a home made with hands but a home made by God. Though separated from you for a time, he is well cared for. After all, to be away from the body as we know it is, for God's children, to be "at home with the Lord" (v. 8). And so he is. Amen.
—David Albert Farmer

The Lord of Our Days

TEXT: Eccl. 3:1–8

We come together today on a sad occasion, the death of Frances Moore. But times like these give us cause to think, and they offer us the possibility of growing stronger. We grow still stronger as we trust in God, depending on him to meet our needs. For it is God who is Lord of our days, our work, our play, our hopes and dreams, and especially of our pain. God ordered Frances's days, and we would do well to consider how he orders ours as we consider this text.

A time to be born (3:2). God is the Lord of creation. He made Frances and he made us, for God created the universe. Genesis 1 teaches that God made all things good. James 1:17 adds that all good gifts come from God, who never changes, never fails to be just and loving. Everything good that Frances did was God's work through her.

Further, God made us for a specific purpose. Men and women are created in God's image and have the capacity to know and love him. The main reason we were born is to love and serve God, who died for us so that we might have eternal life. The book of Ecclesiastes claims that it is not always easy to relate to God, yet urges us to do so. As we walk with the Lord, we find that the God who created us orders our days.

A time to live (3:3–8). The Lord of our days fills our days with important work to do. Frances was a homemaker, one who made living easier for others. You may be a farmer, a computer expert, a secretary, or a teacher, or you may do some other type of worthy work that makes you gather, sew, or plant. All honorable work is given by the Lord of our days to benefit others and to meet our family's needs. In our work we find meaning, and this meaning takes us back to God.

God also gives family, as Frances's gathered loved ones demonstrate. In families we learn to laugh and to weep, to mourn and to dance, and to love and hate. Whatever your family's current level of love and trust, I ask you at this crucial time to draw together. A death reminds us that petty squabbles and old hurts only separate us from those we need most. A death also reminds us that family closeness is a wonderful gift.

Most of all, God gives himself. Work and family enrich our lives, but even these blessings do not match the grace and love of God. Just as you need family now, so you need the love of your heavenly Father. Reach out to him as the Lord of your days who gives good work and good people during the living of your life.

A time to die (3:2). A funeral reminds us that life on Earth ends. We all die. And under normal conditions none of us really longs for death. Yet death is a reality, and we must prepare for it.

Frankly, many of us fear death. Paul speaks of his fear when he mentions that sin is the sting of death (1 Cor. 15:54–55). Why does sin make death sting? Because it separates us from God unless we have believed in Christ. If we commit our lives to the Lord of our days, though, there is no sting in death, for our sins are forgiven (1 Cor. 15:56–57).

Through Christ we need not fear death. He has defeated death on our behalf (1 Cor. 15:54–58). He has promised life after death (John 3:16). He has promised a place where death, separation, and pain—such as we feel today—will no longer exist (Rev. 21:1–8). All who prepare for death by trusting in Christ can claim these promises as their own.

The Lord of our days desires to give us endless days with him. The one who made us, who gave us work and family, desires to spend eternity with us. As we take comfort in these truths, may we learn to walk with the Lord of our days.—Paul R. House

Moving Day: Funeral Sermon for One Who Died Following a Long Illness

TEXT: John 14:1–3

It's never easy to say good-bye. It's hardest to say good-bye on moving day. When we stand among the piled-up boxes of our lives, sadness wells within our hearts. The apartment or house we leave has become our home. Even worse is the pain of moving out-of-state, for we must bid farewell to dear friends.

For [the deceased], moving day has come. We cry because we will miss him. We are sad for he is no longer with us, to share our lives, our laughter, our hopes.

While moving day has its sadness, there is reason for joy. It can be happy. As we load up the last box and head for the open road, a sense of excitement and anticipation grips us. We wonder: What will our new home be like? Will we enjoy the neighborhood? Will we really feel at home?

With certainty, we know moving day was happy for [the deceased], because we know where he moved! John 14:2 speaks of our heavenly Father's house. In this house are many rooms. Right now I imagine [the deceased] is getting settled into his new home. We feel sorry for ourselves, but we must not feel sorry for him. [The deceased] is happy in the presence of Jesus.

Did you know even Christ had a moving day? For three years, the twelve disciples set their vocations aside to follow Jesus. Now his earthly ministry was coming to a head. For the last time, Jesus spoke of his departure. Confused, Simon asked, "Lord, where are you going?" The Savior replied, "Where I am going you cannot follow now, but you will follow later."

Jesus' "moving day" meant he was returning to his Father in heaven. His work on Earth was complete. The disciples wanted to follow him right away, wherever he was going, but Jesus knew that was impossible. Simon and the others still had much to accomplish on Earth. Their time had not yet come. The Lord's departure meant temporary separation, but he gave them a wonderful promise: ultimately he would be reunited with his followers. Jesus assured them, "You will follow later."

The word *disciple* means "follower." Simon and the others were faithful followers of Christ. They called him "Master," and it was more than just a title. In every way, they had forsaken all else to serve Jesus. Because they followed him on Earth, he assured them they would one day follow him to heaven. By the fruit of his testimony, we believe [the deceased] followed Jesus to heaven. When you respond with obedience to the grace of God, God's Word tells us, a "room" is reserved for you in the heavenly Father's house. As sure as I stand here today, for each of us is coming a "moving day." Scripture gives us only glimpses of heaven. We would rather have a detailed photograph, but we are provided with only a shadowy portrait. Despite this, one proposition is sure, as John 14:3 tells us: "I will come back and take you to be with me that you also may be where I am."

Jesus moved away, but one day he will return for a visit. When he does, the bodies of the dead will be transformed. We will be given resurrection bodies. The apostle Paul calls it a "mystery." Even he could not fully understand the nature of our heavenly uniform. What he does say is that what is temporary will become indestructible. What is miserably weak will become incredibly strong. No cancer can harm our resurrection bodies. No disease or infirmity will impair us then. [The deceased] leaves behind a body used up, but when we see him again he will be the [deceased] of strong frame we once knew.

Moving day, from a spiritual standpoint, means giving up what we cannot keep for what we cannot lose. Anyway you look at it, it is to our advantage. For the Christian, heaven becomes our wonderful home. With our resurrection bodies, we will live with Jesus forever. What a promise!

Before moving day came for [the deceased], he gave us an admirable example of trust in God and love for life.—J. Gregory Crofford

Our Very Present Help

TEXT: Ps. 46

We join you today in this painful event as friends who share in your grief and disbelief. We share your sense of deep loss and the profound wish that there might have been some other way. We have no answers or explanations; we, like you, are inclined to search for ways to understand, but we have all already discovered that such a search is in vain. Still, without answers, explanations, or ways to grasp what has happened, we stand alongside each of you with hope and confidence in Jesus Christ that the last word has not been spoken. Even in this situation of what feels to us like finality in the extreme, the God of life will not let it be. The God who gives life—physically and spiritually—has already taken the one you love into his divine arms and welcomed her into her heavenly home.

We understand all too well that those of you nearest to her remain in a state of confusion, heavyhearted and bereaved, lonely and confused. Of course; how could it be any other way? What I have to offer today is a simple reminder that the God who loves and has provided for her eternally also loves you and is ready to help you bear the heavy load. This is the abiding message of the Christian faith and the only basis on which we can face life's grim realities with a sense of hopefulness intact. God loves you, abides with you, and will not forsake you in these moments and in the days of readjustment and reorientation that are ahead of you.

This surely is the message of Psalm 46. Where could we find stronger words of comfort? These are words especially for you today.

Not only are the psalmist's words beautifully rendered and reflective of profound insight, but also the very logic provides a pastoral word of comfort and inspiration. The writer begins with the full force of theological reality, a statement of religious confession and assurance that gives order and hope to his life and to the whole human family. This is the beginning point. This is the lens through which we view world events and the more immediate circumstances affecting our lives. Any other point of departure, any other frame of reference, will distort not only how we see but also how we hope. The psalmist began with God, and so must we.

Not with just any god, mind you, but with the one true God, the creating, redeeming, and loving God. The God on whom his people may depend; and with only a little bit of experience in our uncertain and many times cruel world, we see that this is the God on whom we *must* depend. "God is our refuge and strength, a very present help in trouble" (Ps. 46:1). Therefore, let us come to grips with our grief, anger, fear, and loneliness, which result from this untimely death, by looking first to and through such a God as this, the God to whom Jesus also pointed. Because of his own reliance on God and because God was so much in him, Jesus could say, "Come to me, all who labor and are heavy laden, and I will give you rest . . . rest for your souls" (Matt. 11:28, 20).

The psalmist's assessment of God does stir us to reach out to God because God is reaching out to us in a living presence that helps us fend off enemies from without and enemies from within. God is our refuge; in relationship with God we may take shelter from outward attack, such as a tragedy over which we have absolutely no control. Oh, there will come a time to step out of the shelter and take on the enemy; but even then God will be with us, because God, too, is our strength. The psalmist's summary of theological affirmation is that God is a present help in trouble; come what may, God's presence is what we need to cope and keep on searching for the divine meaning in life. Again, this is where we begin, not with the trouble.

The trouble is real, and God never asks us to ignore it; that would be disastrous. However, in spite of trouble, the psalmist still draws our attention Godward. As an example of trouble, the psalmist recalls a personal experience—perhaps the most horrifying experience he could have imagined: an earthquake. Even in that time when he feared for his own life amid death and destruction all around, he could still affirm that God was his refuge and strength.

What you have been living through for the last several days is like a personal and emotional earthquake—with much of your joy and stability threatened and even dying. Finding peace and courage to rebuild will not be easy. You can find some courage and encouragement that you're not up against it all alone. In both the material and emotional rebuilding and healing, the Lord of hosts is with you; the God of Jacob is your refuge.—David Albert Farmer

LECTIONARY-BALANCED MESSAGES

A third type of sermon is the lectionary-balanced message. As the name implies, the pastor works with one or more lectionary readings from the Sunday closest to the funeral or crisis service. These readings are used to develop a message in which biographical and expository material are balanced fairly evenly. This is a challenging method, likely to be appreciated in traditions that observe and value the lectionary. Even in traditions that do not use a lectionary, the pastor may nevertheless do significant exegetical work with a text and blend it with biographical material. This type of preaching anchors the occasion and the pastoral care offered during the service in the larger life of the church—and not surprisingly, such messages can help those who are bereaved or affected by crisis to cope with anniversaries of their loss. The life of the deceased is remembered primarily in terms of how it reflected the gospel being proclaimed. Therefore, listeners hear fewer personal anecdotes than in the biographical message, but the sermon runs the risk of sounding generic, which can happen if a Scripture-centered message is simply transposed to a new setting with the names changed.

This type of message has other risks. It tends to be longer than the biographical message, because the preacher is simultaneously doing obituary and proclamation. It is difficult to use this method effectively if one did not know the deceased. What is more, there may be Sundays when none of the lectionary texts is a good fit for the occasion at hand.

The Resurrection and the Life

TEXT: John 11:1–44

Our friend and loved one, Dorothy A., has lived a full and rich life among us and has left a treasure of rich memories of her life and service that few can match. A graduate of George Peabody College in home economics, she was dietitian of the college for a number of years.

She was an artist with food and flowers. Not only could she prepare the foods to taste so good, she could also prepare them to look beautiful for the table. The same could be said of her talent with flowers—growing them, arranging them, and teaching others how to do both with them.

She was an excellent Sunday school teacher of teenage girls. And she was a faithful wife to her husband, Fred P., who died many years ago, and a good wife to her second husband, who was a blessing to her and blessed by her.

In the end she died of Alzheimer's disease, after having lived the rich and full life of a caring and loving friend.

A brief message from God's Word: In the Gospel of John there is a story of two sisters and their brother: Martha, Mary, and Lazarus. Many of you know the story, but I want to take part of it and share my thoughts with you. Martha, Mary, and Lazarus were close friends of Jesus, and evidently he would stop by their house when visiting Jerusalem. A short time prior to his Crucifixion he was in Perea (modern Jordan) when Lazarus became ill and the sisters sent word to Jesus asking him to come to help Lazarus. But the Master did not go that very day. He delayed his going two days, which caused some consternation among his disciples. Then he said, let us go to Bethany, where the three lived.

As he and his disciples approached Bethany, word came to Martha, who left immediately to go and meet Jesus. Note the dialogue that took place:

MARTHA: Rabbi [Master or Teacher], if you had been here, my
    brother would not have died. [What great faith she had in her friend
    Jesus.]

JESUS: Your brother shall rise again.

MARTHA: I know that he shall rise again, in the resurrection, at the last
    day. [She thought of the resurrection as an event in the far-off, dim
    future.]

Then Jesus replied with one of the great statements found in the Bible: "I am the resurrection and the life: he that believeth in me, though he were dead, yet shall he live: and whosoever liveth and believeth in me shall never die. Believest thou this?"

There are two references to death in these two verses. "Though he were dead," or die, refers to physical death. "Yet shall he live" refers to spiritual life. In the second instance, verse 26, Jesus restates the truth, "And he that liveth [spiritually] and believeth shall, never die [spiritually]." It is our Lord's way of saying to his disciples that the life he gives is spiritual and eternal and transcends the physical life, which is affected by physical death; death then serves as the gateway into the greater life with the Father forever.

And then the Master makes it very personal: "Do you believe this?"

And Martha comes forth with one of the great confessional statements found in the New Testament: "Yes, Lord, I believe that you are the Christ, the Son of God, he who is coming into the world." Other confessions are found, of John the Baptist, Simon Peter, and Thomas. And I think our friend, Dorothy, if here in the flesh, would rise up from her place and say with Martha, "That's my confession, too; God bless you, Martha!"

The scene changes, and Jesus finds Mary and she cries to him, and the friends wail in their sorrow, and the Master weeps, literally "bursts into tears," thus showing his own humanity but also decrying their failure to understand that he is the answer to their needs and the Comforter while with them.

He then commands someone to move the stone from the cave entrance and in a loud voice cries out, "Lazarus, come forth!"

The crowd is silenced by the authority of his voice and stands in silence. In a moment a man comes out of the cave with his face and legs still wrapped in the grave clothes in which he had been buried. The miracle of returning a grown man to life was the high-water mark of the signs done by Jesus up to that time, as John gives them to us.

When Lazarus came before Jesus, the Master said to those about him, "Loose him and let him go." For a while, at least, the friend and brother would live longer in the flesh to help and bless others. The rest of the chapter is given over to the effects of the miracle on various groups.

But for us the words and the sign speak for themselves.

There was need for the Great Physician, but he waited in order that he might show forth a greater power than healing, the power of raising one from the dead, from the grave, and from the power of Satan!

We see Jesus caring for his friends, amazed at their wailing, grieving with them, and then moving to demonstrate the mighty power of God, even the Son of God.

And that same one is here among us today, in the person of the Holy Spirit, to bring his love and comfort to us all. He is here to say to all of us: death cannot hold you captive. All that is needed is your trust in the Savior and Lord of life. Take comfort in these words and walk with him in high places.

May our heavenly Father be with you one and all, and may his grace be sufficient for you.—G. Allen West Jr.

Memorial Sermon for Jackson Blanchard

TEXT: Acts 9:36–43

If there is any text in the Bible that reminds me of our friend Jackson, it is this one. Not just the story itself, but its placement, too. Acts 9 has to be one of the two most dramatic, pivotal chapters in apostolic history. I think it's wonderful that in the midst of talking about Paul's conversion and Peter's road trip, the author of Acts saw fit to tell the story of a Christian woman who never preached a sermon, never published an article, but who was precious to the Church. It is as though Luke, presenting us with a series of snapshots of the early Church, got to chapter 9, looked out from behind the camera, and said, "Wait a second. Tabitha, come over here. I want you in this picture, standing right here with the major players."

Who was this Tabitha? Well, for starters she was a woman known by two different names. And Jackson, you know, had another name. She wasn't always called Jackson! Tabitha is presented as a woman on her own. She ministered to widows; it may be that she herself was a widow. Or perhaps she had been engaged at one time to a fiancée who died tragically, as happened to Jackson. Tabitha was someone who came to faith in Christ as an adult, but once she did, she gave all of her energy and talents for God, and she became part of a community. Tabitha was someone who labored behind the scenes. While the big names were out on the lecture circuit and attending important conferences, Tabitha and women like her stayed home and kept everything running smoothly. They were the support staff of the early Church.

And then what happened? Tabitha became ill. We don't know what the warning signs were, how it all began, at what point death invaded her mortal body. But no doctor could help. She suffered. She died. And the community mourned. Perhaps especially the women—those who were closest to her, who had known her good works and enjoyed her company, who watched with anguish as her life ebbed away. Christians do weep when they lose someone they love, even though we do not sorrow as those who have no hope.

They called for Peter. We don't know why. But according to the text, they didn't say, "Peter, come and raise Tabitha from the dead," or "Peter, if you had been here our sister would not have died." (That's another story!) They just said, "Peter, please come." Peter came, and after he arrived they told him Tabitha stories. One by one they brought out the gifts she had made. They showed him the labor of her hands. They shared their memories of her thoughtfulness. Peter listened, and after hearing their stories and witnessing their tears, he put them out of the room and closed the door. Peter knelt and prayed, then took her hand and said, "Tabitha, arise." And she opened her eyes and lived. We can imagine the laughter and joy when the other disciples saw her again.

On January 2nd, our Lord came to Jackson's room and shut the door. We cannot see her now. But Jesus took her by the hand and said, "Jackson, arise." And she opened her eyes and saw him. She's been given new life in him—a life where there is no sickness, no pain, no sorrow. And one day Jesus will open that door for you, for me, for all who believe in him. We will see our sister again, and what gladness there will be in that reunion!

That's not the end of the story. It says in Acts that word of what happened was spread throughout Joppa, and many believed in the Lord. It just goes to show that you don't have to have a seminary degree or be a tenured apostle in order to be God's instrument for spreading the gospel! The particulars of Tabitha's life aren't mentioned again in the New Testament. That's okay; the garments, the good works, and the memories are not an end in themselves. They point to Tabitha's Lord. And so it should be for us, as we celebrate the life of Jackson Blanchard.

As I reread this passage in preparation for today, I realized that it sounded like something else I'd read in the New Testament. When I checked, I found it is remarkably similar to the raising of the daughter of Jairus, recorded in Mark 5 and Luke 8. The stories are so alike that some ancient manuscripts of Mark have Jesus saying, *"Tabitha* cumi" instead of "Talitha cumi!" Well, yes, it's true that one event took place during the earthly ministry of Jesus and the other is postresurrection. One miracle was done by Jesus and the other by Peter in the power of Jesus' name. But the sequence is almost identical: A girl or woman is ill. She dies. Someone is sent for by those who love her. He puts them from the room. He takes her hand and says, "Arise." There is new life, and there is joy. The stories are amazingly similar, except for one detail that stopped me in my tracks. In Mark and Luke, after the miracle, Jesus said, "Give her something to eat." In Acts, no food was given. Tabitha did not eat.

And that's the way it was, wasn't it? Jackson could not eat. Her body couldn't keep down the food and drink she tried to consume. It was a cruel irony: Jackson, who with Linda Forbes and student helpers arranged so many receptions and coffee hours here at the seminary; Jackson, the only person I've ever known to offer refreshments when people came to see her at the hospital; Jackson, who loved table fellowship: Jackson could not eat. I believe it is two months today since Jackson had her last meal in this life with others. A few of us gathered in her apartment for an impromptu Christmas Eve service, with Holy Communion. The grape juice we used was actually a can of juice she'd given me a few weeks earlier, when I visited her at Evanston Hospital. The bread, I confess, was taken from a package of communion wafers on the shelf in the seminary kitchen. And in that meal, God took the stuff of ordinary life and transformed it into a means of grace. That drink, originally intended to strengthen her for the remission of cancer, was given instead for the remission of sins. The bread, which was a link to the seminary community she loved, connected her in the end to a much larger community: to a company of apostles and prophets, saints and martyrs, Christians whose names are known only to God, "ten thousand times ten thousand in sparkling raiment bright." Jackson ate and drank, and was thankful. And she is alive in Christ.

Today the same meal is set before us. It is a table that extends all the way to the Upper Room on the night before Jesus gave his life for us. It is a table where Peter and Paul were both fed, a table with a place set for the daughter of Jairus and, I am sure, for Tabitha. It's a table so large that it reaches across the centuries to include Jackson and all the faithful departed; a table where we will meet the disciples of generations yet unborn, when we gather at last with all the blessed for the marriage supper of the Lamb. There's a place for you at the table this morning—a foretaste of the heavenly banquet that is yet to come. So draw near with faith to receive the bread of heaven, to drink the cup of salvation, and to give thanks for the gift of everlasting life in Christ Jesus our Lord.
—Carol M. Norén

Funeral Sermon for Les

TEXT: Luke 12:35–40 (TEV)

Be ready for whatever comes, dressed for action with your lamps lit, like servants who are waiting for their master to come back from a wedding feast. When he comes and knocks, they will open the door for him at once. How happy are those servants whose master finds them awake and ready when he returns! I tell you, he will take off his coat, have them sit down, and wait on them. How happy they are if he finds them ready, even if he should come at midnight or even later! And you can be sure that if the owner of a house knew the time when the thief would come, he would not let the thief break into his house. And you, too, must be ready, because the Son of Man will come at an hour when you are not expecting him.

In John 11:25, Jesus said, I am the resurrection and the life. He who believes in me will live, even though he dies; and whoever lives and believes in me will never die. This is the gospel of the Lord.

In their Sunday morning routine of preparing to come to church, it was not uncommon to hear Les say as he headed to the garage to pull out the car, "Lydia, are you ready?" That was the first call. She knew that meant she had five minutes to wrap things up, grab her Bible, and unplug the coffeepot. Sure enough, like clockwork, the second call came. As Les returned to help her into the car, he'd always say, "Ready, Lydia?" She tells me it was a predictable, familiar dialogue that she could count on every week.

This week was different. It wasn't Lydia who heard the call. It was Les as he died suddenly from a massive stroke this past Sunday morning. He might have experienced what you just heard read from the twelfth chapter in Luke. The master came to Les and may have asked, "Ready, Les?" Les knew the Word of God. He was familiar with this very passage that Lydia found underlined in his personal Bible. It instructs all of us to "be ready for whatever comes because he will come at an hour when you are not expecting him."

The Lord came and knocked, and Les opened the door for him. At once, very quickly, he went. Like Lydia's calls of readiness, Les also had two calls. The first came very early on in his life as a young boy he learned to articulate his faith in his personal Lord and Savior. He used to tell me he couldn't remember the time he was *not* a Christian. It was a way of life for him. The more God entrusted to Les, the more his faith grew and his stewardship strengthened.

Like the servants in the Gospel story waiting for their master to return, Les kept a constant vigil. He demonstrated readiness that Peterson describes in *The Message,* saying, "He is a blessed man if when the master shows up he's doing his job" (Luke 12:43). Blessings were his and continue to be his. In his faithful service to God that Les lived out before us here in this faith community all could see he was dressed for action with his lamp lit (as Luke so aptly puts it). Dressed in the armor of God, Les could stand firm.

It can be a challenge to envision armor when we always saw him in his brown suit or his navy blue suit. Lydia said that, try as she did, she never could get him to dress in any other colors. Colors were not important; what he was dressed for was. Brown or blue, he was dressed for action! Les wore the full armor of God that Paul describes in Ephesians 6. He covered himself and his entire life with the breastplate of righteousness and a belt of truth. He wore a helmet of salvation and carried the sword of the Spirit. And his feet were fitted with the readiness of the gospel. With these he stood firm and did his job! He was ready to open the door at once even if the master should come at midnight or even later. God was happy to find Les prepared as the time came for the second call.

Unlike the five minutes Les gave Lydia to finish preparing for church, he had eighty-five years before that second call came. He proved the words of James 4:14 to ring true: that life is like a "mist that appears for a little while and then vanishes." It matters not that we have five minutes or eighty-five years—it passes by all too quickly.

Lastly, you too must be ready. The hour will come. It came for Les last Sunday morning at 7:15, when he was not expecting the call. The Lord welcomed him home to join the great cloud of witnesses, and heaven rejoiced!

But friends, Lydia, we must remember that Jesus knows both sides: the glory of welcoming Les into the heavenly kingdom and the deep grief and loss experienced here in the earthly kingdom. For us, for Lydia, life is forever changed. It will never be the same again. How well he knows that. In the gospel of John we find the account of the crucifixion in which Jesus was dying and near the foot of the cross stood his mother with the other women. When Jesus saw his mother there, and the disciple whom he loved also standing nearby, he said to his mother, "Dear woman, here is your son," and to the disciple, "Here is your mother." From that time on the disciple took her into his home. In our time of separation, although temporary—until we meet again in the heavenly realm—it is very real and very hard. We need each other. I say to you those same words today that Christ spoke long ago: "Lydia, here is your family," and to the church family, "Here is Lydia." In the great and empowering compassion and comfort of our Lord, may we all be found doing our jobs ready to live out the will of the master and giver of all blessings, now and forever more. Amen.

Let's pray: O God, we give you thanks for Les's life as your faithful servant, beloved husband, and brother in Christ. Comfort and strengthen each one of us today as we say good-bye. Thank you for the love and support we have as your church body. May you find us ready and standing firm together in doing your will until your call comes to us.—Sally Gill

Funeral Sermon for Edward J. Cullman

TEXT: Isa. 25:6–7

The Old Testament Prophet Isaiah describes God's ultimate triumph over death and pain as a festival, a feast of victory over all of God's enemies. This victory banquet will include wonderful, rich, mouthwatering food and aromatic, well-aged wines, the very best wines that the vintner can produce. Invitations to this celebration have gone out to all the peoples of the Earth, and the prophet proclaims that at God's table, death, the greatest enemy of the human heart, shall have no place.

This is what we need to hear as we bow before God and celebrate the life of Edward J. Cullman. Death intrudes into our human lives once again. There is the bitter pain of separation, we are numb with shock and grief; but God, the Lord of life and death, must have the last Word.

God speaks this Word in many voices, especially from the mouths of Job, John, and Jesus. The Word has been prayed and sung. Isaiah sums it up with certainty: He will swallow up death forever. Then, when death is consumed, God will command a feast.

I appreciate the many places where the Bible describes eternal life as a feast or banquet. Death is swallowed up by God as surely as we eat the festive meal with great relish or joyfully drink wine to gladden the human heart (Ps. 104:15)

Ed was a home vintner, a wine maker. He knew the kind of love and care it took to produce a vintage that would be properly aged, flavorful, aromatic, amber or tawny, red or white. Ed gave his vineyard the devotion and attention that only a creator can give, taking great pride and joy in the fruit of his labors.

As we remember today, we think of Ed's Creator and how Ed was chosen in holy baptism, processed, matured, and aged in that growing process we call life.

God's hands created and fashioned this strong, intelligent, loving man who was the fruit of God's creation.

Ed was a man's man. Born in Philadelphia, he grew up tough and strong, and served in the Navy during the Korean War. He worked hard and knew the value of a dollar. He was self-driven and goal-oriented. At the age of forty-four, when most people have left school far behind, Ed graduated from Ohio State University with a BSBA in finance. At fifty-five, he graduated from the University of Phoenix with an MBA. He raised five children, cared for his parents and mother-in-law, and dearly loved his wife, Evie. Let me share his own words: "My marriage to Evie was a significant event in my life. My children and grandchildren have certainly been a joy to my life. I would like to thank all of you for the little time that we have had together; it was all too short. I have looked fondly on the pictures of us in my den many times. May God bless you, each and everyone."

Ed worked hard at Storage Tek and was an active member of this church, faithful in worship and in study. Ed was honored and proud to serve at Advent's altar as a lay assisting minister, offering prayers and assisting with Holy Communion. I know that the memories of serving as an altar boy with the Mass in Latin all came back to him. His questions and comments during Bible studies and other classes amazed me. Ed often said, "I want to learn more about my religion."

Shooting straight from the hip, Ed was practical and pragmatic, and said things the way he perceived them. He enjoyed numbers, statistics, and playing "What If" on his computer. God blessed him with wit and humor, like a fine Sauvignon Blanc, very dry.

All winegrowers know that a suffering vine produces the best grapes. The greatest vineyards are found in the most difficult climates and soils—so poor and barren that little else can take root in them. Again, Ed's words: "I would like to say that since my late twenties I have been plagued with rheumatoid arthritis, the pain has been with me most of the time (day and night). Only after the heart attack in Canada has the pain receded some. This has affected my disposition and consequently made me very grumpy and quiet at times. Forgive me for those times, they were way too frequent and I would exchange them for more pleasant ones if I could. We are dealt situations in life and therefore must make the best we can. I could have done better." Through most of the years I have known him there was great pain and discomfort from his arthritis. Ironically, that pain left him after his major heart attack up in Canada.

That brings us to the heart that failed him. Describing himself as a "cat using up his nine lives," Ed knew that his days were numbered. Everyone prayed and held their breath when Ed and Evie traveled because their last few trips, beginning with the one to Canada, were marred by major heart disease. This last trip was a quest, a pilgrimage, he said, to bury Paula's ashes and to see all of the kids and his brother. His heart held out, but now we know it was his "farewell tour," and it was a gift from heaven. Even though his death seems sudden and abrupt, let us look at it this way. He was given five extra years of family, fun, and life before that bad heart finally stopped beating. Ed did know chronic pain and suffering, it did make him grumpy and quiet at times, but it also gave him a great appreciation of life, family, friends, and God.

Ed was rarely absent from worship. The bread and wine of the Eucharist fed Ed's soul. In the Gospel Jesus says, "I am the bread of life. Whoever comes to me will never be hungry, and whoever believes in me will never be thirsty. This is indeed the will of my Father, that all who see the Son and believe in him may have eternal life; and I will raise them up on the last day." Think of it! Being raised up to take a place at the banqueting table, where the bread of life and the cup of salvation are spread. What a wonderful promise! No cholesterol or calories, only that feast of rich food and well-aged wines that God commands when death is swallowed up forever. This is what Jesus means when he offers himself to us as the Bread of Life, the one who sustains, nourishes, and feeds us. Jesus Christ is that feast upon the mountain, the feast of fine food and wine. Remember his words at the Last Supper: "I tell you, I will never again drink of this fruit of the vine until that day when I drink it new with you in my Father's Kingdom" (Matt. 26:29). When we meet Christ face to face, we will not be hungry, we will not be thirsty. Jesus is the vine and we are the branches. The vintner of heaven and earth will gladden our hearts as we celebrate our arrival at God's party.

So, through the tears, and in our own way, let us raise a toast to Ed as he finds his seat in the Kingdom and feasts on the bread of life and the fruit of God's vine. Amen.—Dennis K. Hagstrom

A Christmas Message of Peace

TEXT: Luke 2:1–14, 21–32

The death of a loved one is never easy, but to experience the death of a husband and father at Christmas is especially difficult. While the rest of the world is celebrating the birth of the Christ child, those of us here will always connect this season with the death of John. At this moment, we are having a difficult time connecting with the joy, the glitter, the excitement of the season. The warmth and hope of Christmas seem like a distant echo to us. So why read Luke's account of the birth of Jesus? Why bring Christmas to a funeral?

Because if the message of Christmas cannot speak to us at this moment, if it cannot address this deep hole in our spirits, it cannot speak to us at the better times of life.

If I were asked to name one word that summarizes the message of Christmas, it would be *peace.* When the angels appeared to the shepherds, they blessed them with the peace born of God's favor. Many of the carols we sing at this season of the year speak directly of or paint the picture of peace—"Silent Night," "Away in the Manger," "O Little Town of Bethlehem," and so on. God came to bring peace on this Earth. It is peace that a broken and hurting world needs desperately. It is a sense of peace that those of us gathered in this place want, for our world has been disrupted by death. We would like for the tumultuous voices of pain and grief to be silenced. We long for that sense of stability and order that death has taken from us. Today we felt like crying with the prophet, "My soul is bereft of peace; I have forgotten what happiness is" (Lam. 3:17 NRSV).

One of my favorite Christmas carols is "It Came Upon the Midnight Clear." One of the verses reads like this:

> All ye, beneath life's crushing load, whose forms are bending low,
> who toil along the climbing way with painful steps and slow,
> Look now! for glad and golden hours come swiftly on the wing:
> O rest beside the weary road, and hear the angels sing.

Will you rest with me beside the weary road of grief for a moment and hear afresh the angels' song of peace?

In Scripture, the word for peace comes from the Hebrew word *shalom*. That word means far more than the absence of conflict, though it surely means that. In its fullest sense, shalom, or peace, describes a sense of wholeness, or completeness, or well-being. It is of that peace the angels sang. It is that peace that surrounds us today.

When I visited John in the hospital shortly before he died, Betty related to me her lifelong concern for his salvation. She also shared with me that the day before he slipped into his coma, he asked God to forgive him and to come into his life. He accepted God's offer of peace. The broken relationship between God and John was reconciled. Betty related to me how after that experience John seemed so much more at peace with himself and what was happening to him. We can celebrate that John found that peace God offers to each of us.

We can also celebrate that John is now at peace. His lifelong struggle with illness is now over. Because of his new relationship with God, we are confident that John is secure in the arms of God. For him all sickness, strife, pain, and death are no more, as John heard a voice from heaven say, "Blessed are the dead who from now on die in the Lord. . . . they will rest from their labors" (Rev. 14:13 NRSV).

We can celebrate God's promise of peace in the midst of our pain and grief. In John's Gospel, after the crucifixion of Jesus, the disciples lock themselves in a room to be alone with their fears and grief. Suddenly Jesus appears in their midst and says, "Peace be with you." From that moment everything changed for them. Jesus' presence transformed their sense of hopelessness and despair into one of hope and excitement. His presence gave them new direction and purpose for living.

When the angel appeared to Mary telling her that she was chosen to give birth to the Messiah, the angel told Mary the name of her son was to be Immanuel, "God with us." Over and over in Scripture, salvation is described as the presence of God among his people. Israel was delivered from Egypt because God intervened in person on their behalf. Moses was able to lead the people through the wilderness because God was in their midst as a pillar of fire or a cloud. Joshua was able to win battles because God was with him. When God is present, all is well.

The message of the Christmas story is that God is present. Jesus is in our midst. Even in the middle of chaotic circumstances, we can live with hope, joy, and purpose, because God has not abandoned us. The same God in whose presence John now stands is with us. He will lead us through the darkest valley and give us rest and strength. The psalmist writes (Ps. 4:6–8 NRSV),

> There are many who say, "O that we might see some good!
> Let the light of your face shine on us, O Lord!"
> You have put gladness in my heart more than when their grain and
>   wine abound.
> I will both lie down and sleep in peace; for you alone O Lord, make me
>   lie down in safety.

The angels' blessing of peace does not have to sound as a distant echo for us this Christmas. If we listen closely with our hearts, we will experience the presence of God with us. In his presence we will find strength, hope, joy, and life.

May the peace of Christ rule in your hearts this Christmas.—Jim Holladay

Funeral Sermon for Thomas Ackerman

TEXT: Matt. 25:34–40

These words of Jesus, recorded by Matthew and read at the Eucharist last Sunday, have been meant for many people, men and women who have given unselfishly of themselves, loving and serving others. Out of the millions of people who have been faithful to this idea, we celebrate the life of one this morning, one for whom we know these words of Jesus were meant: Tom Ackerman.

As we worship together, we remember before God a man who always gave love and concern to the people around him, a man who cared for others, and in doing so witnessed to the love of Jesus Christ. I am confident that we are assembled this morning, not only with tears of grief but also with thanks to God for Tom's life and love. We remember with thanksgiving all that he meant to us and the impressions that he made on individual minds and hearts. We are grateful for his life, seemingly brief at thirty-seven years, but a life that more than made up for its brevity with true caring, friendship, and love. Your presence here today testifies to the quality of that life.

When death strikes down someone in his thirties, we are stunned and shocked. Even when the end comes after a long, hard illness, it is just not right. It is so unnatural. Cancer is a fearful word to us because this illness is so unpredictable and seems to strike at any time. For the last year, Tom and Donna have known what it means to fight that dreadful disease, a fight that ended last Sunday.

Truly, Tom was a fighter. In the times I visited with him, I always saw a man who was doing everything humanly possible to get better. I truly admired his patience in suffering, his acceptance of treatment, the poking, the prodding, and the surgeries. He was not a quitter. Deep in his heart, Tom knew that it was not God's will for him to be sick and dying. During this struggle against cancer, Tom remained the man that he had been all of his life: a loving and devoted husband to Donna; father to Alex, Tate, and Jarod; a loving son to his parents; and a caring brother to Brian, Doug, and Pam.

My lasting impression of Tom will be that he was always giving and putting others and their needs first, including Donna, his boys, and the many others for whom he cared. Having earned a master's degree, he worked for a number of years as a drug and alcohol counselor. But one day he approached Donna with the idea that he would like to stay at home and raise his sons as a "hands-on" father. Because he made that decision, his sons will always remember Dad taking them sledding, ice skating, or swimming whenever they asked. Being at home also made it possible to offer much needed assistance to his father-in-law.

Tom also cared for people whom he did not know. Here at Advent Church, he was a member of the congregation council and the social outreach committee, assisting with our food bank and Habitat for Humanity. He volunteered to be Advent's contact person with Habitat and encouraged our members to go out and help with the building of houses for the homeless. One Sunday he gave a wonderful presentation in our adult forum on the ministry of Habitat for the homeless in our community and around the world.

Tom truly lived our Lord's command to feed the hungry, clothe the naked, build shelter for the homeless, and serve Christ through the people he encountered every day. Tom's service and love to others was a fruit of his Christian faith. Before he became ill, he was regular in his attendance at Sunday worship and at the Lord's Table, building his life on God and God's work. This was his response to God's love and the gift of God's Son, Jesus Christ.

Habitat for Humanity builds houses. Habitat understands the need every human being has for a place of shelter, refuge, and safety, a dwelling where one is protected from cold, storms, and a world that is often an unfriendly place. Every human being needs a place to call home. Without giving it much thought, Tom helped build homes for strangers, strangers in whom Jesus dwells.

In today's Gospel, Jesus proclaims that for everyone who trusts in his death and Resurrection, he is building a habitat in heaven, a dwelling place that is free from cancer, pain, death, and tears, a sanctuary wherein God dwells, an abode where he, our Savior, lives and reigns forever. This is the Father's house, it is the heavenly place we call home.

Indeed, today there are great tears and sadness. It is very difficult to say goodbye to someone so young and in the prime of life, one who has been such a vital influence on his family and friends. Hopefully, through the tears and sadness, there can be the joy that comes from knowing that Tom was truly a child of God for whom Jesus died and rose again, a child of God who took his baptismal covenant seriously by loving and serving others, and a child of God who looked forward to dwelling in the house of the Lord, forever.

"Come, Tom, you that are blessed by my Father, inherit the Kingdom prepared for you." Amen.—Dennis K. Hagstrom

SUNDAY MESSAGES

A fourth kind of sermon included in this collection is the Sunday message. Part of effective ministry to those in crisis and sorrow is instructing them in what the Christian faith says about death, the afterlife, crises, and so on, both before and after these events occur. The congregation may remember and draw on these teachings when the time of need comes. In much of contemporary North America, it has become uncommon to hear Christian preachers talk about heaven and hell—perhaps because in an age of affluence we are so preoccupied with the present that we hold less thought for the future.

The Life to Come

TEXT: 1 Cor. 13:9–13

I. *Heaven is homecoming.* To be absent from the body is to be at home with the Lord! It is, in the language of the Old Testament, "to be gathered to the fathers." Originally, this meant to be buried in the cave with the ancestors. But with the developing revelation of the Old Testament, and especially in the light of the Resurrection of Christ, it meant to be at home with the Lord.

Will we know each other on that glad morning? Our text says, "Now I know in part; but then shall I know even as also I am known." Our knowledge will be more complete, not less complete. We shall know as we are known. We won't have to go around like people at a convention with name tags on our lapels. It will be a glorious meeting with those we have known and loved, and with those we have known only by name.

But in the deepest sense, it will be a homecoming to the one whom having not seen we love. I visualize a corridor to the throne room where I will cast myself at his feet and say, "Thank you, Lord Jesus, for saving my soul—for giving to me, thy great salvation—so full and free." To see him, face to face, is heaven indeed!

II. *Heaven is fulfillment.* Every high and holy spiritual goal in this life is pointing toward heaven. All spiritual values will be brought to completion there. We were created for fellowship with God—but we do not yet know what fellowship really is, and we will not until it is fulfilled in his presence.

And heaven is much more: it is described in the Bible again and again as renewal, as the New Creation. Have you become aware of the tragic toll that the years take upon your life and vitality? The treasures here will fade away; the life here is dying; achievements here are always partial; this world is not our home; we are pilgrims passing through! But heaven is the home for which we were made—it is the New Creation. This old, broken, and dying body will be exchanged for a glorious resurrection body, like the body of our Lord! These tears of sorrow will be wiped away! Behold, he makes *all things new!* Earth has no sorrow that heaven cannot heal.

But lurking in the minds of some is that nagging question: How can it be heaven if there is someone missing? How can there be joy if there is the vacant chair? We will see it as Jesus sees it: he has done all that the love of God can do to reach the last sinner—but he will not force one soul to come into his family.

III. *Who will be there?* This is the most important question of all. The Bible teaches that only those whose names are written in the Lamb's book of life will be there—only those who have washed their robes and made them white in the blood of the Lamb. What does this mean? It means that those who have been given the new life in Christ, who have been born again by the Holy Spirit's power, will be there. Heaven is not composed of all the church members, or all the so-called Christian nations, or a certain favored race. Heaven is the fellowship of those who have been redeemed by faith in Christ and by obedience to his saving word. He will gather his elect from the four corners of the Earth, and the mark that distinguishes them is the banner of the great apostle: "I am crucified with Christ; nevertheless I live; yet not I but Christ liveth in me" (Gal. 2:20).—Wayne E. Ward

Yes, God Can

TEXT: John 19:26–27

One of the great concerns of the dying is for the ones who are going to be left behind. Jesus set the pace in showing us how to die. He wanted to see that the family's needs were adequately met.

That might mean different things for different people. Providing adequate insurance coverage for our loved ones is perhaps the most common way we try to meet that need. Seeing to it that the household is on a sound financial base is so important. Many families have suffered in other ways after their grief experience due to the mess they found themselves in financially.

Obviously, the intensive care unit of the hospital is not the best place for accomplishing this goal. Since we're all in the process of dying—that is, since we are all moving toward that appointment—the time to start preparing for the family's future is now. When you are dying, it will be helpful for you not to have to worry about this matter.

There are other family needs one might want to meet. I have been present when a dying person has called the family members into the room. I have heard them talking to their loved ones about dreams and wishes. I have heard them ask for forgiveness where they have done wrong to someone. I've seen the tears, heard the prayers, watched the embraces, and felt the power of human emotion in times of reconciliation.

The dying one must always recognize that his or her departure from this life will leave an empty place for others. Someone will feel the pain and anxiety. Someone will wonder about what to do. How beautiful it can be when the dying one, like our Lord, looks out for the interests of the living and does everything possible to care for the needs of others.

We might also note that when Jesus turned to John and asked that he care for his mother, it was a way of turning to the network of friends we have and seeking help from them. John was honored to be so recognized by the dying Lord. Many times our friends are more than glad to do the extra thing that will give us comfort and give our loved ones necessary help.

We need our friends in the time of suffering and death.

Grief is harder when there is no established network of friends who can give intimate support in times of sorrow. Each of us needs a group of quality relationships, rather than exclusive dependence on only one or two people.

That's also where a good church family enters the picture. The fellowship of the church and the strength one derives from the people of faith is invaluable to the dying and their loved ones.—Jerry Hayner

What Happens After We Die?

TEXT: 1 Cor. 15:12–20

What happens when we die? That's a question everyone wants to know the answer to, but one that most people are reluctant to talk about. On the one hand, we are repulsed by death—by its finality, by the way it ends our relationships with those we love, by its inevitability. On the other hand, we're attracted by the hope of what might be beyond—escape, new beginnings, freedom from pain. The boxer Joe Louis said it best: "Everybody wants to go to heaven but nobody wants to die."

I want to talk with you about what happens after we die. I can't answer all the questions. I can't even answer most of them. In the end, we're still going to be faced with a mystery. What we do know, we know through Jesus Christ. Just as he is our model for this life, he is also our model for the life to come.

Now, there are many people who believe that nothing happens after we die—that's it, the end, period. They believe that after death we cease to exist, that there's a total void. Our senses support that understanding. The way we know another person is by what we see them do, what we hear them say, the way they touch us, either gently in love or harshly in anger. Death brings an end to all that. Our senses cease to know the person. We have precious memories, and the things the person has taught us continue to affect us deeply. But at the moment of death, all communication, the lifeblood of human relationships, stops.

There is biblical support for that understanding. The Old Testament talks about the dead going to a place called Sheol, a place of darkness and emptiness, a place separated from the life-giving presence of God. The New Testament also understands the finality of death. If death were not such a formidable thing, then Jesus' Resurrection wouldn't be such a big deal. If death were just an automatic passageway from this life into a better one, Jesus' return from death would be a regression. Instead of rejoicing that he returned from the dead, we would feel sorry for him. But the Scriptures say that for three days Jesus was dead and that he was in that vast, empty place the Old Testament calls Sheol, what we call hell.

Yet there is something in the human spirit that knows we are intended to exist beyond our death. From the dawn of time, human beings have been straining to break the boundaries of life that death puts on us. The ancient Egyptians built pyramids to shelter their pharaohs as they journeyed to the afterlife. The Confucians of China built altars in their homes to provide a place for the spirits of their ancestors. We know there must be something about us that was meant to live beyond death; that's why 1 Corinthians 15:26 calls death "the last enemy." It's something that works against what we were created to be.

I think that *Embraced by the Light* was a best-seller because it affirms what so many of us want to believe: that death is really no big deal. But that is not what the Bible teaches. The Bible affirms that death is a big deal, and the only one who can keep us from being destroyed by it is God himself, who sent Jesus Christ to face it head on. It wasn't something he looked forward to. On the night before he died, Jesus prayed in the Garden of Gethsemane that he would be delivered from death. He prayed so hard that he sweat blood. It's only because Jesus Christ himself died and suffered the full power of death and then was raised from its abyss on Easter that there is any hope for us beyond the grave.

Eternal life isn't something that's programmed into us. It's not an automatic event. The Bible calls death our enemy because it has robbed us of eternal life. The power of Christ is that he has reclaimed life for us and that he gives it back to us as a gift. If Jesus had not conquered the power of death by his Resurrection, we would think of him as only another great teacher, perhaps sent by God to enlighten us but not having the power of God to create and restore life. It is through his Resurrection that Jesus is our Savior, and his life and teachings show us how we are to live now that we have been saved from the destruction of death.

So what are those whom we love who have died doing right now? Are they watching over us? Are they enjoying God's presence? Do they know how much we miss them? The Bible doesn't give a detailed account of what we do in those years between our death and the return of Christ. I suspect that's because we would not be capable of understanding such an account if it was provided.

When we think about where the dead are or what they're doing, the only way we can think about them is in ways that we who are alive can conceive. But I suspect that when we die, all the categories of time and knowledge that we use to order our lives will be changed.

My friend George Sweazey once wrote about death, saying that death is not a collapse of the soul but an expansion. He compared the experience of dying to that of a little boy walking through a dark vale full of fears and uncertainties after being away from home. In the darkest and most frightening part of the journey, his father goes out to meet him and takes his hand and leads him the rest of the way until they reach home.

I like George's description. Dying is the scariest part of life's journey, something none of us has ever done before. It's at the moment of our death that God takes us by the hand and holds us until we reach our final destination. We don't reach it the moment we die. It's not until Christ comes again that God will gather all his children into his home. When we die, we are with God, free from pain and worry as we wait for the resurrection of our bodies at the end of time.

We know that there are a lot of things we don't understand, but we also know the one who provides for us. We have many fears about death and questions about resurrection, but we know that whatever is in the future, our Savior Christ is there waiting for us, and that the love and acceptance we know here are but a foretaste of what is to come.—Stephens G. Lytch

Dying in the Lord

TEXT: Rev. 14:13

What could it mean *to die in the Lord?*

I. *To die in the Lord must mean to die in the faith of the Lord.* We die believing. Even faith as small as a grain of mustard seed can remove mountains, said Jesus. Even small faith is great faith.

Jesus said, "Blessed are they that have not seen, and yet have believed." We have not seen the Christ, yet we have faith.

II. *To die in the Lord must mean to die in the grace of the Lord.* Who of us does not need the forgiving grace of Christ? Who of us is without fault, imperfection, incompleteness, sin? But we die in the Lord and we receive his grace and we are made whole. This is a great gospel which is ours.

III. *To die in the Lord is to die in the keeping of the Lord.* The Lord is thy keeper, the Lord shall preserve thy soul. Many a Christian soldier has gone up to the front heroically facing the death of his body, while gloriously aware that no shot nor shell could hurt that which really mattered; the soul of him was in the keeping of God.

It is a great comfort to us when we can commit the souls of our loved ones with faith and confidence into the keeping of God.

IV. *To die in the Lord is to live.* It is the glorious message of Easter. "Death is not a blind alley; it is a thoroughfare." Death is the portal of the soul "into another room." "I am the resurrection and the life," said Jesus. And so to die in him is henceforth to live with him.

V. *To die in the Lord is to receive his peace.* Blessed are the dead who die in the Lord. Yea, that they may rest from their labors. I cannot conceive that heaven is nonactivity. That would not be heaven. But I can conceive that heaven is activity without tensions, without insecurity, without restlessness; activity with peace, the peace of God which passeth all understanding.

VI. *Dying in the Lord, living in the Lord—this is sharing the purposes and will of the Lord.* We get a little insight into that when we are permitted to do good works here and now. The blessedness of being allied to the great and ultimate purposes of God must be blessedness indeed.—M.K.W. Heicher

Ain't No Grave Gonna Hold This Body Down

Text: Matt. 28:1–10 (Easter 1999)

Far be it from me to teach you anything new on this Easter Sunday. My only goal is to teach once again the old, old story that you already know, the story you heard in Sunday school and from the gospel of Matthew just a moment ago: Jesus of Nazareth died on the cross and rose from the dead. The women went to anoint his dead body, but found the stone rolled away from the door of the tomb. An angel dressed in dazzling white gave them the news, "He has risen from the dead and is going ahead of you into Galilee. There you will see him." Because of this story, we deck the sanctuary with lilies, pull out all the stops on the organ, dress in our best clothes and sing, "Hallelujah! For the Lord God omnipotent reigneth!" From childhood I have come to expect all of these things on Easter. I always liked going to church on Easter because everybody looked nice, the hymns were happy, and I had the sense that something very important and wonderful was being celebrated. Besides, I knew I could go home and chow down on those gumdrops and chocolate bunnies in my Easter basket. Today I have no gumdrops or chocolate bunnies, and it doesn't matter. If the sanctuary were stripped of lilies and organ, if we all had on blue jeans, the story that lies at the heart of this day would still be true. Nothing matters more than telling that story as often as we can until we realize it is not just a story but the wonderful Word of life.

So I'm going to shift the scene now from this festive sanctuary and ask you to divert your mind from your Easter dinner plans so that we can go stand together in the cemetery. I have stood in too many cemeteries. At forty-four, I'm old enough to have lost many people dear to me. I lost my father to a slow and agonizing case of colon cancer, and my grandfather to Alzheimer's disease. Nine years ago, one of my dearest friends in all the world ran into a truck and was instantly decapitated. The man who was my great spiritual mentor all through my years at seminary, a former Marine in perfect physical shape, was in the middle of a six-mile run one day when he dropped dead of a heart attack. In my professional life, I've buried little children whose lives were cut short by cancer and leukemia, I've buried young men who committed suicide, I've buried the ravaged bodies of great saints who endured horrible illnesses. Yes, I have stood in too many cemeteries, both as a mourner and as the person who officiates over the mourning. And I'm going to stand in many more until the day the trumpet blows for me.

When I get called to perform a funeral, I immediately put on my professional armor. I have to. Even if I knew the deceased very well, I cannot remain strong and confident for a family that needs my help unless I put my own emotions aside. But this doesn't mean that death ever becomes routine. Every time that final moment comes, every time I stand out in that cemetery and contemplate a casket ready to be lowered into the dark, damp ground, I shudder. I dread it. I think to myself what a wretched and horrible thing death is—no wonder the Bible calls it our "last enemy." In fact, I once had the vivid experience of conducting a graveside service for an overwhelmed family who could not bear the thought of losing Uncle Ralphie. When the casket was carried to its location and placed over the hole that had been dug, the family demanded that it be opened one last time so they could see his face. Although this is somewhat unorthodox, the undertaker did what they asked. Then, after the casket was closed and I had performed the graveside service, the family once again pressured the undertaker to open it up so they could see Ralphie. I was appalled, but the undertaker over-ruled me. When he opened the casket, Ralphie's grieving mother threw herself on top of it while his widow howled in agony with a rage and grief I can still hear. Death is a thief and a robber. It puts an unbridgeable gap between us and the people whom we have loved, with whom we have built lives and relation-ships that are the foundation of our being.

In recent years, death has been rehabilitated by popular culture. Death is now interpreted as just another experience of life, a natural part of the rhythm of the cosmos. Death is one point along the so-called circle of life that moves from birth to maturity to death to rebirth. To those of us who live above the equator, Easter has turned into a big spring festival. As fall turns into winter and then winter into spring, our bodies will wither and age, then die, then pass into the soil where they will give birth to new life forms like flowers and trees. I don't know about you, but this explanation hardly strikes me as tidings of comfort and joy. I've visited my father's grave. In the summer, his old friend Nick plants beautiful red and white geraniums on it. Somehow, I am not filled with gratitude and fulfillment that the body of my father, rotting away in the soil, is providing nutrients for the local flora and fauna. My father was worth more than that. All of the generosity, humor, and goodness that was in him, all of his talents and dreams, all of his tenderness and reverence, are lost to me—and I hate that. I do not feel that a few geraniums are an adequate substitute for the father who gave me life, who loved me, who is lost to me. Nor does the Bible say so, or teach anything about the circle of life. The Bible teaches that death, far from being a natural part of life, was never intended to be part of God's good creation. It came about as a result of sin. The whole story of the Bible is the story of how God entered human history to deal with that sin, so that death would not have the last word.

When Job, one of the most righteous and good men in all Scripture, lost his family and property and then fell ill with horrible disease, he raged about his miserable condition. "My spirit is broken, my days are cut short, the grave awaits me," he cried out in horror. "If the only home I hope for is the grave, if I have to spread out my bed in darkness and call the worms my mother and sister, where then is my hope?" Job was a man full of talents and experiences who had tasted life's good gifts to the fullest. He was outraged and horrified that everything he had said, done, thought, and dreamed was destined for annihilation, to become food for grubs. But Job knew something else. He knew that the God whom he worshipped was more than a force, more than an idea, more than a myth invented to explain the primitive world. His God was personal; he trusted in God as a man trusts in his best friend to stand with him, provide for him, and comfort him. A God who had created Job in God's own image was not about to let that image be defaced and destroyed by the powers of darkness. So, in his misery and confusion, Job was able to say, "I know that my Redeemer lives; and that in the end he will stand upon the earth. And after my skin has been destroyed, yet *in my flesh* I will see God; I myself will see him with my own eyes."

My Redeemer lives; *I myself* shall see him. Those are stunning words. Job fully expects that after he dies, he will live life in all of its fullness. He will not be pushing up daisies or existing as some disembodied soul in a state of suspended animation. He will be himself. He will even be "in the flesh," in a new and transformed body not subject to aging, disease, or decay. How does Job know this? Because he knows who his friend is. Though things look dark at the moment, Job knows that his Redeemer, his friend, remains in control of the universe and will not let him go down into the dust.

My Redeemer lives; *I myself* shall see him. These are the only words that empower me when I stand in the cemeteries. These are the only words that give me hope now that I am getting older and watching my mortal body fall apart. This past January, I lay in a hospital bed and knew I was going to die. This body in which I live had suddenly let me down. Its lungs were filled up with blood clots, its bowels were full of parasites, its immune system had crashed. It was covered with hives and red rashes and swollen with fluid. I knew my doctor thought I was going to die, and I myself longed for the end of my gasping for breath and howling in pain. But I hated the whole experience. Even as I prepared to die, I hated to die because I couldn't bear the thought of the end of me. God creates us with what are called survival instincts. We jump back when faced with a threat; we instinctively cover our heads when something is thrown toward us; adrenaline pumps throughout our bloodstream to alert us to danger. The survival instinct is itself a form of evidence that death is not normal or natural. Even as my body deteriorated, that survival instinct was screaming in my brain. This woman that I am, this woman so rich in friends and experiences, this woman full of dreams and hopes this woman who wants to travel and read more great books and write great poetry, this woman who walks her dog and drives her car and loves to tell jokes—I couldn't bear the thought of the end of her, even as the end seemed near for the flesh in which she was living. I wanted to be more than a wandering spirit on some astral plane. I wanted to be more than a pile of compost producing next spring's hyacinths. I wanted to be *me,* fully *me,* like no one else who had ever lived or ever would live. I wanted to be *me* forever.

And so I will be. I didn't die this time. Someday I will. But I, created in the image of God, saved by the grace of God, called into relationship by the love of God, will hear the voice of my Savior telling me what he told those women so long ago on Easter morning: "Don't be afraid!" And I will sing back to him the words of that old gospel song, "When I hear the trumpet sound, there ain't no grave gonna hold this body down!" For I know that my Redeemer lives, and that my eyes will behold him, myself and my daddy and my friend Bob and my mentor Gene and every Christian soul I've ever buried. That is my Easter joy! Amen!—Joy J. Hoffman

Our Inheritance of Hope

TEXT: 1 Pet. 1:3, 4

The hope of the Christian is a lively hope—not a dead hope, not a languid and languishing hope, but a living, vital, active principle. Its author is God. Its source is mercy. Its medium or channel is through the Resurrection of Christ. It brings to us an inheritance that we begin to enjoy here and shall continue increasingly to enjoy hereafter. For this inheritance is incorruptible, that is, imperishable, immutable, incapable of decay. It is undefiled. It is not tainted by sin; all its enjoyments are right and good and holy. It fadeth not away. It is not like the fading flowers that exhibit their beauty and yield their fragrance only for a short time and then perish. How different it is from the things of Earth! It is reserved in heaven for all believers. It is prepared, or "laid up," there, beyond the reach of all enemies. No wonder the apostle bursts out with such words of grateful emotion as "Blessed be the God," and so on.

These words are the language of experience. It was as though the apostle had said, "I have this hope; I have it now, and I feel its enlivening, cheering, supporting influence. It is a living, vital, life-giving hope of a blessed immortality. Blessed be the God," and so on. It is this element of experience which goes far to make the Resurrection of Christ such a source of joy to the world.

The Christian's hope is well founded. God would never show us a thing he did not mean to give us.—George MacDonald

Things Missing in Heaven

TEXT: Rev. 21:1–7

What a number of "conspicuous absences" there are to be in "the homeland!"

No more sea! John was in Patmos, and the sea rolled between him and his kinsmen. The sea was a minister of estrangement. But in the home country, every cause of separation is to be done away with, and the family life is to be one of inconceivable intimacy. No more sea!

And no more pain! Its work is done, and therefore the worker is put away. When the building is completed, the scaffolding can be removed. When the patient is in good health, the medicine bottles can be dispensed with. And so shall it be with pain and all its attendants. The inhabitant never says, "I am sick!"

And no more death. "The last enemy that shall be destroyed is Death." Yes, he too shall drop his scythe and his lax hand shall destroy no more forever. Death himself shall die! And all things that have shared his work shall die with him. "The former things have passed away." The wedding peal which welcomes the Lamb's bride will ring the funeral knell of Death and all his sable company. —John Henry Jowett

Though He Slay Me, Yet Will I Trust Him

TEXT: Job 13:15

A few years ago I spent some days in Rome and, on a free afternoon, slipped away from the rest of the party and found the Pyramid of Caius Cestius, and the

Protestant cemetery nearby. In that cemetery is the grave of John Keats who, as he was dying at the age of twenty-five, "seemed to feel the flowers growing over him." I knew I would find violets growing on his grave because my father had told me how he, as a youth working in the pits of Castleford, had ordered a copy of the poems of Keats to be sent to him by post. When the parcel arrived, he opened it, still covered as he was with pit muck, and read his favorite poems, and into that book, some years later, he had put some leaves from the violet plants which a friend had brought him from the grave of Keats.

There they were, two Italian gardeners with baggy trousers, tending the grave, and with their permission I collected a few more leaves from the violets to put with my father's. Twenty yards away from the grave of Keats was the grave of Shelley, who died at the age of thirty. For a few moments I was in communion with both of them, and also with my father, who died thirty-four years ago and had never been able to make the pilgrimage to Rome that I made on his behalf. I went there for him, and with him. What I ask you is, was I unreasonable in thinking so?

Now, I myself am in the "sere and yellow leaf" (Macbeth, Act V, Scene 3). After two heart attacks a man must be aware that he cannot live forever. John Donne, the metaphysical poet and Dean of St Paul's, in a situation similar to my own wrote:

> Since I am coming to that Holy room
> Where, with Thy quire of saints for ever more
> I shall be made Thy music; as I come
> I tune the instrument here at the door
> And what I will do then think here before.

So I want you to think with me of our eternal hope, of those "Last Things"; for as Hamlet said, "That fell sergeant, death, is so strict in his arrest."

The Book of Job is a pre-Christian book, yet Job could say, "Though he slay me yet will I trust him." Let me outline the drama to you. The first scene is set in heaven, where God is receiving reports from his angels about the state of the universe. Into his presence comes Satan, an angel but a fallen angel, who has been going to and fro on the Earth. "Have you considered my servant, Job," asks God, "that he is perfect, there is no one like him?" Satan points out how much it suited Job to be upright, for God had blessed him with sons and daughters and with everything his heart could desire. Accepting the challenge of this, God goes on to allow Satan leave to afflict Job in any way he might wish, provided he does not touch him personally. Satan goes out from the presence of the Lord, and blight, plague, and disaster smite Job from every quarter. His children are killed and his crops and livestock are obliterated.

Yet Job sinned not "The Lord gave, the Lord has taken away; blessed be the name of the Lord."

Again the scene is set in heaven, and Satan comes into the presence of the Lord. "Have you considered my servant, Job?" God asks once again. "Skin for skin," says Satan. "Touch him personally and you will see how he will respond." Once again Satan goes out, this time with carte blanche to do anything he wishes to Job, short of death. He strikes Job with painful disease so that, covered in boils, he is left sitting among the ruins of his house scratching himself with a piece of pot. In his extremity his wife approaches him and asks, "Why do you not curse God and die?" and Job responds, "You speak like a foolish woman. Shall we receive good of the Lord, and shall we not receive evil?" In everything Job sinned not.

I cannot help but think that Satan now piles on the agony by sending to Job his three friends, Eliphas, Bildad, and Zophar. For a while they are silent in the presence of Job's grief, but then they open their mouths and go on and on for twenty chapters, trying to prove to Job that he must have sinned to suffer as he is doing. Finally, and this is a nice touch for those young people who always imagine they can improve on their elders, Elihu, a young man, springs into action and, rebuking the old men into silence, goes boringly on for yet another twenty chapters.

Goaded beyond endurance, Job cries out, "Oh that I knew where I might find him, that I might present my case before Him," and in the midst of his torments cries out, "Though he slay me, yet will I trust Him." It is no part of my task today to tell you how the book ends, but I would remind you of one other cry of the tormented Job. In 1921, at Samuel Collier's funeral here, in this hall, Isobel Baillie sang: "I know that my redeemer liveth and that He will stand in the latter day upon the earth; for though worms destroy this body yet in my flesh shall I see God." And you all know how *The Messiah* goes on: "For the trumpet shall sound and the dead shall be raised incorruptible."

Job was reaching out after Christian confidence. What have we to say about that confidence, and our reason for having it? What do I expect "when the present has latched his postern behind my tremulous stay"? Let us together explore the faith we have.

What is the ground of our Hope? It is contained in one word spoken by Jesus: the word *Father*. Someone wrote, "There are some words without which a religion would not be itself, and for Christianity that word is *Father*." God's fatherhood was recognized in embryo in the Old Testament: "Like as a father pitieth his children, so the Lord pitieth them that love Him," and "When Israel was a child I loved him, and brought my son from Egypt." But, uniquely, Jesus spoke of God not as an angry God or as an avenger or judge, but as "Our Father, which art in heaven," and added, "Your Father knows what things you need before you ask him." His last word on the cross was, "Father, into your hands I commit my spirit."

What we learn in the Christian way is that our own fatherhood and motherhood are a pale shadow of the fatherhood and motherhood of God. What earthly parents would give up a precious child? When the fire started in the Epworth Rectory on the night of 1708, everyone made for the exits, except little John Wesley, age five, who was asleep in a room upstairs. Charles, age one, was carried out by his nurse. Suddenly John's face appeared at the window under the burning roof. One man climbed on another man's shoulders and pulled the boy out in the nick of time—"a brand plucked from the burning." Desperate and ineffective, Samuel Wesley, John's father, watched the rescue operation, his hands clasped in prayer. As the little boy was handed into the arms of his mother he cried, "Let the house burn, I am rich enough, I have all my children."

Can we seriously think that our Heavenly Father would allow all the love and fellowship we have glimpsed here to be snuffed out by an accident to a mere physical body? We are more than a chance conglomeration of atoms. When a young man died in tragic circumstances, his father was called to the mortuary to identify him. His word to me was simply, "He was not there." We can sing with Zinzendorf:

> Jesus, thy blood and righteousness
> My beauty are, my glorious dress.
> Midst flaming worlds in these arrayed
> With joy shall I lift up my head.

The Christian believes in the essential goodness, rightness, and justice of the universe. He does not believe that such a universe throws away its greatest treasure. The evidence for this faith is found in Jesus.

He is unique. Two thousand years ago he who was dead became alive again. I do not think it matters how we interpret the Resurrection; it has changed the world and us. About the details of how it was done we may have a reverent agnosticism. For Job, God's face was hidden. We "have seen the glorious gospel day in Jesus' lovely face displayed."

I have to admit to you that the New Testament seems to speak with two voices about what exactly this means. The words of Paul, and the Book of Revelation, seem to imply a period of waiting after death: "How long, O Lord, how long, before you avenge our blood upon the earth," cry the souls beneath the alter slain for the love of Jesus. Paul mysteriously said, "We shall not all sleep, but we shall be changed in a moment, in the twinkling of an eye at the last trumpet." Paul's view seemed to be that those who were in Christ would continue to sleep in him until he awakens us again. Now friends, when I go to sleep I don't notice the passage of time. It could be a few hours, it could be a hundred years, like the sleep of Rip Van Winkle, or it could be a millenium; but what difference does it make if we are "in Christ"? The great day will come when

> Our spirits, too, will quickly join,
> Like theirs with glory crowned;
> And shout to see our Captain's sign
> And hear His trumpet sound.

A few years ago I preached at the Methodist Chapel in Dent in the Yorkshire Dales. It is a building that has been used continuously for worship by the Methodists, and by the Quakers before them. In the lovely evening sunshine I stood outside the door with the society steward, just before the service began. "How long have you had this place?" I asked. "Oh, not long, only since 1842, and it was a Quaker place for two hundred years before we had it." Then he pointed to the graveyard. "There's layers of Quakers buried under layers of Methodists there." With a straight face I said, "This is going to be one of the most crowded places in the Dales on Resurrection Day." I meant it to be a joke, but he didn't seem to think it was funny, and perhaps he was right. Paul said, "The heavens will roll up like a curtain and God will be all in all."

I mentioned a second New Testament view. It is found in the words of Jesus: "I go to prepare a place for you, and if I go I will come again and receive you unto myself, that where I am there you may be also." Christians have taken great comfort from these words, and thousands, like Mr. Valiant For Truth in Bunyan's *Pilgrim's Progress,* have passed over triumphantly and "all the trumpets have sounded for them on the other side."

When I was in the City of Leeds twenty years ago, an old lady in her eighties was taken into hospital to die. She had an only daughter. For two or three nights I watched with them, but on the last night we were joined by a contemporary of the dying Christian, another old lady. As we watched in the early hours, it became clear that the old lady was aware of more than the three of us around her bed. She spoke to others we could not see, and named them. The second old lady became our interpreter: "He was Sunday School Superintendent in 1904," and so on. We two younger people were mere spectators, and as we watched, she slipped quietly away from us and joined them. Gordon Rupp once said that the preachers' obituaries in the yearly Minutes of Conference was the Methodist Calendar of Saints. In saying so, he quoted a story of one of Wesley's preachers who was taken ill while on his circuit, or round. He was taken into someone's home and was near death. Suddenly, about three in the morning, he said to the watchers, "Put out the candles, the morning has already come."

Alexander Whyte called the dying thief the first and greatest of New Testament believers because he believed in Jesus while he was still on the cross and his hope was black as night. He said, "Lord, remember me when Thou comest into thy kingdom," and Jesus answered him, "This day shalt thou be with me in paradise." This is surely why we Methodists shout (and there are no other words for it):

> Bold I approach the eternal throne
> And claim the crown through Christ, my own.

Frankly, friends, I don't care how God does it; let him do it his way. The Resurrection of Jesus shows us that love, care, and personality survive beyond the grave: He broke the bread and they knew him.

Wilfred Callin died in the 1960s and news of his death came to us while we were in the Ministerial Synod. We all remembered his hymn "O Lord of every lovely thing," which ends:

> Until with those who toiled and dreamed
> To build Thy kingdom here.
> With those the world has ne'er esteemed,
> With all the host of Thy redeemed
> We in Thy home appear.

But we, his brethren, chose to sing for our comfort Richard Baxter's hymn "He Wants Not Friends That Hath Thy Love," the last verse of which is:

> The heavenly host world without end
> Shall be my company above;
> And Thou, my best and dearest friend,
> Who shall divide me from Thy love?

That's it. What then is the nature of our hope? How can we know? "Eye hath not seen, ear hath not heard, neither hath it entered into the mind of man to imagine the things that God hath prepared for them that love him." John Baillie, forty years ago, said our hope could all be summed up in one word: *glory*. The poor Cornish preacher, Billy Bray, called himself "the King's son." Someone once complained that he was always interrupting the service by shouting "Amen" or "Hallelujah." "Bless you," he said. "If you shut me up in a barrel, I'd shout *glory* through the bung hole."

What do we mean by glory? It is not an earthly thing, connected with money, or pride of place or circumstance. It has nothing to do with the Big Bang or the Stock Exchange, nor is heaven going to be a constant succession of royal weddings. Most of the words with which we try to paint a picture of it fall short and give way. There used to be a hymn that spoke of the saints eternally "casting down their golden crowns around the glassy sea." How boring. I prefer:

The Lamb there in His beauty without a veil is seen.
It were a well spent Journey though seven deaths lay between.
The King with His fair army doth on mount Zion stand,
And glory, glory dwelleth in Immanuel's land.

I think we have all had glimpses of glory, and there are many things we would like to recapture. For me, I could happily relive those Sunday School anniversaries of my childhood with special singing and a crowded platform. I would like to live again some of the mission anniversaries of the 1950s, when both the Free Trade Hall and the Albert Hall were crammed full of people. You can all recall periods of spiritual intensity, or of great preaching, or of love and praise of a high order when, like St. Paul, we were lifted up to the seventh heaven and saw and heard things it was not lawful for a man to utter. All this will be possible, and continuous, and much more besides, because heaven is a place where time does not exist, and the past, the present, and the future may be enjoyed with unlimited freedom. I still have things I would like to say to my mother and father. "There are things in the letters of our brother Paul," wrote Peter in one of his letters, "which are not easy to understand." You can say that again, and won't it be nice to be able to ask him personally what he meant? I would like to have a word with Shakespeare, and ask Mozart if he has written any more music. How wonderful to think that many of us will not have to listen in vain for a loved one's step on the stairs.

Nor will this be all: heaven, like this world, will be a place of judgment as well as mercy. I am sometimes almost ashamed to be living in our society as it is, and I should hate to think I may never see it put right. We have often imagined judgment to be a big black book with all our miserable peccadilloes written in it. I think we shall be judged on our attitudes rather than on our achievements. "When did we see you hungry?" cried the people on the King's left hand. "It is just because you didn't see that these, the least of my little ones, were hungry that you are going out into the outer darkness," replied Jesus.

Parliament has recently been debating obscenity and in most people's minds this has raised pictures of lonely men in dirty mackintoshes peeping at naked girls. My friends, I think these are the minor obscenities, the minor exploitations of our world. I look for a day in this world, or in the next, when those who corner millions of pounds simply by maneuvering the markets, putting people out of work, and stripping assets; when those who buy the seed corn of the Third World cheap and starve little children to death; when those who sell arms to both sides in a cruel war; and when those who withhold the birthright of a people simply because their skins are black will discover that God's justice, like his mercy, is unlimited.

It will certainly be true that in heaven, if not for everyone here and now, Martin Luther King's dream will be realized, and the best hopes of the Church, which we have struggled so feebly to bring about, will, under the rule of God, be a reality.

I have listened to Midday Service preachers for twenty-three years, and I have only heard one previous sermon on this theme. In the early 1950s, John Huxtable preached such a sermon. He described the death of a Christian as being like a great sailing ship he once saw, fully rigged, going out from a Welsh port into the setting sun. He concluded, "This, without everything else, is worth everything else without this."

I believe that is what is meant by being "in Christ" for now, and for all eternity.

> O Christ, He is the fountain,
> The deep, sweet well of love.
> The streams on earth I've tasted
> More deep I'll drink above.
> There to an ocean's fullness
> His mercy doth expand,
> And glory, glory dwelleth
> in Immanuel's land.

Yes, though he slay me, yet will I trust him.—John Banks

Eternal Life

TEXT: Rom. 6:23

I. Eternal life is man's life when God has spoken his "yes" upon it, once for all, unconditionally and unreservedly, not to be changed any more.

II. Eternal life is man's life lived with God, in his bright light, nourished and sustained by his own life.

III. Eternal life is man's life committed to the service of God and thereby to the service of the neighbor, a life which certainly also serves him best who is allowed to live it.

IV. Eternal life is a strong and no longer weak life, joyous and no longer sad, true and no longer deceitful.

V. Eternal life is man's indestructible life because it comes from God and is sustained by him.—Karl Barth[5]

When Death Comes

TEXT: 2 Cor. 4:16–5:10

Death is an inevitable experience in life and you cannot escape it. As life on this Earth has a beginning, so it has an ending. "Birth and death are the parentheses that bracket the experience of every person."

Death is not, of course, a topic we like to discuss. On the other hand, we must not ignore death, for it is an experience that will come to each of us. And we all have had those moments in our lives when we have asked ourselves the question, "What happens when death comes?" Paul gives us some answers to that question in our text.

First, when death comes, we will be given a reward. This is the truth Paul proclaims in 2 Corinthians 4:17–18.

Paul refers to this reward in verse 17 as an "eternal weight of glory far beyond our comprehension." In other passages, the reward is spoken of in other terms (see Rom. 8:18; James 1:12; 2 Tim. 4:3).

What will this reward be like? Whether it is something God gives to us or simply the experience of heaven itself, Paul says that we will receive this reward after death, and that the reward God has prepared for us will be something so much greater than anything we have ever experienced here on this Earth that there is no comparison.

Second, when death comes, there will be release. This is the truth he proclaims in 2 Corinthians 5. Paul uses two images to express this truth.

In verse 1, he uses the imagery of a heavenly building. As a tentmaker, Paul's comparison of his body to a tent or a tabernacle was a natural one. When the tent of our physical body is taken down, Paul says, God has a far superior building already prepared for us. The superiority of this future building is evident in the contrast.

In verse 2, Paul speaks of a heavenly garment. At death we are stripped of the rudiments of this life, like stripping off dirty clothes to step into the shower. Then we are given a new garment to put on.

What is Paul saying? Does he despise the human body? He knew that, at death, the heavenly body prepared for him would have no such limitations.

When death comes, we will be given a new body that will be unlimited, free of pain, and void of suffering.

Third, when death comes, there will be relationship. That is the truth Paul proclaims in 2 Corinthians 5:5–8. "While we are at home in the body we are absent from the Lord," and "to be absent from the body" is "to be at home with the Lord."

Have you ever wondered what makes hell, hell? And what makes heaven, heaven? A prospect of eternal isolation is more fearful than a thousand burning hells. What makes hell, hell is that it is where we will be eternally separated from the one by whom and for whom we were made. What makes hell, hell is that it is where we will eternally be strangers, pilgrims in a foreign land.

What makes heaven, heaven is that it is where we will enjoy eternal fellowship with our heavenly Father. What makes heaven, heaven is that it is where we will eternally be at home.—Brian L. Harbour

SERMONS FOR TIMES OF CRISIS

The fifth category of sermons in this collection is the crisis message. Like Sunday sermons, crisis messages are classified by the occasion rather than by the proportion of exegesis to biographical and historical information. Some crisis messages are highly contextual, such as Dennis Hagstrom's Columbine sermon. Others could easily be adapted for use in many different kinds of crisis.

A Very Present Help

TEXT: Ps. 46:1

Yes, that is what we need and generally want in time of trouble—we want God. Yesterday we were busy. Yesterday we didn't seem to need him. Occasionally we stopped a moment to remember that God is; this fleeting thought passed through our mind, or in some little emergency we breathed a prayer. But today—trouble, death. We want to be sure of God.

To be sure of God we must first find him in our own hearts. After that we may find him revealed in his handiwork, in the lives of good men, in the Bible. He comes to us in the Christ, but first of all we meet him in our hearts. In the restlessness of our hearts we discover a desire for him. In our consciences we learn that he desires us to be righteous. In our appreciation of truth and beauty and goodness we learn to know him, in the awe that breaks over our souls, in the quiet peace that sometimes descends upon us we touch the hem of his garment. But it is in the life of him who once walked in bodily form upon the earth, and who today is a spiritual presence with us, who has found a way into our lives—by this Christ we know that God is and that he is a very present help in time of trouble.

How does he help us? He gives us strength, or as Jesus said, he gives us comfort. Comfort means being strong together. His presence is our strength. We can lean on him.

God thus becomes our refuge, like a place unto which to fly, like a strong rock under which to hide against the wind and the storm, like a mountain valley where one may find peace.

Strength and refuge bring peace. Jesus said, "Peace I leave with you, my peace I give unto you: not as the world giveth, give I unto you. Let not your heart be troubled, neither let it be afraid." Peace comes as the gift of Christ. It is the peace of adequate spiritual resources, the peace of clean hands and a pure heart—the peace of a presence by our sides and in our hearts. "Lo, I am with you always, even unto the end of the world."

This same psalm of our text speaks of a river the streams whereof make glad the city of God. The river of God's grace brings refreshment, cleansing, power, beauty, buoyancy. There is much to be received from the river of grace that flows from the throne of God. God is a very present help in time of trouble.
—M.K.W. Heicher

Columbine

TEXT: John 10:1–10

For the past month we have been viewing scenes from Kosovo and Yugoslavia. There have been television images of bombings, soldiers, and thousands of refugees fleeing to the borders of Albania and Macedonia, seeking safe haven. We have also seen the faces of women, men, and children who are the victims of the terrors of war, refugees who could not escape bullets and bombs and who died in their search for safety.

Yes, we have turned on NBC, CNN, or Fox News to watch the war in the Balkans. It is so far away.

Over the past several years, we have heard on the news about people being shot and killed here in the United States. Last May 21, in Springfield, Oregon, a student opened fire in a crowded cafeteria at Thurston High School, killing one student and injuring twenty-three. On March 24, 1998, four female students and a teacher were killed and ten people were wounded during a false fire alarm at a Middle School in Jonesboro, Arkansas, when two boys, ages eleven and thirteen, opened fire from the woods. Again, we turned on NBC, CNN, or Fox News to be saddened and concerned by tragedy that is still so far way.

But on Tuesday, April 20, our world here in Denver, Colorado, changed forever. Tragedy was no longer far away; it came right here to the foot of our beautiful Rocky Mountains. Turning on the television we saw the horror, not from Kosovo, or Oregon, or Arkansas, but from Littleton, in Colorado, only forty-five minutes from here.

We are horrified that there could be a school shooting here. At first, it seemed that maybe there were no fatalities. True, wounded students had been taken to the hospital. At first, no deaths were reported. But then, as the afternoon wore on, we learned that there were fatalities. It was unbelievable: twelve students and one teacher dead, along with the two killers, who committed suicide.

The Denver community has been overcome by tears, pain, and despair. Evil appeared on Tuesday afternoon and demanded our time and attention. The initial feelings of shock have dissolved into grief and questioning: Why? Why would those boys commit such a horrible act? How could this have happened? Is there any way that this could have been prevented? In the weeks and months to come there will be much discussion and many attempts to answer all of these questions and others, as people step back from the tragedy and try to resume their normal lives.

As Christians, we rely on our faith in times such as these. Even as we may ask God, "Why?" we seek God's comfort and hope in the midst of grief and fear. Today, the fourth Sunday of Easter, is, as it is every year, Good Shepherd Sunday. The appointed readings center on Jesus Christ as the loving Shepherd of the sheep, the one who lifts us up and carries us on his strong shoulders. Believe me when I say that there is hope given in God's promise as we read these Scriptures in the light of what happened in Littleton on Tuesday.

We read of Jesus as the Shepherd who calls his sheep by their own names and leads them out and into life. "He goes ahead of them, and the sheep follow him because they know his voice." Because the sheep hear his voice and know his voice, they follow him in the firm confidence of faith. This is the Shepherd who leads them in right paths and beside still waters, making them to lie down in green pastures. The Risen Lord, Jesus Christ, is the Good Shepherd in whom we put our trust.

Christ calls us to faith in him, promising us that in him we may know the love of God and that we will dwell in the house of the Lord, forever. This is always the message of Good Shepherd Sunday.

The Good Shepherd does not lead us astray or betray us. The Littleton tragedy was not "caused" by God nor "sent" by God to teach us a lesson. What happened was not God's will.

Evil has reared its ugly head with a magnitude that is overwhelming. People have no choice but to hurt, mourn, and be perplexed by what has happened in a community where "these things never happen!"

The Good Shepherd also wept over people, people who sought evil rather than the good. There is evil in the world and it is real. Our human freedom is essential, flawed, and often tragic. While the two killers have to bear much of the blame, we also need to mourn over the entire situation. This is a context full of hate; teenagers lack self-esteem and feelings of worth and therefore grab it in perverse ways. This situation is the fruit borne of the gun and bomb violence in our country. This situation is full of a lack of credibility in nonviolence as a lifestyle. This situation just cries out for peace. This situation is full of the reality of sin at any age.

Where is the gospel? As evil launched this attack, where was the gospel of the Good Shepherd who is the Risen Lord? Actually, we saw it almost immediately. It was there in the bold caring for one another and in the way the community responded. God's love was made manifest in the caring and helping hands of others—teachers, paramedics, police, crisis counselors, and clergy.

The Gospel was proclaimed as friends risked their own lives to save the lives of others. The cross of Christ was emblazoned on a teacher who gave up his life for his students, and on a seventeen-year-old Christian woman whose last words were, "Yes, I believe in God." Truly the blood of these martyrs witnessed to the gospel, following the Shepherd who lays down his life for the sheep and says, "This is my commandment, that you love one another as I have loved you. No one has greater love than this, to lay down one's life for ones friends. You are my friends if you do what I command you" (John 15:12–14). Would we have the courage and conviction of our faith to make that ultimate sacrifice, to look down the barrel of a gun and say with our last breath, "Yes, I am a Christian?"

Some may ask, "Where was God on Tuesday afternoon?" My answer is very simple. God was right there, in Littleton, Colorado, no less than God was there on Calvary as his beloved Son hung bleeding and dying on the cross. We believe that God is in the midst of those being shot or terrorized, as the one who knows the suffering of violence and who promises the new life of resurrection—a resurrection life that comes complete with nail prints and scars. The message of the cross is that God is present in the midst of human suffering and pain, God knows full well what it means to cry, and God weeps with us today.

Here is a message from Rocky Mountain Synod Bishop, Allan Bjornberg:

> How is it possible that our children should kill our children? The whole Denver community is reeling from the shootings yesterday at Columbine High School in Littleton, a Denver suburb.
>
> ELCA pastors were on the scene throughout the day, providing care for students and faculty who escaped the gunfire and explosions. Lutheran Family Services is providing counselors experienced in trauma counseling as many area congregations plan worship services followed by small group conversations. Area ELCA parishes have been deeply affected. Members and friends attend Columbine. Anne-Marie Hochhalter, a member of Christ Lutheran, Highlands Ranch [and a cousin to Advent's own Andrea Johnson], remains in critical condition in an area hospital.

The Bishop continues:

> When such unspeakable evil overwhelms us, we can only claim the grace and power of Christ alive among us. We are in Mark's Gospel, walking with the women to the tomb, tearfully asking, "Who will roll away the stone for us?" This tragedy has swept us back to Ash Wednesday while we cling desperately to Easter life.
>
> As we gather to pray, to weep, to struggle with this reality, we claim the power of the Resurrection. Please join your prayers to ours. Victims, families, perpetrators, and caregivers are lifted up to God's mercy with the plea, "Help us, we pray, in the midst of things we cannot understand, to believe and trust in the communion of saints, the forgiveness of sins, and the resurrection to life everlasting."

The reality of Tuesday's tragedy reminds us how precious life is, and that if we take life and the love of family and friends for granted, some day we may truly regret it. Take the time now to mend a broken relationship and to give someone an extra hug. Life is God's gift to us and we are to live it to the fullest.

Today, as we in Colorado and people all across our nation continue to struggle with this senseless tragedy and seek the healing that is so necessary, we can offer up this prayer of confidence to the Good Shepherd, for ourselves and all of Tuesday's victims, faithfully trusting that he calls our names and leads us to him: "Though I walk through the valley of the shadow of death, I shall fear no evil; for you are with me; your rod and your staff they comfort me. . . . Surely your goodness and mercy shall follow me all the days of my life, and I will dwell in the house of the Lord forever."—Dennis K. Hagstrom

They Said So!

TEXT: Ps. 107:1–9

Fred Craddock shares a story that has a pointed relevance for this All Saints' Day. Craddock tells of returning to the little church of his childhood in the hills of Tennessee. He had not been there in years. Walking into the sanctuary, he noticed that they had purchased new stained glass windows since he had been there. Admiring the windows, he noted that set at the bottom of each window was the name of the donor of the window, but he recognized none of the names. "You must have had many new folks join this church since I was a boy," said Fred to one of the members. "I don't recognize a single name."

"Oh those people aren't members here," replied the member. "This town hasn't grown a bit since you were a child, neither has our church. We bought these windows from a company all the way over in Italy. They were made for a church in St. Louis and when they arrived none of them would fit. So the company said they were sorry, they would make new windows, and told the church in St. Louis to sell them wherever they could. We bought the windows from them."

"But don't you want to remove these names?" asked Craddock.

"Well, we thought about it. But we're just a little church. Not many here, never any new people. So we like to sit here on Sunday morning surrounded by the names of people other than ourselves."

So, we sit here this morning, surrounded by the names and the faces of people other than ourselves. Since Wednesday afternoon I have met many saints; some of the names and faces are familiar—faces that I see almost every Sunday, names you can find in the membership directory. I have also encountered other saints, through prayer, Bible Study, reading, and reflecting on the events of the past four days—saints who speak to us from the pages of Holy Scripture, saints who teach us to sing from the pages of the hymnal, saints whose witness in the life of the Barrington United Methodist Church has shaped our life and witness today. I have met some less familiar saints this week: a young girl named Chelsea who stopped by with her mother on Thursday morning and gave me a five dollar bill from her allowance because, as she told me, "I want to help you rebuild the church"; the saint named Noel who gave me a check because, as he told me, "I was married at the church forty-seven years ago, and the church means a lot to me." Many saints have called on the phone, have written notes, have been here with us to lend comfort and support as we have walked through the valley. Yes, we gather this morning surrounded by the saints visible and invisible. The communion of saints has seldom, if ever, been more real to me than this morning. And I rejoice and give thanks for this "blest communion, fellowship divine."

These saints speak to us this day, as the psalmist reminds us in our text for this morning. As the redeemed of the Lord, they remind us to join with them in giving thanks to the Lord our God: "O give thanks to the Lord for God is good; for God's steadfast love endures forever." They said so, and we this morning say so! The psalm is one of thanksgiving to God, for deliverance from various difficult, threatening situations. In our text, the situation described is one of wandering in "the desert wastes," the wilderness, the place where the spirit withers for want of nourishment, where the soul faints because of hunger and thirst. The wilderness is a threatening place, a place where one feels lost, hopeless, displaced; a place where the spirit cries out for meaning and the soul for assurance. So we find ourselves in just such a wilderness this morning and our spirits, too, cry out for comfort, for reassurance, for hope. Israel had experienced the wilderness, the desert wastes, and knew what it meant to have their souls faint within them. In those moments of exile and utter despair, they cried out to the Lord and, writes the psalmist, "God delivered them from their distress, God led them by the straight way until they reached an inhabited town." Our voices too cry out from our distress, cry out for strength, cry out for sight to see beyond the ashes and rubble, cry out for deliverance.

"O give thanks to the Lord, for God is good, for God's steadfast love endures forever. Let the redeemed of the Lord say so!" Such is the cry of the saints. The saints are those who have known the power of God to deliver them from their distress, to know the power of God in Christ Jesus to satisfy the thirst of the spirit for meaning and joy; to fulfill the hunger of the soul for assurance and hope. And they say so! They say so in the lives they lead, the witness they make, the legacy they leave. They are signs to remind us when we find ourselves in those situations where our spirits are thirsty and our souls are hungry, where we faint under the burden of grief, where our pain seems overwhelming—O give thanks to the Lord, for God is good, for God's steadfast love endures forever! As we say so—as we give thanks to God in Christ Jesus—we too are set free to live confidently, to experience our lives renewed, to know our hungers and thirsts satisfied.

These past days have been difficult. We grieve not simply the devastation of a building, but also the loss of a symbol of our faith, a place where we celebrated God's love in Christ Jesus in word and song and sacrament, in fellowship and study, and in mission and ministry. We find ourselves this morning wandering in the desert of the spirit. But, dear friends, listen to the saints, the redeemed of the Lord—God hears our cry, Christ Jesus walks with us and will deliver us; the Spirit will nourish our spirits, give drink to our parched spirits, fill our hungry souls. The saints, the redeemed of the Lord, say so! And I believe it! We believe in the one who makes it a priority to bring new life out of death, new structures out of ashes, new hope out of barrenness, new joy out of grief. The good news for us is that our God is a redeeming God, the one whose gracious love reaches out to us in the midst of tragic loss to comfort us, to sustain us, and most important of all, to deliver us to new life. We grieve this morning, but we have a word from the saints, a promise that though a building has been devastated by fire, the church is still present; though hearts are heavy, new strength will be given; though spirits hunger and thirst, God in Christ will lead us into an exciting future.

A friend tells of a museum in New York City where there is found a Romanesque lintel taken from a church in France. On the lintel is carved a scene of Jesus' entry into Jerusalem on Palm Sunday. A most interesting and telling processional is depicted: first, Jesus riding on a donkey; then some children waving palm branches, followed by adults; and last, more adults dressed in modern clothing. What a powerful reminder that we too have joined the procession of the saints. And so, just as they say, "We cried out to the Lord in our distress, and God delivered us. O give thanks to the Lord, for God is good, for God's steadfast love endures forever!" so we now, this morning, in the midst of our grief, in the midst of our pain, in the midst of our anguish, also say so. We gather at the table to eat and drink with all the saints, to hear them once again say so, and then we go from the table to say so ourselves—God in Christ is good, and the gracious love of our God will strengthen us and deliver us and fill our lives and our life together with hope. Thanks be to God! Amen!—James M. Wilson

The Heroism of Going On

Up in the Highlands of Scotland, a little group of people were talking about heroism: they were saying that everybody had sooner or later to practice some kind of heroism. A young man turned to an old woman; she looked so ordinary and so serene. He did not know that life had been for her a series of tragic things. "And what kind of heroism do you practice?" he said with an obvious air of thinking that he did not believe there could be any kind of heroism in a life like hers. "I?" she said. "I practice the heroism of going on."

There is great need for us, especially at certain times, to practice "the heroism of going on."

I. *The heroism of going on in faith.* There is something inexorable about the death of a loved one. One is forced to say, "This is a fact." The fact is inexorable, relentless, undeniable.

Facing the fact, the bereaved may then say, "This is my faith. I have faith in God. God is our refuge and strength."

II. *The heroism of going on in love.* Love for the departed does not cease; it may be wonderfully deepened. Grief may be transmuted into love for others. The comfort that is received by faith becomes the comfort that we in love give to others (1 Cor. 1:3, 4).

III. *The heroism of going on in hope.* How the words of Jesus kindle and strengthen our hope: "I am the resurrection and the life." "In my Father's house are many rooms. . . . I go and prepare a place for you." This is the heroism that the present hour and the coming days demand of us—the heroism of going on, in faith, in love, and in hope.—M.K.W. Heicher

Suffering Triumphantly

TEXT: Heb. 12:11

A man who was imprisoned in a tower was trying to attract the attention of passers-by in order to get a message to a friend. He had a number of coins in the tower with him. He dropped one. A man came by and noticed the coin, picked it up, and rushed on without looking up. The prisoner tried again. This time he dropped a gold piece. A passer-by snatched it up quickly and hurried on without looking up. The man in the tower recognized that this procedure was bringing no results. He found a stone and dropped it on the next man who passed. The stone struck the man and pained him and he immediately looked up to see who had thrown it, and so the man in the tower got his message through.

God drops his blessings on us continually in material, temporal, and spiritual benefits; but we snatch them up and rush on without giving attention to the source. Then God may allow troubles to drop into our experience, in the form of disappointments, tragedies, or physical pain. In the hour of pain, men look to God and ask why. It is in a time of tribulation that God brings comfort, with spiritual and physical healing. Thus his love is manifested in the hour of darkness.

I. The problem of suffering needs to be realistically faced by everyone. Many have gone through intense suffering without profit to themselves or to others when they might have been heroically triumphant. Understand certain things: one of the outstanding reasons for suffering is that men and women ignore the great moral and spiritual laws that God has woven into the fabric of the universe. We may try to break them, but we break ourselves instead.

II. How can we meet suffering and emerge as real heroes?

(a) Many meet suffering and pain with resentment. They blame the Almighty, become hardened and callused.

(b) Others react to suffering with self-pity. They center on their ills in morbid introspection.

(c) Another class reacts to suffering by calling it an illusion. They say that suffering is not a reality.

(d) Many react to suffering by trying to drown it in a whirlpool of excitement.

(e) Others submit to suffering with spineless resignation.

(f) The Christian way of meeting suffering is revealed by Christ. He not only suffered, but he suffered triumphantly. He turned the agony of the cross into a glorious symbol of victory. He has blazed the way for Christians to follow (Matt. 26:39).

III. What may we gain from suffering? The desert of suffering is a proving ground in which a man's spirit may develop to its full capacity.

(a) Suffering provides men with keener insight and sympathy for their fellow men.

(b) Patience is also a product of suffering. "Tribulation worketh patience" (Rom. 5:3). Many of us never learn patience without suffering.

(c) Someone says, "Must this suffering go on endlessly?" No, this message would not be complete unless it pointed beyond suffering. Hear these encouraging words: "I saw a new heaven and a new earth" (Rev. 21:1–4).—Rev. Arthur

Holding It Together

Text: Col. 1:11–20

I caught her out of the corner of my eye as I dashed into the study. Mary Beth was sitting on the floor in the hallway, holding her beloved blanket and cuddling her stuffed dog. There had been a brief testing of wills between her and her mother, and I thought better of inquiring immediately as to why she was sitting on the floor in the hallway. After checking messages, I came out of the study to see Mary Beth still sitting there. Now the time seemed right, so I inquired, "Good morning, Mary Beth; why are you sitting here?" She looked up with tearful eyes and announced, "Daddy, I very, very sad." I replied, "I'm sorry you are sad. What makes you sad this morning?" She sighed and said, "My church had a big fire and my Duffy went away." Our cocker spaniel, Duffy, died the week before the fire. Mary Beth's world had been badly shaken; things important to her three-year-old life—her church and her dog—were gone; her world seemed to be coming apart and she was sad. She probably was scared, and definitely had been angry as well. I picked her up, gave her a hug, and said, "Daddy is sad, too. But Jesus will help us."

Most of us know what Mary Beth was experiencing. We have encountered those moments when everything seems to be coming apart, when our world seems to crumble down around us, when our lives are fractured by illness or job loss or a broken relationship, or by a child who wanders from the fold; when our hope withers as dreams fade or as the forces of oppression and injustice work their destruction. Yes, we know what it is to have life begin to unravel, to have the center give way, to feel our very being under attack by the principalities and powers. Have we not been left very, very sad or very, very scared, wondering, "Who's in charge here?" I did not lie to Mary Beth, nor did I discount her hurt with a pious platitude when I said to her, "But Jesus will help us." I spoke to her what I consider to be the bedrock of our faith. I wanted her, in this moment of great ambiguity, to hear the Word of Promise. The same Word of Promise I need to hear when I find my life coming apart. The same Word of Promise each of us longs to hear when life seems to spin in centrifuge and we realize our powerlessness to do anything about it; when all our answers and explanations seem so very irrelevant. This same Word of Promise Paul sets before the Christians in Colossae.

I would be hard pressed to offer a text more fitted to express this promise of God, especially on this last Sunday after Pentecost, this Sunday that the Church celebrates as Christ the King Sunday. Our text is one of the great christological hymns of the New Testament, comparable to the other great hymns, such as the ones found in the second chapter of the Letter to the Philippians or in the first chapter of the Gospel of John. The hymn celebrates the Lordship of Jesus Christ over the whole of creation—indeed, over the whole of the cosmos. No small thinking here! Listen to the wonderful litany of affirmations celebrating the power and authority of Christ Jesus: "He is the image of the invisible God, the firstborn of creation. In him all things were created; he is before all things. In him all things hold together; he is the firstborn from the dead. In him the fullness of God was pleased to dwell; through him all life is reconciled." What bold affirmations! What a powerfully comforting Word to us, who must contend with the principalities and powers. Yet what a poetic Word to the Church—a Word calling the Church to live in the light of the bold, sweeping claims of the hymn; to witness with our words and our deeds to the Lordship of Christ Jesus announced by these powerful lyrics.

As the preexistent wisdom, Christ Jesus was the firstborn, the head of the created order. The Risen One, he is resurrection's first child, the head of the New Creation. With a mighty crescendo, the hymn proclaims that the center has been established in Christ Jesus; the principalities and powers no longer have ultimate say—Christ Jesus is now in charge. What a comforting thought! What an empowering reality from which and in which to live! Think about this. Whatever happens, whatever we experience—whether a fire or a scary diagnosis, oppression or moral chaos, tragedy or death of a loved one—the center may shake, there may be disruptions, chaos may surround, but Christ Jesus is Lord; the gracious, life-affirming love of the invisible God is at the center; in him all things, our very lives, hold together.

Whenever life seems to come apart, either through tragedy or illness, someone will inevitably say, "It is the will of God," as if such an explanation should provide comfort, or if not, at least bully us into silence. These words have been uttered frequently in certain circles as of late. I realize, for the most part, that people utter such a statement because words seems to fail in tragic moments, so ascribing the situation to God's will is an attempt to comfort. But such a statement is not only lousy theology, it is also, as Leslie Weatherhead reminded us longer before Rabbi Kushner did, simply not true. It simply is not true that God wills churches to burn, or people to contract cancer, or automobiles to crash, or hurricanes to wreak devastation and destroy life. Someone, a stranger, said to me on the afternoon of October 28th that the fire must somehow be the will of God. I turned and gently but firmly replied (at least I hope this is what I said), "Nonsense. God does not burn down churches—at least not the God I know." Others since have repeated those words, and each time I respond with a firm, "No, that is not true. God does not burn down churches. Certainly not the God who comes to us in Christ Jesus." Weatherhead points out, in his little classic of some fifty years ago entitled *The Will of God,* that Jesus Christ expresses the will of God. God wills our salvation, our wholeness of life, our freedom, our joy. God wills justice and peace and moral order. God wills a New Creation, a vital church, a loving community. The cross stands as a reminder of the decisive victory of God's will and God's purpose over all those forces of evil, destruction, and death. Life full, whole, and abundant is God's will for you and for me, a claim made visible in Christ Jesus, the Risen Lord.

It is in him, the Risen One, that life, indeed the whole cosmos, holds together. I find this the most comforting of all the affirmations the hymn makes about Christ. Christ Jesus is celebrated as the glue that holds all things together, the one in whom all reality coheres, the one who brings life together in a new way, the Lord of Life. Every time we pray these familiar words, "Thy Kingdom come," we are celebrating the victory. Each time we offer grace before a meal, we announce that Christ Jesus is Lord and that the world and all it offers are subject to his gracious rule. Every time we gather to celebrate the Eucharist or baptize a little one, we proclaim the center, the one who holds all things together. Each time an act of kindness is done, mercy is offered, or justice is promoted, we witness to the claim that God is in charge—the God made visible in Christ Jesus. When we gather to worship, to sing praise to God, to remember our past, to rejoice in our present, to eagerly anticipate our future, we announce that no fire can diminish us, no sorrow can deter us, no tragedy can dissuade us from celebrating that gracious love that holds us together.

A story is told about a man who emerged from a bomb shelter in London after a night of terrible bombing. Amid the rubble there was a newspaper vendor hawking that morning's newspaper. The vendor asked the old man, "Don't you want to buy a newspaper? Don't you want to find out who won the battle last night?"

"I don't need to read the papers," replied the old man. "I don't need to read the papers and find who won the battle because I already know who has won the war."

That's us! In our daily skirmishes with the powers of this world, we can live with hope and confidence. The foundations may shake, but the center holds! We can act faithfully and live courageously. We will face some tough struggles, but we know already who has won the war: the one in whom all things hold together—Jesus the Christ. As we move through these days of grieving, of dislocation, and of stress, may the Spirit open us for this Word—this Word that announces that the center holds, that God in Christ is at work among us to redeem and to renew.

No, I didn't lie; I didn't even play with the truth in my response to Mary Beth. Nor did I give her religious platitudes. I gave her what Paul gave to the Colossians, and to each of us: the wonderful, powerful Word of Promise, a Word that proclaims that in Christ Jesus—this image of the invisible God, this one who is the firstborn of all creation, this one who is the firstborn from the dead, this one through whom all life is reconciled—all of life, all of your life and my life, is held together. Indeed, Jesus will help us to newness of life. May our lives celebrate this promise. Thanks be to God! Amen!—James M. Wilson

Remembrance of the Dead

TEXT: Matt. 25:31, 34–40

Many among us have taken part in services in memory of victims of violence who were killed because of their religious beliefs and because of their preaching in word and action the biblical message of redemptive love. At times we may have marked the occasion with red programs, signifying the blood of martyrs; other times we have preferred the green of hope. We have never been able to present a scroll that could list all those who throughout history have given their lives that we might be liberated.

When we honor those forebears, we do so having made the passage from initial devastation to peaceful remembrance. We can even rejoice that these men and women were so struck by the gospel message that they cared enough for others to sacrifice their own well-being in serving them.

For many here at this assembly, the death of someone we love may be too recent for us to consider these moments of contemplation a celebration. We can at least be grateful for the Church's encouragement to us tonight to pause and recall memorable times with those who are now safely in the hands of God.

Well-meaning friends often urge us to seek distractions, to move on with our lives. The gospel suggests actions that are memorials of loving care, signs of our faith that in reaching out to others we are following in the steps of the first Christians. I doubt that any one of us could have been more tempted than Mary to ask, "Why?" as she kept the death watch of her son with John and the other disciples. Yet after a quiet, somewhat hidden life, she accepted the commission, "Woman, behold your son," and widened her motherhood beyond that of Jesus to the Church being born. Certainly her remembrances were both bitter and sweet, like gall and honey; on that Friday, the peace and well-being associated with the mystery of resurrection were yet to come.

Yet, even before that assurance of Sunday morning, Mary and John turned outward to each other in faithful obedience to the testament of Jesus. That care, that compassion of two sorrowing persons for each other, was soon extended to the frightened people gathering in the Cenacle, then to puzzled followers as the Easter message spread, and on to the cheering thousands at Pentecost. Mary and John, united at the moment of the violent death of Jesus, continue to inspire us with their role in the founding era of a community pledged to justice through peace, to a sect whose members in their love and care for one another were always open to welcoming others.

In any naming of the dead, we all know that the list of the faithful is incomplete, that any roll call is limited. Tonight as we name loved ones, let us think of them as representative of those no longer in need of any conversion of life. May we ask for the grace we need so we too will hear one day, "Truly I tell you, just as you did it to one of the least of these who are members of my family, you did it to me."—Grace Donovan

The Cost of Being Found

TEXT: Luke 15:1–10; 1 Tim. 1:12–47
(preached the Sunday after the Starr Report was published)

Several years ago I was part of an adult Sunday School class that was asked to change its name. The church was growing and the minister had read that newcomers were more likely to join new groups than long-established classes. I guess he thought we could fool repeat visitors into thinking we were creating something novel if we came up with a new moniker. Well, we spent most of class time one Sunday trying to come up with a suitable name. Someone suggested "The Disciples Class," but Jerry reminded us that the church membership class already had that title. "The New Beginnings Class"—Barbara thought that sounded like a divorce recovery workshop. The Wesley Class—no, the pastor wanted something that would be recognizable to non-Methodist newcomers. Tongue in cheek, I said, "Hey, why don't we call ourselves the Scribes and Pharisees? Jesus was always talking to them, and in the Sermon on the Mount he said, "Unless your righteousness exceeds that of the Scribes and Pharisees, you will never enter the kingdom of Heaven."

To my amazement, the class took me seriously. They thought it was a great idea, and promptly changed their name to the Scribes and Pharisees. You don't have to know much of what's written in the New Testament to realize that the Scribes and Pharisees got a lot of bad press. Jesus accused them of extortion, vanity, greed, neglecting justice, and straining at gnats but swallowing camels.

He called them hypocrites seven times in the course of one sermon, recorded in Matthew 23. He likened them to serpents, a brood of vipers, blind guides, and whitewashed sepulchers; they looked good on the outside but were full of rottenness within. Of course there were exceptions, such as the scribe mentioned in Mark 12, whom Jesus praised, saying, "You are not far from the Kingdom of God"; Nicodemus, who brought myrrh and aloes to care for the body of the crucified Savior; and the Pharisees mentioned in Luke 13:31, who advised Jesus to "get away from here, for Herod wants to kill you." But these were the exceptions. The Gospels generally portray the Scribes and Pharisees as self-righteous, judgmental hypocrites; a religious clique that stood in opposition to Jesus. Not much to love about them.

This morning's reading from the Gospel offers us one more reason to view the Scribes and Pharisees in a negative light. Here they are, acting holier-than-thou and daring to criticize Jesus. Their suspicion toward the Messiah had been building for some time. The scribes, who were the lawyers and judges, claimed that Jesus ignored or manipulated the law whenever it suited him. They had evidence he didn't conform to the Sabbath rules. He told stories that cast other religious leaders in the role of the bad guy, like in the parable of the Good Samaritan. He insulted them at dinner parties and violated the standards of ritual purity to which the Pharisees had devoted their lives.

As this chapter in Luke begins, they lodged another complaint against Jesus, and though it may seem strange to us at first, Jesus took it seriously. So should we. The Pharisees and Scribes organized a public protest to complain, "This man receives sinners and eats with them." Other translations of the Bible read, "He welcomes sinners." There were several things at stake here. Let's start with welcoming or receiving. An English friend of mine had the distinction of getting M.B.E. (Member of the British Empire) early this year. He and his family were invited to Buckingham Palace, he was presented to the Queen, and she gave him the award. My friend is no royalist, but he was nevertheless thrilled to be received by the Queen. It is an honor, a Kodak moment, maybe even the thrill of a lifetime when a famous person pays tribute or attention to you. Jesus was becoming increasingly well-known in his time and place. People talked about what he said and did. You might even call him a celebrity. To be the focus of his gracious attention was to be honored. The Scribes and Pharisees also charged him with dining with sinners. This irked them because in Jewish tradition mealtime was sacred. A blessing was said at the beginning and at the end of every meal. There were rules about what food and drink could be offered, and about how they were to be served. And beyond that, breaking bread with someone was and is a sign of trust and friendship, a means of healing broken relationships.

Our Redeemer's critics were angry because he received sinners and ate with them. They believed—quite rightly, in my opinion—that those people had done nothing to merit such an honor. They were convinced—and so am I—that God would hold Jesus and those sinners accountable for their behavior. They wanted the traditions and rules of their faith respected, not ignored or cast aside. And when we consider the "sinners" with whom Jesus kept company, we can understand the critics' indignation. The tax collectors were cheats. Diverting revenue for their personal use was all in a day's work. They lied to people about what was owed, and as long as their superiors got their cut, the government turned a blind eye to it. Not a pretty picture. The "sinners" mentioned in verse 2 included prostitutes, adulterers, drunkards, and people who profaned the Mosaic law or disregarded it altogether. We're talking about cheating, lying, sexual immorality, substance abuse, and lawlessness. Common sense tells us that these are more than personal transgressions, more than private matters. They have consequences for everyone around the person who commits them. Everyone in that first-century society suffered because of their wrongdoing—through broken families, damaged reputations, children physically or emotionally abandoned, people left in poverty, violence related to alcohol abuse, widespread cynicism and distrust, an increase in corrupt business practices—well, each of you could add to the list. It all sounds familiar, doesn't it? No wonder the Scribes and Pharisees were disgusted.

Jesus did not disagree with their assessment of the situation. He didn't argue with their conclusions. On the contrary, the parables he told after hearing the protest validated their objection. Those people were sinners. They were guilty. In fact, Jesus' story pushed their point even further; the way he presents it, they're so depraved, so lacking an inner moral compass, so lost in sin that they are incapable of finding their own way back. Sheep, to use his example, wander aimlessly, thinking no further than the next clump of grass. Sheep are ruled by their appetites; they lack the will and means to find the shepherd when they become separated from him. A lost coin is incapable of acting on its own, because it isn't even alive. The law of gravity causes it to be lost and it has no power of resistance. It is ruled by forces outside itself. Downright pathetic. That is how our Lord describes the people disdained by the Scribes and Pharisees.

The most outrageous thing about it is that they matter to Jesus. He loves them, and tells us each one is important to God. Some of you have seen shepherds at work. You know that when one goes after a lost sheep, upon finding it he doesn't shoot it on the spot or tell it never to come near the farm again. No. The shepherd may have to grab it by the crook or carry it in a way the sheep doesn't enjoy, but it is all done because he values it. He rejoices to find what is his. In a similar way, the woman whose coin has disappeared doesn't say, "Oh well, it wasn't worth that much anyway." She spends time and effort to recover that missing drachma because she is invested in it. It is precious to her. This last week, a Northbrook businessman offered a million dollars for one Major

League baseball whose market value is perhaps $10. There was nothing intrinsically special about that baseball. What made it worth more than a million was Mark McGwire's connection to it. With lost sheep and lost coins, sinners and tax collectors, it is Jesus who gives them value.

We can read in Scripture what happened to sinners who were found by the seeking love of Christ. The difference was apparent. Matthew left his tax office when Jesus came to him; he rose and followed the Messiah. His old job and way of life were left behind. Mary Magdalene was liberated from a life of prostitution and became the first witness to the Resurrection. Being found by Christ so transformed Zacchaeus that he gave half his goods to the poor, and he repaid those he had defrauded fourfold. Redeemed sinners bore fruits that befit repentance, to quote John the Baptist—but only the grace of Christ made it possible. Did Jesus brush off the seriousness of their sin? Not at all; he died on the cross for it. God's justice is not negated or compromised, but as Scripture reminds us, the Lord is forbearing toward us, not wishing that any should perish, but that all should reach repentance (2 Pet. 3:2).

This is good news. And perhaps we can take special joy that the Bible shows that the Good Shepherd's care extends not only to tax collectors and notorious sinners, but even to the most self-righteous, zealous Pharisee. According to the New Testament, Jesus seeks other people who are just as lost but in a different wasteland. The apostle Paul, for example, was found by Christ, who sought him. Paul was out hunting down Christians, not Christ, when the Lord came to him on Damascus Road and claimed him as his own. Saul, a man who had boasted in his pedigree that he was "a Pharisee, a Hebrew born of Hebrews, as to zeal a persecutor of the church, as to righteousness under the law blameless" (Phil. 3:5, 6), came to refer to himself as the foremost of sinners—but once saved by the mercy of Christ, who sought him out and gave him new value and a new name. The persistent love of God Incarnate appeared in the Upper Room to his so-called friends, who had nevertheless denied and abandoned him. It approached the disciples when they lost their direction and purpose at the Sea of Galilee. And the seeking love of God is found in communities as well as individuals. Ananias and the early Church took a big risk in believing that the Lord had truly found Paul. But as they obeyed the divine command and went looking for the man, they became agents in Christ's transforming work, and what a difference that made for the spreading of the gospel throughout the world.

You and I are living in a time of crisis. We struggle with issues of justice and forgiveness, discernment and decision making. We wonder who can be trusted. In our families, our church, our nation, we may be tempted to label some as Pharisees and hypocrites, denounce others as sinners beyond the pale. You may be the victim of someone else's labeling. Whatever voices clamor for your attention, listen first to the Shepherd, who said, "I have come to call not the righteous, but sinners, to repentance." Remember that all have sinned and fall short of the glory of God (Rom. 3:23), that whoever keeps the whole law but fails one point has become guilty of all of it (James 2:10), that God's Word declares, "none is righteous, no, not one. All have turned aside, together they have gone wrong" (Rom. 2:10, 12).

The cost of being found by Christ has been paid at Calvary, because he loves us. The cost of being found without Christ if we deny our lostness is eternal. And the mark of those who are found is that they join our Lord in his search for others who are equally precious to him. As Paul writes in 1 Timothy, "I received mercy for this reason, that in me, the foremost of sinners, Jesus Christ might display his perfect patience for an example to those who were to believe in him for eternal life." Disciples of Jesus are admonished, "If a man or woman is overtaken in any trespass, you who are spiritual should restore that one in a spirit of gentleness" (Gal. 6:1). So pray for our nation and those in authority. Pray for Scribes and Pharisees, tax collectors and sinners, for those neighbors and coworkers and family members who appear to have wandered far from the fold of God. Let the beauty and goodness and holiness of the one who loved us while we were yet sinners be seen in your life, and give thanks that his mercy has found you.—Carol M. Norén

SERMON OUTLINES

A sixth type of resource is the basic outline for crisis and funeral messages. The pastor builds a message for the occasion on such an outline.

There Is a River

TEXT: Ps. 46:4

"There is a river." A copious fountain or flowing stream makes the hearts of its beholders glad. And there is a city. What is suggested here is the security and happiness and ample supplies for the spiritual Church, "the city of God."

I. "There is a river": It is a gladdening stream. "Shall make glad the city of God." Beauty. Fertility. Thirst-quenching. Health-giving. Life-saving.

II. "There is a river": It flows a copious stream of truth and grace. The gladdening river is an emblem of many great and joyous truths. The river of grace. The river of mercy. The river of peace. Well is the grace of God compared to a river. (a) Large in volume. (b) Perpetual in movement. (c) Saving in character.

III. "There is a river": The manner of it. (a) Gentle in flow. (b) Endless in continuance. (c) Ever tranquil. (d) Eternal fullness.

IV. "There is a river": The river is God himself. It is the outflow, the self-communication of his own being, the blessings to the souls of men.

V. "There is a river": The effects of it. (a) It is a stream of spiritual supply. (b) It brings spiritual refreshment and happiness to God's people. (c) The river flows through the city, cleanses, purifies, beautifies, nourishes, brings prosperity. "There is a river, the streams whereof shall make glad the city of God." —M.K.W. Heicher

Life's Record

TEXT: Job 19:23

I. Job is longing for a permanent record or memorial. This seems the natural desire of many. But Job need not have made that plaintive cry, for his words were written. They have permanent entry here in the Word of God. But indeed all our words are written in the Lamb's Book of Life—every thought we think, every word we say, every deed we do. They are written "with a pen of iron and a point of diamond," both upon our very being and upon our human hearts. Learn: Let us do what we have to do and say what we have to say now, and not wait for a dying hour.

II. Let us be careful to say and do nothing in life which we shall long by and by to unsay and undo.

III. Let us above all speak for God and the Gospel now. The influence will last even better than a book.—J. G.

On Knowing God

TEXT: John 14:1

I. Some of us might say that we know very little about God. But the fact is that we know a great deal about him, and this should give us great comfort.

(a) *God is nearby now.* A father writing to his son serving in the overseas armed forces closed his letter with these words: "Remember, my son, no one is ever far from God."

(b) *God is good.* That means that God is just. It is most difficult for us to be just in our judgments of one another, because we do not know one another through and through. We do not know what weaknesses are due to heredity and environment. We do not know what ideals are held in the person's mind. But God knows. God is our loving Father. How much we know about God!

II. But to receive the deep comfort of God one must not only know about God; one must also know God. One may know about another and not know him at all. To know another you must open your mind and heart and soul to him; in other words, you must give yourself to him. Then you will know how full of love and grace and comfort God is. "Ye believe in God, believe also in me," said Jesus. Again he said, "Lo! I am with you always." "Let not your heart be troubled."—M.K.W. Heicher

The Evergreen Disciple

TEXT: Acts 21:16

Mason was a very young old man who "carried in his breast the fountain of perpetual youth."

An old disciple has these marks: (a) He is eminent for strength of faith and steadfastness of character. (b) He possesses a spirit of resignation. (c) He has a rich legacy of happy memories. (d) He is in full sympathy with the true spirit of progress. (e) He is wise in council because he is rich in experience. (f) He has before him the most glorious prospect.

Let not the aged be ashamed of the gray beard. Let the young remember that a righteous youth is the first step toward a happy old age.—J.O.D.

The Difference Christ Makes

TEXT: 2 Cor. 6:9–10

(a) We are able to get our grief out, to express it. (b) We are able to overcome our guilt through his presence. (c) We are able to remove self-pity and resentment. (d) We are able to have a new perspective on eternity through the viewpoint of love that helps us to stand anything that happens to us.

Our sorrow is transformed into hours of certainty when we are sure of God and his love. This enables us to thank God and take up our tasks with courage and bravery, to comfort those who mourn, and to live and die with victory. —Lance Webb

Comfort for Mourners

TEXT: Matt. 5:4

There are four spiritual elements that bring comfort to those who mourn.

I. There is no agony in death itself. There may have been severe suffering previous to death, but death is enveloped in a merciful unconsciousness.

II. The loved one who has passed on is not dead but is alive forevermore. Thought, mind, spirit—these in their fundamental nature are timeless. The body is temporal and passes away, but the soul is eternal and so endures.

III. The life of the departed loved ones does not continue in lonely isolation. It emerges into a realm where like cleaves to like in happy fellowship.

Although the loved one cannot return to you, you can go to him.—H. M. Ratliff Jr.

A Funeral Meditation

TEXT: John 11:25

The resurrection and eternal life of a man do not rest in any condition of nature. A grain of wheat is planted; it will grow if the conditions and circumstances are right—soil, sunshine, rain. But circumstances do not determine whether or not a man's soul shall live. Whether he was rich or poor, lived here or there, achieved high position or only low, circumstances have no final word. The final word is Christ's: "I am the resurrection and the life."

The resurrection and eternal life of a man do not rest in others. A family cannot say, "Our brother shall live," except in faith. A friend cannot say, "He shall live!" It was only Jesus who could say to Martha and Mary, "Thy brother shall rise again."

The eternal life of a man does not rest in himself. He does not achieve it as a man achieves a position in a community. He does not make it as he makes a fortune. He accepts it as one accepts a gift. It is by the grace of Christ that eternal life is given to a believing soul.

I am glad that this is so. Nature is too erratic to be depended on: So many seeds are planted that never live. Our families and friends are so forgetful. We ourselves too often sacrifice a higher for a lesser good.

So this gift is in the proper hands—hands that are pure, hands that care, hands that are kind, hands that are loving.

Into His hands we commend the souls of our loved ones, and we have comfort in the thought of him who watcheth over them.—M.K.W. Heicher

SERMON ILLUSTRATIONS AND POETRY

The best place for a pastor to find poetry suitable for inclusion in a funeral or crisis-related service is in the hymnal used by the congregation. The hymn lyrics have two distinct advantages: they have the ring of familiarity for listeners and they have the endorsement of the larger church. The most likely source for relevant and engaging sermon illustrations is also the most accessible: the world in which the pastor and congregation live. Such stories should not violate any confidentiality, of course, but drawing on common history and experience has the potential to connect listeners to the gospel with powerful immediacy.

Although the hymnal and the congregational context may be the first place to look for evocative material for Christian worship, the search should not end there. We are not all equally creative or gifted in expression. Sometimes an image or poem from literature or film will carry your point and open up new worlds and opportunities to your listeners. A congregation traumatized by crisis or loss may be able to latch on to a visual image or apt phrase more readily than they can follow the explication of a concept. That being the case, we have a responsibility to discern and employ the best metaphors and language available to us.

The illustrations and poetry in this section are drawn from *The Minister's Manual* and other sources. They were selected to evoke or depict a wide range of experiences and emotions. Your discernment is necessary to determine which of them is suitable for the occasion for which you are preparing. Following are some of the questions to be asked in the discernment process:

1. Will this help communicate the gospel, obscure the gospel, or contradict it? Some amusing stories about heaven, for example, have nothing to do with the promises of the Bible.

2. Is the language or imagery intelligible and appropriate for this culture? A poem that is deeply moving to one generation may impress another as mawkish or absurd. (And be aware that your taste is not necessarily better—or worse—than the congregation's!)

3. Does the poem or illustration truly fit the theme of the service or the point of the sermon, or is it filler—being considered only because it is someone's favorite? If the latter is the case, perhaps a better place to share the story or poem is at the repast after the committal.

When including poetry in the sermon or elsewhere in the service, keep in mind that most congregations can listen to only brief excerpts during the course of a sermon. They will hear most effectively if the portion you are using is memorized or nearly memorized, so that you can say the words with conviction, as though they were your own.

My final suggestion in using these or other resources is simple: let your illustrations make the Good News as vivid and believable as any bad news in your message. It may be easier—and necessary—to present bad examples of one thing or another, but we must guard against making problems more real and believable than solutions! Weight your sermon in favor of the hope that is ours through God's promises in Christ.

Illustrations for Preaching

In Uppsala, Sweden, stands the medieval Church of the Holy Trinity. Still home to an active congregation, it began as a place where artisans and farmers worshipped during construction of the great cathedral nearby. A small, fenced-in area by an outside wall protects a small, simple monument with this inscription:

To those who come after us:
Give us a little space. Let two spouses have rest together
Until the Spirit comes.
If you need this place,
Let us lie under your feet or
Give us from your property
Another little room
Where our bones may enjoy their rest.
We were enough like you.
We were people. We were Christians.

I remember hearing an evangelist at an evening meeting where a solemn hymn had been sung, of which the refrain was "Eternity! Eternity!" break the silence which followed the singing with the impressive question, "Where will you spend it?" The purpose of the question was laudable, yet it conveyed an idea which most of his hearers already held, and of which it would have been well if they could have been disabused—that eternity is a tract of duration lying wholly on the other side of death. If they had been asked where eternity begins, most of them would have promptly answered, "at death." The common conception is that the grave is the point at which time ends and eternity begins. But time does not end, neither does eternity begin; and there is great moral as well as metaphysical confusion in conceiving of any such boundary line. The kind of life which possesses the power of continuance is a kind of life which has as much to do with the present moment as with any future moment of duration. If one is living it now, no questions need be asked about the future, that will take care of itself; and to the one who refuses to live it now, expectations about the future are vain.—Washington Gladden[1]

Heaven is not a dull place. It is not a worn-out mansion with faded curtains, and outlandish chairs, and cracked ware. No; it is as fresh, and fair, and beautiful as though it were completed yesterday. The kings of the earth shall bring their honor and glory into it.

A palace means splendor of apartments. Now, I do not know where heaven is, and I do not know how it looks, but, if our bodies are to be resurrected in the last day, I think heaven must have a material splendor as well as a spiritual grandeur. Oh, what grandeur of apartments when that Divine hand which plunges the sea into blue, and the foliage into green, and sets the sunset on fire, shall gather all the beautiful colors of earth around His throne, and when that arm which lifted the pillars of Alpine rock, and bent the arch of the sky, shall raise before our soul the eternal architecture, and that hand which hung with the loops of fire the curtains of morning shall prepare the upholstery of our kingly residence!—DeWitt Talmage[2]

Some days are little, and some days are large, and in all those days, common-place and ordinary and routine days, Jesus says: "I will be with you." And then when come life's testing days—days big with meaning, with terror, with pain, with duty, with trial—Jesus stands there to fortify us as we go on clinging to Him.—George W. Truett[3]

Have you any appreciation this evening of the good and glorious times your friends are having in heaven? How different it is when they get news there of a Christian's death from how it is here. It is the difference between embarkation and coming into port. Everything depends upon which side of the river you stand when you hear of a Christian's death. If you stand on this side of the river, you mourn that they go. If you stand on the other side of the river, you rejoice that they come. Oh, the difference between a funeral on Earth and a jubilee in heaven—between requiem here and triumphal march there, parting here and reunion there. Together! Have you thought of it? They are together. Not one of your departed friends in one land and another in another land; but together in different rooms of the same house—the house of many mansions. Together! I never appreciated that thought so much as recently, when we laid away in her last slumber my sister Sarah. Standing there in the village cemetery, I looked around and said: "There is father, there is mother, there is grandfather, there is grandmother, there are whole circles of kindred"; and I thought to myself, "Together in the grave—together in glory." I am so impressed with the thought that I do not think it is any fanaticism when someone is going from this world to the next if you make them the bearer of dispatches to your friends who are gone, saying, "Give my love to my parents, give my love to my children, give my love to my old comrades who are in glory, and tell them I am trying to fight the good fight of faith, and I will join them after a while." I believe the message will be delivered, and I believe it will increase the gladness of those who are before the throne. Together are they, all their tears gone. No trouble getting good society for them. All kings, queens, princes, and princesses. In 1751, there was a bill offered in your English Parliament, proposing to change the almanac so that the first of March should come immediately after the 18th of February. But oh, what a glorious change in the calendar when all the years of your earthly existence are swallowed up in the eternal year of God!—DeWitt Talmage[4]

Heaven is a new world; it is a city. It does not have the monotony of the country. It is a city, but it is not like ours. There are no dark rooms. There are no fine streets on one side and filth on the other. It is 1,200 miles long and broad, and it is fairer than an earthly dream. Verse 11 speaks of light. We have all watched a sunset play with colors among the clouds. No artist's pallet was ever so rich. Or perhaps we have seen the colors in Switzerland and the clear air. We delight in the colors of nature, and that too shall be satisfied in heaven. There is an indication that the nature that now pleases us shall still be there. There is a flowing river, there are groves of trees with wondrous fruits. We shall not forever be standing stiff with harps, but breathing souls full of joy.—Walter Rauschenbusch[5]

There comes a last earthly day—the day of death. Somebody asked Dwight L. Moody if he had dying grace, and he said, "Why, no. I have living grace, but when I come to die I shall have dying grace." And when they carried him home from a meeting he was conducting in Kansas City, where a fatal sickness had seized him, there propped up on his pillows, with his loved ones around him, he looked at them, and then looked up into the open heavens, and said: "The world is receding. Heaven is opening. God is calling me, and I must be away." He had dying grace when death came.—George W. Truett[6]

Sigrid Undset won the Nobel Prize for her epic novel, *Kristin Lavransdatter*. In the last chapter of the book, the death of the title character is depicted by means of a moving confession of faith: "It seemed to her a mystery that she could not fathom, but which she knew most surely nonetheless, that God had held her fast in a covenant made for her without her knowledge by a love poured out upon her richly and in spite of her self-will, in spite of her heavy, earthbound spirit; somewhat of this love had become *part* of her, had wrought in her like sunlight in the earth, had brought forth increase which not even the hottest flames of fleshly love nor its wildest bursts of wrath could lay waste wholly. A handmaiden of God had she been—a wayward, unruly servant, oftenest an eye-servant in her prayers and faithless in her heart, slothful and neglectful, impatient under correction, but little constant in her deeds—yet had he held her fast in his service, and under the glittering golden ring a mark had been set secretly upon her, showing that she was his handmaid, owned by the Lord and King who was now coming, borne by the priest's anointed hands, to give her freedom and salvation."—Sigrid Undset[7]

From a divine revelation to St. Catherine of Siena: "I want to be merciful to the world and provide for my reasoning creatures' every need. But the foolish take for death what I give for life, and are thus cruel to themselves. I always provide, and I want you to know that what I have given humankind is supreme providence. I gave you a will to love, making you a sharer in the Holy Spirit's mercy, so that you might love what your understanding sees and knows. All this my gentle providence did, only that you might be capable of understanding and enjoying me and rejoicing in my goodness by seeing me eternally."—Catherine of Siena[8]

A minister was calling on a friend in the hospital. The friend was dying. He wanted some indication about the afterlife. He said to the minister, "Tell me what heaven is like." That is an awfully hard question to answer in a few moments. While he was thinking, the minister heard a scratching on the hospital room door. He recognized the barks of his little dog. He had left the dog out in his parked car. But the dog had chased him into the hospital, down the hallway, and to this room. So the minister said, "Do you hear that bark and the scratching on the door?" "Yes." "That is my little dog. He has never been in this hospital. He doesn't know what is on this side of that door. He knows only one thing: I am here. And when I open the door, you will see how happy he is. What a welcome he will give me when he bounds through the door."—Theodore C. Mayer[9]

Great religious leaders often die as they lived: with a confession of faith on their lips. John Wesley's last words were, "The best of all is, God is with us," and Martin Luther is reported to have said, "Father in heaven, though this body is breaking away from me, and I am departing this life, yet I know that I shall forever be with thee, for no one can pluck me out of thy hand."

How great shall be that felicity, which shall be fainted with no evil, which shall lack no good, and which shall afford leisure for the praises of God, who shall be all in all:

For I know not what other employment there can be where no lassitude shall slacken activity, nor any want stimulate to labor. I am admonished also by the sacred song, in which I read or hear the words, "Blessed are they that dwell in Thy house, O Lord; they will be still praising Thee." All the members and organs of the incorruptible body, which now we see to be suited to various necessary uses, shall contribute to the praises of God, for in that life necessity shall have no place, but full, certain, secure, everlasting felicity. For all those parts of the bodily harmony, which are distributed through the whole body, within and without, and of which I have just been saying that they are present, elude our observation, shall then be discerned, and along with other great and marvelous discoveries which shall then kindle rational minds in praise of the great Artificer, there shall be the enjoyment of a beauty which appeals to the reason. What power of movement such bodies shall possess, I have not the audacity rashly to define, as I have not the ability to conceive. Nevertheless I will say that in any case, both in motion and at rest, they shall be, as in their appearance, seemly; for into that state nothing which is unseemly shall be admitted. One thing is certain, the body shall forthwith be wherever the spirit wills, and the spirit shall will nothing which is unbecoming either to the spirit or to the body. True honor shall be there, for it shall be denied to none who is worthy, nor yielded to any unworthy person so much as sue for it, for none but the worthy shall be there. True peace shall be there, where no one shall suffer opposition either from himself or any other. God Himself, who is the Author of virtue, shall there be its reward; for, as there is nothing greater or better, He has promised

Himself. What else was meant by His word through the prophet, "I will be your God, and ye shall be my people," than, I shall be their satisfaction, I shall be all that men honorably desire—life, and health, and nourishment, and plenty, and glory, and honor, and peace, and all good things? This, too, is the right interpretation of the saying of the apostle, "That God may be all in all." He shall be the end of our desires who shall be seen without end, loved without cloy, praised without weariness. This outgoing of affection, this employment, shall certainly be, like eternal life itself, common to all.—St. Augustine[10]

Cotton Mather, the noted American clergyman, uttered on his deathbed, "Is this dying? Is this all? Is this what I feared when I prayed against a hard death? Oh, I can bear this! I can bear it."

"And I think that God is loved with the whole soul by those who through their great longing for fellowship with God draw their soul away and separate it not only from their earthly body but also from every corporeal thing. For them no pulling or dragging takes place even in putting off their lowly body (cf. Phil. 3:21), when the time allows them to take off the body of death through what is supposed to be death. For which one of those who groan in this tent (cf. 2 Cor. 5:4) because they are weighed down by a corruptible body would not also give thanks, first saying, "Who will deliver me from this body of death?" And when he sees that he has been delivered from the body of death by his confession, he will make the holy proclamation, "Thanks be to God through Jesus Christ our Lord!" (Rom. 7:25).—Origen[11]

Charlotte Brontë, the daughter of an Anglican clergyman, never preached a sermon from a pulpit, but put her testimony in the mouths of the characters in her novels. In *Jane Eyre,* one such witness to faith is given by Helen Burns, a young girl dying of consumption:

> "I am very happy, Jane; and when you hear that I am dead, you must be sure and not grieve: there is nothing to grieve about. We all must die one day, and the illness which is removing me is not painful; it is gentle and gradual: my mind is at rest."
>
> "But where are you going to, Helen? Can you see? Do you know?"
>
> "I believe; I have faith: I am going to God, my Maker and yours, who will never destroy what he created. I rely implicitly on his power, and confide wholly in his goodness: I count the hours till that eventual one arrives which shall restore me to him, reveal him to me."
>
> "You are sure, then, Helen, that there is such a place as heaven; and that our souls can get to it when we die?"
>
> "I am sure there is a future state; I believe God is good; I can resign my immortal part to him without any misgiving. God is my father; God is my friend: I love him; I believe he loves me."

"And shall I see you again, Helen, when I die?"

"You will come to the same region of happiness: be received by the same might, universal Parent, no doubt, dear Jane."—Charlotte Brontë[12]

Fear of death is a property of nature due to disobedience, but terror of death is a sign of unrepented sins. Christ is frightened of dying but not terrified, thereby clearly revealing the properties of his two natures.—John Climacus[13]

Angelus Silesius was the pen name of Johann Scheffler, a German mystic of the seventeenth century. His work, *The Cherubinic Wanderer,* is a collection of aphorisms and couplets touching on a wide range of theological subjects. Some of these pertain to death:

Death is a blessed thing; if it be vigorous, the life that springs from it will be more glorious.

If He should live in you, God first Himself must die. How would you, without death, inherit His own life?

I say that nothing dies; just that life eternal is given us through death, even the death infernal.

Time's like eternity, eternity like time, unless you do yourself between them draw a line.—Angelus Silesius[14]

Humbert of Romans was an early Dominican best known for his treatise on the formation of preachers. However, he also wrote about the value of prayer and actions on behalf of souls in purgatory. Whatever one believes about purgatory itself, some of Humbert's suggestions are unobjectionable to the most ardent Protestant. Humbert prescribes making offerings at the altar, undertaking penance and making amends on behalf of the dead, giving alms, doing acts of kindness, and carrying out some good plan which the dead person had. All these are pleasing to God and honor the memory of those being mourned.

In October 1943, a physician in Copenhagen devised a strategy for saving more than two thousand Jews from the Nazis in the course of a dozen or more funerals. Dr. Karl Koster organized funeral processions through the streets of the city, ending up at the cemetery on the grounds of Bispebjerg Hospital. From the graveside, they broke into small groups and went to various buildings in the hospital complex, where they were hidden and fed until they could be smuggled out of the country. One might say that standing at an open grave was the entry into new life for them. Even so, for Christians the grave does not represent the end, but the continuation of a pilgrimage to heaven.

Death is the common denominator of life. By it we are reduced to exactly what we are: no more, no less. The grave is the portal through which everyone must pass to enter into the timeless eons of eternity. One's view of death will depend on one's view of life. While the nature of man is to pass from life into death, the nature of the "new creature in Christ" is to pass from death into life. It is this principle and pattern which Jesus came to reveal. At death, man's worth is not increased one iota by his silver and his gold. Every life must be weighed on the same balance, and the scale is tipped by one thing only: faith in the risen Lord. Passing from death into life begins with renunciation of self and a turning to the Lord of life. The life that weighs the most is the life that has lost itself in the greater, eternal life of God.—Richard Bennett Sims

Death is a disorder. The Bible makes this crystal clear. The death of human beings points to an ultimate disorder. It should *not* be; the grim boundary markers should *not* stand between us and the eternal life of God. And precisely for that reason this whole unnatural state, this disorder, this "brokenness" of the world, gives way when Jesus Christ comes and lays his ordering and healing hand on his fellow humans.—Helmut Thielicke

Halford Luccock said, "Christianity made its way throughout the Roman world by the communication of wonder!" I believe it did. For men had had enough of household deities, and gods of small utility. This new faith caught hold of their farthest-flung imagination, for He took His time by such surprise that it could only sputter, as it staggered back from Him: "Why, we have seen strange things today!"

> He scandalized society!
> He ruffled every tradition that they knew!
> See! God on earth: an intimate divinity.
> Death on a Cross: a loving Saviour! And an open tomb: eternal life!

They stood enchanted, and at last when breath broke through, they sang, *Gloria in Excelsis!*—Win Blair Sutphin

Almighty God and glorious Savior, "who died for us, that whether we wake or sleep, we shall live together with him" (1 Thess. 5:10). God has honored and crowned His creation, dressed him with dignity, given him the opportunity to make choices, and enabled him to reason and think. He gave His Son that we might have a way to the Almighty. Without God, life would be an endless vacuum with no incentive or purpose. Life without God would be a cheat. God has made life a challenge, a thrill of conquest. He gives strength far beyond ourselves. He encourages the downcast heart.

Isaiah, the mighty statesman of the Old Testament, said: "Thou wilt keep him in perfect peace whose mind is stayed on thee: because he trusteth in thee" (Isa. 26:3).—W. E. Thorne

St. Francis of Assisi, hoeing his garden, was asked what he would do if he were suddenly to learn that he was to die at sunset that very day. He replied: "I would finish hoeing my garden." If we were to live nobly, then we must redeem this present moment, this present hour, this present day.

Nikos Kanzantzakis tells of an earnest young man who visited a saintly old monk on a remote island. He asked him, "Do you still wrestle with the devil, Father?" The monk answered, "Not any longer, my child. I have grown old, and he has grown old with me. He no longer has the strength. Now I wrestle with God." "With God!" exclaimed the young man in astonishment. "Do you hope to win?" "Oh, no, my son," came the reply, "I hope to lose."—John N. Gladstone

Only in one place can we find an assurance that God is love, and loves us eternally, and that is in Christ. He is the Revealer of God to men, and Guide of men of God. "God is Christlike, and in Him is no un-Christlikeness at all," was Michael Ramsey's way of putting it. "God," said Paul, "proves His love for us in that, while we were yet sinners, Christ died for us." In Jesus Christ, incarnate, crucified, and risen from the dead, the love of God is communicated to our wondering hearts, and we are forever sure that nothing can ever separate us from it.—John N. Gladstone

I remember once near Interlaken waiting for days to see the Jungfrau, which was hidden in mists. People told me it was there, and I should have been a fool to doubt their word, for those who told me lived there and they knew. Then one day the mists were gone, and the whole great mountain stood revealed. Next day the mists were back, but now I had seen, and knew myself it was true. Men and women, let us trust the saints, the people who have a right to speak about the fellowship of Christ, because they have lived in that country all their lives. Yes, and let us trust our own moments of vision: what does it matter if there are days when the mists come down and the face of God is hidden? We have seen, and we know forever this is real, so real that by it we can live and die.—James S. Stewart

We know that we shall not be equal in glory; the equality . . . lies in this, that each soul is fulfilled to its full extent with the delights of God's house. And we know that there can be no murmuring or envying in that manifestation of the sons of God. We shall, I imagine, have no time to say, "Who could have thought of seeing you there?" We shall be too engrossed in the reflection, "Who would have thought of seeing me here?"—Ronald A. Knox

THE GOOD FIGHT.   This is a great retrospect. *I have finished my course.* Life is made up of ends and of beginnings. Death is but the greatest crisis of many, and all crises are like Janus in the Roman pantheon: two-faced. The end of one crisis is the beginning of another. But with all the ebbs and flows of life there must be a unity, some grand unity that constitutes life's reality. For us that unity is, in Paul's phrase, *"For me to live in Christ,"* that is, Christ is my career.

The unity of our life is therefore objective, outside ourselves. It is not in the evolution of life but in its goal. When Wordsworth writes of life whose days are bound each to each by natural piety, he is not truly Christian. When a man is truly Christian, each day is bound to Christ, is devoted to him, is lived in him. Life is not realizing a plan but fulfilling a mission. Thus a broken column in a churchyard, symbolizing a broken life, is an anachronism. There is no such thing as a broken life for the man of faith. All life is complete in Christ, and always complete; no matter when the end comes, the course is finished.—P. T. Forsyth

I know nothing about what form life will take in the beyond, but I know that it will not be an unincarnate, abstract, impersonal world of ideas, of pure anonymous spirits or phantoms. I know that I shall retain my personal identity; and it is a fact here below, in personal fellowship, in the person-to-person relationship when it is true, that I find a foretaste of heaven.—Paul Tournier

DARING TO HOPE.   If we dare to hope not only for the living but also for the dead and those still unborn, if we hope not only for the human race but for the whole of nature as well, we will repent of all petty visions of the future that absolutize the interests of a particular group. With the apostle Paul we will express our solidarity in hope with all of the groaning creation that restlessly awaits God's coming redemption (Rom. 8:21–23).—Daniel L. Migliori

GOING HOME.   How rich this Earth seems when we regard it—crowded with the loves of home! Yet I am now getting to go home—to leave this world of homes and go home. When I reach that home, shall I even then seek yet to go home? Even then, I believe, I shall seek a yet warmer, deeper, purer home in the deeper knowledge of God—in the truer love of my fellow men. Eternity will be—my heart and my faith tell me—a traveling homeward, but in jubilation and confidence and vision of the beloved.—George MacDonald

I remember hearing Sidney Montague of the Northwest Mounted Police tell of the thrill he felt when, in the midst of his explorations in the virgin forest of the Canadian Rockies, he came suddenly for the first time upon a breathtaking view, the grandeur of which was overwhelming, making him vividly aware that that moment was freighted with an unforgettable memory of splendor. It was then he said that he realized, as he had not realized before, that life is a matter of moments and that one only lives as one gets the most from each moment's experience. And later he wrote a poem that began: "This moment is your life."—Clayton E. Williams

IMMORTAL SYMPHONIES.   Winter is on my head, but eternal spring is in my heart. The nearer I approach the end, the plainer I hear around me the immortal symphonies of the world to come. For half a century I have been writing my thoughts in prose and verse, but I feel that I have not said one-thousandth part of what is in me. When I have gone down to the grave, I shall have ended my day's work, but another day will begin the next morning. Life closes in the twilight but opens with the dawn.—Victor Hugo

Rabbi Jacob taught, "This world is like a vestibule before the world to come. Prepare thyself in the vestibule that thou mayest enter into the hail." He used to say, "Better is one hour of repentance and good deeds in this world than the whole life of the world to come. However, better is one hour of the blissfulness of spirit in the world to come than the whole life of this world."—Cited by William E. Silverman

LIFE EVERLASTING.   A pastor in Portland, Oregon, learned from his physician that his life on earth was limited. Knowing how troubled his faithful flock would be at the news, he entered the pulpit the next Sabbath, and with his vibrant Christian faith, he shared the news with his people. Then he added:

> I walked out where I live, five miles out of this city, and I looked at the river in which I rejoice, and I looked at the stately trees that are always God's own poetry to my soul. Then, in the evening, I looked up into the great sky, where God was lighting his lamps, and I said: "I may not see you many times more, but river, I shall be alive when you cease running to the sea; and stars, I shall be alive when you have fallen from your sockets in the great down-pulling of the universe."

—Ernest J. Lewis

Some call death paying the debt of nature, but Spurgeon said it is more like taking in a paper note and getting gold in exchange. American paper money used to be a silver certificate that could truly be exchanged for silver. That is no longer the case, but the illustration holds true. When we die, we exchange the paper for the real thing.

McCullough wrote, "How irrational it would be to think of the Parthenon standing for thousands of years and the Phidians living a paltry three score years and ten; of Handel's *Messiah* existing but not Handel; of da Vinci's *Last Supper* continuing but da Vinci gone forever; of Michelangelo's *Moses* remaining but Michelangelo forever dust!"

A MATTER OF DEATH AND LIFE.   When there is a real emergency, we often say that it is a matter of life and death. Christians know, however, that our time on Earth is just the opposite: a time of death and life! We are not dying people in the land of the living. We are living people in the land of the dying.

The last song Mario Lanza ever sang was "I'll Walk with God." He recorded it for the movie version of *The Student Prince.* Just afterward he became ill and died. What a great way to end one's life, declaring, "I'll walk with God"!

Black-bordered death notices are still commonly seen in Eastern Europe, posted in public places. Commonly one sees a star and knows that the deceased was a Communist or a cross and knows that the deceased was a believer. One such notice was posted for a Christian physician. He had suffered through a long battle with cancer and must have known that he was dying. Without doubt he chose the three verses of Scripture that were printed on his death notice. No star, no cross, but three verses from the Bible. One was 2 Timothy 4:7: "I have fought a good fight." Another was John 11:25: "I am the resurrection and the life." Most impressive was Romans 14:8: "If we live, we live to the Lord, and if we die, we die to the Lord, so whether we live or we die, we belong to the Lord." What a philosophy for both death *and* life.

Queen Milica had the horrible experience of losing both her husband and her two sons in the same day on the same battlefield. After the battle was over, she had someone bring to her the weapons her sons had carried. From them she made a lamp to hang inside the church in the convent where she spent the rest of her life. It was a new way of "beating swords into plowshares." We all respond to grief in different ways, but it's helpful to look for constructive ways to express our sorrow and constructive ways to perpetuate the memory of those we love.

They couldn't decide whether or not to tell the old man that he was terminally ill. Finally the family agreed that he should be told. So they gently explained to him that he was not expected to recover. They said, "It's only a matter of time." Wisely he answered, "That's what it's always been—only a matter of time." He spoke truly. From the moment we were born, it has been "only a matter of time." Some die sooner and some later, but this Earth is not the permanent home of any of us, and it's always only a matter of time.

After a rather lengthy and extensive apologetic for the resurrection of the dead and the final triumph of God in Christ, the apostle Paul writes, "If only for this life we have hope in Christ, we are to be pitied more than all men" (1 Cor. 15:19 NIV). We are confronted by the affirmation that the Christian life is one lived out under the presence of death, but not under its power. This life, as we live it and know it and breathe it, is to be valued as the place of our enrichment and personal growth. Yet this life has been transcended, extended if you will; it has been given a new horizon, the borders have been pushed to the limits, which are no longer limits at all.—Albert J. D. Walsh

The stream of life through millions of years, the stream of human lives through countless centuries. Evil, death and dearth, sacrifice and love—what does "I" mean in such a perspective? Reason tells me that I am bound to seek my own good, to seek to gratify my desires, to win power for myself and admiration from others. And yet I "know"—know without knowing—that in such a perspective nothing could be less important. A vision in God *is.*—Dag Hammarskjold

In a harbor two ships sailed: one setting forth on a voyage, the other coming home to port. Everyone cheered the ship going out, but the ship sailing in was scarcely noticed. And a wise man said, "Do not rejoice over the ship that is setting out to sea, for you cannot know what storms it will encounter, what fearful dangers it may have to endure. But rejoice rather over the ship that has safely reached port, and brings home all its passengers in peace."

And this is the way of the world: when a child is born, all rejoice; when a man or woman dies, all weep. We should do the opposite. No one can tell what trials and travails await a child; but when a mortal dies in peace, we should rejoice, for he has completed his long journey and is leaving this world with the imperishable crown of a good name.—Adapted from *The Talmud*

Dr. James S. Stewart, the noted minister of the Church of Scotland and Chaplain to the Queen, said that once when he was in a home in Scotland, he walked back to the kitchen and over the kitchen sink, printed on a card, he saw these words: "Divine worship will be held here three times daily."

Brother Lawrence, a member of the Carmelite religious order several centuries ago, showed us how it is possible to do everything for the love of God, even to the picking up of a straw from the floor.

When one sees the significance of the commonplace, this humdrum world can be made a veritable garden of God.—James W. Cox

Before I was old enough to go to school, I delighted in visiting the elderly couple in the big old house across the road. Downstairs were large spacious rooms that were fun to explore. I do not remember the furnishings of these rooms, but I still recall the graciousness of the small gray-haired lady whose cookie jar seemed to be always full.

Sometimes I was allowed to go up the broad stairs, through a large bedroom, and into a world of mystery and beauty—the studio of the artist daughter. The many sizes of brushes, the tubes of paint, and what the artist did with them were endlessly fascinating.

I recapture that long-ago feeling with happiness and expectancy as I consider the many rooms that Jesus told us are in his Father's house.—Mary Louise Williams[15]

GOD SEES.   The sum of it is from a story told in the terrible days of the blitz in London. It is said that a father, holding his small son by the hand, ran from a building which had been struck by a bomb. In the yard was a shell hold, and seeking shelter the father jumped in, then held up his arms for his son to follow. But the small boy, hearing his father urging him to jump, replied, "I can't see you." The father, however, could see his son outlined against the night sky, standing hesitant and anxious, and replied, "But I can see you. Jump!" So the faith that enables us to confront death with dignity is not that we can see, but that we are seen; not what we know, but that we are known; not that death denies life, nor life denies death, but that both are part of God's gift. Neither can separate us from his love. And that faith *does* give dimension and dignity to life—Gene E. Bartlett

Not many years ago, a sixteen-year-old girl lay dying in a Phoenix hospital. A dear friend was a Carmelite priest. The last time he saw her, he must have looked dreadfully upset. As he tells it, "She looked up into my worried and harried face and said, 'Don't be afraid.'" Such, at its most profound, is the Christian theology of death: "Don't be afraid." It is most profound when a child can say to an adult, a girl to a priest, when it is the dying who can say to the living: "Don't be afraid."—Walter J. Burghardt

The dead and the living are not names of two classes which exclude each other. Much rather, there are none who are dead. The dead are the living who have died. Whilst they were dying, they lived, and after they were dead, they lived more fully. All live unto God. God is not the God of the dead, but of the living. Oh, how solemnly sometimes that thought comes up before us, that all those past generations which have stormed across this earth of ours, and then have fallen into still forgetfulness, live yet. Somewhere, at this very instant, they now verily are. We say they were—they have been. There are no have-beens. Life is life forever. To be is eternal being. Every man that has died is at this instant in the full possession of his faculties, in the most intense exercise of all his capacities, standing somewhere in God's great universe, ringed with the sense of God's presence, and feeling in every fiber of his being that life which comes after death is not less real but more real, not less great but more great, not less full and intense, but more full and intense than the mingled life which, lived here on earth, was a center of life surrounded with a crust and circumference of mortality. The dead are the living. They lived whilst they died, and after they die, they live on forever.—Alexander MacLaren

LIVING HALF-LIVES.   At Atlantic City, on the one hand of the boardwalk are all the glittering, changing trifles which entertain and please us for a moment. On the other hand is the wideness of the open sea. But, curiously enough, the benches along the boardwalk are so arranged that people who pause to rest must sit with their backs to the sea. And many people live that way, moving from one pleasure to another until they are weary, and then resting with their eyes fixed on the things that are here today and gone tomorrow. It isn't even half of life, to live in only one world, to face the care and the monotony of long years, to suffer pain, and to know sorrow with your back turned on the realities of the spiritual world.

The Christian turns toward the sea, gathers into his soul all of its wideness and depth and strength, and sees each particular event against that background, in its proper setting.—Harold Elliott Nicely

A noble death reveals a noble life. 1 John 3:16 reminds us, "Hereby perceive we the love of God because he laid down his life for us." A long life of loving service may prove the love that inspires it, and a long career of patriotic service may prove one's patriotism; but we are all more immediately impressed by a patriotic death, or a death of devoted self-sacrifice. No higher evidence can one give than to die, and while all our soldiers were men of like passions with ourselves, those who died for us gave a proof of a noble patriotism which rises above criticism. The gentle unselfishness of the brave is a well-known trait, and suggests sacred depth of character which we may well revere.

In the south of England is an old churchyard. It is difficult to read more than a word on most of the gravestones. But there is one stone on which a full line can still be read clearly. It says: "Gone away with a Friend."—Raymond W. Fenn

The final journey will be the most wonderful leg of our trip. The arrival will be the most exciting, for we are destined to travel to a place that has been gloriously described in Scripture: "There shall be no night there, neither sinning, nor sorrow, nor death." It shall be a place of song and joy and everlasting life. It will mean reunion with our loved ones. The landing will be as sudden as is the landing of our plane dipping down from the sky to the airport below. So live each day to the fullest with God, and heaven has already begun in you. Keep walking life's way with him, and he will lead you into fairer pastures, until finally you shall go with him to the other shore.—Reubin K. Youngdahl

I think of death as a glad awakening from this troubled sleep which we call life, as an emancipation from a world which, beautiful though it be, is still a land of captivity.—Lyman Abbott

A newspaper reporter interviewed an old lamplighter on his round in the early hours of the morning. "What a dismal task yours must be of putting out lights!" the reporter said, "Not so," replied the lamplighter, "for there is always another light waiting for me. It's a cheering prospect." The reporter remonstrated, "But when you come to the last light and put it out, what then?" "Then," said the old man, "comes the dawn."—Aaron N. Meckel

In 1899, in the midst of a great revival in Kansas City, Dwight L. Moody became ill and was rushed home to Massachusetts, where in his last moments he said to his son, "This is no dream, Will. If this be death, it is inexpressibly sweet. Earth is receding, heaven is opening, God is calling, and I must go."—S. F. Marsh

Every new experience with Christ tells us more about heaven. In the days before the discovery of America, the Spanish coins carried a picture of the Pillars of Hercules at the Strait of Gibraltar and the inscription, "Ne plus ultra," meaning "There is nothing beyond." But after the courageous voyage of Columbus, the inscription was altered to read "Plus ultra," meaning "Something beyond." Before the world knew Christ and his Resurrection, the knowledge of heaven was meager, but in his presence we are always saying "Plus ultra," and that something we call heaven.—A. Purnell Bailey

Heaven is like the life of Jesus with all the conflict of human sin left out. Heaven is like the feeding of the multitude in the wilderness, with everybody sure to get ample to eat. Heaven is like the woman sinner from the streets who bathed the feet of Jesus in her tears and wiped them with her hair. I do not want more than that. It is peace, joy, victory, triumph—it is life, it is love, it is tireless work, faithful and unselfish service going on forever. The way to achieve all this is to try to follow Christ today, tomorrow, and the day after, through prayer and right living.—Henry van Dyke[16]

When Michael Faraday, the nineteenth-century English physicist, was dying, some of his conferees were eager to obtain from him a brief statement of his final conclusions. "What," they asked, "are your speculations?" "Speculations!" he exclaimed. "I have none. I am resting on certainties. For I know whom I have believed and am persuaded that he is able to keep that which I have committed unto him against that day."—Fred R. Chenault

Our answer to death can only be a theological answer. No doctor, no medicine, no mechanism, no man can save us. Only the ultimate power of God can reach us when we have passed beyond the reach of men. There is no other alternative than trusting in him. Only in this trust, only in him, can we die and live courageously.—Albert C. Journey[17]

E. Stanley Jones once saw some rug weavers in northern India. Patiently, week after week and month after month, they wove the rug. Dr. Jones felt that the work seemed futile, for the rug was filled with many imperfections. But he was looking at the wrong side of the rug, and when he went around to the weaver's side and saw the beautiful pattern that was unfolding, he understood the meaning of patience. So as we look upon the human scene with its pain and suffering, we see the wrong side of God's pattern. One day we shall see his purpose. Now we see the blotches, blurs, and imperfections, but we may also know something of his plan, purpose, and patience in it all.—John A. Lensink

If there be a design in this universe and in this world in which we live, there must be a designer. Who can behold the inexplicable mysteries of the universe without believing that there is a design for all mankind and also a designer? Who would persuasively contend that this work of the Great Designer could only end in oblivion, in destruction without a trace? Who will contend that this—the noblest work of the Great Designer—man, with dominion over all living things; man, with a brain and a will, with a mind and a soul; man, with intelligence and divinity—should come to an end when the Spirit forsakes its earthly temple?—Everett M. Dirksen

I am standing upon the seashore. A ship at my side spreads her white sails to the morning breeze and starts for the blue ocean. She is an object of beauty and strength, and I stand and watch her until at length she hangs a speck of white cloud just where the sea and sky come down to mingle with each other. Then someone at my side says: "There! She's gone!"

Gone where? Gone from my sight—that is all. She is just as large in mast and hull and spar as she was when she left my side, and just as able to bear her load of living freight to the place of destination. Her diminished size is in me, not in her; and just at the moment when someone at my side says, "There! She's gone!" there are other eyes watching her coming, and other voices ready to take up the glad shout, "There she comes!"

People think God is destroying them because he is tuning them. The violinist screws up the key till the tense cord sounds the concert pitch; but it is not to break it but to use it tunefully that he stretches the string on the musical rack.—H.W.B.

Some specialists train canaries to sing by putting them in a dark room. After a bit they turn on a music box. That is how God taught some of us to sing. We are made perfect through suffering, and we would never have learned the heavenly music but for the suffering and the dark valley.

That is the eastern light which fills the valley of time with wonderful beams of glory. It is the great dawn in which we find the promise of our own day. Everything wears a new face in the light of our Lord's Resurrection. I once watched the dawn on the East Coast of England. Before there was a gray streak in the sky everything was held in grimmest gloom. The toil of the two fishing boats seemed very somber. The sleeping houses on the shore looked like the abodes of death. Then came gray light, and then the sun, and everything was transfigured! Every window in every cottage caught the reflected glory, and the fishing boats glittered in morning radiance. So everything is transfigured in the Risen Christ.—John H. Jowett

In years gone by and in some areas today, we are accustomed to seeing storm cellars or man-made caves for protection from cyclones or violent winds. Those cellars served as protection only for those who took refuge in them. The storm would continue, but he who took refuge within was safe. So it is with those who trust in God, who has revealed his goodness and love in Jesus Christ. He knoweth them that put their trust in him. And only God knows. He is the final Judge of the measure of our faith.—John Arend Lensink

In an Eastern land was an ancient tomb which, men said, had been raised above a mighty conqueror. Now, this tomb was cunningly devised, to the intent that no one should enter it. For generation upon generation it remained closed. But after many, many years an ingenious craftsman found wherein the secret of the entrance lay and opened the door that had been shut for two thousand years.

Then men entered into the tomb with awe. They found in the midst thereof the body of the ancient king, embalmed with spices, and in his shriveled hand lay the root of a lily.

One took the bulb, which had lain in the dead king's palm for sixty generations, and planted it in the ground; and the Earth gave it of her fatness, and the clouds spared it of their moisture, and the sun smiled upon it and gave it warmth, so that it burst into life. In the springtime it put forth leaves above the Earth, and in the summer it bore a flower of exceeding beauty, which men came to look upon and admire. At last a wise man saw it and, as he marveled at its loveliness, said, "If thy Maker can recall thee to life after two thousand years, surely he can recall me also."—John Jowett

A little boy had been put to bed by his father in a bedroom next to the study. There was no light save the shaded study lamp by which the father was reading. Soon there came a call from the next room: "Daddy, I want a drink of water." The father rose and gave the boy a sip of water. Then there came another call: "Daddy, are you still there?" "Yes, my son, go to sleep." "Daddy, are you going to stay right there?" "Yes, my son, go to sleep." And the final call was, "Daddy, is your face turned toward me?" When the same answer came, the boy, assured of safety, fell quietly asleep.

Today we all want to make sure that God's face is still turned toward us. We know that in time the clouds will lift and the sun will shine again. Peace, love, and joy must return to the world as long as God has his face turned toward us.—F. S. Eitelgeorge

On a certain date in 1946, a lover of beauty stopped overnight in San Francisco to see the Golden Gate Bridge. To his dismay he found it enveloped in fog. Just before he had to leave in order to catch the train, he watched the fog begin to rise. Soon he could see the upright piers and all that lay between, but nothing of the anchorage at either end. He could look at the suspension span, but not at what supported that massive structure. Thus he beheld a parable of life on earth. Life comes out of an eternity that we cannot see and leads into another eternity that we cannot know. But still we need not fear about the span that we call life. We know the Builder and Maker. His name is God. We trust him for time and for eternity. Why? Because of the Resurrection!—Andrew W. Blackwood

In the ruins of Ross Castle at Killarney are the graves of the ancient kings of Ireland. On their tombstones may still be deciphered the symbols of royalty; but close beside them are other monuments, marked with the transverse sword and cross. "These," said the guide, "are the tombs of crusaders."

> Their swords are rust;
> Their good steeds dust;
> Their souls are with their God, we trust.
> —D.J.B.

REMEMBRANCE OF HEROES.   There is no royal road to renown. There is no soft couch of ease for him who would win his way to honor and fame, or gain a noble name. There is a way that is hard, a hill called "Difficulty" to be met and overcome. All our blessings, in one way or another, are associated with suffering.—E. J. Nickerson

God grant that all who watch today
Beside their sepulchers of loss,
May find the great stone rolled away
May see at last, with vision clear,
The shining angel standing near,
And through the dimly lighted soul
Again may joy's evangel roll
The glory of the cross.
—Julia H. Thayer

Edward Gibbon's sneers at Christianity are well known. He takes his place among the greatest historians of all time, yet—as Dean Stanley once observed—his sneers do not alter the fact that his great history entitled *The Decline and Fall of the Roman Empire* might equally have been called *The Rise and Progress of the Christian Church.* And there, surely, is the true measure of what it has meant and still means "to know Christ and the power of his Resurrection."
—Rev. J. S. Whale

THE NEW SENSE OF PATRIOTISM.   With all of these scars and wounds and pains of separation, we come to Memorial Day with a new sense of patriotism, a new conception of sacrifice, a new horror for war, a new viewpoint of freedom and an increased appreciation of the "land of the free and home of the brave." We come with a hope for the future and a longing for our posterity, praying God to forbid that war again shall molest our homes and disorganize the world.

The day means that while they sleep, with their ears deaf to the sound of cannon and eyes closed to the flash of the Sword, we will decorate with our flowers, weep with our tears, remember with our minds, and cherish with our hearts, thinking first, last and always of our country's fairest manhood, who fell for homes, friends, and freedom.

Poetry

So here hath been dawning
Another blue Day;
Think, wilt thou let it
Slip useless away?
Out of Eternity
This new Day is born;
Into Eternity
At night, will return.
—Matthew Arnold, from "Rugby Chapel"

Oh, say, "He has arrived!"
And not that "He has gone."
May every thought of him
Be in that Land of Morn.
Arrived! To hear His voice
And see His welcoming smile;
And then to greet again
Those he has lost a while.
Arrived! To tread no more
The weary path of pain,
Nor feel the waning strength
The body feels, again.
To be forever free
From all that limits love
In joyful service thus
He now may tireless move.
Then say not, "He has gone,"
Nor think of him as dead;
But say, "In the Father's House
He has arrived"—instead.
—Author unknown

There is not room for Death,
Nor atom that his might could render void:
Thou—*Thou* art Being and Breath,
And what *Thou* art may never be destroyed.
—Emily Brontë, from "Last Lines"

A precious one from us has gone,
A voice we loved is stilled;
A place is empty in our hearts
That never can be filled.
God in his wisdom hath recalled
The boon that he had given;
And though the body slumbers here
The soul is safe in heaven.
—Anonymous poem on a funeral card, 1905

So live, that when thy summons come to join
The innumerable caravan, which moves
To that mysterious realm, where each shall take
His chamber in the silent halls of death,

Thou go not, like the quarry slave at night,
Scourged to his dungeon, but, sustained and soothed
By an unfaltering trust, approach thy grave
Like one who wraps the drapery of his couch
About him, and lies down to pleasant dreams.
—William Cullen Bryant, from "Thanatopsis"

More homelike seems the vast unknown,
Since they have entered there;
To follow them were not so hard,
Wherever they may fare;
They cannot be where God is not,
On any sea or shore;
Whate'er betides, Thy love abides,
Our God, forever more.
—John White Chadwick, from "Auld Lang Syne"

When Death, the angel of our higher dreams,
Shall come, far ranging from the hills of light
He will not catch me unaware; for I
Shall be as now communing with the dawn.
For I shall make all haste to follow him
Along the valley, up the misty slope
Where life lets go and Life at last is born.
There I shall find the dreams that I have lost
On toilsome earth, and they will guide me on,
Beyond the mists unto the farthest height.
I shall not grieve except to pity those
Who cannot hear the songs that I shall hear.
—Thomas Curtis Clark, "The Journey"

Though dead, not dead;
Not gone, though fled;
Not lost, though vanished.
In the great gospel and tree creed,
He is yet risen indeed;
Christ is yet risen.
—Arthur Hugh Clough, from "Easter Day"

Let them in, Peter, they are very tired;
Give them the couches where the angels sleep.
Let them wake whole again to new dawns fired

With sun, not war. And may their peace be deep.
Remember where the broken bodies lie . . .
And give them things they like. Let them make noise.
God knows how young they were to have to die!
Give swing bands, not gold harps, to these our boys.
Let them love, Peter—they have had no time—
Girls sweet as meadow wind, with flowering hair . . .
They should have trees and bird song, hills to climb—
The taste of summer in a ripened pear.
Tell them how they are missed. Say not to fear;
It's going to be all right with us down here.
—Elma Dean

O may I join the choir invisible
Of those immortal dead who live again
In minds made better by their presence: live
In pulses stirred to generosity,
In deeds of daring rectitude, in scorn
For miserable aims that end with self,
In thought sublime that pierce the night like stars,
And with their mild persistence urge man's search
To vaster issues.
—George Eliot, from "O, May I Join the Choir Invisible"

At the round earth's imagined corners, blow
Your trumpets, Angels, and arise, arise
From death, you numberless infinities
Of souls, and to your scattered bodies go,
All whom the flood did, and fire shall o'erthrow,
All whom war, dearth, age, agues, tyrannies,
Despair, law, chance, hath slain, and whose eyes
Shall behold God, and never taste death's woe.
But let them sleep, Lord, and me mourn a space,
For if above all these, my sins abound,
'Tis late to ask abundance of thy grace,
when we are there; here on this lowly ground,
Teach me how to repent; for that's a good
As if thou hadst sealed my pardon, with thy blood.
—John Donne, *Holy Sonnets VII*

Who struggles up the tortuous peaks
Roams the hills with easy stride.

Who storms across the widest seas
Embarks upon a pond with casual mien.
Who beholds the majesty of God
Is fearless in the presence of mortality.
—Franklin Elmer Jr.

The Body of
B Franklin Printer,
(Like the Cover of an old Book
Its Contents torn out
And stript of its Lettering and Gilding)
Lies here, Food for Worms,
But the Work shall not be lost;
For it will (as he believ'd) appear once more,
In a new and more elegant Edition
Revised and corrected,
By the Author.
—Benjamin Franklin

When I go down to the sea by ship,
And Death unfurls her sail,
Weep not for me, for there will be
A living host on another coast
To beckon and cry, "All hail!"
—Robert Freeman, from "Beyond the Horizon"

Prayer the Church's banquet, Angels' age,
God's breath in man returning to his birth,
The soul in paraphrase, heart in pilgrimage,
The Christian plummet sounding heaven and earth;
Engine against th'Almighty, sinners' tower,
Reversèd thunder, Christ-side-piercing spear,
The six-days world transposing in an hour,
A kind of tune, which all things hear and fear;
Softness, and peace, and joy, and love, and bliss,
Exalted Manna, gladness of the best,
Heaven in ordinary, man well drest,
The milky way, the bird of Paradise,
Church-bells beyond the stars heard, the souls blood,
The land of spices; something understood.
—George Herbert, from "Prayer"

Build thee more stately mansions, O my soul,
As the swift seasons roll!
Leave thy low-vaulted past!
Let each new temple, nobler than the last,
Shut thee from heaven with a dome more vast,
Till thou at length are free,
Leaving thine outgrown shell by life's unresting sea!
—Oliver Wendell Holmes, from "The Chambered Nautilus"

If I should suddenly be called to go
With Death, on some far journey, on a day
When Life besought me joyously to stay—
Why should I then consider him my foe!
He has appeared so often—now I know
That he is but the guide upon the way
To such divine adventures as we may
Not even dream of here on earth below.
Death takes the film of earth-dust from our eyes
And frees the spirit from its flesh outworn,
That we may journey through the morning skies
Within the everlasting arms upborne,
Till on our new-found vision shall arise
The glory of our resurrection morn.
—Annie Lees Huget, "If I Should Suddenly Be Called"

And Jesus took his own hand and wiped away her tears,
And he smoothed the furrows from her face,
And the angels sang a little song,
And Jesus rocked her in his arms,
And kept a-saying: Take your rest,
Take your rest.

Weep not, weep not,
She is not dead;
She's resting in the bosom of Jesus.
—James Weldon Johnson, "Go Down, Death," from *God's Trombones*

If everything is lost, thanks be to God
If I must see it go, watch it go,
Watch it fade away, die
Thanks be to God that He is all I have
And if I have Him not, I have nothing at all

Nothing at all, only a farewell to the wind
Farewell to the grey sky
Goodbye, God be with you evening October sky.
If all is lost, thanks be to God,
For He is He, and I, I am only I.
—Dom Julian, "If Everything Is Lost"

(Bass drum beaten loudly.)
Booth led boldly with his big bass drum—
(Are you washed in the blood of the Lamb?)
The Saints smiled gravely and they said: "He's come."
(Are you washed in the blood of the Lamb?)
Walking lepers followed, rank on rank,
Lurching bravos from the ditches dank,
Drabs from the alleyways and drug fiends pale—
Minds still passion-ridden, soul-powers frail—
Vermin-eaten saints with moldy breath,
Unwashed legions with the ways of Death—
(Are you washed in the blood of the Lamb?)
(Banjos.)
Every slum had sent its half-a-score
The round world over. (Booth had groaned for more.)
Every banner that the wide world flies
Bloomed with glory and transcendent dyes.
Big-voiced lasses made their banjos bank;
Tranced, fanatical they shrieked and sang;
"Are you washed in the blood of the Lamb?"
Hallelujah! It was queer to see
Bull-necked convicts with that land make free.
Loons with trumpets blowed a blare, blare, blare
On, on upward thro' the golden air!
(Are you washed in the blood of the Lamb?)
(Bass drum slower and softer.)
Booth died blind and still by faith he trod,
Eyes still dazzled by the ways of God.
Booth led boldly, and he looked the chief,
Eagle countenance in sharp relief,
Beard a-flying, air of high command
Unabated in that holy land.
(Sweet flute music.)
Jesus came from out the court-house door,
Stretched his hands above the passing poor.

Booth saw not, but led his queer ones there
Round and round the mighty court-house square.
Then, in an instant all that blear review
Marched on spotless, clad in raiment new.
The lame were straightened, withered limbs uncurled
And blind eyes opened on a new, sweet world.
(Bass drum louder.)
Drabs and vixens in a flash made whole!
Gone was the weasel-head, the snout, the jowl!
Sages and sibyls now, and athletes clean,
Rulers of empires, and of forests green!
(Grand chorus of all instruments. Tambourines to the foreground.)
The hosts were sandalled, and their wings were fire!
(Are you washed in the blood of the Lamb?)
But their noise played havoc with the angel-choir.
(Are you washed in the blood of the Lamb?)
Oh, shout Salvation! It was good to see
Kings and Princes by the Lamb set free.
The banjos rattled and the tambourines
Jing-jing-jingled in the hands of Queens.
(Reverently sung, no instruments.)
And when Booth halted by the curb for prayer
He saw his Master thro' the flag-filled air.
Christ came gently with a robe and crown
For Booth the soldier, while the throng knelt down.
He saw King Jesus. They were face to face,
And he knelt a-weeping in that holy place.
Are you washed in the blood of the Lamb?
—Vachel Lindsay, "General William Booth Enters Heaven"

Where are Elmer, Herman, Bert, Tom and Charley,
The weak of will, the strong of arm, the clown, the boozer, the fighter?
All, all are sleeping on the hill.
One passed in a fever,
One was burned in a mine,
One was killed in a brawl,
One died in a jail,
One fell from a bridge toiling for children and wife—
All, all are sleeping, sleeping, sleeping on the hill.
Where are Ella, Kate, Mag, Lizzie and Edith,
The tender heart, the simple soul, the loud, the proud, the happy one?—

All, all are sleeping on the hill.
One died in shameful child-birth,
One of a thwarted love,
One at the hands of a brute in a brothel,
One of a broken pride, in the search for heart's desire;
One after life in far-away London and Paris
Was brought to her little space by Ella and Kate and Mag—
All, all are sleeping, sleeping, sleeping on the hill.
Where are Uncle Isaac and Aunt Emily,
And old Towny Kincaid and Sevigne Houghton,
And Major Walker who had talked with venerable men of
   the revolution?—
All, all are sleeping on the hill.
They brought them dead sons from the war,
And daughters whom life had crushed,
And their children fatherless, crying—
All, all are sleeping, sleeping, sleeping on the hill.
Where is Old Fiddler Jones
Who played with life all his ninety years,
Braving the sleet with bared breast,
Drinking, rioting, thinking neither of wife nor kin,
Nor gold, nor love, nor heaven?
Lo! He babbles of the fish-frys of long ago,
Of the horse-races of long ago at Clary's Grove,
Of what Abe Lincoln said
One time at Springfield.
—Edgar Lee Masters, "The Hill," from *Spoon River Anthology*

There is no death! The stars go down
To rise upon some other shore,
And bright in heaven's jeweled crown
They shine for evermore.
There is no death! The forest leaves
Convert to life the viewless air;
The rocks disorganize to feed
The hungry moss they bear.
There is no death! The dust we tread
Shall change beneath the summer showers
To golden grain, or mellow fruit,
Or rainbow-tinted flowers.
And ever near us, though unseen,

The dear immortal spirits tread;
For all the boundless universe
Is life—there are no dead!
—John L. McCreery, from "There Is No Death"

I am not resigned to the shutting away of loving hearts in the
    hard ground.
So it is, and so it will be, for so it has been, time out of mind:
Into the darkness they go, the wise and the lovely. Crowned
With lilies and with laurel they go; but
I am not resigned.
—Edna St. Vincent Millay, from "Dirge Without Music"

You are not dead—Life has but set you free!
Your years of life were like a lovely song,
The last sweet poignant notes of which, held long,
Passed into silence while we listened, we
Who loved you listened still expectantly!
And we about you whom you moved among
Would feel that grief for you were surely wrong—
You have but passed beyond where we can see.
For us who knew you, dread of age is past!
You took life, tiptoe, to the very last;
It never lost for you its lovely look:
You kept your interest in its thrilling book;
To you Death came no conqueror; in the end—
You merely smiled to greet another friend!
—Roselle Mercier Montgomery, "On the Death of an Aged Friend"

I shall go forth some day
Forgetting the foolishness of song and rhyming,
And slowly travel life's road until twilight
Whispers: "This is the end of earth's journey;
Your pathway
Is now up, past the stars;
Keep on climbing."
With quick intake of breath,
Eyes wide with wonder at the white gleaming
Chalice of exquisite revelation . . .
I shall drink, and drinking know the renascence
From death,

And be done with all doubt,
And all dreaming.
—John Richard Moreland, from "The Final Quest"

Pilot, how far from home?—
Not far, not far tonight,
A flight of spray, a sea-bird's flight,
A flight of tossing foam,
And then the lights of home.
And, yet again, how far?
And seems the way so brief?
Those lights beyond the roaring reef
Were lights of moon and star,
Far, far, none knows how far!
Pilot, how far from home?
The great stars pass away
Before Him as a flight of spray,
Moons as a flight of foam!
I see the lights of home!
—Alfred Noyes, "Lights of Home"

In the beginning was God,
Today is God,
Tomorrow will be God.
Who can make an image of God?
He has no body.
He is as a word which comes out of your mouth.
That word! It is no more,
It is past, and still it lives!
So is God.
—Pygmy hymn

Tomorrow I shall die.
I feel the coming of my grave.
Hereafter I shall fly
On wings of morning. Death's cold wave
Affrights me not at all;
I schooled me at the school of Christ.
And when in death I fall,
I answer to a holy tryst.
—Bishop William Alfred Quayle, "The Passionate Man's Pilgrimage"

Give me my scallop shell of quiet,
My staff of Faith to walk upon,
My Scrip of Joy, Immortal diet,
My bottle of salvation;
My gown of glory, hope's true gage,
And thus I'll take my pilgrimage.
Blood must be my body's balmer,
No other balm will there be given
Whilst my soul like a white Palmer
Travels to the land of heaven, Over the silver mountains,
Where spring the Nectar fountains;
And there I'll kiss
The Bowl of bliss,
And drink my eternal fill
On every milken hill.
My soul will be a dry before,
but after it, will ne'er thirst more.
And by the happy blissful way
More peaceful Pilgrims I shall see,
That have shook off their gowns of clay,
And go appareled fresh like me.
I'll bring the first
To slake their thirst
And then to taste those Nectar suckets
At the clear wells
Where sweetness dwells,
Drawn up by Saints in crystal buckets.
And when our bottle and all we,
Are filled with immorality:
Then the holy paths we'll travel
Strewed with Rubies thick as gravel,
Ceilings of diamonds, sapphire floors,
High walls of Coral and Pearl Bowers.
From thence to heaven's Bribeles hall
Where no corrupted voices brawl,
No Conscience molten into gold,
Nor forg'd accusers bought and sold,
No cause defend, nor vain spent journey,
For there Christ is the King's Attorney:
Who pleads for all without degrees,
And he has Angels, but no fees.

When the grand twelve million Jury,
Of our sins with sinful fury,
Gainst our souls' black verdicts give,
Christ pleads his death, and then we live,
Be thou my speaker taintless pleader,
Unblotted Lawyer, true proceeder,
Thou movest salvation even for alms:
Not a bribed lawyer's palms.
And this is my eternal plea,
To him that made Heaven, Earth and Sea,
Seeing my flesh must die so soon,
And want a head to dine next noon,
Just at the stroke when my veins start and spread
Set on my soul an everlasting head.
Then am I ready like a palmer fit,
To tread those blest paths which before I writ.
—Sir Walter Raleigh (allegedly written shortly before his execution)

I have lived
Because the faith within me that is life
Endures to live, and shall, till soon or late,
Death, like a friend unseen, shall say to me
My toil is over and my work begun.
—Edwin Arlington Robinson

Sometimes I think God grew tired of making
Thunder and mountains and dawn redly breaking;
Weary of fashioning gorges and seas,
Sometimes I think God grew tired of heating
The earth with the sun, and of fully completing
The whole of the world! God grew tired, and so
He took just a bit of the soft afterglow,
He took just a petal or two from a flower,
And took a songbird from a sweet scented bower.
The dewdrops He took from the heart of a rose,
And added the freshness of each breeze that blows
Across long green meadows. He took all the love
Left over from his heaven above.
His kind fingers mixed them—God's hand and no other—
And made, for the first time, the soul of a mother.
—Margaret E. Sangster, "The Soul of a Mother"

The waves of the ocean imitate the rolls of the
Heavenly music that rolls in heaven.
O le ul lum ul la, O le ul lum ul la,
O glory to God for this heavenly display.
The wheels of a time-piece imitate the flows of the
Heavenly love that flows in heaven.
Chorus.
The wings of an eagle imitate the seraphim that soar
In the heavens of heavenly love.
Chorus.
—Shaker Song

Peace, peace! He is not dead, he doth not sleep—
He hath awakened from the dream of life—
'Tis we, who lost in stormy visions, keep
with phantoms and unprofitable strife.
—Percy Bysshe Shelley, from "On the Death of John Keats"

Sunset and evening star,
And one clear call for me!
And may there be no moaning of the bar,
When I put out to sea,
But such a tide as moving seems asleep,
Too full for sound and foam,
When that which drew from out the boundless deep
Turns again home.
Twilight and evening bell,
And after that the dark!
And may there be no sadness or farewell,
When I embark;
For tho' from out our bourne of Time and Place
The flood may bear me far,
I hope to see my Pilot face to face
When I have crost the bar.
—Alfred, Lord Tennyson, "Crossing the Bar"

Death, and darkness get you packing,
Nothing now to man is lacking,
All your triumphs now are ended.
And what Adam marr'd, is mended;
Graves are beds now for the weary,
Death a nap, to wake more merry;

Youth now, full of pious duty,
Seeks in thee for perfect beauty,
The weak, the aged tir'd, with length
Of daies, from thee look for new strength,
And Infants with their pangs Contest
As pleasant, as if with the brest;
Then, unto him, who thus hath thrown
Even to Contempt thy kingdome down,
And by his blood did us advance
Unto his own Inheritance,
To him be glory, power, praise,
From this, unto the last of daies.
—Henry Vaughan, "Easter Hymn"

I cannot think that thou are far,
Since near at need the angels are,
And when the sunset gates unbar
Shall I not see thee, waiting, stand,
And white against the evening star
The welcome of the beckoning hand.
—John Greenleaf Whittier

Yet Love will dream, and Faith will trust
(Since He who knows our need is just)
that somehow, somewhere, meet we must.
Alas, for him who never sees
The stars shine through his cypress-trees!
Who, hopeless, lays his dead away,
Nor looks to see the breaking day
Across the mournful marbles play!
Who hath not learned, in hours of faith,
The truth to flesh and sense unknown,
That Life is ever lord of Death,
And Love can never lose its own!
—John Greenleaf Whittier, from "Snow-Bound"

I know not what the future hath
Of marvel or surprise,
Assured alone that life or death
His mercy underlies.
And if my heart and flesh are weak
To bear an untried pain;

The bruised reed He will not break
But strengthen and sustain.
And Thou, O Lord, by whom are seen
Thy creatures as they be;
Forgive me if too close I lean
My human heart on thee.
And so beside the silent sea
I wait the muffled oar;
No harm from Him can come to me
On ocean or on shore.
I know not where His islands lift
Their fronded palms in air;
I only know I cannot drift
Beyond His love and care.
—John Greenleaf Whittier, from "The Eternal Goodness"

It seemeth such a little way to me,
Across to that strange country, the Beyond;
And yet, not strange, for it has grown to be
The home of those of whom I am so fond;
They make it seem familiar and most dear,
As journeying friends bring distant countries near.
So close it lies that when my sight is clear
I think I almost see the gleaming strand;
I know, I feel, that those who've gone from here
Come near enough sometimes to touch my hand;
I often think, but for our veiléd eyes,
We should find heaven right about us lies.
And so for me there is no sting to death,
And so the grave has lost its victory;
It is but crossing with abated breath
And white, set face, a little strip of sea,
To find the loved ones waiting on the shore,
More beautiful, more precious than before.
—Ella Wheeler Wilcox, from "The Beyond"

She lived unknown, and few could know
When Lucy ceased to be;
But she is in her grave, and, oh,
The difference to me!
—William Wordsworth, from "Lucy"

Opening Sentences and Calls to Worship

T he first words you say in worship are very important, and perhaps even more so at funerals and crisis-related services than on Sundays, where you are more likely to have choir and organ helping to prepare the congregation. Your tone of voice and body language, as well as the words you speak, set the tone of the service and help (or hinder) the congregation in worshiping God.

The following opening sentences and calls to worship are arranged simply. Those from Scripture are given before those that come from other sources. The first six are equally suitable for crisis-related services and funerary rites. After the general calls to worship, opening sentences suitable for the funerals of infants and children and for the funerals of suicides are presented. Most of these calls to worship are said by the leader and require no congregational response; this means that printing a bulletin is not necessary.

FOR SERVICES OF CRISIS OR SORROW

Cast your burden on the Lord, and God will sustain you (Ps. 55:22a).

Blessed be the God who consoles us in all our affliction, so that we may be able to console those who are in any affliction with the consolation with which we ourselves are consoled by God (2 Cor. 1:3a, 4).

Blessed be the Lord, who has heard the voice of my supplications! The Lord is my strength and my shield, in whom my heart trusts (Ps. 28:6–7a).

The Lord is near to the brokenhearted, and saves the crushed in spirit (Ps. 34:18).

God is our refuge and strength, a very present help in trouble (Ps. 46:1).

God, you are near to all who call on you honestly. You fulfill the desire of all who fear you; you hear their cry, and save them (Ps. 145:18–19).

FOR FUNERALS

Our help is in the name of the Lord, who made heaven and earth, and in our Savior Jesus Christ, who abolished death and brought life and immortality to light through the gospel (Ps. 124:8; 2 Tim. 1:10).

This is indeed the will of my Father, that all who see the Son and believe in him may have eternal life; and I will raise them up on the last day (John 6:40).

Jesus said, "I am the resurrection and the life. He that believeth in me, though he were dead, yet shall he live, and whosoever liveth and believeth in me shall never die" (John 11:25–26).

All of us who were baptized in Christ Jesus were baptized into his death. We were therefore buried with him through baptism into death in order that, just as Christ was raised from the dead through the glory of the Father, we too may live a new life. If we have been united with him in his death, we will certainly also be united with him in his Resurrection (Rom. 6:3–5).

We do not live to ourselves, and we do not die to ourselves. If we live, we live to the Lord, and if we die, we die to the Lord; so then, whether we live or whether we die, we are the Lord's. For to this end Christ died and lived again, so that we might be Lord of both the dead and the living (Rom. 14:7–9).

As it is written, things which eye saw not, and ear heard not, and which entered not into the heart of man—whatsoever things God prepared for them that love him. But unto us God revealed them through the Spirit; for the Spirit searcheth all things, yea, the deep things of God (1 Cor. 2:9–10).

Dying, Christ destroyed our death. Rising, Christ restored our life. Christ will come again in glory. As in baptism [name of deceased] put on Christ, so in Christ may [name of deceased] be clothed with glory. Here and now, dear friends, we are God's children. What we shall be has not yet been revealed; but we know that when he appears, we shall be like him, for we shall see him as he is. Those who have this hope purify themselves as Christ is pure.

LEADER: What is your only comfort in life and in death?

PEOPLE: That I am not my own, but belong, body and soul, in life and in death, to my faithful Savior Jesus Christ.—from *The Heidelberg Catechism*[1]

Dearly beloved: We are gathered today to pay our final tribute of respect to that which was mortal of our deceased loved one and friend. To you members of the family who mourn your loss, we especially offer our deep and sincere sympathy. May we share with you the comfort afforded by God's Word for such a time as this: [*followed by several Scripture sentences*].—Ritual of the Church of the Nazarene[2]

Friends, we have gathered here to praise God and to witness to our faith as we celebrate the life of [name of deceased]. We come together in grief, acknowledging our human loss. May God grant us grace, that in pain we may find comfort, in sorrow hope, in death resurrection.

O Lord our God, in Whom we live, and move, and have our being,

Have mercy upon us.

O Lord our God, Who dost not afflict willingly, nor grieve the children of men,

Leave thy peace with us.

O Lord our God, Who hast brought life and immortality to light through Jesus Christ our Savior,

Bless us and comfort us, we humbly pray.—Ritual of the Moravian Church

Let us worship God and remember before him his servant [name of deceased]. In the name of the Father, the Son, and the Holy Spirit. Amen.—Ritual of the Evangelical Covenant Church

Blessed is our God always, now, and ever, and unto ages of ages.
Amen.

The grace of the Lord Jesus Christ and the love of God and the fellowship of the Holy Spirit be with you all.

And also with you.

The grace and peace of God our Father and the Lord Jesus Christ be with you.

And also with you.

The grace and peace of God our Father, who raised Jesus from the dead, be always with you.

And also with you.
May the Father of mercies, the God of all consolation, be with you.
And also with you.[3]

너희는 마음에 근심하지 말라.
Pronunciation: Nuh hee nan mah eum eeh kan shim hah jee mahl lah.
Translation: Let not your hearts be troubled.

FOR THE FUNERAL OF A STILLBORN CHILD, INFANT, OR CHILD

As a father has compassion on his children, so the Lord has compassion on those who fear him; for he knows how we are formed, he remembers that we are dust. But from everlasting to everlasting the Lord's love is with those who fear him, and his righteousness with their children's children (Ps. 103:13, 14, 17).

Dear friends, we have gathered here in our grief to draw on the strength the Lord provides and to witness to our faith in Christ, who is the Resurrection and the Life. We acknowledge the human loss of [name of the deceased], son/daughter of [name of deceased's mother] and [name of deceased's father]. A precious life was conceived. Sadly we accept this death. May the Lord grant each of us grace, that in the midst of our pain we may find comfort; in our sorrow, hope; in death, resurrection.

FOR A SUICIDE

Brothers and sister, we meet together in perplexity, confusion, and anguish. Some of us may perhaps be burdened with inexplicable guilt. Our brother/sister [name of deceased] has taken his/her own life. We gather together to ask for healing and peace. We have great need of the Holy Spirit of God. Let us first attend to our feelings of guilt, whether these are justified or unjustified. Let us ask for God's forgiveness and that of our community, for us and for our deceased brother/sister, in the age-old words of King David. He was an impulsive man, capable of great sin but capable also of immense humility, repentance, and generosity. [*Here follows a reading from Ps. 51.*][4]

We come today as a thirsty land crying out for rain, as a hungry heart longing for nourishment, as a lonely and frightened sheep pleading for rescue by the Good Shepherd, as that same sheep safe in the arms of the rescuer.

We hear the voice of our heavenly Father say, "Come to me, all you who are weary and burdened, and I will give you rest. Take my yoke upon you and learn from me, for I am gentle and humble in heart, and you will find rest for your souls."

Even though we are hurting and have unanswered questions, may "the peace of God, which passes all understanding . . . guard your hearts and your minds in Christ Jesus." May the Father of compassion and the God of all comfort be with each of us as we now bow in prayer before him.[5]

Scripture Readings

The following readings are appropriate for funerals and worship in times of crisis. The left-hand column gives the citation. The right-hand column notes whether it is especially appropriate for a particular part of the service, such as opening sentence, unison recitation, and so on, or for a particular type of service, such as the funeral of a child.

Reading	Key Phrase or Idea	Part of Service
Old Testament and Apocrypha		
Genesis 15:15	Abraham's death	Funeral of aged person
Exodus 15	Canticle of deliverance	
Numbers 6:24–26	The Lord bless you and keep you	Benediction
Deuteronomy 33:27	The eternal God is your refuge	Opening sentence
Joshua 1:9	Be strong and of good courage	Opening sentence
Joshua 3:14–4:7	Crossing over Jordan	
2 Samuel 12:18–24	On the seventh day the child died	Child's funeral
Proverbs 31:10–12, 28–31	Her children rise up, call her blessed.	Woman's funeral
Job 1:21	The Lord gives, the Lord takes away	
Job 5:17–26	Come to grave in ripe old age	Funeral of old person
Job 14:1–14	Man that is born of woman . . .	

Reading	Key Phrase or Idea	Part of Service

Old Testament and Apocrypha, continued

Reading	Key Phrase or Idea	Part of Service
Job 19:25–27	I know that my Redeemer lives	Committal
Ecclesiastes 3:1–15	To everything there is a season	
Isaiah 25:6–10	God will swallow up death	
Isaiah 26:1–4, 19	Thou wilt keep him in perfect peace	Crisis or funeral
Isaiah 35:1–6, 10	Zion restored	
Isaiah 40:1–11	Comfort, comfort my people	
Isaiah 40:6b, 8	The grass withers, the flower fades	After readings
Isaiah 40:28–31	They that wait upon the Lord	Crisis or funeral
Isaiah 41:10	Fear not, for I am with you	Opening sentence
Isaiah 43:1–3	I have called you by name	Crisis or funeral
Isaiah 55:1–3, 6–13	Seek the Lord while he may be found	
Isaiah 65:17–25	New heavens and new earth	Untimely death
Isaiah 66:13	As a mother comforts you	Opening sentence
Jeremiah 31:15	Rachel weeping for her children	Stillbirth, miscarriage
Lamentations 3: 22–26	The steadfast love of the Lord	Crisis or funeral
Ezekiel 34:11–16	Shepherd of Israel	
Ezekiel 37:1–14, 21–28	These bones shall live	
Daniel 12:1–3	The final consummation	
Hosea 6:1–3	Come, let us return to the Lord	Healing after tragedy
Jonah 2:1–9	God's mercy to Jonah	
Micah 6:6–8	What does the Lord require?	
Micah 7:18–20	God pardons our iniquity	

Reading	Key Phrase or Idea	Part of Service
Old Testament and Apocrypha, continued		
Nahum 1:7	The Lord is a stronghold in trouble	Crisis, opening
Zechariah 8:1–8	I will return to Zion, and will dwell	
Wisdom 3:1–5	Souls of the righteous in God's hand	
Psalms		
1	Blessed is the one who walks	Crisis or funeral
4	Answer me when I call	The dying, crisis
16:1–2, 5–11	Preserve me, Lord, for I take refuge	
22:1–5, 19, 22–24	My God, why have you forsaken me?	
23	The Lord is my shepherd	Unison recitation
24:3–5	Who may ascend the Lord's hill?	Opening sentence
25:1–7, 10, 14–18, 20–22	To thee, O Lord, I lift up my soul	
27	The Lord is my light	
34	Thanksgiving for deliverance	
34:18	The Lord is near the brokenhearted	Tragic/untimely death
39:4–13	Lord, let me know my end	Funeral of old person
42	As the hart pants for the water	
43	You are the God in whom I take refuge	
46	God is our refuge and strength	
55:22a	Cast your burden on the Lord	Opening sentence
62	For God alone my soul waits	Dying or bereaved
71	In thee, Lord, do I take refuge	
84	How lovely is your dwelling place	
90	Lord, you have been our dwelling place	

Reading	Key Phrase or Idea	Part of Service

Old Testament and Apocrypha, continued

Reading	Key Phrase or Idea	Part of Service
91	He who dwells in the shelter	Dying or bereaved
103	Bless the Lord, O my soul	
116	I love the Lord, because he heard	Crisis or funeral
118	The Lord is my strength and my song	
119:9–12	How can a young man cleanse his way?	
121	I will lift up my eyes to the hills	
124:8	Our help is in the name of the Lord	Opening sentence
126:5–6	Those who sow in tears	Funeral of a child
130	Out of the depths I cry to thee	Suicide, crisis
131	O Lord, my heart is not lifted up	Funeral of a child
139	O Lord, you have searched me	Suicide, crisis
145:18	The Lord is near to all who call	Opening sentence
146	I will praise the Lord as long as I live	
147:3, 5	The Lord heals and binds	Opening sentence

Gospels

Reading	Key Phrase or Idea	Part of Service
Matthew 5:1–12	Blessed are the poor in spirit	Church member
Matthew 6:19–21	Treasures in heaven	
Matthew 11:28–30	Come unto me, all who labor	Crisis or funeral
Matthew 18:1–5, 10	Unless you become like children	Funeral of a child
Matthew 19:13	Let the children come to me	Funeral of a child
Matthew 25:31–40	I was hungry and you gave me food	Church member
Matthew 28:1–10	Resurrection of Jesus	
Mark 4:35–41	Jesus calms the storm	Crisis

Reading	Key Phrase or Idea	Part of Service
Gospels, continued		
Mark 5:35–43	Raising daughter of Jairus	Funeral of a child
Mark 10:13–16	Let the children come to me	Funeral of a child
Luke 7:11–17	Widow of Nain's son raised	Funeral of a youth
Luke 12:37–40	Blessed are those servants	Unexpected death
Luke 15:11–32	The prodigal son	Suicide, other tragedy
Luke 24:1–6	Resurrection of Jesus	
Luke 24:13–35	The Emmaus road encounter	Funeral with Eucharist
John 3:3–17	God so loved the world	
John 5:19–29	The Father raises the dead and gives them life	
John 6:35–40	I am the bread of life	Funeral with Eucharist
John 10:1–18	Jesus the Good Shepherd	
John 11:23–25	Your brother will rise again.	
John 11:25	I am the Resurrection and the Life	Opening sentence
John 12:23–26	Unless a grain of wheat falls	Committal service
John 14:1–6	Let not your heart be troubled	
John 15:1–17	Jesus, the true vine	
John 16:12–22, 33	Sorrow into joy	
John 20:1–18	Resurrection of Jesus	
John 21:1–14	Post-Resurrection meal by the sea	Funeral with Eucharist
Epistles		
Acts 9:36–42	Raising of Tabitha	Funeral of woman
Acts 10:34–43	Peter's sermon on resurrection	
Acts 16:25–34	Paul and Silas in prison	Crisis
Romans 5:1–11	We are justified by faith	Crisis or funeral
Romans 8:14–23	All who are led by the Spirit of God	Crisis or funeral
Romans 8:25–28	The Spirit intercedes for us	
Romans 8:31–39	If God is for us, who is against us?	Crisis or funeral

Reading	Key Phrase or Idea	Part of Service
Epistles, continued		
Romans 14:7–9	Living or dying, we are the Lord's	
Romans 15:13	The God of hope fill you with all joy	Benediction
1 Corinthians 1:2	Grace and peace from God	Benediction
1 Corinthians 15: 20–28	For as in Adam all die	
1 Corinthians 15: 35–58	The nature of the Resurrection	
2 Corinthians 1:3–4a	God consoles us in affliction	Miscarriage, stillborn
2 Corinthians 4:7–18	Treasure in earthen vessels	
2 Corinthians 5:1	A house not made with hands	Opening sentence
2 Corinthians 5:5–8	Absent from body, present to the Lord	
2 Corinthians 12:1–9	My grace is sufficient for you	Crisis
2 Corinthians 13:14	The grace of the Lord Jesus Christ	Benediction
Ephesians 1:3–10	In Him we have redemption	
Ephesians 1:15–23	Our hope in Christ	
Ephesians 3:14–19	Being rooted and grounded in love	Benediction
Philippians 3:20–21	Our commonwealth is in heaven	
Philippians 4:7	The peace which passes understanding	Benediction
Colossians 1:11–20	May you be strengthened with power	Crisis
Colossians 3:1–17	Raised with Christ	
1 Thessalonians 4: 13–18	The trumpet shall sound	
1 Thessalonians 5:23	The God of peace sanctify you	Benediction
2 Thessalonians 2: 16–17	God's comfort and good hope	Benediction
1 Timothy 1:2	Grace, mercy, and peace	Benediction

Reading	Key Phrase or Idea	Part of Service
Epistles, continued		
2 Timothy 1:10	But now has been revealed	Opening sentence
2 Timothy 2:8–13	Jesus Christ, risen from the dead	
2 Timothy 4:6–8	I have fought the good fight	
Hebrews 2:5–18	Christ's saving work	
Hebrews 4:14–16	A high priest who sympathizes	
Hebrews 9:26–28	Death and judgment	A sermon about death
Hebrews 11:1–3, 6–7, 12–16	The roll call of the faithful	
Hebrews 12:1–2	Surrounded by a cloud of witnesses	
Hebrews 13:5b–8	I will never leave you nor forsake you	
Hebrews 13:20–21	The God of peace who brought back	Benediction
James 5:7–11	Therefore be patient	Dying, crisis
1 Peter 1:3–9	Our hope through the resurrection	
1 Peter 1:3, 4	Our hope through the resurrection	Opening sentence
2 Peter 3:9–13	The Lord is not slow in his promise	
1 John 1:5–9	God is light and in him is no darkness	
1 John 3:1–3	Beloved, we are God's children now	
Jude 24–25	The presence of God's glory	Benediction
Revelation 1:5–6	Unto him that loved us	Benediction
Revelation 7:9–17	The great multitude in heaven	
Revelation 14:12–13	Blessed are the dead	Committal
Revelation 21:1–7	God shall wipe away every tear	
Revelation 22:1–5	Tree and river of life	
Revelation 22:12–14	Behold, I am coming quickly	

Invocations and Opening Prayers

After calling the congregation to worship, an invocation both invites the Spirit of God to be present in worship and leads the congregation into communion with God. An opening prayer also usually acknowledges the occasion of the gathering, whether it is the Lord's Day, a funeral, or something else. Like most collect-form prayers, the invocation contains a petition and, usually, a closing ascription, such as "through Jesus Christ our Lord." The prayer facilitates the transition to music or Scripture readings that follow. The first four of the following opening prayers are suitable for crisis-related services as well as for funerals.

You may want to compose your own invocations, reflecting the season of the church year or mentioning particulars of the situation that has brought people together for worship. Extemporaneous prayer is also appropriate. As you develop your own opening prayers, remember that they should be fairly brief and be prayed in Jesus' name. They will be easier to compose and easier for the congregation to comprehend if they follow collect form.

FOR FUNERALS OR CRISIS-RELATED SERVICES

Grant, we beg of you, Almighty God, unto us who know that we are weak, and who trust in you because we know that you are strong, the gladsome help of your loving-kindness, both here in time and hereafter in eternity. Amen.—Roman Breviary, 11th century and earlier[1]

Comfort, O merciful Father, by your Word and Holy Spirit, all who are afflicted or distressed, and so turn their hearts unto you, that they may serve you in truth, and bring forth fruit to your glory. Be, O Lord, their succor and defense; through Jesus Christ our Lord. Amen.—Philip Melanchthon[2]

Look upon us, O Lord, and let all the darkness of our souls vanish before the beams of your brightness. Fill us with holy love, and open to us the treasures of your wisdom. All our desire is known unto you; therefore, perfect what you have begun, and what your Spirit has awakened us to ask in prayer. We seek your face; turn your fact unto us and show us your glory. Then shall our longing be satisfied and our peace be perfect; through Jesus Christ our Lord. Amen.—St. Augustine[3]

Almighty God, the fountain of all life: thou art our refuge and strength; thou art our help in time of trouble. Enable us, we pray, to put our trust in thee, that we may obtain comfort, and find grace to help in this and every time of need; through Jesus Christ our Lord. Amen.[4]

FOR FUNERALS

O Jesus Christ, our Risen Lord, who in death has gone before us: Grant us the assurance of your presence, that we who are anxious and fearful in the face of death may confidently face the future, in the knowledge that you have prepared a place for all who love you. Amen.

O God, our Father, creator of all, giver and preserver of all life: We confess to you our slowness to accept death as part of your plan for life. We confess our reluctance to commit to you those whom we love. Restore our faith that we may come to trust in your care and providence; through Jesus Christ our Lord. Amen.

O God, the Lord of life, the conqueror of death, our help in every time of trouble, who does not willingly grieve or afflict your children: Comfort us who mourn, and give us grace, in the presence of death, to worship you, that we may have sure hope of eternal life and be enabled to put our whole trust in your goodness and mercy; through Jesus Christ our Lord. Amen.[5]

Almighty God, unto whom all hearts are open, all desires known, and from whom no secrets are hid: cleanse the thoughts of our hearts by the inspiration of your Holy Spirit, that we may perfectly love you, and worthily magnify your holy name, through Christ our Lord. Amen.—Leofric, Bishop of Exeter, 11th century[6]

O God, whose mercies cannot be numbered: Accept our prayers on behalf of thy servant [name of deceased], and grant him/her entrance into the land of light and joy, in the fellowship of thy saints; through Jesus Christ thy Son our Lord, who liveth and reigneth with thee and the Holy Spirit, one God, now and for ever. Amen.[7]

Almighty God, those who die in the Lord still live with you in joy and blessedness. We give you heartfelt thanks for the grace you have bestowed upon your servants who have finished their course in faith and now rest from their labors. May we, with all who have died in the true faith, have perfect fulfillment and joy in your eternal and everlasting glory; through your Son, Jesus Christ our Lord. Amen.[8]

Almighty God and Father, it is our certain faith that your Son, who died on the cross, was raised from the dead, the first fruits of all who have fallen asleep. Grant that through this mystery your servant [name of deceased], who has gone to his/her rest in Christ, may share in the joy of his Resurrection. We ask this through our Lord Jesus Christ, your Son, who lives and reigns with you and the Holy Spirit, one God, for ever and ever. Amen.

DEACON: Have mercy upon us, O God, according to thy great mercy, we beseech thee: hearken, and have mercy.

CHOIR: Lord, have mercy. *(thrice)*

DEACON: Furthermore, we pray for the repose of the soul of the servant of God departed this life, [name of deceased]; and that thou wilt pardon all her/his sins, both voluntary and involuntary.

CHOIR: Lord, have mercy. *(thrice)*

DEACON: That the Lord God will establish his/her soul where the just repose.

CHOIR: Lord have mercy. *(thrice)*

DEACON: The mercies of God, the kingdom of heaven, and the remission of his/her sins, we entreat of Christ, our King Immortal and our God.

CHOIR: Grant it, O Lord.

DEACON: Let us pray to the Lord.

CHOIR: Lord, have mercy.

EXCLAMATION: For thou art the Resurrection, and the Life, and the Repose of thy departed servant, [name of deceased], O Christ our God, and unto thee we ascribe glory, together with thy Father who is from everlasting, and thine all-holy, and good, and life-giving Spirit, now, and ever, and unto ages of ages. Amen.[9]

Benedictions

May almighty God bless you, the Father, and the Son and the Holy Spirit. *Amen.*

The grace of the Lord Jesus Christ, and the love of God, and the fellowship of the Holy Spirit, be with you all, now and evermore. *Amen.*

May the love of God and the peace of the Lord Jesus Christ bless and console us and gently wipe every tear from our eyes: in the name of the Father, and of the Son, and of the Holy Spirit. *Amen.*[1]

With the souls of the righteous dead, give rest, O Savior, to the soul of thy servant, preserving it unto the life of blessedness which is with thee, O thou who lovest mankind. In the place of thy rest, O Lord, where all thy Saints repose, give rest, also, to the soul of thy servant: For thou only lovest mankind. Glory to the Father, and to the Son, and to the Holy Spirit. Thou art the God who descended into hell, and loosed the bonds of the captives: Do thou give rest, also, to the soul of thy servant. Now, and ever, and unto ages of ages. Amen. O Virgin along Pure and Undefiled, who without seed didst bring forth God, pray thou unto him that his/her soul may be saved.[2]

Let us go forth in the name of Christ.
Thanks be to God.

The God of peace, who brought again from the dead our Lord Jesus Christ, the great Shepherd of the sheep, through the blood of the eternal covenant, make you perfect in every good work to do his will, working in you that which is well pleasing in his sight; through Jesus Christ, to whom be glory for ever and ever. *Amen.*

> Alleluia. Christ is risen.
> *The Lord is risen indeed. Alleluia.*
> Let us go forth in the name of Christ.
> Thanks be to God.

The peace of God, which passeth all understanding, keep your hearts and mind in Christ Jesus our Lord; and the blessing of God Almighty: the Father, the Son, and the Holy Spirit, be with you and remain with you always. *Amen.*

May the presence of God the Father give you strength; may the presence of God the Son give you peace; may the presence of God the Holy Spirit give you comfort and love.[3]

> God be in your head, and in your understanding.
> God be in your eyes, and in your looking.
> God be in your mouth, and in your speaking.
> God be in your heart, and in your thinking.
> God be at your end, and at your departing.[4]

The God of grace, who hath called us unto the eternal glory by Christ Jesus, make you perfect, establish, strengthen, settle you. To him be glory and dominion for ever and ever. *Amen.*

Unto him that loved us, and washed us from our sins in his own blood, and hath made us a kingdom, priests to his God and Father—to him be glory and dominion for ever and ever. *Amen.*

May God be merciful to us, and bless us. May he cause his face to shine upon us. May the grace of our Lord Jesus Christ, and the love of God the Father, and the fellowship of the Holy Spirit, be with you all, both now, and on into eternity. *Amen.*[5]

> Que la gracia, la misericoria y la paz de nuestro Señor Jesucristo sean con ustedes ahora y para siempre. *Amen.*
>
> *Pronunciation:* Kay la grass-ee-a, la mee-ser-ee-cor-dee-a la pass de noo-estro Sain-yor Hey-soo-kree-so con oo-sted-ace a-ho-ra-ee see-em-pay. A-main.

Translation: May the grace, the mercy, and the peace of our Lord Jesus Christ be with you now and forever. *Amen.*—Wayne Weld

El Señor los bendiga y los guarde, almas afligidas; el Señor haga resplandecer su rostro sobre ustedes, y tenga de ustedes misericordia. El Señor los ilumine con la laz de su presencia y los de la paz.

Pronunciation: Ail Sain-yor los bain-de-ga ee los goo-är-de, all-mas a-flee hee-das; Ail Sain-yor aw-gaw ray-splan-day-sayr soo row-strow sow-bray oo-sted-ace, ee tain-gaw day oo-sted-ace mee-sayr-ree-cor-dee-a. All Sain-yor lows ee-loo-mee-nay cohn la loose day soo pray-sain-see-a ee lows day la pass. *A-main.*

Translation: The Lord bless you and keep you, afflicted souls; the Lord make his face to shine on you, and have mercy on you. The Lord illumine you with the light of his presence and give you peace. *Amen.*[6]

ONE: The Lord said to Abraham,

MANY: Do not be afraid.

ONE: The Lord said to Isaac,

MANY: Do not be afraid.

ONE: Moses said to the people,

MANY: Do not be afraid.

ONE: Joshua said to the people,

MANY: Do not be afraid.

ONE: Boaz said to Ruth,

MANY: Do not be afraid.

ONE: Jonathan said to David,

MANY: Do not be afraid.

ONE: The angel of the Lord said to Joseph,

MANY: Do not be afraid.

ONE: The angel said to Mary,

MANY: Do not be afraid.

ONE: The angel said to the shepherds,

MANY: Do not be afraid.

ONE: The angel said to the women at the tomb,

MANY: Do not be afraid.

ONE: The Lord said to Paul,

MANY: Do not be afraid.

ONE: And Jesus said,

MANY: Do not be afraid; just have faith.

ONE: Let us not be afraid as we go into the world, fully alive in the love of God through Jesus Christ, our Sovereign and Savior.

ALL: Amen.[7]

Pastoral Prayers

It is often the custom for the pastor to say one or more long extemporaneous or written pastoral prayers during the course of a worship service. These prayers are in addition to the invocation or opening prayer, benediction, and committal prayers. While these vary in length, they are appropriate for use during the service in addition to the specific categories already mentioned.

The length of pastoral prayers may tax the attention span of the congregation. When you pray extemporaneously, you can help them stay focused and truly give voice to their silent prayers by observing a few guidelines. First, have a single theme in the prayer, or if several themes are to be addressed, divide them into focused units, like the sample prayer from the Church of Scotland's *Ordinal and Service Book* provided in this section. Second, let the petitions imply the situation that gives rise to them rather than explaining the situation at length. In the prayer from the *Directory of Public Worship,* for example, grief is acknowledged but not described as though God had no idea of the concept. Third, keep the style consistent throughout the prayer. A prayer that begins by addressing God directly invites the congregation to address God with you. If halfway through you turn and speak to someone else, as in "I ask you to pray for the family, that they may know God's comfort," or "Let us all resolve right now to follow Jesus all the way"—you have, in effect, interrupted a conversation. This bewilders and distracts the congregation as they try to pray with you.

The first three of these prayers is suitable for a crisis-related or funeral service. The fourth prayer may be adapted for a service of cleansing or rededication of things profaned, such as after vandalism or violence in the church—an event almost certainly to be viewed as a crisis by the congregation.

FOR FUNERALS OR CRISIS-RELATED SERVICES

Almighty and most merciful God, who art the strength of the weak, the refreshment of the weary, the comfort of the sorrowful, the help of the tempted, the life of the dying, and the God of all consolation: thou knowest full well the inner weakness of our nature and how we cannot bear our crosses without thy divine aid. Help us, O eternal God, to possess our souls in patience, to maintain unshaken hope in thee, to keep that childlike trust which feels the Father's heart hidden beneath the cross. So shall we be strengthened with power according to thy glorious might, in all patience and long-suffering. So shall we be enabled to endure pain and sorrow, and in the very depth of our sorrow to praise thee with a joyful heart.—Johann Habermann

O holy Father, whose mercies are from everlasting to everlasting, to Thee alone can Thy children flee for refuge in their affliction, trusting in the assurance of Thy love. From the grief that burdens our spirits, from the sense of solitude and loss, from the doubt and fainting of the soul in its trouble, we turn to Thee. Strengthen our feeble faith, we implore Thee; comfort our hearts, and by the Gospel of Thy beloved Son speak peace to our souls. Grant this, O heavenly Father, for Jesus' sake. Amen.[1]

O Lord, support us all the day long of our troublous life, until the shadows lengthen and the evening comes, and the busy world is hushed, and the fever of life is over, and our work is done. Then in Thy mercy grant us a safe lodging, and a holy rest, and peace at the last, through Jesus Christ our Lord. Amen.—John Henry Newman[2]

FOR CLEANSING OR RECONSECRATION OF THINGS PROFANED

Almighty God, by the radiance of your Son's appearing, you have purified a world corrupted by sin: We humbly pray that you would continue to be our strong defense against the attacks of our enemies; and grant that [name of item] and whatsoever in this church has been stained or defiled through the craft of Satan or by human malice may be purified and cleansed by your abiding grace; that this place, purged from all pollution, may be restored and sanctified, to the glory of your name; through Jesus Christ our Lord, who lives and reigns with you and the Holy Spirit, one God, now and for ever. Amen.[3]

FOR FUNERALS AND MEMORIAL SERVICES

O King of saints, who hast not entered into thy triumph alone but attended by ten thousand times ten thousand, we bless thee for those with thee whom we have known and loved. Let their presence on the heights draw us upwards as we toil and struggle; let their victory make us of good courage; let their faith and patience be our inspiration and our power, and by thy grace may we too someday stand above all that today tempts and soils and casts us down, and in the heavenly places find our eternal home. Amen.[4]

Grant, O Lord, to all who are bereaved, the spirit of faith and courage, that they may have strength to meet the days to come with steadfastness and patience, not sorrowing as those who have no hope, but in thankful remembrance of thy great goodness in the past, and in the sure expectation of a joyful reunion in the heavenly places. This we ask in the Name of Jesus Christ our Lord. Amen.

Almighty and eternal God, who amid the changes of this mortal life art always the same, we frail children of Earth do humble ourselves in thy presence. We bow in reverence before thy judgments, saying, "The Lord gave, and the Lord hath taken away; blessed by the Name of the Lord." In the silence of this hour speak to us of eternal things, and comfort us with the assurance of thine everlasting love, through Jesus Christ our Lord.

God of all grace, who didst send thy Son our Savior Jesus Christ to bring life and immortality to light, most humbly and heartily we give thee thanks that by his death he destroyed the power of death, and by his glorious Resurrection opened the kingdom of heaven to all believers. Grant us assuredly to know that because he lives we also shall live, and that neither death nor life, nor things present nor things to come, shall be able to separate us from thy love which is in him.

Help us now to wait upon thee with reverent and submissive hearts, that as we read the words of eternal life we through patience and comfort of the Scriptures may have hope, and be lifted above our darkness and distress into the light and peace of thy presence, through Jesus Christ our Lord. Amen.[5]

Our loving Father, comfortingly look upon us in our sorrow, and abide with us in our loneliness. O thou who makes no life in vain, and who lovest all that thou hast made, lift upon us the light of thy countenance, and give us peace. Amen.

We pray that thou wilt keep in tender love the life which we shall hold in blessed memory. Help us who continue here to serve thee with constancy, trusting in thy promise of eternal life, that hereafter we may be united with thy blessed children in glory everlasting, through Jesus Christ our Lord. Amen.[6]

O God, we thank thee for thy love revealed in Jesus Christ. In this hour it comforts us to know that the friendship of our souls with thee is an eternal friendship and nothing in life or death is able to separate us from thee. Help us so to commit ourselves to thy fatherly care that we may be more than conquerors over doubt and sorrow, and may, through the experience of the cross, be able the better to help those who are bowed down with grief. Assured that thy love will never let us go, may we face the future with calm confidence, knowing that whatever comes, thou art with us and wilt uphold us; through Jesus Christ our Lord. Amen.[7]

Dear God of eternity, life is so precious to each of us that all that is within us says no to death. We see death as the dark, mysterious enemy that destroys the good that you have created.

Help us to see death as you see it: not the end but the beginning, not a wall but a doorway, not a dark road but a path that leads to eternal light and life.

We will miss our loved one, but we thank you, Lord, for memory. May our minds and hearts be filled with the wonderful recollections of the past. Help our sadness to wear a smile as the passing of time wipes the tears away. Time can be a great physician, healing the void that we now feel.

Every life is a gift from you, dear Father. Thank you for sharing this special person's life with us. We will cherish the memory forever. Amen.[8]

Our heavenly Father, we give thanks to you for the life you have given to our loved one and friend, [name]. We thank you for the talents she/he had and used for your service, and we thank you for the influence of her/his life. Take the words of your servant and the expressions of love of friends to comfort the family and strengthen them for the days ahead. In Jesus' name. Amen.

God of our memories, lest we forget those who died on the battlefield, those who came back sore and sick, those who came back tried and true: God bless them all! Bring to a war-wearied world peace—the peace of the nations, neighbors of a new world; the peace of the races, brothers and sisters all by a universal soul; "the peace of God, which passeth all understanding." Bring to a war-wearied world happy, honorable, and lasting peace. We ask in the name of Christ, the Prince of Peace. Amen.—S. G. Spottswood

Gather us up, O Father of us all, and hold us in thine everlasting arms as lambs in thy bosom. For sometimes, as we think of the transience and mortality of life, we are made a little afraid and need to be held close. We need to hear thy voice as it whispers in our hearts, so that we shall not be afraid. Then as one by one we slip away, it shall not be with fear and dread, but quietly and sweetly as "one who wraps the draperies of his couch about him and lies down to pleasant dreams" Quicken and sanctify, O Lord, the memories that we cherish. Let them throng our hearts; Let them be part and parcel of our lives; that we who have known thy saints in the flesh may still have blessed communion with them in the spirit.—William Frederick Dunkle Jr.

We thank thee, O God, for the difference that thy Son's coming among us has made in the history of the world and in the trend of human thought and life. We thank thee who hast given us the victory over dark despair, over futile impotence, over transient earthiness, and over the apparent finality and dread of death. We thank thee for a message and a life and a power that bring comfort to the anguished, assurance to the doubting, enduring faith to the bewildered and unsettled, and great joy to the sad. We give thanks unto thee, O God, for thy revelation unto us, and for all that thou hast made possible in us and through us. In the name of Christ. Amen.—R.K.M.

LITURGICAL RESOURCES FOR PASTORAL CARE

The fifth chapter of this book is a lengthy discussion of the pastoral care needs of the dying, the bereaved, and those who have gone through other crises. Ministry to people in these situations may take many forms; among these are prayer and other liturgical acts.

The prayers that follow may be said by you or a layperson who is making pastoral calls, or they may be printed out and given to the people being visited, for their own use later on. There are times when people have difficulty putting into their own words the deep questions and pain they are experiencing. Written prayers may help give them voice and also reassure them that they are not alone in their circumstances and feelings.

There are two types of materials in this section: resources for individual prayer, followed by those that may be used for corporate worship.

Jesus, you rewarded Mary's seeking with the consolation of your risen presence. Give me the grace not to cling to my old relationship to [name of deceased] but to rejoice in his or her transformed presence. Amen.[9]

[Mother or] Father God:

You have taught me much about life. Now I need to be taught about death. I have sadness, emptiness, a hole in my life. I know I can live without my loved one, but I do not want to have to.

I do not want to be too selfish. I know that this dear one had to live and die his life. But I was not ready. I guess I never would have been. I hope that he was ready, from your perspective.

My prayer had been for him not to die until he felt very loved by all of us and by you. I am convinced that he did feel loved. I am grateful.

However you continue life beyond life as we know it, I trust You. You are gracious forever. But that does not heal the loss.

Thank you for the blessing of love shared between us. Thank you for maturity we learned through our problems, shared. Somehow through my tears I trust that in you he rests in peace and that in you all of us touched by him can also live in your peace.

I do not understand, but I trust that your peace does pass all understanding. Amen.[10]

    O God,
    I come to you now
    as a child to my Mother
    out of the cold which numbs
    into the warm who cares.
    Listen to me inside,
    under my words
    where the shivering is,
    in the fears
    which freeze my living,
    in the angers
    which chafe my attending,
    in the doubts
    which chill my hoping,
    in the events
    which shrivel my thinking,
    in the pretenses
    which stiffen my loving.
    Listen to me, Lord,
    as a Mother,
    and hold me warm
    and forgive me.
    Soften my experiences
    into wisdom,
    my pride
    into acceptance,
    my longing
    into trust,
    and soften me
    into love
    and to others
    and to you.[11]

Compassionate God, [name of deceased] was loved and cherished by me; unlock the floodgates of my tears that I may pour out my lamentation to you. For you are God of Infinite Compassion. Amen.[12]

I am distressed, O Lord, and bitterly downcast because [reason]. Though I know so little, help me to go on believing in thy love when I cannot understand and when the path of reason is darkened. Let the light of faith shine in my heart. Amen.

Nothing can make up for the absence of someone whom we love, and it would be wrong to try to find a substitute; we must simply hold out and see it through. That sounds very hard at first, but at the same time it is a great consolation, for the gap, as long as it remains unfilled, preserves the bonds between us. It is nonsense to say that God fills the gap; God doesn't fill it, but on the contrary, keeps it empty and so helps us to keep alive our former communion with each other, even at the cost of pain.[13]

As I conclude this book, I am both exhausted and exhilarated. Exhausted because the fatigue caused by the cancer is overwhelming. Exhilarated because I have finished a book that has been very important to me. As I write these final words, my heart is filled with joy. I am at peace.

It is the first day of November and fall is giving way to winter. Soon the trees will lose the vibrant colors of their leaves and snow will cover the ground. The Earth will shut down, and people will race to and from their destinations bundled up for warmth. Chicago winters are harsh. It is a time of dying.

But we know that spring will soon come with all its new life and wonder.

It is quite clear that I will not be alive in the spring. But I will soon experience new life in a different way. Although I do not know what to expect in the afterlife, I do know that just as God has called me to serve him to the best of my ability throughout my life on Earth, he is now calling me home.

Many people have asked me to tell them about heaven and the afterlife. I sometimes smile at the request because I do not know any more than they do. Yet, when one young man asked if I looked forward to being united with God and all those who have gone before me, I made a connection to something I said earlier in this book. The first time I traveled with my mother and sister to my parents' homeland of Tonadico di Primiero, in northern Italy, I felt as if I had been there before. After years of looking through my mother's photo albums, I knew the mountains, the land, the houses, the people. As soon as we entered the valley, I said, "My God, I know this place. I am home." Somehow I think crossing from this life into life eternal will be similar. I will be home.

What I would like to leave behind is a simple prayer that each of you may find what I have found—God's special gift to us all: the gift of peace. When we are at peace, we find the freedom to be most fully who we are, even in the worst of times. We let go of what is nonessential and embrace what is essential. We empty ourselves so that God may more fully work within us. And we become instruments in the hands of the Lord.

As I have said so often, if we seek communion with the Lord, we must pray. One of my favorite prayers is attributed to Saint Francis of Assisi. Let us conclude by reciting it together:

> Lord, make me an instrument of your peace.
> Where there is hatred, let me sow love.
> Where there is injury, pardon.
> Where there is doubt, faith.
> Where there is despair, hope.
> Where there is darkness, light.
> Where there is sadness, joy.
> O Divine Master, grant that I may not so much seek
> To be consoled as to console;
> To be understood, as to understand;
> To be loved, as to love;
> For it is in giving that we receive,
> It is in pardoning that we are pardoned.
> It is in dying that we are born to eternal life.[14]

O merciful Father, who hast taught us in thy holy Word that thou dost not willingly afflict or grieve thy children. Look with pity upon the sorrows of thy servant for whom our prayers are offered. Remember him/her, O Lord, in mercy, nourish his/her soul with patience, comfort him/her with a sense of thy goodness, lift up thy countenance upon him/her, and give him/her peace; through Jesus Christ our Lord. Amen.[15]

Eternal Lord God, you hold all souls in life: Give to your whole Church in paradise and on Earth your light and your peace; and grant that we, following the good examples of those who have served you here and are now at rest, may at the last enter with them into your unending joy; through Jesus Christ our Lord, who lives and reigns with you, in the unity of the Holy Spirit, one God, now and for ever. Amen.[16]

> Ever-living God, this day revives in us memories of loved ones who are
>   no more.
> What happiness we shared when they walked among us.
> What joy when, loving and being loved, we lived our lives together.
> *Their memory is a blessing for ever.*

Months or years may have passed, and still we feel near to them.
Our hearts yearn for them.
Though the bitter grief has softened, a duller pain abides;
for the place where once they stood is empty now.
The links of life are broken, but the links of love and longing
   cannot break.
Their souls are bound up in ours for ever.
We see them now with the eye of memory,
  their faults forgiven, their virtues grown larger.
So does goodness live, and weakness fade from sight.
We remember them with gratitude and bless their names.
Their memory is a blessing for ever.
And we remember as well the members
  who but yesterday were part of our congregation and community.
To all who cared for us and labored for all people, we pay tribute.
May we prove worthy of carrying on the tradition of our faith,
  for the task is now ours.
Their souls are bound up in ours for ever.
We give you thanks that they now live and reign with you.
As a great crowd of witnesses,
  they surround us with their blessings,
  and offer your hymns of praise and thanksgiving.
They are alive for ever more. Amen.[17]

Let us remember and thank God whom we worship for making us your children by grace and for sustaining us with the bread of life:

We thank you, Lord.

For your presence wherever we have gathered:

We thank you, Lord.

For the pardon of our sins, especially when Christians have martyred Christians, which restores us to the fellowship of your faithful people, the saints:

We thank you, Lord.

For the faith of those who have gone before us, for their encouragement to us, and for the fellowship of the saints:

We thank you, Lord.

For [*opportunity for all to name the faithful departed who have been significant in their Christian life*] and

For the great cloud of witnesses, the saints:

We thank you, Lord.

Yours, O Lord, is the greatness, the power, the glory, the victory, and the majesty:

For everything in heaven and on Earth is yours.

Yours, O Lord, is the Kingdom:

And you are exalted as head over all. Amen.

Merciful Lord, who art the strength of sufferers and the comfort of those who are heavy of heart: incline thine ear, we beseech thee, to the prayers of all who cry unto thee in their troubles; succor the distressed, uphold the fainting, relieve the suffering, console the sad, and make thy face to shine upon them, O Lord, thou lover of souls.—F. B. Macnutt, *The Ministers Manual 1970.*

Most merciful God, whose wisdom is beyond our understanding, surround the family of [name of deceased] with your love, that they may not be overwhelmed by their loss but have confidence in your goodness, and strength to meet the days to come. We ask this through Christ our Lord. Amen.[18]

May our Lord Jesus Christ be near us to defend us, within us to refresh us, around us to preserve us, before us to guide us, behind us to justify us, above us to bless us. Who lives and reigns with the Father and the Holy Ghost, God for evermore. Amen.—Tenth century

Committal Prayers

Several prayers may be said in the course of a committal service: an opening prayer, a commendation, the actual words of committal, the Lord's Prayer, a collect, and so on. Following are various prayers that may be used in such a ritual.

Man that is born of a woman has but a short time to live and is fully of misery. He comes up and is cut down like a flower; he flees as it were a shadow, and never continues in one stay.

In the midst of life we are in death; of whom may we seek for succor, but of you O Lord, who for our sins are justly displeased.

Yet, O Lord God most holy, O Lord most mighty, O holy and merciful Savior, deliver us not unto the bitter pains of eternal death.

You know, Lord, the secrets of our hearts; shut not your merciful ears to our prayers, but spare us, Lord most holy, O God most mighty, O holy and merciful Savior, most worthy Judge eternal, suffer us not at our last hour for any pains of death, to fall from you.[1]

> Lord, have mercy upon us;
> *Christ, have mercy upon us.*
> Lord, have mercy upon us;
> *Christ, hear us.*
> Lord God, Father, hear us as we pray:
> [*The Lord's Prayer is said by all*]
> Lord God, Son, thou Savior of the world,
> *Be gracious unto us.*
> By thy human birth, by thy prayers and tears, by the grief and anguish of
> thy soul, by thy cross and passion, by thine atoning death, by thy rest in

the grave, by thy triumphant resurrection and ascension, by thy sitting at
the right hand of God, by thy divine presence, by thy coming again to thy
Church on Earth, or our being called home to thee,
Bless and comfort us, gracious Lord and God.
Lord God, Holy Spirit,
Abide with us forever. Amen.
I am the Resurrection and the Life, saith the Lord; he who believes in me,
though he were dead, yet shall he live. And whosoever lives and believes
in me shall never die. Therefore, blessed are the dead who die in the Lord
from henceforth; yea, says the Spirit, that they may rest from their labors.
O death, where is thy sting? O grave, where is thy victory? The sting of
death is sin; and the strength of sin is the law; but thanks be to God, who
gives us the victory through our Lord Jesus Christ.
[Congregation sings:]
Now to the earth let these remains in hope committee be,
Until the body changed attains blest immortality.
Keep us in everlasting fellowship with the Church Triumphant, and let us
rest together in thy presence from our labors.
Hear us, gracious Lord and God.
Glory be to him who is the Resurrection and the Life, who quickens us
while in this dying state and, after we have obtained the true life, does
not suffer us to die any more.
Glory be to him in the Church which waits for him, and in that which is
around him, forever and ever.
Amen.
[Congregation sings:]
The Savior's blood and righteousness
My beauty is, my glorious dress;
Thus well arrayed, I need not fear,
When in his presence I appear.
The peace of God, which passes all understanding, keep your hearts and
minds in the knowledge and love of God, and of his Son, Jesus Christ,
our Lord; and the blessing of God Almighty, the Father, the Son, and the
Holy Spirit, be with you all. Amen.[2]

Almighty God, by the death and burial of Jesus, your anointed, you have
destroyed death and sanctified the graves of all your saints. Keep our
brother/sister, whose body we now lay to rest, in the company of all your
saints and, at the last, raise him/her up to share with all your faithful people
the endless joy and peace won through the glorious Resurrection of Christ our
Lord, who lives and reigns with you and the Holy Spirit, one God, now and
forever.[3]

In sure and certain hope of the resurrection to eternal life through our Lord Jesus Christ, we commend to almighty God our brother/sister [name] and we commit his/her body to the ground/the deep/the elements/its resting place; earth to earth, ashes to ashes, dust to dust. The Lord bless him/her and keep him/her. The Lord make his face to shine upon him/her and be gracious to him/her. The Lord look upon him/her with favor and give him/her peace. Amen.[4]

O God, by whose mercy the faithful departed find rest, bless this grave, and send your holy angel to watch over it. As we bury here the body of [name], welcome him/her into your presence, that he/she may rejoice in you with your saints for ever. We ask this through Christ our Lord. Amen.

Almighty and ever-living God, in you we place our trust and hope, in you the dead, whose bodies were temples of the Spirit, find everlasting peace. As we take leave of [name], give our hearts peace in the firm hope that one day he/she will live in the mansion you have prepared for him/her in heaven. We ask this through Christ our Lord. Amen.[5]

With the souls of the righteous dead, give rest, O Savior, to the soul of thy servant, preserving it unto the life of blessedness which is with thee, O thou who lovest mankind. In the place of thy rest, O Lord, where all thy saints repose, give rest, also, to the soul of thy servant: for thou only lovest mankind.

Glory to the Father, and to the Son, and to the Holy Spirit.

Thou art the God who descended into hell, and loosed the bonds of the captives: Do thou give rest, also, to the soul of thy servant. Now, and ever, and unto ages of ages. Amen. O Virgin alone Pure and Undefiled, who without seed didst bring forth God, pray thou unto him that his/her soul may be saved.[6]

O God, our help in ages past, our hope for years to come, into thy gracious keeping we commit the soul of our beloved brother/sister, thanking thee for all he/she has meant to us and praying that through the grace of our Lord Jesus Christ thou wilt grant him/her an abundant entrance into thine eternal kingdom. Comfort, we beseech thee, the hearts that are heavy with sorrow, and grant that they may find in thee a friend who is equal to all their needs. Sanctify to each of us the memories of this solemn hour. Here in this place with its tender associations, may we dedicate ourselves anew to thy service, that with chastened desires and nobler motives we may return to our homes and to the duties that await us; through Jesus Christ our Lord. Amen.[7]

Almighty God, who by the death of thy dear Son Jesus Christ hast destroyed death, by his rest in the tomb hast sanctified the graves of the saints, and by his glorious Resurrection hast brought life and immortality to light: Receive, we beseech thee, our unfeigned thanks for that victory over death and the grave which he had obtained for us and for all who sleep in him. Keep us in everlasting fellowship with all that wait for thee on Earth, and with all that are with thee in heaven, in union with him who is the Resurrection and the Life, who liveth and reigneth with thee and the Holy Spirit, ever one God, world without end. Amen.[8]

Now the body of [name] returns to the earth, becomes again earth, earth to earth returning, the matter of the body dissolving back into the great source of all life and becoming compost for the nourishment of new living things. . . . Our human spirit must let go of the perishable form to be transformed into imperishable spirit. This is a great mystery which we do not pretend to understand. But we trust with that faith of little children who put their hand into the hand of a loving parent, knowing they will be led aright. So we trust, even without knowledge, in that great Creator-Spirit from which all life comes, and to which it returns, to raise this human spirit to immortal life. Take back now our sister/ brother into your bosom, O Wisdom-Spirit. In faith we entrust her/him into your arms. Amen.[9]

Father of all, we pray to you for those we love but see no longer: Grant them your peace; let light perpetual shine upon them; and in your loving wisdom and almighty power, work in them the good purpose of your perfect will; through Jesus Christ our Lord. Amen.[10]

Into your hands, O merciful Savior, we commend your servant [name]. Acknowledge, we humbly beseech you, a sheep of your own fold, a lamb of your own flock, a sinner of your own redeeming. Receiving him/her into the arms of your mercy, into the blessed rest of everlasting peace, and into the glorious company of the saints in light. Amen.[11]

Eternal God, you have shared with us the life of [name]. Before he/she was ours, he/she is yours. For all that [name] has given us to make us what we are, for that of him/her which lives and grows in each of us, and for his/her life that in your love will never end, we give you thanks. As now we offer [name] back into your arms, comfort us in our loneliness, strengthen us in our weakness, and give us courage to face the future unafraid. Draw those of us who remain in this life closer to one another, make us faithful to serve one another, and give us to know that peace and joy which is eternal life; through Jesus Christ our Lord. Amen.[12]

하나님 아버지 그리스도 안에서 모든 성도가 부활 할것을 믿습니다.

Pronunciation: Hah nah nim, ah buh jee,

Gha rhee sêdoh ahn eeh suh

Moh Dan seong doh gah

Booh hwahl hal guh sê

Miht sê nee dah.

Translation: Our Father in heaven, we/I believe that, in Christ, all the saints will be raised to life. —Jacob Kim

그리스도 안에서 모든 사람이 살리라.

Pronunciation: Gha rhee sa doh Ahn eek such Moh dan sa ram yi Sahl Lee Rah.

Translation: In Christ, all will be made alive.

Resources for Funerals of Children

The structure of the funeral or memorial service for a child is not substantially different from the structure of any other funeral. The content, however, will be slightly different, for both theological and pastoral reasons. First, we are reminded of Jesus' special regard for children, and their state of relative innocence. Second, the death of a child, whether stillborn, miscarried, or at any stage before maturity, can be a crushing loss for the family. It presents particular pastoral care needs. Scripture readings, prayers, and hymns should acknowledge these factors even as they offer thanksgiving to God who is the giver of all life, however brief or long.

In planning the funeral of an infant or child, you will want to keep in mind a few logistical considerations. Obviously, six pallbearers are not needed to carry a very tiny coffin. Having one friend or family member carrying it can be wrenching for that person and for those who witness it. One thoughtful compromise is to have the funeral home staff, whether one or two people, carry or guide the coffin into the church, escorted by honorary pallbearers. This acknowledges the closeness of the relationship to the child without limiting participation to only one or two persons.

A second consideration is the likelihood that other children will be attending the service, particularly siblings of the deceased child. You will have had opportunities for conversation with immediate family members prior to the service and will have some sense of their comprehension of what has happened and of appropriate ways to address their grief. If the children are old enough to attend regular Sunday worship, their presence at the funeral should be encouraged—provided, of course, that there are loving adults to sit with them and offer moral support. A children's sermon during the service may or may not be part of your tradition, as may the singing of particular hymns. You will want to plan a service that invites their participation by using language and music with which they are familiar. In addition, you may want to protect siblings or friends of the deceased child from well-intentioned adults who may try to pressure them into performing (by singing or telling a story, for example), stifling their emotions, or engaging in ritual acts for which they have had no preparation or counsel, such as kissing the corpse.

SCRIPTURE READINGS

The Scriptures suggested earlier in this section of the book include readings that may be especially suited for the funeral of a child.

HYMNS

The following hymns and songs are suggested:

"Children of the Heavenly Father"

"Fairest Lord Jesus"

"I Sing a Song of the Saints of God"

"Jesus Loves Me"

"Jesus Loves the Little Children"

"Safe in the Arms of Jesus"

"Tell Me the Stories of Jesus"

"The Lord's My Shepherd, I'll Not Want"

"This Is My Father's World"

"Thy Holy Wings, O Savior"

"What a Friend We Have in Jesus"

"Will the Circle Be Unbroken"

PRAYERS FOR A MISCARRIAGE, STILLBORN CHILD, OR INFANT

Almighty God, Creator of life, whose ways are hidden from our finite, temporal sight, yet whose marvelous works are experienced every hour, our hearts go out to these parents in the loss and disappointment they feel with the premature death of one for whom they had yearned. It has come so shortly after birth (or prior to birth). Bless now the mother who has carried this child lovingly. Bless also the father who sorrows here this day. You know their heaviness of heart. You share our griefs and sorrows. You know our broken dreams. You invite us to cast our burdens on you and find in your eternal arms the comfort and strength to go on.

Your Son, our Savior, has said, Let the little children come to me, and do not hinder them; for the Kingdom of God belongs to such as these. We commit to your loving arms this little life to dwell in your presence forever. Receive [name] into your loving arms. Receive us also that we may experience your healing in days to come. This we pray in the name of our resurrected, living Savior, even Jesus Christ the Great Shepherd of the sheep. Amen.[1]

Lord Jesus, whose Mother stood grieving at the foot of the cross, look kindly on these parents who have suffered the loss of their child [name]. Listen to the prayers of Mary on their behalf, that their faith may be strong like hers and find its promised reward, for you live for ever and ever. Amen.[2]

All-loving and caring God, parent of us all, know our grief in our loss, for you too suffered the death of your child. Give us strength to go forward from this day, trusting, where we do not understand, that your love never ends. When all else fails, you still are God.

We thank you for the life and hope that you give through the Resurrection of your Son Jesus Christ. We pray to you for one another in our need, and for all, anywhere, who mourn with us this day. To those who doubt, give light; to those who are weak, strength; to all who have sinned, mercy; to all who sorrow, your peace. Keep true in us the love with which we hold one another.

And to you, with your Church on Earth and in heaven, we offer honor and praise, now and for ever. Amen.[3]

Blessed Jesus, lover of children, in lowliness of heart we cry to you for help. Expecting the life of a child, we have witnessed his/her death. Our despair is profound, and we know you weep with us in our loss. Help us to hear your consoling voice, and give healing to our grief, merciful Savior. Amen.[4]

Lord God, ever caring and gentle, we commit to your love this little one, [name], who brought joy to our lives for so short a time. Enfold him/her in eternal life. We pray for his/her parents, who are saddened by the loss of their child/baby/infant. Give them courage and help them in their pain and grief. May they all meet one day in the joy and peace of your Kingdom. We ask this through Christ our Lord. Amen.[5]

PRAYERS FOR A CHILD

O Thou God of our fathers, we come to thee as children of thy loving and watchful care, to pray for those who have loved and labored for this little child whom thou hast called unto thy eternal rest. Our minds, O God, are unable to understand the meaning of thy purposes for our lives, but we are well-assured that no sorrow thou dost ask us to bear is without a divine meaning. In the name of Jesus Christ, the Good Shepherd of the sheep whose love does embrace us all and especially the little children, we pray that the tears of farewell may one day, as thou hast promised, become the joy of morning and gladness. Amen.[6]

Almighty God, our Heavenly Father, thou who hast strengthened thy children with thy light and power in all ages, hear us now as we beseech thee to give us faith in thy love that will not let us go.

Enable us to wait upon thee in our time of tribulation. We pray with our Savior that thy will be done in our lives. Grant unto us the privilege of hearing thy will, the vision to perceive it, and the courage to fulfill it.

Thy tender mercies remind us that we are not alone in our sorrow and loss. As we have suffered, so thou hast suffered in giving of thine only begotten Son. As we have loved, so thou hast loved more and loved first. If there is pain and death in our lives, so there has been a cross and a crown of thorns in thine. O God, Thou art ever near when we are afflicted, for thou hast suffered with us.

In our moment of grief, guide our steps, that we may place our trust in thee. Into thy hands we commit our lives. And having abided in faith, hope, and in love, may we yet see the radiance of a new day. In the name of him who leads the way out of darkness into light, who conquered the cross with the Resurrection, in the name of Christ, we turn to thee. Amen.[7]

LEADER: The Lord Jesus is the lover of his people and our only sure hope. Let us ask him to deepen our faith and sustain us in this dark hour.

You became a little child for our sake, sharing our human life. To you we pray:

PEOPLE: Bless us and keep us, O Lord.

LEADER: You grew in wisdom, age, and grace and learned obedience through suffering. To you we pray:

PEOPLE: Bless us and keep us, O Lord.

LEADER: You comforted those who mourned the loss of children and friends. To you we pray:

PEOPLE: Bless us and keep us, O Lord.

LEADER: You took upon yourself the suffering and death of us all. To you we pray:

PEOPLE: Bless us and keep us, O Lord.

LEADER: You promised to raise up those who believe in you, just as you were raised up in glory by the Father. To you we pray:

PEOPLE: Bless us and keep us, O Lord.[8]

O most compassionate and loving Savior, who, when on Earth, didst gather the little children into thine arms and put thy holy hands upon them to bless them, we commit to thee this little child which our Heavenly Father hath now taken away. Be thou the tender Shepherd of this lamb. Carry it in thy bosom into the green pastures and beside the still waters of thy paradise among the happy company of the glorified children, and at the last day restore it to those yearning hearts, when the mystery of thy providence shall be unveiled from all faces. Hear us, O God, for Jesus our dear Redeemer's sake, to whom, with thee, O Father, and the ever blessed Spirit, the Comforter, be all praise and glory, world without end. Amen.[9]

O God, you are present here. You sit beside each person. When a hand touches another, or arms meet arms, or eyes look deeply into other eyes, or words are spoken, you are here—in a handshake, an embrace, a gaze, a voice.

You are present here, even if we are not sure, for nothing can separate us from you and your love.

It is a time of absence, a time of questions, a time of tears. Help us to feel your presence. Accept our thoughts and feelings, no matter what they are. Help us to accept our thoughts and feelings, no matter what they are.

Grant us the grace to live with our memories in ways that will help us.

Give us the peace that knows there is hope on the other side of crying and separation.

Give us your love as we let go of [name] and walk through our grief.

Bless this family; bless [names of parents, siblings, grandparents].

Give to them strength and peace. Amen.[10]

Holy God, your goodness is everlasting, and your mercies never fail. Yours is the beauty of childhood and yours is the fullness of years. Comfort us in our sorrow, strengthen us with hope, and breathe peace into our troubled hearts. Assure us that the love in which we rejoiced for a time is not lost, and that this child is with you, safe in your eternal love and care. We ask this in the name of Jesus Christ, who took little children into his arms and blessed them. Amen.[11]

Our heavenly Father, you were willing to give up your only beloved Son to face death on our behalf. You know the pain that comes in the loss of one dearly loved. Fill us with your grace to face this loss now of [name]. We entrust him/her to your eternal arms, to enjoy the bliss of your eternal mansions forevermore. We recall the words of your Son who said, Let the children come to me, for of such is the kingdom of heaven.

We pray that your love and peace might surround the sorrowing parents and all the members of the family. Show compassion to them and comfort them this day and in the days that follow. May things unseen and that which is eternal grow more clear to them and to all of us. May we long for that future promised resurrection when we who know Christ are united forever in your perfect heavenly Kingdom. This we pray in the name of our living Savior, who holds the keys to death and life. Amen.[12]

O God, whose beloved Son did take little children into his arms and bless them: Give us grace, we beseech thee, to entrust this child, [name], to thy never-failing care and love, and bring us all to thy heavenly Kingdom; through the same, thy Son Jesus Christ our Lord, who liveth and reigneth with thee and the Holy Spirit, one God, now and for ever. Amen.[13]

O God, our heavenly Father: let the light of your countenance shine upon us and draw us into your presence in our deep sorrow. We do not always understand the things that happen in this life. Comfort those who mourn this child and preserve them through Jesus Christ, who is the friend of children. Let your Holy Spirit bear witness in our hearts to the promise of eternal life, and give them assurance that they shall be reunited with their dear child in your heavenly Kingdom, through Jesus Christ our Lord. Amen.[14]

God our Father, your love gave us life, and your care never fails. Yours is the beauty of childhood, and yours the light that shines in the face of age. For all whom you have given to be dear to our hearts, we thank you, and especially for this child you have taken to yourself. Into the arms of your love we give his/her soul, remembering Jesus' words: Let the children come unto me, for of such is the kingdom of heaven.

To your love we also commend the sorrowing parents and family. Show compassion to them as a father to his children, comfort them as a mother comforts her little ones. As their love follows their hearts' treasure, help them to trust that love they once have known is never lost, that the child taken from their sight lives for ever in your presence.

Into your hands we also give ourselves, our regret for whatever more we might have been or done, our need to trust you more and to pray, all our struggle for a better life. Comfort us all. Keep tender and true the love in which we hold one another. Let not our longing for you ever cease. May things unseen and eternal grow more real for us, more full of meaning, that in our living and dying you may be our peace. Amen.[15]

Theme Song. When Israel had passed through the water as it had been dry land, and had escaped from the malice of the Egyptians, they cried: Let us sing praises unto our deliverer and our God.

Refrain. Give rest to the child, O Lord.

Hymns. O Word of God, who didst humble thyself even unto the flesh, and wast graciously pleased to become a babe, yet without change: Ordain thou that this child whom thou hast accepted may be received into Abraham's bosom, we beseech thee.

Thou wast beheld a little child, thou who existest before all the ages, and forasmuch as thou art good, unto children hast promised thy Kingdom: Number therein this child here present.

Glory be to the Father, and to the Son, and to the Holy Spirit.

Thou hast taken unto thyself, O Christ the Savior, this spotless child, ere he/she had been tempted of earthly pleasures, bestowing upon him/her thine eternal good things; forasmuch as thou lovest mankind.

Now, and ever, and unto ages of ages. Amen.

Hymn to the Birth-giver of God. O thou who, in wise inexpressible, didst hear the Wisdom and Word of the Father, heal thou the cruel wound of my soul, and soothe the pang of my heart.[16]

Holy Spirit, source of all understanding, fill our bereft and bewildered hearts with the warm breath of your consolation. While [name] was alive, we poured on him/her all our love. Let this be our quiet confidence: life is changed, not taken away. Amen.[17]

LEADER: Let us thank God for the gift of this child and offer our petitions to God.

That as [name] was reborn in the waters of baptism, she/he may enjoy eternal happiness in heaven,

ALL: Merciful Lord, hear us.

LEADER: For the consolation of this family and their friends,

ALL: Merciful Lord, hear us.

LEADER: That we may be patient with ourselves when we are visited with anguish, or despair,

ALL: Merciful Lord, hear us.

PRESIDER: In thanksgiving for all the joy, happiness, and tenderness which [name] gave her/his family in her/his short life,

ALL: Merciful Lord, hear us.

LEADER: That we may realize that [name] life is changed, not taken away,

ALL: Merciful Lord, hear us.[18]

To you, O Lord, we humbly entrust this child, so precious in your sight. Take him/her into your arms and welcome him/her into paradise, where there will be no sorrow, no weeping nor pain, but the fullness of peace and joy with your Son and the Holy Spirit for ever and ever. Amen.[19]

With faith in Jesus Christ, we must reverently bury the body of [name]. Let us pray with confidence to God, in whose sight all creation lives, that he will raise up in holiness and power the mortal body of this little child, for God has chosen to number his/her soul among the blessed.[20]

Music

HYMNS FROM DENOMINATIONAL AND OTHER MAJOR HYMNBOOKS

Key

BH	*Baptist Hymnal* (1976)
CH	*The Covenant Hymnal* (Evangelical Covenant Church)
COH	*The Collegeville Hymnal* (Roman Catholic)
H1982	*The Hymnal 1982* (Episcopal)
HFG	*Hymns for the Family of God*
LBW	*The Lutheran Book of Worship*
MH	*Hymnal and Liturgies of the Moravian Church*
NCH	*The New Century Hymnal* (United Church of Christ)
PH	*Presbyterian Hymnal*
UMH	*The United Methodist Hymnal*

Title	BH	CH	COH	H1982	HFG	LBW	MH	NCH	PH	UMH
A Mighty Fortress Is Our God	37	464			118	228–229	428	439–440	260	110
A Multitude Comes from the East and the West					313					
Abide with Me	217	757	431	662	500	272	382	99	543	700
All Creatures of Our God and King	9	55		400	347	527		455	62	
Amazing Grace	165	341	447	671	107	448	321–322	547–548	280	378
Around the Throne, a Glorious Band			335							
Because He Lives		744			292					364
Be Still, My Soul		455			77			488		534
Behold a Host Arrayed in White		764				314				
Blest Be the Tie That Binds	256				560	370	485–486	393	438	557
Canticle of Redemption										516
Cast Thy Burden upon the Lord		453			53		538			
Children of the Heavenly Father	207	87			89	474		487		141
Christ Is Alive		259	269	182					108	318

Christ the Victorious				358			367		653
Close to Thee	61			405					407
Come, Christians, Join to Sing				342				150	158
Come, Come Ye Saints	210								
Come, Gracious Spirit, Heavenly Dove			499						
Come, Let Us Join Our Friends Above						250			709
Come, We That Love the Lord (Marching to Zion)	505	577		392	550	6	379, 382		733
Come, Ye Disconsolate						548			510
Come, Ye Faithful, Raise the Strain			247	199–200		143, 144	230	114, 115	315
Commit Thou All That Grieves Thee				669		177			
Countless Hosts Before God's Throne						561			
Even as We Live Each Day					350				
Face to Face	489				128				
Faith of Our Fathers	143	584	634	558	526	500	253	381	710

Title	BH	CH	COH	H1982	HFG	LBW	MH	NCH	PH	UMH
Fix Me, Jesus										655
For All the Saints	144	767	336	287	614	174	560	299	526	711
For All Your Saints, O Lord						176				
Forever with the Lord!							554			
Give Rest, O Christ, to Your Servant				355						
Give Thanks for Life								297	528	
Give to the Winds Thy Fears								404		129
Glimpses of Glory		749								
Great Is Thy Faithfulness	216	78			98			423	526	140
Guide Me, O Thou Great Jehovah	202	408		690	608	343	431	18–19	281	127
He Leadeth Me	218	404			606	501	429			128
Here from All the Nations		762								
How Blest Are They Who Trust in Christ								365		654
How Firm a Foundation	383	437	452	636–637	32	507	535	407	361	529
I Call You to My Father's House			413							

Hymn										
I Have a Future All Sublime		743								
I Know Not What the Future Hath		492								
I Know of a Sleep in Jesus' Name						342				
I Must Tell Jesus		462			49			486		
If Death My Friend and Me Divide										656
If Thou but Suffer God to Guide Thee		203		635		453	544	410	282	142
I'll Fly away								595		
I'll Praise My Maker		7		429					253	60
Immortal, Invisible	32	10	566	423	319	526	163	1	263	103
Immortal Love, Forever Full		329				196		166		
In Heaven Above		754			131	330				
In Paradisium			411							
In the Bulb There Is a Flower		752						433		707
In the Garden		428			588			237		314
In the Sweet By and By		495	747							

Title	BH	CH	COH	H1982	HFG	LBW	MH	NCH	PH	UMH
Into Paradise May the Angels Lead You				354						
It Is Not Death to Die							555			
It Is Well with My Soul	339	451			495	346		438		377
Jerusalem, My Happy Home	488		469	620		331		378		
Jerusalem, the Golden				624		347	563			
Jerusalem, Whose Towers Touch the Skies						348				
Jesus, I Live to Thee							556			
Jesus Lives, and So Shall I		248			288					
Jesus Lives, Thy Terrors Now			287	194–195						
Jesus, Lord, Your Resurrection			410							
Jesus, Lover of My Soul	172	369		699	222		380–381	546	304	479
Jesus, Priceless Treasure		459			277	457–458	365	480	365	532
Jesus, Remember Me		561							599	488
Jesus, Son of Mary				357						
Jesus, Still Lead On							432			
John Saw the Heavens		776								

Hymn Title	1	2	3	4	5	6	7	8	9	10
Leaning on the Everlasting Arms	254				87					133
Let Hope and Sorrow Now Unite		756								
Light's Abode, Celestial Salem				621						
Like a River Glorious		463			497					
Lo, What a Cloud of Witnesses				545						
Lord of the Living		753							529	
Love Divine, All Loves Excelling	58	439	454	657	27	315	364	43	376	384
Make My Calling and Election							562			
May Choirs of Angels Lead You				356						
May the Angels Lead You into Paradise			412							
Mil Voces para Celebrar										59
More Love to Thee, O Christ		384			476		345	456	359	453
My Faith Looks up to Thee	382	343		691	84	479	332		383	452

Title	BH	CH	COH	H1982	HFG	LBW	MH	NCH	PH	UMH
My Hope Is Built	337	433			92	293–294			379	368
My Jesus, as Thou Wilt							534			
My Jesus, I Love Thee	76	370			456		353			172
My Life Flows on in Endless Song								476		
My Shepherd Will Supply My Need		91	458	664	66			247	172	
My Times Are in Thy Hand							541			
Near to the Heart of God	354	85			35				527	472
Nearer, My God to Thee	333						459	606		528
Nobody Knows the Trouble I See										520
Now Let the Earth with Joy Resound			339							
O By and By	506									
O Exalt and Praise the Lord	564									
O, for a Thousand Tongues to Sing	69	299		493	349	559	216	42	466	57
O God, Our Help in Ages Past	223	422	457	680	370	320	166	25		117

Hymn										
O God, Whose Will Is Life and Good					435	552				
O Holy City, Seen of John			620							
O Holy Spirit, Enter in					459					
O How Blest to Be a Pilgrim		758								
O Lord, Let Now Your Servant					339					
O Lord of Life, Where'er They Be								530		
O Love That Wilt Not Let Me Go	368			404	324	360		384	480	
O Thou, in Whose Presence									518	
O What Their Joy			623				385		727	
Oh, Happy Day When We Shall Stand					351					
Oh, Happy They in God Who Rest		460								
Oh, That I Had a Thousand Voices					560			475		
On Eagle's Wings		81							143	
On Jordan's Stormy Banks I Stand	490	759							754	

Title	BH	CH	COH	H1982	HFG	LBW	MH	NCH	PH	UMH
Out of the Depths I Cry to You	246								240	515
Praise, My Soul, the King of Heaven	8	35	513	410	339	549	27		478	66
Precious Lord, Take My Hand					611			472	404	474
Psalm 23	173									
Pues Si Vivimos (When We Are Living)								499	400	356
Remember Me	491									
Rock of Ages, Cleft for Me	163		685		108	327	333–334	596	361	361
Saints of God, Come to His/Her/Their Aid			414							
Saranam, Saranam (Refuge)										523
Saviour, Blessed Saviour							347			
Shall We Gather at the River	496							597		723
Sing Alleluia Forth in Duteous Praise				619						
Sing Hallelujah, Praise the Lord!							565			

	C1	C2	C3	C4	C5	C6	C7	C8	C9	C10
Sing We the Song of Those										
Someday Soon		748								706
Soon and Very Soon		750								
Stand by Me		447								512
Steal Away to Jesus								599		704
Sweet Hour of Prayer	401	389			439		445	505		496
Swing Low, Sweet Chariot										703
Thank God for the Promise					110					
The Church's One Foundation	236	579	489	525	547	369	242	386	442	545
The Day of Resurrection		260	278	210		141	132	245	118	303
The God of Abraham Praise	25	37		401	332	544	161	24	188	.116
The King of Love My Shepherd Is	215	84	460	645–646		456	372	248	181	138
The Lord My God My Shepherd Is				663						
The Lord's My Shepherd, I'll Not Want	341	92	479	451	40, 42		184	479	170	136
The Old Rugged Cross	430	235			256			195		504
The Saviour Lives, No More to Die							138			

Title	BH	CH	COH	H1982	HFG	LBW	MH	NCH	PH	UMH
The Strife Is O'er		257	276	208		135	139–140	242	119	306
There Is a Land of Pure Delight	504									
There Is a Road That Goes to Heaven		745								
Thine Be the Glory		243			291	145		253	122	303
Thou Hidden Source of Calm Repose										153
Thy Holy Wings, Dear Savior		80								502
Thy Word, O God, Declareth							568			
'Tis So Sweet to Trust in Jesus	375	458			91					462
To Christ, Whose Hands Will Bless		456								
To God We Render Praise							566			
Under His Wings		97			412					
Up from the Grave He Arose		245			298					322
We Are the Lord's, His All-Sufficient Merit						399				

We Shall Walk Through the Valley	501	454								
We Will Lay Our Burden Down		589								
What a Friend We Have in Jesus	403	399			466	439	163	506	403	526
What Wondrous Love Is This	106	226	530	439	283	385		223	85	292
Whate'er My God Ordains Is Right							549			
When Aimless Violence Takes Those We Love		457								
When Grief Is Raw	461									
When in the Hour of Deepest Need						303				
When My Lips Can Frame No Sound							557			
When the Roll Is Called up Yonder	503									
When We All Get to Heaven	491	755								701
Ye O Holy Angels Bright		760		625						

OTHER MUSIC RESOURCES

Recordings

Charlotte Church, *Voice of an Angel*

Cutting Edge

Phil Coulter, *Serenity*

Delirious? *King of Fools*

Greg Ferguson, *Leave a Light On*

David Haas, *Blest Are They*

Willie Nelson, *The Troublemaker*

Passion

Twila Paris, *How Beautiful*

Matt Redman, *The Heart of Worship; The Father's Son*

Adrian Snell, *Feed the Hungry Heart*

Songs and Prayers from Taizé

John Michael Talbot, *Beginnings; Heart of the Shepherd; Meditations in the Spirit*

Vineyard Music, *Live from London*

Choral Music

Adams, Stephen	"The Holy City"
Bach, J. S.	"Jesu, Joy of Man's Desiring"
	"Nach Dir, Herr, Verlanget Mich"
	"Now Let Every Tongue Adore Thee"
	"Ah, How Fleeting"
Barnby, J.	"Crossing the Bar"
Barnby-Lewis, Joseph	"Now the Day Is Over"
Brahms, Johannes	"How Lovely Is Thy Dwelling Place"
Chadwick, George Whitefield	"When Our Heads Are Bowed with Woe"
Christiansen, Fredrik Melius	"I Know a Home Eternal"
Dawson, William	"Soon Ah Will Be Done"
Durufle, Maurice	"In Paradisum"
Fauré, Gabriel	"In Paradisum" from *Requiem*
Franck, Cesar	"Panis Angelicus" (O Lord Most Holy)

Franck, Johann Wolfgang	"O Jesus, Grant Me Hope and Comfort"
Gaul, A. R.	"Great and Marvelous" from *The Holy City*
	"No Shadows Yonder" from *The Holy City*
	"They Shall Hunger No More"
Gounod, Charles	"Forever with the Lord"
	"O Divine Redeemer"
	"Unfold, Ye Portals Everlasting," from *Redemption*
	"Sanctus," from *St. Cecilia's Mass*
Greene, Maurice	"I Will Lay Me down in Peace"
Grieg, Edward	"Jesus, Friend of Sinners"
Haas, David	"Blest Are They"
Hairston, Jester	"In Dat Great Gittin' Up Mornin'"
Handel, George Fredrich	"Come Unto Him," from *Messiah*
	"He Shall Feed His Flock," from *Messiah*
	"I Know That My Redeemer Liveth," from *Messiah*
Handel, George Fredrich, and Milligan, Harold Vincent	"Immortal Love"
Harris, William H.	"Almighty and Most Merciful Father"
Haydn, Franz J.	"Lo, My Shepherd Is Divine"
Herbert, J. B.	"Let Mount Zion Rejoice"
Kelly, Bryan	"Te Deum"
Kingsley, R.	"Immortality"
Lauridsen, Morten	"O Nata Lux," from *Lux Aeterna*
MacDermid, James G.	"In My Father's House"
Malotte, Arthur Hay	"The Lord's Prayer"
Manz, Paul	"E'en So, Lord Jesus, Quickly Come"
Matthews, John Sebastian	"I Heard a Voice from Heaven"
Mendelssohn, Felix	"Forever Blest Are They" (men's voices)
	"Happy and Blest Are They"
	"He That Shall Endure to the End"
Noble, T. Tertius	"The Souls of the Righteous"
Palestrina, Giovanni	"Sicut Cervus" (As Pants the Hart)

Parker, Horatio William	"The Lord Is My Light"
Peery, Charles H. H.	"God Shall Wipe away All Tears"
Prentiss, Elizabeth, and Harlan, Benjamin	"More Love to Thee"
Rilsky, Neophyte	"The Day of the Resurrection"
Rutter, John	"In Paradisum"
	"God Be in My Head"
Schubert, Franz	"Ave Maria"
Shelley, Harry Rowe	"Crossing the Bar"
	"Hark, Hark, My Soul"
Spohr, Louis	"Blest Are the Departed"
Stainer, John	"God So Loved the World"
	"My Hope Is in the Everlasting"
Stanford, Charles	"Nunc Dimittis"
	"Oh, for a Closer Walk with God"
Thompson, Randall	"He That Ruleth," from *The Last Words of David*
Thompson, Virgil	"The King of Love My Shepherd Is"
Tschaikovsky, Peter, and Cain, Noble	"O Blest Are They"
Tschesnokoff, Paul	"Salvation Is Created"
Ward-Stephens	"In My Father's House"
Willeby, C.	"Crossing the Bar"

Instrumental Music

Bach, J. S.	"Before Thy Throne, My God, I Stand"
	"Blessed Jesu, at Thy Word"
	"Hark! A Voice Saith, All Is Mortal"
	"In Thee, Lord, Have I Put My Trust"
	"Jesu, Joy of Man's Desiring"
	"Now Thank We All Our God"
	"Our Father, Who Art in Heaven"
Brahms, Johannes	"Blessed Ye Who Live in Faith Unswerving"
	"Deck Thyself, My Soul"
	"A Lovely Rose Is Blooming"

	"O God, Thou Faithful God"
	"O Sacred Head, Now Wounded"
	"O World, I Now Must Leave Thee"
Bridge, Frank	"Adagio in E Major"
Buxtehude, D.	"Now, Holy Spirit, We Pray to Thee"
Darke, Harold	"Chorale Prelude on St. Peter"
Drischner, Max	"If Thou But Suffer God to Guide Thee"
Dupré, Marcel	"Cortege et Litanie"
	"He, Remembering His Great Mercy"
Elmore, Robert	"Chorale Prelude on *Seelenbrautigam*"
Franck, Cesar	"Andante" from *Grande Piece Symphonique*
	"Chorale in B Minor"
Greenfield	"Prelude in Olden Style"
Guilmant, Alexandre	"Funeral March and Song of the Seraphs"
	"Prelude and Cradle Song"
Karg-Elert, Sigfrid	"Adorn Thyself, O My Soul"
	"Now Thank We All Our God"
	"O God, Thou Faithful God"
	"Rejoice Greatly, O My Soul"
Mendelssohn, F.	"Adagio" from *The First Organ Sonata*
Muffat, Georg	"Adagio" from *Toccata*
Oldroyd, George	"My South Hath a Desire and Longing to Enter the Courts of the Lord"
Peeters, Flor	"Aria"
	"O God, Thou Faithful God"
Purvis, Richard	"Communion"
Vaughan Williams, Ralph	"Rhosymedre"
Verne, Louis	"Prelude in C Minor"
Walther, Johann	"Lord Jesus Christ, Be Present Now"

NOTES

PART ONE

Chapter One: Theological Foundations
of Ministry to the Bereaved

1. Pannenberg, W. "Did Jesus Really Rise from the Dead?" Lecture delivered at several seminaries in the United States in 1963, drawn from his book *Christologie*, translated as *Jesus: God and Man* by L. R. Wilkins and D. A. Priebe. Philadelphia: Westminster Press, 1977.

2. Tiller, G. C. "Face to Face." In *Tabernacle Hymns*, Vol. 4. Chicago: Tabernacle, 1941, p. 18.

3. Avery, R. K., and Marsh, D. S. "We Are the Church." Carol Stream, Ill.: Hope, 1972. Reprinted in *The United Methodist Hymnal*. Nashville: Abingdon Press, 1989, no. 558.

4. Seitz, C. Brochure advertising 2001 Scholarly Engagement with Anglican Doctrine conference, "Nicene Christianity: The Future for a New Ecumenism," Charleston, S.C., Jan. 2001.

5. Wainwright, G. *Doxology*. New York: Oxford University Press, 1980, p. 192.

6. Stone, S. J. "The Church's One Foundation," 1866. Reprinted in *The [Episcopal] Hymnal 1982*. New York: Church Publishing, 1982, p. 525.

7. Hoffman, J. J., quoted in *The Tribune-Democrat*, Johnstown, Pa., June 18, 1999.

8. Küng, H. *Eternal Life*. New York: Crossroad, 1996, p. 127.

9. Sheppy, P. "Toward a Theology of Transition." In P. C. Jupp and T. Rogers (eds.), *Interpreting Death*. Washington, D.C.: Cassell, 1997, p. 47.

10. Sheppy, 1997, p. 47.

11. Wainwright, *Doxology,* pp. 444–445.

12. "Heaven." In F. L. Cross (ed.), *Oxford Dictionary of the Christian Church.* (2nd ed.) New York: Oxford University Press, 1974, p. 623.

13. Thurian, M. *The Eucharistic Memorial.* Quoted in Hanson, A. T. "The Communion of Saints." In J. G. Davies (ed.), *New Westminster Dictionary of Liturgy and Worship.* Philadelphia: Westminster Press, 1979, p. 114.

14. Mastantonis, G. *A New-Style Catechism on the Eastern Orthodox Faith for Adults.* St. Louis: Logos Press, 1969, p. 155.

15. *Book of Common Prayer.* New York: Oxford University Press, 1990, p. 862.

16. Stone, S. J. "The Church's One Foundation." *United Methodist Hymnal.* Nashville: Abingdon Press, 1989, no. 545, stanza 5.

17. McNeill, J. T. (ed.). *Calvin: Institutes of the Christian Religion.* Philadelphia: Westminster Press, 1960, p. 997.

18. Wainwright, *Doxology,* p. 450.

19. Eichrodt, W. *Theology of the Old Testament.* London: S.C.M., 1967, p. 515.

20. Wainwright, G. "Theology of Worship." In J. G. Davies (ed.), *New Westminster Dictionary of Liturgy and Worship.* Philadelphia: Westminster Press, 1986, p. 505.

21. Howatch, S. *Ultimate Prizes.* New York: Ballantine Books, 1989, pp. 286, 313.

22. DeWolf, L. H. *A Theology of the Living Church.* New York: HarperCollins, 1953, p. 143.

Chapter Two: Communities of Faith

1. "Association of Theological Schools Survey." D. S. Schuller (ed.), *Theological Education.* Vandalia, Ohio: Association of Theological Schools, Spring 1988, p. 4.

2. An agape was a common meal shared in the Christian community on a regular basis. Related to the Eucharist, it was an occasion for the display of Christian love and usually included distribution of food to the needy. Davies, J. G. "Burial." In J. G. Davies (ed.), *New Westminster Dictionary of Liturgy and Worship.* Philadelphia: Westminster Press, 1986, p. 117.

3. Newns, B. "Medieval and Roman Catholic Burial." In J. G. Davies (ed.), *New Westminster Dictionary of Liturgy and Worship.* Philadelphia: Westminster Press, 1986, p. 119.

4. Nageleisen, J. A. *Charity for the Suffering Souls: An Explanation of the Catholic Doctrine of Purgatory.* Rockford, Ill.: Tan Books, 1982, p. 218.

5. Niebergall, A., and Lathrop, G. "Lutheran Burial." In J. G. Davies (ed.), *New Westminster Dictionary of Liturgy and Worship.* Philadelphia: Westminster Press, 1986, p. 124.

6. Buchanan, C. O. "Anglican Burial." In J. G. Davies (ed.), *New Westminster Dictionary of Liturgy and Worship.* Philadelphia: Westminster Press, 1986, p. 120.

7. Douglas, A. "Heaven Our Home: Consolation Literature in the Northern United States, 1830–1880." In D. E. Stannard (ed.), *Death in America.* Philadelphia: University of Pennsylvania Press, 1975, p. 51.

8. Watts, I. "O God, Our Help in Ages Past," 1719. *United Methodist Hymnal.* Nashville: Abingdon Press, 1989, no. 117.

9. Hewitt, E. E. "When We All Get to Heaven," 1898. In D. Hustad (ed.), *Hymns for the Living Church.* Carol Stream, Ill.: Hope, 1974, p. 546.

10. Saum, L. O. "Death in the Popular Mind of Pre–Civil War America." In D. E. Stannard (ed.), *Death in America.* Philadelphia: University of Pennsylvania Press, 1975, p. 41.

11. Westergreen, N. O., unpublished letter to S. Westergreen, Dec. 19, 1898.

12. Black, K. *Worship Across Cultures.* Nashville: Abingdon Press, 1998, p. 126.

Chapter Three: Funerals and Other Memorial Services

1. Black, *Worship Across Cultures,* pp. 98, 126.

2. Funeral directors are required by law to provide potential customers with an itemized list of expenses. In addition, most states and counties cover the cost of a simple funeral and cremation for people who receive public assistance. If, however, families want substantial upgrades on the basic service, they are responsible for paying the difference. The situation may be compared to renting a car; if your voucher is good for a Metro, you cannot expect a Mercedes for the same price.

3. Black, *Worship Across Cultures,* p. 158.

4. Lazor, P. "Orthodox Burial." In J. G. Davies (ed.), *New Westminster Dictionary of Liturgy and Worship.* Philadelphia: Westminster Press, 1986, p. 118.

5. Hapgood, I. F. *Service Book of the Holy Orthodox-Catholic Apostolic Church.* New York: Antiochian Orthodox Christian Archdiocese, 1975, pp. 607–608.

6. Ford, J. M. *The Silver Lining: Wake Services.* Mystic, Conn.: Twenty-Third Publications, 1987, p. 55.

7. Willimon, W. H. *Worship as Pastoral Care.* Nashville: Abingdon Press, 1979, p. 115.

8. Senn, F. C. *Christian Liturgy: Catholic and Evangelical.* Minneapolis: Augsburg Fortress, 1997, p. 672.

9. There is a Roman Catholic funeral liturgy that can be said outside the Mass. The rite may be used on solemnities of obligation, on Holy Thursday and the Easter Triduum, and on the Sundays of Advent, Lent, and the Easter season. The rite may also be used in places or circumstances where it is not possible to celebrate the funeral Mass before the committal—for example, if a priest is not available.

International Commission on English in the Liturgy. *Order of Christian Funerals.* Chicago: Liturgy Training Publications, 1990, p. 93.

10. Conversation with staff of Leak & Sons Funeral Home, Chicago, July 19, 2000. In my own experience, more than 50 percent of funerals for black Christians have been held during evening hours.

11. Wallis, C. L. (ed.). *Funeral Encyclopedia: A Source Book.* New York: HarperCollins, 1953, p. 307.

12. Black, *Worship Across Cultures,* p. 33.

13. Black, *Worship Across Cultures,* p. 51.

14. Mitford, J. *The American Way of Death Revisited.* New York: Vintage Books, 1998, p. 111.

15. Sullivan, G., quoted in "Remains of the Day," *Chicago Tribune Magazine,* Feb. 12, 1995, p. 10.

16. The national flag may be used at funerals of active members and veterans of all branches of the armed forces. Flags for active duty personnel are provided by the branch of service; veterans' flags are supplied by the Department of Veteran Affairs. The average pastor does not need to be concerned with how to conduct a full military funeral because these are led by military chaplains.

17. Black, *Worship Across Cultures,* p. 147.

18. Walter, T. "Committal in the Crematorium: Theology, Death and Architecture." In P. C. Jupp and T. Rogers (eds.), *Interpreting Death: Christian Theology and Pastoral Practice.* London and Washington, D.C.: Cassell, 1997, p. 206.

19. Engle, P. E. (ed.). *Baker's Funeral Handbook.* Grand Rapids, Mich.: Baker, 1996, pp. 116–117.

20. Black, *Worship Across Cultures,* p. 145.

21. http://www.webcaskets.com, p. 5.

22. A memorial service need not involve a funeral home at all; the funeral director's work may be limited to arranging for cremation and, if desired, arranging interment of the cremains. The bereaved thus avoid the costs of embalming and preparing the body for viewing, purchasing or renting a coffin (the container in which the body is cremated is not the one used at the wake or funeral), renting a room for the visitation, transporting the body from the funeral home to the church and from the church to the cemetery, and so on.

23. Evangelical Covenant Church. *Covenant Book of Worship.* Chicago: Covenant Press, 1981, p. 171.

24. Black, *Worship Across Cultures,* pp. 41, 81, 99, 147, 159, 194, 216.

25. Clemons, J. T. (ed.). *Sermons on Suicide.* Louisville, Ky.: Westminster/John Knox Press, 1989, p. 17.

26. Lutheran Church in American. *Lutheran Book of Worship.* Minneapolis: Augsburg Fortress, 1978, p. 331.

27. Church of the Brethren. *For All Who Minister: A Worship Manual for the Church of the Brethren.* Elgin, Ill.: Brethren Press, 1993, p. 400.

28. *Book of Common Worship.* Louisville, Ky.: Westminster/John Knox Press, 1993, p. 911.

29. Tsoukalas, S. *Masonic Rites and Wrongs: An Examination of Freemasonry.* Phillipsburg, N.J.: Presbyterian and Reformed Publishing, 1995.

30. DeSpelder, L. A., and Strickland, A. L. *The Last Dance: Encountering Death and Dying.* Mountain View, Calif.: Mayfield, 1983, pp. 22–23.

31. Conversation with Officer Andrew P. Norén, Chicago Police Department, July 24, 2000.

32. Black, *Worship Across Cultures,* pp. 52, 159.

Chapter Four: Is There Any Word from the Lord?

1. Long, T. G., and McCarter, N. D. *Preaching in and out of Season.* Louisville, Ky.: Westminster/John Knox Press, 1990, p. 14.

2. Ware, H., Jr. "Happy the Home When God Is There." *United Methodist Hymnal.* Nashville: Abingdon Press, 1989, no. 445.

3. Allen, R. J. *Preaching the Topical Sermon.* Louisville, Ky.: Westminster/John Knox Press, 1992, p. 20.

4. Proctor, S. D. *Preaching About Crises in the Community.* Philadelphia: Westminster Press, 1988.

5. Telephone conversation with the Rev. James Wilson, Barrington, Ill., July 2000.

6. Letter from Dennis K. Hagstrom, July 26, 2000.

7. ABC World News Tonight with Peter Jennings, broadcast July 26, 2000.

8. Wainwright, G. "Preaching as Worship." In R. Lischer (ed.), *Theories of Preaching.* Durham, N.C.: Labyrinth Press, 1987, p. 355.

9. Wainwright, "Preaching as Worship," p. 358.

10. Wainwright, "Preaching as Worship," p. 361.

11. Sider, R. J., and King, M. A. *Preaching About Life in a Threatening World.* Philadelphia: Westminster Press, 1987, p. 12.

12. Greimel, H. "German Town in Mourning for Its Thirteen Concorde Victims." *Chicago Tribune,* July 27, 2000, p. 7.

13. Worship bulletin from All Saints Episcopal Church, Chicago; the Rev. Bonnie Perry, pastor; Feb. 15, 1999.

14. Unknown African poet, cited in Harding, V. "Introduction." In H. Thurman, *For the Inward Journey: The Writings of Howard Thurman.* Orlando: Harcourt Brace, 1984. Reprinted in bulletin from All Saints Episcopal Church, Chicago, Feb. 15, 1999.

15. Proctor, *Preaching About Crises in the Community*, pp. 81, 84, 87.

16. Neu, D. L. "Telling Love's Story: Remembering and Responding to AIDS." In K. Cherry and Z. Sherwood (eds.), *Equal Rites: Lesbian and Gay Worship, Ceremonies, and Celebrations*. Louisville, Ky.: Westminster/John Knox Press, 1995, pp. 44–49.

17. Neu, "Telling Love's Story," pp. 47–48. In one prayer, the "Compassionate Holy One" is asked to "open our hearts and minds and hands"; in the other prayer, the "Nourishing One" and "Thirst Quencher" is blessed for giving us bread to strengthen us for the long journey and water to keep us alive in the desert.

18. Dawn, M. *Reaching Out Without Dumbing Down*. Grand Rapids, Mich.: Eerdmans, 1995, p. 76.

19. "A Service of Hope After Loss of Pregnancy." In *United Methodist Book of Worship*. Nashville: Abingdon Press, 1992, pp. 623–626.

20. Ruether, R. R. *Women-Church: Theology and Practice*. New York: HarperCollins, 1986, p. 150.

Chapter Five: Pastoral Care Issues

1. Williams, W. (words), and Hughes, J. (music). "Cwm Rhondda," 1745/1907. Translated from the Welsh by P. Williams and others, 1771. *Hymns and Psalms*. London: Methodist Publishing, 1983, no. 437.

2. Boswell, J. *Life of Johnson*. New York: Modern Library, Sept. 19, 1777.

3. The five stages she observed were denial, anger, bargaining, depression, and acceptance. Kübler-Ross, E. *On Death and Dying*. Old Tappan, N.J.: Macmillan, 1969.

4. Kübler-Ross, E. *To Live Until We Say Good-Bye*. Englewood Cliffs, N.J.: Prentice-Hall, 1978, p. 152.

5. Kübler-Ross herself has said, in reference to working with the bereaved, "Once the patient dies, I find it cruel and inappropriate to speak [to the bereaved] of the love of God." While a responsible pastor will refrain from mouthing platitudes that do not take seriously the depth of loss the bereaved may be experiencing, after a death is nevertheless when mourners need to hear that God loves them and understands their sorrow. Kübler-Ross, *On Death and Dying*, p. 156.

6. Long, T. G. "Why Jessica Mitford Was Wrong." *Theology Today*, 1999, *55*(4), 500.

7. Oden, T. *Pastoral Theology: Essentials of Ministry*. New York: HarperCollins, 1983, p. 298.

8. *Education for Physicians on End of Life Care, Trainer's Guide*. Unit I: *Gaps in End of Life Care*. Chicago: American Medical Association, 1991, p. 91.

9. Bonhoeffer, D. *Spiritual Care* (J. C. Rochelle, trans.). Minneapolis: Augsburg Fortress, 1985, p. 59.

10. De Hennezel, M. *Intimate Death: How the Dying Teach Us How to Live* (C. B. Janeway, trans.). New York: Vintage Books, 1998, p. 142.

11. Cousins, N. *Anatomy of an Illness as Perceived by the Patient: Reflections on Healing and Regeneration.* New York: Norton, 1979, p. 154.

12. Browe, P. "Viaticum." In F. L. Cross and E. A. Livingstone (eds.), *Oxford Dictionary of the Christian Church.* (2nd ed.) New York: Oxford University Press, 1974, p. 1436.

13. Crichton, J. D. "Unction." In J. G. Davies (ed.), *New Westminster Dictionary of Liturgy and Worship.* Philadelphia: Westminster Press, 1986, p. 511.

14. Bonhoeffer, *Spiritual Care,* p. 59.

15. "Prayers at Time of Death." *Book of Common Prayer,* pp. 464–465.

16. Oden, *Pastoral Theology,* p. 249.

17. Gonda, T. A., and Ruark, J. E. *Dying Dignified: The Health Professional's Guide to Care.* Menlo Park, Calif.: Addison-Wesley, 1984, p. 157.

18. Gonda and Ruark, *Dying Dignified,* p. 294.

19. DeSpelder and Strickland, *The Last Dance,* pp. 283–284.

20. Telephone conversation with staff of Private Autopsy Incorporated, Aug. 14, 2000.

21. Vanauken, S. *A Severe Mercy.* New York: HarperCollins, 1976, p. 176.

22. Nuland, S. B. *How We Die: Reflections on Life's Final Chapter.* New York: Knopf, 1993, p. 122.

23. Kettering, T. *The Elephant in the Room.* Colorado Springs: Bereavement Publishing. Reprinted with permission in Ann Landers's column, *Chicago Tribune,* Feb. 12, 2000.

24. Sjogren, S. *Conspiracy of Kindness.* Ann Arbor, Mich.: Vine Books, 1993.

25 Bonhoeffer, *Spiritual Care,* p. 74.

26. Willimon, *Worship as Pastoral Care,* p. 104.

27. DeSpelder and Strickland, *The Last Dance,* p. 215.

28. Howatch, S. *Absolute Truths.* London: HarperCollins, 1994, pp. 144–145.

29. I acknowledge that there may be extraordinary circumstances that could require you to officiate at the funeral of a family member. For example, you may be in a place where there are no other Christian clergy or where no one else speaks your language, or relations with all other Christian clergy may be so hostile that they refuse to conduct a funeral for your loved one. Very few of us are in such circumstances, thank God.

30. Willimon, *Worship as Pastoral Care,* p. 102.

31. "How Firm a Foundation." In Rippon's *A Selection of Hymns,* 1787. Reprinted in *The United Methodist Hymnal.* Nashville: Abingdon Press, 1989, no. 529.

32. Letter from the Rev. James Huskins, Edenton, N.C., Aug. 7, 2000.

33. Quarantelli, E. L., and Dynes, R. R. *Images of Disaster Behavior: Myths and Consequences,* 1973, p. 67; and Baker, Chapman, 1962, quoted in Rogers, G. O., and Nehnevajsa, J. *Behavior and Attitudes Under Crisis Conditions: Selected Issues and Findings.* Washington, D.C.: Federal Emergency Management Agency, 1984, pp. 104, 105.

34. Institute for Ethics. "Module 2: Communicating Bad News." *Education for Physicians on End-of-Life Care: Trainer's Guide.* Chicago: American Medical Association, 1999, p. 2.

35. Letter from the Rev. James Huskins, Edenton, N.C., Aug. 7, 2000.

36. Rogers and Nehnevajsa, *Behavior and Attitudes Under Crisis Conditions,* p. 77.

37. Chrisholm, T. O. "Great Is Thy Faithfulness." Carol Stream, Ill.: Hope, 1923. Reprinted in *The Covenant Hymnal: A Worshipbook.* Chicago: Covenant Press, 1996, no. 78.

38. Wilson, J. M. "They Said So!" Sermon preached Nov. 1, 1998, Barrington, Ill.

39. McMahon, C. "West Joins Race to Save Sub Crew." *Chicago Tribune,* Aug. 17, 2000, sec. 1, p. 24. The icon in the photograph was not clear but it may have been St. Nicholas, the patron saint of Russia and of sailors.

40. Coniaris, A. M. *Introducing the Orthodox Church: Its Faith and Life.* Minneapolis: Light and Life, 1982, pp. 171, 175.

41. Prayer of Humble Access, from "Service of Word and Table IV." *United Methodist Book of Worship.* Nashville: Abingdon Press, 1992, p. 50. Adapted from *Book of Common Prayer,* 1990.

PART TWO

Sermons and Sermon Briefs

1. Bosco, R. (ed.). *The Puritan Sermon in America.* Delmar, N.Y.: Scholars Facsimiles and Reprints, 1978.

2. Lloyd, D. S. *Leading Today's Funerals.* Grand Rapids, Mich.: Baker Books, 1997, pp. 110–112.

3. Tillich, P. *Systematic Theology,* vol. 3. Chicago: University of Chicago Press, 1963, p. 57.

4. Delaney, W. G. "God's Ultimate Claim." In J. Clemons (ed.), *Sermons on Suicide.* Louisville, Ky.: Westminster/John Knox Press, 1989, pp. 43–48.

5. Barth, K. *Deliverance to the Captives.* 1961. Reprinted in *The Minister's Manual 1969.*

Sermon Illustrations and Poetry

1. Gladden, W. "Where Does the Sky Begin?" In C. Fant Jr. and W. M. Pinson Jr. (eds.), *A Treasury of Great Preaching,* Vol. 6. Dallas: Word, 1971, 1995, p. 210.

2. Talmage, D. "The Spider in Palaces." In Fant and Pinson, *A Treasury of Great Preaching,* Vol. 5, p. 305.

3. Truett, G. W. "A Promise for Every Day." In Fant and Pinson, *A Treasury of Great Preaching,* Vol. 8, p. 149.

4. Talmage, D. "The Ministry of Tears." In Fant and Pinson, *A Treasury of Great Preaching,* Vol. 5, p. 300.

5. Rauschenbusch, W. "The New Jerusalem." In Fant and Pinson, *A Treasury of Great Preaching,* Vol. 7, p. 165.

6. Truett, G. W. "A Promise for Every Day." In Fant and Pinson, *A Treasury of Great Preaching,* Vol. 8, p. 149.

7. Undset, S. *Kristin Lavransdatter: The Cross.* New York: Knopf, 1929, p. 383.

8. Catherine of Siena. "Divine Providence." Reprinted in R. J. Payne (ed.), *Classics of Western Spirituality: Catherine of Siena.* New York: Paulist Press, 1980, p. 277.

9. Mayer, T. C. "If a Man Die." In V. A. Myers (ed.), *I'll Give You a Daisy a Day: Sermons for Funerals.* Lima, Ohio: C.S.S., 1978, pp. 107–108.

10. St. Augustine, *The City of God.*

11. Origen. "An Exhortation to Martyrdom." Reprinted in R. J. Payne (ed.), *Classics of Western Spirituality: Origen.* New York: Paulist Press, 1979, p. 42.

12. Brontë, C. *Jane Eyre.* Garden City, N.Y.: Literary Guild of America, 1954, pp. 69–70.

13. Climacus, J. "On Remembrance of Death." (C. Luibheid and N. Russell, trans.) Reprinted in R. J. Payne (ed.), *John Climacus: The Ladder of Divine Ascent.* New York: Paulist Press, 1982, p. 132.

14. Silesius, A. *The Cherubinic Wanderer.* (M. Shrady, trans.) Reprinted in R. J. Payne (ed.), *Classics of Western Spirituality: Angelus Silesius.* New York: Paulist Press, 1986, pp. 40–41.

15. Williams, M. L. *Sorrow Speaks.*

16. van Dyke, H. *The Treasure Chest.* New York: HarperCollins, 1965.

17. Journey, A. C. *Presbyterian Life.*

Opening Sentences and Calls to Worship

1. *The Heidelberg Catechism.* Grand Rapids, Mich.: Eerdmans, 1964, p. 3.

2. Engle, *Baker's Funeral Handbook,* p. 38.

3. International Commission on English in the Liturgy, *Order of Christian Funerals,* p. 81.

4. Ford, J. M. *The Silver Lining: Wake Services.* Mystic, Conn.: Twenty-Third Publications, 1987, p. 55.

5. Engle, *Baker's Funeral Handbook,* pp. 116–117.

Invocations and Opening Prayers

1. Quoted in Wright, V. H. (ed.). *Prayers Across the Centuries.* Wheaton, Ill.: Harold Shaw, 1993, p. 74.

2. Quoted in Wright, *Prayers Across the Centuries,* p. 89.

3. Quoted in Wright, *Prayers Across the Centuries,* p. 59.

4. *Methodist Book of Worship.* Nashville: Methodist Publishing, 1944, p. 413.

5. *Methodist Book of Worship,* pp. 32–33.

6. *United Methodist Book of Worship.* Nashville: Abingdon Press, 1992, p. 33.

7. *Book of Common Prayer.*

8. *Lutheran Book of Worship.*

9. Hapgood, *Service Book of the Holy Orthodox-Catholic Apostolic Church.*

Benedictions

1. International Commission on English in the Liturgy, *Order of Christian Funerals,* p. 121.

2. Hapgood, *Service Book of the Holy Orthodox-Catholic Apostolic Church,* p. 393.

3. Adapted from United Methodist Clergywomen's Consultation, USA; printed in *United Methodist Book of Worship,* no. 563.

4. Sarum Liturgy, England, thirteenth century. In Wright, *Prayers Across the Centuries.*

5. Engle, *Baker's Funeral Handbook,* p. 129.

6. *Book of Common Prayer,* p. 114.

7. Cherry and Sherwood, *Equal Rites,* pp. 51–52.

Pastoral Prayers

1. *Directory of Public Worship.* Quoted in Office of the General Assembly, *The Book of Order.* Louisville, Ky.: Presbyterian Church USA, 1999, sec. W-4.10000.

2. Newman, J. H. Quoted in *The Book of Worship for Church and Home.* Nashville: Methodist Publishing, 1964, p. 222.

3. Standing Liturgical Commission. *The Book of Occasional Services* (Episcopal). New York: Church Hymnal Corporation, 1979, p. 203.

4. Coffin, H. S. *Joy in Believing.* New York: Scribner's, 1956. Quoted in *The Minister's Manual 1970.*

5. *Ordinal and Service Book,* The Church of Scotland. London: Oxford University Press, 1940.

6. Ritual of the Methodist Episcopal Church. *The Methodist Hymnal.* Nashville, Methodist Book Concern, 1936.

7. Morrison, J. D. "The Funeral Service." In Wallis, *The Funeral Encyclopedia,* p. 23.

8. Murchison, R. B. In A. Cadenhead Jr. (ed.), *The Minister's Manual for Funerals.* Nashville: Broadmand Press, 1988, p. 196.

9. Ford, J. M. *Welcoming Heaven.* Mystic, Conn.: Twenty-Third Publications, 1990, p. 114.

10. Bohler, C. *Prayer on Wings.* San Diego: Luramedia, p. 57.

11. Loder, T. *Guerillas of Grace: Prayers for the Battle.* San Diego, Calif.: Luramedia, 1984, p. 16.

12. Ford, J. M. *Welcoming Heaven,* p. 119.

13. Attributed to Dietrich Bonhoeffer.

14. Bernadin, J. L. *The Gift of Peace.* Chicago: Loyola University Press, 1997.

15. *Book of Common Prayer,* p. 831.

16. *Book of Common Prayer,* p. 253.

17. *United Methodist Book of Worship,* p. 548.

18. International Commission on English in the Liturgy, *Order of Christian Funerals,* p. 351.

Committal Prayers

1. *African Methodist Episcopal Church Hymnal,* no. 804.

2. *Hymnal of the Moravian Church.* Bethlehem, Pa.: Moravian Church in America, Northern and Southern Provinces, 1969, pp. 119–121.

3. *Lutheran Book of Worship,* p. 212. Reprinted by permission of Oxford University Press.

4. *Book of Common Prayer,* p. 501.

5. International Commission on English in the Liturgy, *Order of Christian Funerals,* pp. 182–183.

6. Hapgood, *Service Book of the Holy Orthodox Catholic Apostolic Church,* p. 393.

7. Wallis, *The Funeral Encyclopedia,* p. 9.

8. Engle, *Baker's Funeral Handbook,* p. 135. From Board of Christian Education of the Presbyterian Church in the United States of America, *Book of Common Worship.* Philadelphia: Board of Education of the Presbyterian Church in the United States of America, 1946.

9. Ruether, *Women-Church,* pp. 212–213.

10. *Book of Common Prayer,* p. 504.

11. *Book of Common Prayer,* p. 499.

12. *United Methodist Book of Worship,* p. 157.

Resources for Funerals of Children

1. Engle, *Baker's Funeral Handbook,* p. 108.

2. International Commission on English in the Liturgy, *Order of Christian Funerals,* p. 146.

3. *United Methodist Book of Worship,* p. 171.

4. *United Methodist Book of Worship,* p. 170.

5. International Commission on English in the Liturgy, *Order of Christian Funerals,* p. 184.

6. Wallis, *The Funeral Encyclopedia,* pp. 18–19.

7. Snavely, F. R. In Wallis, *The Funeral Encyclopedia,* p. 21.

8. International Commission on English in the Liturgy, *Order of Christian Funerals,* pp. 144–145.

9. Wallis, *The Funeral Encyclopedia,* p. 22.

10. *For All Who Minister,* pp. 432–433.

11. *For All Who Minister,* p. 434. Reprinted from *The Funeral: A Service of Witness to the Resurrection* (Supplemental Liturgical Resource 4). Philadelphia: Westminster Press, 1986.

12. Engle, *Baker's Funeral Handbook,* pp. 112–113.

13. *Book of Common Prayer,* p. 470.

14. Kyrkohandbok för Metodistkyrkan I Sverige [Church Handbook for Methodist Church in Sweden] (C. M. Norén, trans.). Örebro, Sweden: Libris-Verbum, 1987, pp. 105–106.

15. *United Methodist Book of Worship,* p. 162.

16. Hapgood, *Service Book of the Holy Orthodox-Catholic Apostolic Church,* pp. 424–425.

17. Ford, *The Silver Lining,* p. 5.

18. Ford, *The Silver Lining,* p. 7.

19. International Commission on English in the Liturgy, *Order of Christian Funerals,* p. 141.

20. International Commission on English in the Liturgy, *Order of Christian Funerals,* p. 194.

BIBLIOGRAPHY

Baxter, R. *The Saints' Everlasting Rest.* London: Epworth Press, 1962. A theological treatise on the nature of heaven and how Christians may attain everlasting rest, written from a Reformed perspective.

Black, K. *Worship Across Cultures.* Nashville: Abingdon Press, 1998. Catalogues what is currently happening in United Methodist churches in the United States whose congregations are made up of ethnic minorities. Weighted toward Asian American worship and includes a few African congregations.

Blackwood, A. *The Funeral.* Philadelphia: Westminster Press, 1942. A classic text, covering traditional issues pertaining to Christian funerals, such as service materials, pastoral concerns, and so on. Some of Blackwood's presuppositions will strike the reader as dated or odd (he deplores viewing the remains or wearing black, for instance), but his advice on pastoral method is still worth reading.

Blair, R. *The Funeral and Wedding Handbook* Joplin, Mo.: College Press, 1998. The author is a Church of Christ minister. Most of the funeral section was previously published in 1990 by Baker Book House as *The Minister's Funeral Handbook.* Includes a bibliography of nine books. Among the book's useful resources are Scripture lists, poems, and hymns. Does not include theological reflection or discussion of the legalities of funerals.

Blanchard, C. A. *Modern Secret Societies.* Chicago: National Christian Association, 1938. (Originally published by the author in 1903.) Blanchard was president of Wheaton College from 1882 to 1925. Mainly an argument against Freemasonry, this book also addresses temperance, insurance, and other lodges. Eight pages deal with burials.

Bohler, C. *Prayer on Wings.* San Diego, Calif.: LuraMedia, 1990. The prayers for times of grief, worry, and crisis may be useful for pastoral care of the bereaved.

Bonhoeffer, D. *Spiritual Care* (J. C. Rochelle, trans.). Minneapolis: Augsburg Fortress, 1985. Bonhoeffer's priestly voice is at the forefront in his sections on ministry to the sick and ministry at the deathbed.

Bosco, R. A. (ed.). *The Puritan Sermon in America, 1630–1750: New England Funeral Sermons.* Delmar, N.Y.: Scholars' Facsimiles and Reprints, 1978. Collection of sermons that can serve as a theological and homiletical resource as you prepare funeral sermons.

Braaten, C. E., and Jenson, R. W. (eds.). *Sin, Death, and the Devil.* Grand Rapids, Mich.: Eerdmans, 2000. The chapter by V. Guroian, "O Death, Where Is Your Sting?" is a good pastoral care resource for bereaved parents.

Cadenhead, A., Jr. *The Minister's Manual for Funerals.* Nashville: Broadman Press, 1988. Cadenhead has written for Baptists and other clergy in free church traditions. While most of the book is a collection of funeral sermons, the reader will also find theological reflection about funerals, good pastoral advice, and brief resources for planning the entire service.

Cherry, K., and Sherwood, Z. (eds.). *Equal Rites: Lesbian and Gay Worship, Ceremonies, and Celebrations.* Louisville, Ky.: Westminster/John Knox Press, 1995. Cherry is a national ecumenical officer with the Metropolitan Community Church and Sherwood is an Episcopal priest. The chapter on funerals and memorial services is not explicitly Christian or even necessarily religious. The first "rite" they note involves throwing all the deceased person's "Fiesta ware" into the fireplace.

Clemons, J. T. (ed.). *Sermons on Suicide.* Louisville, Ky.: Westminster/John Knox Press, 1989. Primarily lectures or sermons for people dealing with suicide. The introduction and sermon by Clemons are particularly helpful.

Coniaris, A. M. *Introducing the Orthodox Church: Its Faith and Life.* Minneapolis: Light and Life, 1982. An accessible primer on Orthodoxy, with sections on "what we believe about eschatology or life after death" and "what we believe about prayers for the dead."

Cousins, N. *Anatomy of an Illness as Perceived by the Patient: Reflections on Healing and Regeneration.* New York: Norton, 1979. Can help clergy and others get in touch with the perspective and anxieties of a critically ill person.

Daniels, E. *The Funeral Message: Its Preparation and Significance.* Nashville: Cokesbury Press, 1937. This older book provides excellent guidelines for preparing different types of sermons for funerals and memorial services.

Davies, J. G. (ed.). *New Westminster Dictionary of Liturgy and Worship.* Louisville, Ky.: Westminster/John Knox Press, 1986.

De Hennezel, M. D. *Intimate Death: How the Dying Teach Us to Live.* New York: Vintage Books, 1998. The author is a psychologist in a hospital for the terminally ill in Paris. Useful as a pastoral care resource.

DeSpelder, L. A., and Strickland, A. L. *The Last Dance: Encountering Death and Dying.* Palo Alto, Calif.: Mayfield, 1983. Reads like a college freshman's textbook—lots of sidebars and photographs. Contains some good material as a starting point for other research and outlines the legal requirements for settling an estate.

Duck, R. C. *Bread for the Journey: Resources for Worship.* New York: Pilgrim Press, 1981. Contains a funeral service and resources for Easter, which may be useful in planning funerals and memorial services.

Education for Physicians on End-of-Life Care: Trainer's Guide and Video Tapes. Chicago: Institute for Ethics, American Medical Association, 1999. Doctors often have difficulty communicating with terminally ill patients and their families. This resource, intended for physicians, is also useful for hospital chaplains and pastors.

Emswiler, S., and Neufer, T. *Sisters and Brothers Sing!* Normal, Ill.: Wesley Foundation Campus Ministry, 1977. Includes songs and a few other resources that may be useful for funerals and memorial services.

Engle, P. E. (ed.). *Baker's Funeral Handbook.* Grand Rapids, Mich.: Zondervan Press, 1996. Contains outlines for various denominational services and a brief compilation of worship resources. Includes no theological reflection about the services, and nothing for free church, Roman Catholic, or other more formal liturgical traditions.

Federal Emergency Management Agency. *Behavior and Attitudes Under Crisis Conditions: Selected Issues and Findings.* Washington, D.C.: U.S. Government Printing Office, 1984. Lists fifty-one different crisis events, from air pollution to water shortage, and discusses responses to each.

Filkins, K. *Comfort Those Who Mourn: How to Preach Personalized Funeral Messages.* Joplin, Mo.: College Press, 1992. Filkins is a Church of Christ minister who writes in a chatty and accessible style about composing funeral messages that are neither exposés nor hagiographies.

Ford, J. M. *The Silver Lining: Wake Services.* Mystic, Conn.: Twenty-Third Publications, 1987. A collection of liturgies allegedly for wakes, though only a sermon or eulogy and a committal are needed to make them full blown memorial services.

Ford, J. M. *Welcoming Heaven: Prayers and Reflections for the Dying and Those Who Love Them.* Mystic, Conn.: Twenty-Third Publications, 1990. Can serve as a devotional book for those who face death and as a pastoral care resource for extending ministry to those who mourn.

Frankl, V. E. *The Doctor and the Soul.* New York: Vintage Books, 1986. An existential analysis of the meaning of suffering, death, and so on.

Garrison, W. *Strange Facts About Death.* Nashville: Parthenon Press, 1978. Written anecdotally but nevertheless has a useful glossary. Some customs are described succinctly.

Gonda, T. A., and Ruark, J. E. *Dying Dignified: The Health Professional's Guide to Care.* Menlo Park, Calif.: Addison-Wesley, 1984. A basic psychology text for nurses, hospice workers, and other health care professionals.

Haggard, F. D. *The Clergy and the Craft.* Fulton, Mo.: Ovid Bell Press, 1970. Written by a minister who is also a mason who claims that Freemasonry is not a religion nor a substitute for religion. The book contains a section on funerals, and discusses how clergy and lodge can work together harmoniously.

Hampe, J. C. *To Die Is Gain: The Experience of One's Own Death.* Atlanta: John Knox Press, 1979. A philosophical discussion of death from a medical, theological, and psychological perspective.

Hapgood, I. F. *Service Book of the Holy Orthodox-Catholic Apostolic Church.* Englewood, N.J.: Antiochian Orthodox Christian Archdiocese, 1975. A readable description of Orthodox burial rites.

Harvard Medical School, Department of Continuing Education. *Spirituality and Healing in Medicine: With Special Emphasis on Death and Dying.* Workbook for Harvard Medical School conference in Boston, 1998.

Hersey, N. L. *Worship Services for Special Occasions.* New York: World, 1970. Covers all kinds of services that may not be included in denominational service books. The liturgies for dedication of memorial items, from headstones to paraments, will be useful to clergy in traditions without guidelines for such occasions.

Hiltner, S. *The Christian Shepherd: Some Aspects of Pastoral Care.* Nashville: Abingdon Press, 1959. Of interest for ministry in crisis and sorrow is Chapter Three, "Shepherding Grief and Loss."

Hiltner, S. *Pastoral Counseling.* Nashville: Abingdon Press, 1949. Part Two includes discussion of preparation for grief.

James, J. W., and Cherry, F. *The Grief Recovery Handbook: A Step-by-Step Program for Moving Beyond Loss.* San Francisco: HarperCollins, 1988. Written from a nonreligious viewpoint.

Jupp, P. C., and Rogers, T. (eds). *Interpreting Death: Christian Theology and Pastoral Practice.* London: Cassell, 1997. Put together on behalf of the Churches' Group on Funeral Services at Cemeteries and Crematoria, this book is written from a British cultural perspective.

Kreeft, P., and Tacelli, R. K. *Handbook of Christian Apologetics.* Downers Grove, Ill.: InterVarsity Press, 1994. A simple, strongly evangelical book, its strength is that it gives lots of biblical citations and is written in plain English.

Kübler-Ross, E. *On Death and Dying.* Old Tappan, N.J.: Macmillan, 1969. Kübler-Ross's classic, in which she describes the five stages of grief.

Kübler-Ross, E. *To Live Until We Say Goodbye.* Englewood Cliffs, N.J.: Prentice Hall, 1978. A collaborative work with Mal Warshaw, a photographer, that documents the "final journey" of several terminally ill people.

Küng, H. *Eternal Life? Life After Death as a Medical, Philsophical, and Theological Problem* (E. Quinn, trans.). New York: Crossroad, 1996.

Kutscher, A. H., and Kutscher, L. G. (eds.). *For the Bereaved.* New York: Frederick Fell, 1971. Very brief essays on everything from pet bereavement to etiquette to a section on Judeo-Christian perspectives. Unfortunately, most of the essays are brief and cursory.

Laderman, G. *The Sacred Remains: American Attitudes Toward Death, 1799–1883.* New Haven: Yale University Press, 1996. Covers many of the same issues as *Death in America.*

Levine, S. *Who Dies? An Investigation of Conscious Living and Conscious Dying.* New York: Anchor Books, 1982. Levine is a disciple of Elisabeth Kübler-Ross and Ram Dass. Discusses the needs of those who are dying and suggests ways we may prepare ourselves for whatever lies ahead.

Lloyd, D. S. *Leading Today's Funerals.* Grand Rapids, Mich.: Baker Books, 1997. Written in simple language, this book is accessible to those without any seminary education. It lacks significant theological reflection, however. For example, among the nine reasons given for having funerals, worshiping God is not mentioned.

Loder, J. E. *The Transforming Moment: Understanding Convictional Experiences.* New York: HarperCollins, 1981. Loder provides a theological framework for understanding divine action and transformation in the midst of crisis experiences.

Lukeman, B. *Embarkations: A Guide to Dealing with Death and Parting.* Englewood Cliffs, N.J.: Prentice Hall, 1982. A Jewish psychologist reflects on death and gives the reader exercises to do.

Maclean, N. *Death Cannot Sever.* New York: Fleming H. Revell, n.d. "An outspoken plea for psychical research to be taken seriously by the churches and regarded as an ally of the Christian faith." Not at all scholarly, but the chapter on "the resurrection body" is interesting.

McNeill, J. T. (ed.). *Calvin: Institutes of the Christian Religion,* vols. 10, 11. Philadelphia: Westminster Press, 1960. Calvin presents a theology of death and resurrection in a logical, lucid fashion.

Mitford, J. *The American Way of Death.* New York: Simon & Schuster, 1963. A groundbreaking book that led to Federal Trade Commission regulations affecting the funeral industry.

Motter, A. M. (ed.) *Preaching About Death.* Minneapolis: Augsburg Fortress, 1975. Includes sermons by preachers from Protestant, Catholic, and Orthodox backgrounds, including Paul Washburn, Walter Burghardt, and James Cox.

Myers, V. A. (ed.). *I'll Give You a Daisy a Day: Sermons for Funerals.* Lima, Ohio: C.S.S., 1978. The introduction gives a theory of preaching for funerals that is useful in contemplating ministry to those who mourn.

Nagleson, J. A. *Charity for the Suffering Souls: An Explanation of the Catholic Doctrine of Purgatory.* Rockford, Ill.: Tan, 1982. Purgatory is explained in terms intelligible to those outside Roman Catholicism.

Norris, K. *The Cloister Walk.* New York: Riverhead Books, 1996. The chapters "The Nursing Home on Sunday Afternoon" and "One Man's Life" reflect on end-of-life issues.

Nuland, S. B. *How We Die: Reflections on Life's Final Chapter.* New York: Knopf, 1994. Nuland, a doctor, describes the physiological process of death from a number of causes, including stroke, heart attack, AIDS, cancer, and so on. He also discusses psychological ramifications. Well-researched, but may be too simple for physicians and too technical for most laity.

Oden, T. C. *Pastoral Theology: Essentials of Ministry.* San Francisco: HarperCollins, 1983. Section Five explores crisis ministry, including pastoral care of the dying.

Order of Christian Funerals (Roman Catholic). Chicago: Liturgy Training Publications, 1989. Liturgical resources for a variety of services in the Catholic tradition.

Phipps, W. E. *Death: Confronting the Reality*. Atlanta: John Knox Press, 1987. Chapter Nine, on life after death, may be helpful, though it's hardly a confession of faith.

Proctor, S. D. *Preaching About Crises in the Community*. Philadelphia: Westminster Press, 1988. More Proctor's own take on crises in the community and his theology of ministry rather than presentation of a method.

Richmond, K. D. *A Time to Die: A Handbook for Funeral Sermons*. Nashville: Abingdon Press, 1990. The author offers examples of "difficult" funerals and provides guidelines and sample sermons for each.

Rowell, G. *The Liturgy of Christian Burial*. London: Society for the Propagation of Christian Knowledge, 1977. This book is out of print, but it is a classic for those who want more information on the history of funeral liturgies.

Rutherford, R. *The Death of a Christian: The Order of Christian Funerals*. (Rev. ed.) Collegeville, Minn.: Liturgical Press, 1990.

Schonwetter, R. (ed.). *Hospice and Palliative Medicine: Core Curriculum and Review Syllabus*. Dubuque, Iowa: Kendall/Hunt, 1999. Written in the oddly detached, clinical language of the medical profession. One chapter's title, for example, is "The Process of Dying and Managing the Death Event."

Sider, R. J., and King, M. A. *Preaching About Life in a Threatening World*. Philadephia: Westminster Press, 1987. The chapter on social justice preaching is also a useful primer for preaching on crisis.

Sobel, M. *Trabelin' On: The Slave Journey to an Afro-Baptist Faith*. Westport, Conn.: Greenwood Press, 1979. Includes information on race relations at antebellum funerals.

Stannard, D. E. (ed.). *Death in America*. Philadelphia: University of Pennsylvania Press, 1974. A description of historical developments that affect funeral practices in the United States today.

Tilson, E., and Cole, P. *Litanies and Other Prayers for the Common Lectionary: Year B*. Nashville: Abingdon Press, 1990. Some of the resources for Easter, Memorial Day, and All Saints Day may be useful for funerals and memorial services.

Tsoukalas, S. *Masonic Rites and Wrongs: An Examination of Freemasonry*. Phillipsburg, N.J.: Presbyterian and Reformed, 1995. Provides examples of masonic burial services from different state lodges.

Tucker, K.B.W. "Christian Rituals Surrounding Death." In P. F. Bradshaw and Hoffman, A. L. (eds.), *Life Cycles in Jewish and Christian Worship*. Notre Dame, Ind.: University of Notre Dame Press, 1996.

Vanauken, S. *A Severe Mercy*. New York: HarperCollins, 1977. The author, a friend of C. S. Lewis and professor at Lynchburg College, describes his conversion to Christianity and the death of his wife.

Wainwright, G. *Doxology: The Praise of God in Worship, Doctrine and Life.* New York: Oxford University Press, 1980. Wainwright presents a theology of death and resurrection as expressed through worship.

Wallis, C. L. (ed.). *The Funeral Encyclopedia: A Source Book.* New York: HarperCollins, 1953. The value of this volume is its three hundred pages of readings and sermons. Includes little explicit theological reflection on what we do when we conduct funerals.

Ward, H., and Wild, J. *Human Rites: Worship Resources for an Age of Change.* London: Mowbray, 1995. Creative liturgies from a more christocentric perspective than *Equal Rites.*

Willimon, W. H. *Worship as Pastoral Care.* Nashville: Abingdon Press, 1979. Willimon is wise, plainspoken, and orthodox in his reflection on worship and his suggestions for pastors.

Winter, M. T. *Woman Prayer Woman Song.* Oak Park, Ill.: Meyer, Sone, 1987. Some of the resources from the section on liberation rituals may be useful for funerals and memorial services.

Wright, V. H. (ed.). *Prayers Across the Centuries.* Wheaton, Ill.: Harold Shaw, 1993. The prayers in this anthology are organized according to era, not subject. Nevertheless, some of them may be useful for ministry in times of crisis and sorrow.

Zaleski, C., and Zaleski, P. *The Book of Heaven: An Anthology of Writings from Ancient to Modern Times.* New York: Oxford University Press, 2000. A collection of writings from various religions.

Zinner, E. S., and Williams, M. B. (eds.). *When a Community Weeps: Case Studies in Group Survivorship.* New York: Brunner/Mazel, 1998. Case studies about events such as the *Challenger* disaster, the sinking of the *Estonia,* and the Oklahoma City bombing.

HYMNALS

African Methodist Episcopal Church Hymnal. Nashville: African Methodist Episcopal Church, 1984.

Baptist Hymnal. Nashville: Broadman Press, 1975.

Bock, F. (ed.). *Hymns for the Family of God.* Nashville: Paragon Associates, 1976.

Covenant Hymnal: A Worshipbook. Chicago: Covenant, 1996.

Fettke, T. (ed.). *The Hymnal for Worship and Celebration.* Waco, Tex.: Word Music, 1986.

Hustad, D. (ed.). *Hymns for the Living Church.* Carol Stream, Ill.: Hope, 1974.

Hymnal of the Moravian Church. Elk Grove Village, Ill.: Moravian Church in America, 1969.

Lutheran Book of Worship. Minneapolis: Augsburg Fortress, 1978.

McKenna, Ed. J. (ed.). *The Collegeville Hymnal.* Collegeville, Minn.: Liturgical Press, 1990.

New Century Hymnal. Cleveland: Pilgrim Press, 1995.

Presbyterian Hymnal: Hymns, Psalms, and Spiritual Songs. Louisville, Ky.: Westminster/John Knox Press, 1990.

United Methodist Hymnal. Nashville: United Methodist Church, 1989.

Web Sites

About.com [http://dying.about.com/health/dying/mbody.htm]. A general resource on death and dying.

Americans for Better Care of the Dying. [www.abcd-caring.org]. Dedicated to better support and care systems for the seriously ill.

Arrangements.com [www.arrangements.com]. Will help you plan every aspect of a funeral service.

Cemetery Records Online [www.interment.net/help/research.htm]. How to find a lost burial.

Compassionate Friends [www.compassionatefriends.org]. Provides grief support after the death of a child.

Department of Veterans Affairs National Cemetery Administration [www.cem.va.gov]. A starting point for learning about benefits for veterans.

FinalThoughts.com [www.finalthoughts.com]. People who join this Web site can write electronic messages that will be delivered after they die.

Funeral Consumers Alliance [vbiweb.champlain.edu/famsa/index.htm].

Internet Cremation Society [www.cremation.org/home.html]. Not for when your hard drive crashes and burns.

Last Acts [www.lastacts.org]. Funded by the Robert Wood Johnson Foundation project to improve end-of-life care. Provides resources, news updates and guides to coping with grief and loss.

Legacy.com [www.Legacy.com]. On-line service that presents obituaries and life stories, intended to complement newspaper obituaries and other traditional means of death notification.

National Hospice and Palliative Care Organization. [www.nhpco.org]. Features a large database of hospice and palliative care programs throughout the United States.

National SHARE Office [www.NationalSHAREOffice.com]. Bereavement support group for people who have experienced stillbirth or miscarriage.

Pet Loss and Grieving Resource Pages [www.teleport.com/ ~ twscan/Pages/Pethome.htm]. Includes information on pet cremation and burial.

Private Autopsy Service [www.privateautopsyservice.com]. Provides information about arranging a private autopsy (as opposed to one required by law and performed at a hospital or medical examiner's office).

Regional Organ Bank of Illinois. [www.robi.org]. Provides referrals to other state organ banks. Among other things, offers a brochure called *A Guide for Religious Caregivers,* which states briefly the position of major religions on organ and tissue donation.

WebCaskets [www.webcaskets.com]. Buy a casket on-line.

Wilbert Funeral Services [www.wilbertonline.com]. Burial vaults, cremation services, urns and urn vaults.

GLOSSARY

Aspergillum. A brush or perforated globe used for sprinkling holy water at a Roman Catholic funeral.

Aspersion of the corpse. The sprinkling of holy water at a Roman Catholic funeral.

Awakening. All-night funeral celebration in Tongan American churches.

Bell tolling. It is customary in some European countries for the church bell to toll either at the time of a person's death or when the death is announced during the main Sunday service. At one time, the number of strokes, tone of the bell, and interval between tolls functioned as a code for the sex and age of the deceased.

Bier. A stand on which a casket is placed. Biers sometimes have wheels so that the casket can be moved from one location to another without lifting.

Bier lights. Six tall, unbleached candles that may surround the coffin during a wake or funeral.

Bikabika. An all-night worship service that precedes a funeral in the Fijian American community. Literally translated, it means "mourners" (Black, 1998, p. 234).

Casket. A lined and usually upholstered oblong box in which a person is buried. Caskets may be made of metal, wood, cloth, or cardboard. *Casket,* rather than coffin, is the word preferred by the funeral industry in the United States.

Catafalque. Similar to a bier but more commonly used for someone "lying in state"; it cannot be moved.

Censing or *Incensation.* Perfuming the air around the corpse with incense, done as part of Roman Catholic and some other funeral services.

Cerecloth. Cloth treated with melted wax or gummy matter and formerly used for wrapping a dead body.

Chapelet. A wreath that may adorn the head of the deceased.

Christian year. The liturgical seasons observed by a majority of the world's Christians, beginning with Advent and ending with Christ the King and Judgment Sunday.

Churchyard. A burial ground adjacent to a church. Normally, only those who belonged to the church may be buried there.

Cloth money. Money given in Chinese American communities to the family of the deceased at or before the memorial or funeral service to assist the family in buying the white cloth for the service (Black, 1998, p. 235).

Coffin. A wooden burial box or chest in the shape of an enlongated hexagon or kite. It is widest at the shoulders and may or may not be lined or upholstered. *Coffin* is the term often used in religious service books.

Columbarium. A structure of vaults lined with recesses for cinerary urns (which contain the ashes of the cremated dead). May be a room or building constructed solely for the purpose, or may be incorporated into the wall of a church building or garden.

Commendation. Used in two senses when speaking about funerals: it is synonymous with *committal,* that is, the words said as the coffin is placed in the ground or retort; or it is a prayer of commendation (commending the soul to God) sometimes said over a person at the time of death.

Committal. Words said at the graveside or crematorium, commending the deceased into God's hands and reminding worshipers of their hope in Christ.

Conditionalism. A Seventh-day Adventist belief that the dead rest in the grave until the resurrection. Seventh-day Adventists do not believe that a person has an immortal soul with a separate, indefeasibly immortal existence apart from the body (*New Westminster Dictionary of Liturgy and Worship,* p. 131).

Corridor of flowers. At the conclusion of a funeral in the traditional black church, ushers carry all the flowers to the rear of the church and place them on both sides of the path down which the pastor, pallbearers, and family will walk.

Cortege. A funeral procession.

Cremains. The ashes of a cremated human body.

Cremate. To reduce a dead body to ashes by the action of fire.

Crematorium. Where cremations occur. In the United States, crematoria are usually privately owned and do not incorporate chapels. In Europe, the crematorium often has a chapel attached, and the committal or entire funeral service may take place there.

Crypt. A place for burials underneath the nave (where the congregation sits) of the church.

Death-mask. More common before the advent of photography, a death mask was an effigy of wax or plaster formed by pressing the substance against the face of the deceased. Death masks were objects of respect and sometimes scholarly interest to those who wanted to retain a likeness of the deceased.

Distribution of mourning signs or bands. Strips of white cloth wrapped around the forehead or upper arm of mourners, or rectangular cloth pinned to the lapel as part of Vietnamese American mourning rituals. Worn from the time of the prayer meeting and viewing of the body until after the burial.

Enbalming. Preserving a dead body by removing blood and internal organs and injecting a dyed and perfumed solution of formaldehyde, glycerin, borax, phenol, alcohol, and water (Mitford, 1963, p. 46).

Eternal life. Life that is not bound by time. In Christian theology, eternal life begins when a new person is baptized into Christ, though eternal life is more commonly spoken of as life that continues after physical death.

Eulogy. From the Greek *eulogia*, meaning "praise." A commendatory formal statement about a person, usually made at a funeral or memorial service. The eulogy may be incorporated into the sermon, or it may be a discrete element of the service. Sometimes the eulogy is labeled *naming* or *witness.*

Funeral. A worship service at which the body of the deceased is present; interment or cremation occurs afterward.

Funeral chapel. A place where dead bodies are prepared for burial or cremation. The term *chapel* suggests that the mortuary has facilities for hosting religious funeral services.

Funeral director. A person licensed to arrange for the legal disposition of dead bodies, who may also conduct or arrange rites, offer psychological support and advice for the bereaved.

Funeral home. A place where dead bodies are prepared for burial or cremation. The term *home* suggests intimacy and family, and is reminiscent of a time when the wake and funeral were held in the home of the deceased.

Funeral meats. Fellowship meal served to mourners after the interment or memorial service.

Furoshiki. A square white cloth that covers the box containing the ashes of someone cremated in the Japanese tradition (Black, 1998, p. 236).

Ghat. Literally a landing place with stairs descending to the Ganges in India, it is also the word for the place of open-air cremation along the river.

Grave liner. A metal or concrete box that holds the casket. Cemeteries claim that the grave liner is necessary to prevent the earth from sinking as the body and casket decompose. It may also protect the body and casket from the elements.

Graveyard. A term for *cemetery* that is out of favor in English-speaking cultures.

Hearse. A vehicle for conveying the dead to the grave. In the United States, the hearse is usually a specially built automobile resembling a station wagon.

Heaven. In Christian theology, the eternal dwelling place of God and the blessed dead.

Hell. In Christian theology, the abode of the damned, where they suffer eternal separation from God.

Holy card. In some traditions, a card with a religious picture on one side and a brief biography of the deceased and a brief devotional poem on the other side. May be distributed at the wake or funeral.

Holy water. Water that has been blessed by a priest for making things or people holy; reminiscent of baptism.

Homegoing. A term used in the traditional black church for the funeral service.

Interment. The placing of the body or ashes in the ground, a mausoleum, or a columbarium.

Ipkwonsik. In Korean tradition, the ceremony of laying the body of the deceased in the coffin, and the brief worship service that follows. Often the deceased is clad in Korean dress. A Bible and other items may also be placed in the coffin.

Kaddish. A traditional Jewish prayer said for the dead.

Kolyva. A traditional dish served after an Orthodox funeral. The kolyva contains wheat, sugar, and almonds. It is decorated with resurrection symbols and placed in front of an icon before serving.

Lectionary. A calendar of suggested readings from the Old Testament, Psalms, New Testament, and Gospels, used by the worshiping community to cover all the major portions of the Bible in a three-year cycle.

Lichgate. In England, a covered entrance to a churchyard, where the funeral process stops for a moment.

Lictor. An assistant to the director of a funeral procession.

Masonic services. Memorial services or funerals led by Freemasons. Sometimes incorporated into the Christian funeral, sometimes held at another location at another time, or sometimes serving as a substitute for a Christian funeral.

Mass card. A card made available during visitation to those paying their respects; may be filled out to request that a requiem mass be said for the deceased. It is customary to make a monetary contribution for this special mass.

Mausoleum. An above-ground building for entombment of the dead. Usually built of stone.

Memorial park. Sometimes used as a synonym for *cemetery.* Other times a memorial park is a burial ground where individual markers are not permitted.

Memorial service. A worship service at which the body of the deceased is not present; may occur days, weeks, or even months after the interment or cremation.

Memory Eternal. A phrase sung by all at the conclusion of an Orthodox burial.

Month's mind, year's mind. A mass said on the monthly or yearly anniversary of a death.

Morgue. Any place where dead bodies are kept until released for burial or cremation.

Mortician. A person who prepares dead bodies for burial or cremation and offers a variety of goods and services to the bereaved. This term is out of fashion in the United States.

Mortuary. An out-of-fashion term for a funeral home. Strictly speaking, a building where dead bodies are kept until burial or cremation.

Nave. The part of the church building where the congregation sits during worship.

Nunc Dimittis. A prayer sometimes used at funerals, based on the words of the prophet Simeon, as recorded in Luke 2:29–32.

Obituary. A notice of a person's death, usually with a biographical account.

Obliquies. An obsolete term for *funeral.*

Office. A short service of praise and thanksgiving with the body present, including Bible readings and psalms.

Pall. A heavy cloth draped over a casket during the funeral. It serves two functions in worship; first, by making all caskets, whether expensive or cheap, appear the same, it communicates our equal status before God. Second, when a pall has liturgical symbols on it, it helps communicate various Christian beliefs.

Pallbearer. A person who carries, or sometimes simply accompanies, the casket at a funeral.

Paradise. In Christian theology, usually used as a synonym for *heaven.*

Paraments. Decorative cloths adorning the altar, lectern, and pulpit. Different colors are used for different seasons in the Christian year. Usually decorated with liturgical symbols.

Paschal candle. A candle lit on Easter (often during the Easter vigil) to symbolize and announce the Resurrection of Jesus Christ from the dead. Lit before the funeral or memorial service begins to remind mourners of the promise of resurrection.

Purgatory. In traditional Catholic theology, a place or state of purification where those judged worthy of heaven are gradually prepared for it.

Relic. A term used in two ways with respect to death: may be part of the body of a revered person, or may be any object venerated because of its association with a saint or martyr.

Repast. Term used in the traditional black church for the meal served after the interment or memorial service.

Requiem. A mass for the repose of one or more departed souls, commonly sung at funerals and on All Souls' Day.

Requiescat. A prayer for the repose of a dead person.

Retort. The cremation chamber, in which the body is consumed by fire.

Rosary. A string of beads used to count prayers, especially in the Roman Catholic Church. It is customary for someone (usually a layperson) to lead the mourners in saying the rosary during the vigil.

Sarcophagus. A stone coffin.

Sempiternity. Without beginning and without end; transcending time. Humans may have eternal life, but only God is sempiternal.

Shiva. Jewish custom of seven days of mourning following the death of a family member. The mourners spend this period in the family home and receive meals and condolence calls from friends. They do not work, attend school, watch television, or shave while sitting shiva, but use the time to reflect on the life of the deceased.

Shroud. A loose-fitting burial garment that looks something like a hooded nightgown. No longer used in the United States, shrouds and burial gowns are still used in parts of the United Kingdom.

Trisagion. The prayer, "Holy God! Holy and Mighty! Holy and Immortal! Have mercy on us!" which is recited at intervals during an Orthodox funeral liturgy.

Troparia. Sung responses to the psalm in an Orthodox funeral liturgy.

Undertaker. A seldom-used synonym for funeral director.

Urn. A container for cremated remains. May be shaped like an urn, a stone or wooden box, or some other form. The size may vary from a child's shoe box to a 12-inch by 10-inch urn.

Vault. See *grave liner.*

Viaticum. Holy Communion administered to or received by one who is dying. Derived directly from the Latin, it means provision for a journey, that is, the journey into eternity (*New Westminster Dictionary of Liturgy and Worship,* 1986, p. 540).

Viewing. Synonymous with *wake* and *visitation.*

Vigil. When pertaining to funerals, it is synonymous with *wake.*

Visitation. Set hours at a private home, funeral home, or church where people may come and pay their respects to the bereaved prior to the funeral. The casket may be open or closed during visitation.

Wake. A watch held over the body of a dead person prior to burial, usually at a funeral home. In modern funeral jargon, the term *visitation* has largely replaced *wake,* and the primary emphasis is on greeting the bereaved rather than watching the deceased. The casket is normally open during a wake. In some traditions, there will be singing, prayers, and testimonies about the life of the deceased.

Winding sheet. Another term for *shroud,* no longer used.

THE AUTHOR

Carol M. Norén is a native of Chicago and an ordained minister in the United Methodist Church. She has served urban and suburban churches in the United States, was pastor of two inner-city churches and hospital chaplain in Manchester, England, and has participated in street evangelism programs in England and Germany. She has taught at Princeton Theological Seminary, Duke University Divinity School, and North Park Theological Seminary. In addition, she has been guest lecturer at denominational seminaries in Europe and Australia and across the United States. Norén is author of *The Woman in the Pulpit* (1991) and *What Happens Sunday Morning: A Layperson's Guide to Worship* (1992).

NAME INDEX

POETRY INDEX

Titles are listed in italics to distinguish them from first line references. When a title is similar to the first words of the opening line of a poem, only the first line reference is listed. Names of poets appear in all capital letters.

TOPICAL INDEX